Islam, Law, and Equality in Indonesia

In Indonesia, the world's largest Muslim-majority country, Muslims struggle to reconcile radically different sets of social norms and laws, including those derived from Islam, local social norms, and contemporary ideas about gender equality and rule of law. In this new study, John Bowen explores this struggle, through archival and ethnographic research in villages and courtrooms of Aceh province, Sumatra, and through interviews with national religious and legal figures. He analyzes the social frameworks for disputes about land, inheritance, marriage, divorce, Islamic history, and, more broadly, about the relationships between the state and Islam, and between Muslims and non-Muslims. The book speaks to debates carried out in all societies about how people can live together with their deep differences in values and ways of life. It will be welcomed by scholars and students across the social sciences, particularly those interested in anthropology, cultural sociology, and political theory.

JOHN R. BOWEN is Dunbar-Van Cleve Professor in Arts and Sciences, Professor of Anthropology, and Chair of the Program in Social Thought and Analysis at Washington University in St. Louis. He is the author of *Sumatran Politics and Poetics* (1991), *Muslims through Discourse* (1993), *Religions through Practice* (2nd edition 2001), and the co-editor of *Critical Comparisons in Politics and Culture* (Cambridge University Press, 1999).

"Westerners seldom appreciate the array of competing religious and social norms among which Muslims must navigate. Bowen skillfully demonstrates that for these Indonesians the quest for meaning among alternative legal and practical values is at the very heart of the tension between local practice and universal faith. His cogent examples and superb eye for their surround bring home with great poignancy and insight, both for Indonesia and the broader Muslim world, the 'principled reflections' that inform the lives of Muslims in the present day."

Lawrence Rosen, William Nelson Cromwell Professor of Anthropology, Princeton University and Adjunct Professor of Law, Columbia Law School

"*Islam, Law and Equality in Indonesia* is an engaging, rich work, a work of many parts, many levels, and great subtlety. It is at once about Islamic public spheres, about the contradictions of everyday village life in Sumatra, about the relationship between the state and religion, about gender and inequality in Southeast Asia, about the negotiation of difference in a bewilderingly complex, normatively diverse world. But, above all, it is about the way in which the law – increasingly, across the globe – is deployed to manage the unmanageable, to resolve the unresolvable, to deal with the incommensurable. As this suggests, you are about to read a study whose ethnographic depth is matched by the breadth of its theoretical reach."

John Comaroff, Harold H. Swift Distinguished Service Professor of Anthropology, University of Chicago, and Senior Research Fellow, American Bar Foundation

Islam, Law, and Equality in Indonesia

An Anthropology of Public Reasoning

John R. Bowen

CAMBRIDGE
UNIVERSITY PRESS

PUBLISHED BY THE PRESS SYNDICATE OF THE UNIVERSITY OF CAMBRIDGE
The Pitt Building, Trumpington Street, Cambridge CB2 1RP, United Kingdom

CAMBRIDGE UNIVERSITY PRESS
The Edinburgh Building, Cambridge, CB2 2RU, UK
40 West 20th Street, New York, NY 10011-4211, USA
477 Williamstown Road, Port Melbourne, VIC 3207, Australia
Ruiz de Alarcón 13, 28014 Madrid, Spain
Dock House, The Waterfront, Cape Town 8001, South Africa

http://www.cambridge.org

First published 2003

Printed in the United Kingdom at the University Press, Cambridge

Typeface Times 10/12 pt   *System* LATEX 2$_\varepsilon$ [TB]

A catalogue record for this book is available from the British Library

ISBN 0 521 82482 6 hardback
ISBN 0 521 53189 6 paperback

To Entan Mah Seri

Contents

Illustrations

Figures

Map

Tables

Acknowledgments

This volume is the third (or the fourth, if you count my dissertation) in which I have drawn on my fieldwork in the Gayo highlands of Aceh province, Indonesia. It is, therefore, to my many Gayo friends that I owe the first words of thanks. Since 1978, they have helped me to see a good number of problems from their perspective. Time and again I have returned to the highlands to situate and reconsider broad issues of religious variation, cultural change, and, as in this volume, the complexities of law, Islam, and social equality, from a vantage point I have come to know very well. Such is the ethnographic approach. Many in the highlands are mentioned in chapter 1, but I must here repeat my gratitude to Abang Evi, my lifelong companion in exploring things Gayo, and to his family.

My own family has helped me in countless ways to write, and to play. Vicki, Jeff, and Greg have their own lives to lead, but they always have remained supportive of the travels and concerns that make up the ethnographic life. My parents sometimes wonder what, after all, I do, but they read some of what I write and remain diffusely embracing of the kind of career I have chosen. Colleagues at Washington University and elsewhere have provided many hours of encouragement and suggestions. Over the years Jack Knight has tried valiantly to refine my arguments regarding political theory, as have, at particular moments, Jim Bohman and Susan Miller Okin. I have learned much about sociology from Michèle Lamont and Rogers Brubaker, and about Islamic law from David Powers. Daniel Lev, Joel Kuipers, Martin van Bruinessen, Robert Hefner, and Andrée Feillard have offered insightful comments from their knowledge of Indonesia. Colleagues too numerous to mention have commented usefully on presentations given at Yale, Harvard, Stanford, Berkeley, UCLA, the University of Chicago, the Centre d'Etudes et de Recherches Internationales (Paris), the Institute for Ismaili Studies (London), the Mosquée Ad-Dawa (Paris), and the International Institute for the Study of Islam in the Modern World (Leiden). Sally Merry's scholarly reading helped me revise the manuscript, as did the skilled editing eyes of Carol Fellingham Webb, and the several editors at Cambridge – Helen Barton, Helen Francis, Pat Maurice, Jackie Warren – who stepped in at a difficult moment to constitute an anthropology editing collective.

Most scholars depend for their livelihood on institutional support, and I have been most fortunate to have taught and thought at Washington University since 1985. I doubt that any university provides a more encouraging atmosphere for intellectual and pedagogical innovation than does my own. I owe a special debt to Bill Van Cleve and Georgia Dunbar Van Cleve for their support of my professional life. The National Science Foundation provided initial research support in 1994. In 1995–96, the Center for Advanced Study in Palo Alto (with funding provided by the National Science Foundation) gave me the opportunity to think about how to turn massive field notes into something readable. Two French institutions then provided further occasions to write, read, and discuss. In 1999, the Maison Asie-Pacifique in Marseille, and in particular Charles Macdonald, allowed me to present findings to an excellent group of area specialists and ethnologists. In 2001, the Centre d'Etudes et de Recherches Internationales in Paris provided another such opportunity and allowed me to begin comparative work on France. Christophe Jaffrelot made that visit possible, as did the initial encouragements of Fariba Adelkhah, Gilles Kepel, and Riva Kastoryano. I continue to enjoy delightful, productive collaborations with those colleagues and with many others in Paris with an interest in Indonesia, including Andrée Feillard, Romain Bertrand, Daniel Sabbagh, Hichem Elarafa, Dhaou Meskine, Ahmad Jaballah, and Hakim El Ghissassi.

Some of the material presented here has appeared previously, and I thank copyright owners for their willingness to allow me to present more refined analyses in book form. Some of the material in chapter 5 first appeared in *Law and Society Review* (2000), published by the Law and Society Association. Material from chapter 6 was part of an article in *Islamic Law and Society* (1998), and appears with permission from Brill Academic Publishers. Chapter 7 includes material that was published in *History of Religions* (1998), copyrighted by the University of Chicago Press. The map was drawn by Jim Railey.

Glossary

Important terms that recur in the text from Indonesian (I), Arabic (Ar), Gayo (G), Dutch (D), or Acehnese (Ach) languages are listed; derivations are given only if some speakers are aware of the word's origin, or when the word exists in both Indonesian and Arabic Islamic lexica. Indonesian words commonly used by Gayo speakers are listed only as Indonesian. Terms that only appear once or twice in the text, and always with translations, are not included.

adat **(I<Ar 'āda):** rules and practices of social life, a culturally appropriate sense of propriety, tradition and custom (see also *ëdët*).

adatrecht **(D),** *hukum adat* **(I),** *adat law*: sets of rules and procedures pertaining to social and political life characteristic of a particular geographical area in the Dutch East Indies and, subsequently, Indonesia, and having legal value.

adil **(I):** just, as in *keadilan*, "justice."

ahlul kitab **(I<Ar** *ahl al-kitâb*): "people of the book," a category generally applied to Christians and Jews to indicate the history of revelation and worship they share with Muslims, but sometimes extended to other religious groups.

angkap nasab **(G):** a uxorilocal marriage arrangement whereby the couple is obliged to remain in the wife's village to care for her parents.

bangsa **(I):** nation, people, sometimes combining both senses.

bupati **(I):** head of a district (*kabupaten*).

camat **(I):** head of a subdistrict (*kecamatan*), below a *bupati*.

cerai **(I):** divorce; in legal proceedings further subdivided into *cerai talaq*, divorce suits brought by the husband, and *cerai gugat* (*gugat* = challenge, litigate), divorce suits brought by the wife.

dakwah **(I<Ar** *da'wa*): "call," instruction to other Muslims about religion, practiced by *dâ'i*.

Dewan Dakwah Islamiyah Indonesia (DDII): Indonesian Islamic Dakwah Council, an organization dedicated to promoting awareness among Muslims of the basics of their religion and of the value of maintaining distinctions and boundaries between religious groups.

ëdët **(G):** Gayo traditions, practices, fundamental social norms; also, the official enforcing those norms.

farâ'id **(I<Ar):** the fixed shares allocated to heirs; *'ilm al-farâ'id*: the knowledge of how to allocate shares, the "science of shares." The Gayo cognate *pera'il* or *pera'id* is used in the same sense, or to designate a woman who receives a fixed share.

faskh **(Ar),** ***fasakh*** **(I),** ***pasakh*** **(G):** a form of divorce, or more precisely annulment of a marriage, in practice nearly always initiated by the wife.

fatwa **(I<Ar *fatwâ*; Ar. pl. *fatâwa*):** legal opinions provided by Islamic scholars or jurists.

fiqh **(I<Ar):** jurisprudential interpretation.

Gerakan Acheh Merdeka (GAM) **(I):** Aceh Liberation Movement, rebels fighting Indonesian troops in Aceh province.

hak **(I,G<Ar):** right; *hak milik*, an individual right in property; *hak ulayat*, rights to land held in the name of a community; *hak asasi* (*manusia*), basic human rights.

hakam **(I<Ar):** mediator, appointed by judges to mediate a divorce.

hakim **(I<Ar):** judge.

halal **(I<Ar *halâl*):** permitted.

haram **(I<Ar *harâm*):** forbidden.

harta **(I):** wealth, estate; *harta bersama*, communal or marital property (acquired by a couple during a marriage); *harta bawaan*, "brought property," preexisting wealth contributed by one party to the marriage (= G *erta*).

hiba, hibah **(I,G<Ar):** a gift given according to rules of Islamic law; *hibah wasiat*, "bequest gift," a term combining two different modes of transferring wealth used in Gayo, Minangkabau, and some other Indonesian societies (see *wasiat*).

hukum **(I,G<Ar):** law in general (*hukum negara*, positive law); regularities in the social or natural world (as in *hukum akal*, "the law of reason"); Islamic law as opposed to adat; the religious value of any action; the legal consequences of an act. (Note that a number of Indonesian words pertaining to law derive from the same Arabic trilateral root *hkm: hak, hakam, hakim, hukum*.)

ijma' (**I<Ar ijmâ'**): consensus over a matter of legal interpretation among knowledgeable Muslims.

ijtihâd (**I<Ar**): (re)interpretation by individuals of Islamic sources.

'illa (**Ar**): the reason (for the revelation of a verse of the Qur'ân).

Inpres, Instruksi Presiden: an executive order.

Institut Agama Islam Negeri (IAIN): State Islamic Institute.

jilbab (**I<Ar**): Islamic dress for women, usually consisting of a loose dress and headcovering.

juëlën (**G**): virilocal marriage form, lit. "sold"; also referred to as *ango*, "brought."

Kantor Urusan Agama (KUA): Office of Religious Affairs.

kaum muda (mudë) (**I,G**): "young group," modernist religious reformers inspired by the Salafiyyah movement of the late nineteenth and early twentieth centuries, opposed to the *kaum tua*, the "old group," who advocated continuing to adhere to teachings of the Shâfi'î legal school predominant in Indonesia.

Kompilasi Hukum Islam di Indonesia: Compilation of Islamic Law in Indonesia.

madhhab (**I<Ar**): legal school or tradition.

mahar (**I,G<Ar mahr**): a gift made directly from the groom to the bride, required for a marriage to be valid in Islam.

Majelis Ulama Indonesia (MUI): Council of Indonesian Ulama, with national, provincial, and local bodies.

manat (**G**): a request or a legacy.

masyarakat adat (**I**): "adat society," people living under local social norms.

milik (**I<Ar**): (individual) ownership.

Muhammadiyah: the second largest Islamic association in Indonesia, after NU (but the most influential association on Sumatra), generally advocating reinterpretations of established religious practices and the heritage of the Salafiya modernist movement.

musyawarah (**I**): deliberation, a process of reaching consensus, a meeting held to resolve a dispute; *musyawarah mufakat* (G. *mupakat*), "consensus through consultation/deliberation," a platform of the Indonesian state ideology, the Pancasila.

Nahdlatul Ulama (NU): the largest of Indonesia's Islamic organizations, based on Java, and in particular in Javanese religious schools (*pesantrens*), and generally following Shâfi'î teachings.

niët (G<Ar *nîya;* I *niat*): intent or intention.

nikah (I<Ar): marriage.

pematang, umë pematang (G): land designated by parents for the child or children who care for them in old age; literally the land lying between main rice plots, suggesting its insignificance.

pemohon (I): the plaintiff in a lawsuit, literally "requesters"; defendants are *termohon*, "those requested."

pengadilan (I): court, judicial procedure; *Pengadilan Agama*, religious court (formerly, in Aceh, *Mahkamah Syariah*, Sharî'a Tribunal); *Pengadilan Negeri*, civil court.

perdata (I): civil cases.

pesaka (G): inherited wealth (= I *pusaka*).

Piagam Jakarta: Jakarta Charter, a draft preamble to the 1945 Constitution written by nine of the authors of the Constitution, and containing a phrase obliging the state to enforce Islamic law for Muslims.

pidana (I): criminal cases.

poh roh (G<Ach): wealth jointly created by a husband and wife, from an Acehnese phrase meaning "to work fallow [land]."

qadi (I,G<Ar *qâdî*): judge; religious official.

qiyâs (I<Ar): an analogy in Islamic reasoning.

sharî'a (I,G<Ar *sharî'a*): the path or way pointed out by God and His Messengers for all humans; the norms and rules that guide a Muslim on that path; a body of positive laws putatively reflecting those norms and rules.

siyasah sharî'a (Ar): sharî'a policy, government laws and actions based on, or designed to promote, sharî'a.

syiqoq (I<Ar): irreconcilable differences, as grounds for divorce; the procedure leading to such a divorce, involving the appointment of mediators.

talaq (I<Ar): repudiation of a wife by her husband; a form of divorce; *ikrar talaq*, the husband's pronouncement of the divorce formula.

ta'lik talaq (I<Ar): a deferred or conditional talaq agreed to at marriage, and usually declared to have occurred by a judge.

taqlîd **(I,G<Ar):** to follow a madhhab (legal tradition), rather than engaging in ijtihâd.

tengku **(G):** a man learned in religious matters.

teniron **(G):** "requested" goods, asked for by the bride's family, most of which is passed on to the bride (thus as "indirect dowry").

ulama **(I,G<Ar):** Muslim scholars of Islam; jurists (as used in Indonesia).

umma(h) **(I<Ar):** the worldwide Muslim community.

wali **(I,G<Ar):** guardian.

waqf **(I<Ar):** endowment or trust.

warisan **(I,G<Ar):** inheritance; *pewaris*, the person leaving an estate; *ahli waris*, heir; *ahli waris pengganti*, "substitute heir," a relative who inherits by taking the place of a linking relative (usually a grandchild taking the place of his or her predeceased parent).

wasiat **(I<Ar *wasîyya*):** bequest; *wasîyya wâjibah*, an "obligatory bequest," a mechanism designed to provide an estate share for relatives whose link of entitlement to the deceased had been broken by the death of a linking relative.

Part 1

Village repertoires

1   Law, religion, and pluralism

What follows is an exploration, through ethnography, of how some people have reasoned about difficult problems of law, religion, and ideals of equality in a pluralistic society, Indonesia. I examine struggles over how best to apply the legal traditions and religious norms of Islam to family life. In Indonesia and elsewhere, disputes over this issue also have been disputes about political allegiance, religious toleration, and, indeed, the very survival of pluralistic societies. Debates and conflicts in Indonesia, the world's largest Muslim-majority country, have a strong bearing on one of our most significant human debates, about how people can live together, admitting their deep differences of values and forms of life, and forging ways to tolerate and accept those differences.

In Europe and North America, philosophers and political theorists have framed this debate as a question for liberal political theory: How far can the tradition of Locke, Hobbes, Kant, and Mill be stretched to fit political communities composed of differing subcommunities, each with its own set of values and rules for social life? Some theorists have answered that all such subcommunities should agree on a core set of liberal principles; others have argued that when no such core set can be found, which is often the case, we should look instead for a *modus vivendi*, a way to get along without agreeing on a set of basic political principles.[1]

This debate will continue among theorists. My work here is that of an anthropologist; I offer an ethnographic account of how Indonesians are grappling with the problems of living in a deeply pluralistic world, one characterizable as a struggle to achieve, not complete agreement, but a way of living that allows for the coexistence, and some degree of recognition, of differing ideas of justice. I trace the diverse ways in which villagers, judges, jurists, social activists, and many others have argued and deliberated over a quite particular form of what philosophers call "value-pluralism." Indonesia is the site of long-standing, diverse efforts to shape lives in an Islamic way, but also of even longer-standing

---

[1] In current debates, the first position is most famously upheld by John Rawls (1996, 1999), and in a different version, by Will Kymlicka (1995); the second, by John Gray (2000), Stuart Hampshire (2000), and in modified forms by Bhikhu Parekh (2000), and Avishai Margalit (1996).

and more diverse efforts to shape them according to local complexes of norms and traditions called *adat*, some 300-plus of them according to conventional calculations – and all this further complicated by shifting sensibilities regarding gender equality and the "rule of law." Indonesians have been trying to work out ways to reconcile this normative florescence, and to do so within resolutely centralizing forms of state rule, under the Dutch, under the democracy, real and then "guided," of the first president, Sukarno, under the authoritarian New Order regime of his successor, Suharto, and now, under what looks increasingly like "unguided chaos" under a succession of short-term presidents: B.J. Habibie, Abdurrahman Wahid, and most recently Megawati Sukarnoputri.

At first glance, looking to Indonesia for ideas about how people might live together seems a singularly bad idea. In 2002, Indonesia is entering the fifth year of its post-Suharto "Reform Era," but the nation-state seems to be pulling itself apart at the seams. Former political allies turn on one another savagely. Local communities engage in bloody struggles over land and work, sometimes refitting their combats in the language of *jihad* or the defense against jihad. Since September 11, 2001, some have called for a jihad to Afghanistan; other Muslim leaders have been appalled at such a call. Neither police nor army tries very hard to keep order. Everyone seems to want *otonomi*, the provinces from Jakarta, and the districts from their provincial centers.

But these centripetal movements are not the reflections of precultural urges or "ancient tribal hatreds." They are shaped by ideas about society and nation, morals and religion, as well as by political, social, and economic interests. Some provincial leaders express their desire to reshape laws and, thereby, everyday life, around *sharî'a*, an Islamic way of life. Some people argue that they would be better off governing themselves according to older sets of norms and practices, adat. Advocates for law reform plead for greater protection for human rights and women's rights, citing English-language categories such as "marital rape" and "gender analysis" as new norms to guide legislation and adjudication. In the early years of the new century, these myriad appeals have become sharper in the climate of reduced state power and heightened fears about national disintegration and international terrorism. But they remain principled, grounded in reasoning about appropriate and legitimate forms of local, national, or international governance.

These calls to reform and reformulate Indonesian social life involve a double movement of reference. One direction is inward, towards indigenousness, authenticity, and Indonesian values, in an effort to find local points of support in the face of global moral corruption. The other direction is outward, towards universality, modernity, and transcultural values of social equality, in the hope that these values may help overcome local injustices. Even the same set of cultural or legal texts can point in both directions. The term "adat" can signify localness and self-government, in contrast to past domination and corrupt rule from Jakarta, but it also can signify an appeal to pan-Indonesian norms of human equality and a respect for widely shared "feelings," in contrast to the mechanical application of particular laws. While "sharî'a" refers to a universal Islamic way of life, it reminds some people of past Islamic kingdoms, others of a future time when girls and boys will dress modestly and observe the fast – and for some men it may promise mainly the right to marry more than one wife. Even appeals to carry out *analisis jender* can be buttressed by references to Western laws, or to Indonesian rural practices of job-sharing, and usually to both.

Indonesian society thus is criss-crossed by competing claims about how people ought to live and about what Indonesian society ought to become. These claims draw on highly local ideas, on national values, *and* on universal rights and laws. To make matters still more complicated, ideas of what is at stake change from one level of society to another. In a village, what might matter most are the rules by which people gain or preserve their control of land. In town, it might be the ways in which judges, administrators, or ordinary people justify their claims in terms of Islamic law, the norms of adat, or state regulations. In national-level debates, at stake might be (and increasingly are) the past, present, and future identities of Indonesians: as religiously Muslims, Christians, or Hindus; as ethnically Acehnese, Javanese, or Balinese; or as, together, members of a single "nation-people" (a *bangsa*).

Repertoires of reasoning

So, perhaps, Indonesia, precisely because of its troubled self-reflecting about what the nation should be and its daily struggling over norms, laws, and social order, *is* an apt place to study ways in which people reason about competing norms. In the rest of this book, I chart this Indonesian normative entanglement, looking at places where norms collide, where something is worth the fight, for more than reasons of self-interest (not that self-interest is not omnipresent). My primary objects of study are socially embedded forms of public reasoning – interpretations, justifications, argumentations – about norms and laws concerning marriage, divorce, and inheritance. These topics lead to others, because it turns out that a great deal is at stake in arguments and conflicts over these norms: at the very least, access to land, religious identity, a sense of local control, women's rights, respect for the ancestors, modernity, the rule of law, and the problem of holding together a nation. The constant element in the narrative concerns gender, the equality of rights and relationships among men and women, and the relative claims that religion, tradition, and universalist norms have on people's conduct.

I start from the level of village disputes and work upwards, following the issues where they take me. I begin the account with the intricacies of kinship-shaped access to land in a village in the Gayo highlands of Sumatra, a place where I have pursued fieldwork since the late 1970s. In Gayo society, as in many other parts of Indonesia, women and men are engaged in debates about the relative merits of adat, Islam, and state laws. Colonial officials created a map of Indies/Indonesian social life that privileged the specifics of *adatrecht*, but this culture-by-culture idea of norms was, and still is, challenged in the name of universal Islamic rules for transmitting property. Here struggles are primarily about how "family" is to be understood and reproduced: as a part of a locally meaningful system of norms and practices, or as the outcome of applying universal Islamic rules for marrying, divorcing, and inheriting wealth.

Courts increasingly intervene in these struggles. It is mainly women who have seized on the opportunities provided by Islamic courts to acquire land rights. But judges on Islamic and civil courts alike have tried to balance claims made in the name of Islam against those made in the name of adat, and the central chapters of the book treat the legal reasoning pursued by judges over recent decades. I point out that their arguments have changed over the decades in response to shifts in society and politics, showing that discourses of compromise and reconciliation among normative systems can be arrived at in more than one way, but that values of gender equality and "harmonious reconciliation" continue to form part of judges' repertoires of justification. Here the debates about Islam and family are firmly situated in a framework of law and "metalegal" arguments about which set of laws ought to govern Indonesia's Muslims.

These arguments are amplified at the level of the nation, often counterposing religious and national allegiances in debates about equality, pluralism, and political legitimacy. Gender equality challenges received understandings of Islamic law, and those Indonesians engaged in this challenge are overturning older ways of interpreting scripture, and encountering strong resistance in the process. Muslims also disagree over how porous the boundaries ought to be between religious communities: should one marry, adopt, or even greet those people who adhere to another religion? Should religious obligations take precedence over national belonging, or vice versa? Finally, is it the state, or God, who has the last legal word? Who gets to say how Muslims ought to marry or divorce, and is there a way to square the circle, underscoring the state's legitimacy while recognizing Muslim claims to the supremacy of scripture? The three issues overlap; all bring up ideas about the equality of rights and relationships among men and women, and the relative claims that religion, tradition, and universalist norms have on people's conduct.

These three issues have engaged many Indonesians in a continual effort to finesse sharp disagreements over ideas of knowledge, legitimacy, and sociabil-ity. We shall encounter much of this "reasoned finessing." In earlier studies, also based on fieldwork in Gayo society, I considered other ways in which Indonesians have tried to persuade others, or, at the very least, live with differences among them.[2] The present work continues a discussion (Bowen 1993b) of the discursive forms that have characterized an "Islamic public sphere" in Southeast Asia, but now targeting the social norms that lie at the intersection of civil society and the state, the area of family norms and law that for many define the limit of legitimate state authority in religious matters.

Justification and social norms

Viewed analytically, then, my interest lies in the ways people select from their "repertoires of justification," a phrase associated with a recent, broadly based social science effort to understand how actors justify what they do in specific, generally conflict-ridden, social settings (Boltanski and Thévenot 1991; Dupret 2000; Lamont and Thévenot 2000; Tilly 1997). Some of these studies (Kastoryano 1997; Lamont 1992), influenced by Durkheim, ask how people occupying particular class or status positions create boundaries between themselves and others (see also Bourdieu 1984). Others, following Weber, ask how members of particular societies judge distributional claims against criteria of legitimacy in a society (Elster 1995) or in a particular social domain, as in Michael Walzer's (1983) idea of "spheres of justice."

The new pragmatic "sociology of justification" has roots in the approaches of American pragmatists (e.g., Goffman 1974) as well as Durkheim and Weber. In France, it also is a moment in a continuing dialectic of social theory, where sociologists are seeking to correct an overly strategic emphasis in the work of Pierre Bourdieu by reinjecting ideas of moral worth and cultural meaning.[3] In Britain and the United States, emphasizing the processes and repertoires that occupy a particular social domain has attracted social scientists seeking to reconcile the emphasis on individual interests and strategies most associated with political science, and the emphasis on norms and systems of meaning most associated with anthropology and cultural sociology (Barth 1987; Bowen and Petersen 1999; Laitin 1992; Petersen 2001; Swidler 1986; Tarrow 1995).

---

[2] These studies include the analysis of changing forms of debate and persuasion involved in resolving disputes (Bowen 1991), poetry designed to convince people to change their religious ideas (Bowen 1993a), debates over alternative understandings of Islamic ritual, and tacit forms of toleration of different understandings (Bowen 1993b).

[3] Bourdieu had framed his initial work as a practice-oriented correction of the over-reliance on publicly enunciated norms in the work of structuralists, in particular Lévi-Strauss; the latter had represented his own philosophical intervention as a scientific corrective to the voluntarism and idealism of post-war philosophy. The critique of Bourdieu, much of it as yet "oral tradition," has a double focus on his over-emphasis on the strategic element in action (such as Bourdieu 1990), and on the shared, monolithic quality of cultural space in his macrosociological accounts of culture (such as Bourdieu 1984; see Lamont 1992).

This direction of research ought to be particularly receptive to the social anthropological tradition of closely studying disputes and modes of reasoning. At least since Malinowski (1926), anthropologists have been concerned with the complex relationship between social norms and values, on the one hand, and the actions observed in everyday life, on the other. Indeed, "rules" *vis-à-vis* "processes" became a shorthand for a tension within legal anthropology (Comaroff and Roberts 1981; Moore 1986). More recently, and somewhat more broadly, studies in "law and society" have turned from studying the pluralism of legal systems to considering the dynamic relationship between legal and other normative orders (Merry 1992), and it is this view of legal pluralism as a continually shifting and contested set of domains (rather than as a single legal field) that informs the present work.

Anthropological interest in disputes and justification is far broader than the phrase "legal anthropology" might suggest. Analyzing disputes and interpretations of events has long been a particularly illuminating way to understand how a wide range of actions are shaped by ideas, norms, and interests. One of the best studies of how one constructs an elaborate justification of a social action remains Evans-Pritchard's (1937) study of oracles and sorcery accusations in Azande society of Central Africa, and similar studies continue to produce excellent accounts of how people reason through misfortune (e.g., Whyte 1997). Indonesianists have provided a wealth of such accounts; indeed, it has become a particular subspeciality within Indonesian studies to show how ideas of responsibility and causality are given cultural shape in the process of working out a dispute, whether in a courtroom setting (F. von Benda-Beckmann 1979; K. von Benda-Beckmann 1984; Just 2001; Slaats and Portier 1993) or in other forums in everyday life (Kuipers 1990; Steedly 1993; Watson and Ellen 1993).

These and other studies point out the comparative advantage of an *anthropology* of reasoning and justification, one based on long-term intimacy with people in a particular place, and a sense of the history, language, and everyday social life associated with those people. The ethnographer's "local knowledge" (Geertz 1983) allows her or him to show in microsociological detail how individuals deploy their social resources to achieve their goals, and how their goals and resources draw their value from a larger cultural system. An anthropology of reasoning and justification allows a full appreciation of conflict, incompatibility, and change in social life, and it provides analytical room for distinct levels of reasoning with respect to the same topic. As actors search for compromise or reconciliation among opposing positions, they constitute new levels of reasoning, "metalevels" of reasoning about how to understand positions taken by others (see Urban 2001). This level may be just as consequential as that of the initial argumentation; indeed, this is the level of reasoning on which judicial reasoning takes place, as judges seek a set of principles that can allow them to take account of positions taken by opposing sides (Sunstein 1996).

Islamic sociolegal reasoning

An anthropology of public reasoning has particular advantages as a way of studying the intersections of Islam, law, and social life.[4] Far from being an immutable system of rules, Islamic jurisprudence (*fiqh*) is best characterized as a human effort to resolve disputes by drawing on scripture, logic, the public interest, local custom, and the consensus of the community.[5] In other words, it is as imbricated with social and cultural life as is Anglo-American law, or Jewish legal reasoning.

Recent studies by historians and anthropologists have highlighted Islamic legal reasoning as a set of social practices, moving away from older presentations of sharî'a as a set of rules (e.g., Schacht 1964) to take account of the social contexts within which jurists and others engage in interpretation and justification. Approaching law as a species of social reasoning has allowed scholars to trace the ways in which jurists and judges take account of both the normative immediacy of sacred texts and the social import of legal outcomes. Historians (e.g., Hallaq 1995; Masud et al. 1996; Powers 1994; Tucker 1998) have emphasized the social contexts and processes of communication and mutual reading among jurists and judges that preceded legal decisions or opinions. Historians and anthropologists also have examined changes in legal structures and legal ideology (for example, the codification of law) that occurred as part and parcel of colonial domination (Buskens 1993; Christelow 1985; Eickelman 1985; Messick 1993).

Although anthropological and sociological studies of Islamic law all look at the place of cultural ideas in legal processes, one finds a range of emphases in this literature. Some studies (e.g., F. von Benda-Beckmann 1979; Dupret 2000; Hirsch 1998; Stiles 2002) have emphasized the practices of seeking justice in an Islamic court, and have given case materials and courtroom discourse a central place in their analyses. Others have drawn on what transpires in courtrooms as evidence for their accounts of broader cultural ideas. Geertz (1983) and Rosen (1989, 1995), for example, have characterized Arabo-Islamic law as a cultural system, in terms of ideas about truth, rights, and personhood. A growing body of work (Hirsch 1998; Moors 1995; Mundy 1995; Tucker 1998; see also Esposito 1982) focuses on the gendered features of Islamic laws, judges' decisions, and courtroom events.

Despite their methodological differences, these studies converge on the finding that, since early in the history of Islamic legal reasoning, judges and jurists have tried to reconcile a number of distinct sources of law. From a formal

---

[4] Elsewhere (Bowen 1993b) I have discussed what I see as the advantages of studying Islam through the practices, and especially the discursive practices, that constitute it, and more recently (2002), I generalized this approach to the study of religious practices in general.

[5] For accounts of Islamic jurisprudential reasoning, see Hallaq (1997) and Vogel (1993).

perspective, these sources are arranged hierarchically, with a clear text of the Qur'ân counting more than a statement of the Prophet Muhammad, and the latter more than a customary practice.[6] But in the practice of reasoning about cases and justifying decisions reached, Muslim authorities and ordinary Muslims always have found themselves having to tack among competing values, norms, and commands.

We find ourselves facing the topic of this book, the entanglement of these imperatives in the lives of Muslim Indonesians. Said in such an abstract way, the story could be about almost any place. Indeed, one of my purposes in writing this book is to show that the specificities of Indonesian law and society point toward some issues facing citizens in all areas of the world. How can differences in fundamental commitments be reconciled within a unified legal system? How can self-rule guarantee equal rights? What forms of public reasoning characterize societies in which many citizens consider religious principles to be legitimate bases for constructing a political and legal system?

Indonesia has some clear advantages as a place to consider such issues. It is one of those rambling collections of political pasts, ways of life, and religious commitments that have proved so difficult to bring together into *national* pasts, presents, and futures (Anderson 1991). Partly because of Dutch ways of administering, and partly because of its size and diversity, it became one of the major sites for writing about legal pluralism. It also contains among its people the largest Muslim population of any country. If we are interested in studying social diversity, political ideas, and religious commitment, all as they bear on law, then Indonesia remains a most interesting place for research and reflection.

The possibility of Islamic public reasoning

I stress "reflection" because I believe that the interest of this study extends beyond Indonesia to contemporary debates about justice and culture. My focus is on struggles by Indonesians to reconcile, or select among, competing sets of values and norms. It considers the social practices in which reasoning about these issues takes place: not political theory or public reason, but socially contextualized political theorizing and public reasoning in the face of competing commands. An anthropological study of such matters in Indonesia can, I believe, add to the current discussions in Europe and North America concerning the mechanisms through which constitutional democratic states can encompass cultural and religious diversity.

In particular, the Indonesian case challenges the analytical adequacy of Western political theory for the comparative study of political and legal reasoning. A number of prominent contemporary liberal political theorists (e.g., Kymlicka

---

[6] For an analysis of early ways in which jurists incorporated custom into law, see Libson (1997).

1995; Rawls 1996, 1999; Raz 1994) have tried to extend political theory to encompass pluralistic or "multicultural" societies. Their strategies differ, but they all involve trying to arrive at a universal core of principles to which people in all societies can subscribe. Will Kymlicka and Joseph Raz define the core of principles in terms of the autonomy of the individual, and his or her capacity to form and revise an idea of "the good life." John Rawls has moved over the years from holding a position close to that of Raz, to attempting to carve out from culture and religion a narrow area of political principle on which all parties can agree. Rawls distinguishes between two sets of ideas and principles. On the one hand is a secular "political conception of justice," which will be shared by all within a society (he uses the phrase "overlapping consensus"), and which defines the limits of "public reason." On the other hand are all the varying "background cultures" specific to each of the several religious and cultural groups in the society, each composed of its own set of distinct "comprehensive doctrines" of the good life, including religious doctrines.

And yet, applying these quite reasonable accounts of justice across cultures raises serious objections. Liberal characterizations of political justice are shaped by the particular cultures from which these theorists come. As Bhikhu Parekh (2000) argues, valuing autonomy and "the good life" are outcomes of a particular Western intellectual and social history, in which Greek philosophy, Christianity, and colonialism each contributed to liberal doctrine. People from other backgrounds have developed different, equally principled bases for politics and justice. For example, many Muslims argue that their religious texts provide a God-given set of political and social ideas, and do not see why they should be rejected in favor of liberal ideas. For them, "public reasoning" *should* derive its principles from religious texts.

Furthermore, in Indonesia, India, Egypt, and elsewhere there is more than one "political conception of justice." One's religious identity determines under which laws one will marry, divorce, and divide one's estate. This structure regulates distributive justice, the legal statuses of men and women, and, at a legal metalevel, the relationship between positive law and religious law. In these societies, there continue to be strong disagreements among different social groups about what this relationship ought to be. In other words, there is neither a single political structure regulating issues of basic justice, nor an overlapping consensus on the current pluralistic legal arrangements – and for principled reasons, not merely as a compromise born of expediency.

I will argue that in Indonesia, much public reasoning *retains* its foundation in comprehensive doctrines, and in particular its foundations in specific understandings of Islam and particular adat-based conceptions of the world. The ensuing debates often concern the legitimacy, in Islamic terms, of efforts to interpret religious texts in such a way that they are compatible with other ideals, for example, that of equal treatment of men and women. In these instances, the

Indonesian Muslims in question endorse, not a political conception of justice as in Rawls, but a reasonable conception of justice that is *public and also Islamic*.

I use "public," therefore, in a broader sense than in Rawls, to include the many kinds of reasoning processes about justice and rights that contain implications for basic structures of society, and that one finds across all levels of society, articulated by village leaders, jurists and judges, national political figures, social activists, and by other, ordinary people. My intention is not to offer a competing version of political theory, a reconstruction of society from first principles. Rather, I offer an anthropological account of such reasoning, the ways in which citizens take account of their own pluralism of values as they carry out their affairs.

Indonesian pluralism

The political and cultural history of Indonesia, of the Dutch East Indies, and of the many kingdoms and societies of the archipelago, has given rise to a particular way of studying pluralism. I find in the region of Southeast Asia as a whole a particular awareness of an "internalized pluralism," a consciousness of other societies at the core of each society's self-definition. One finds origin myths that proceed by differentiating a society from its neighbors, sometimes through a story of the wanderings of two brothers, by receiving an initial charter from a distant power, sometimes strengthened by a marriage between a foreign man and a local princess, or by postulating the new society as the continuation of an older center, accompanied by the transmission of sacred books. This consciousness may be the result of the region's outward orientation, its history in commerce, religion, politics, and art of receiving and transforming objects and ideas that have come from elsewhere, often across the seas.[7]

Southeast Asia borrows in order to create what defines it – a paradoxical formulation that one sees across nearly all human domains in the area. The Javanese *wayang* shadow puppet theater has the power it does precisely because it refers to figures of power who originated elsewhere, as do the Buddhist statues and monasteries of Burma and Thailand, or the Catholic images and dances of the lowland Philippines. One also finds a tendency to produce indigenous social theory about differences across groups, rather than theory that encompasses difference in unity – as one finds, for example, in India and China.

In Indonesian law, adat, Islam, and the positive law of statutes and decrees are each considered to be sources of law, each providing rules that have legal force. From a statist perspective, the distinctions among the three are of mere historical

---

[7] Indeed, the two major histories of Southeast Asia, by Denys Lombard (1990) and Anthony Reid (1988, 1993), have taken the seas, rather than the land masses, as the definitive geographical feature of the area. Both historians were inspired by the work of Fernand Braudel on the Mediterranean.

interest, as bodies of knowledge from which the state has taken its commands. But as debated, lived, and applied, these kinds of law represent three distinct ways of thinking about law, norms, and the state. By inspecting processes in which these categories are invoked, we can discern distinct "metarules" proper to each, rules about what law is, and how it is to be found or created. These ideas about adat, Islam, and positive law will become clearer in subsequent chapters. For the moment schematic contrasts must suffice.

Adat and community

In Indonesia, the sense of a pluralism of norms and values usually is couched in the terms of adat, the Indonesian word with the strongest connotations of localism (though of Arabic origin). Adat can refer to the rules or practices of social life, to feelings and a sense of propriety, or to a somewhat thinner sense of tradition and custom. It may be used to refer to local ways of resolving disputes, rather than to substantive rules, and has been so used in recent appeals to adat ways of overcoming hostility in Ambon and Kalimantan, the sites of violent clashes between social groups. Often it is counterposed to Islamic law or state law. Recently it has been used to mean "local" as opposed to "national," such that the phrase *masyarakat adat*, "adat society," refers to people living under local social norms, and *perempuan adat*, "adat women," really means something like "women speaking for local interests and values" against Jakarta-instigated corruption and repression.

Adat also has a narrower sense, that of "adat law" (*hukum adat*), an expression whose systematic use dates from the period of Dutch colonial rule. To the extent that colonial rulers in the Dutch East Indies wished to rule indirectly, they tried to determine what the local laws might be, and those they consolidated into what they termed adatrecht, adat law. Anthropologists and administrators compiled manuals of the laws in each "adat area" in the Dutch East Indies, and in some regions judges continue to rely on these colonial-era manuals in making decisions. These processes of creating adat law did not so much "invent" it, the term often used for the parallel processes in Africa (Adas 1995; Chanock 1985; Moore 1986), but made into rules those expressions and proverbs that once had been public starting-points for complex political processes. These older processes did not apply rules, but sought out equitable solutions to social problems (F. von Benda-Beckmann 1979; Ellen 1983; Geertz 1983).

Since Indonesian independence the matter has become much more complex. In the late 1950s, shortly after independence, the Indonesian Supreme Court claimed that the revolution had propelled Indonesians toward a new, national kind of adat law, in which the equality of men and women was a notable principle. The dissonance between this claim and actual social practices left to local courts the problem of figuring out how to decide what adat law was or was to be. Was a norm part of local adat law if it guided the current handling of local affairs, or if it was how old men said affairs used to be handled, or if it is how the Supreme Court said all Indonesians ought to conduct their affairs? Put another way, is *adat* to be discovered, remembered, or prescribed (see Lev 1962, 1965)?

Sharî'a and jurisprudence

With adat there is one term and multiple uses, multiple ideas about how it comes to be and is to be found and applied. With "Islamic law," at least three Indonesian terms of Arabic origin are involved: *hukum*, *sharî'a*, and *fiqh*. Hukum has three quite distinct meanings in Indonesia. In its broadest use it refers to "law" in general, and includes statutes, anything given legal status in courts, and broader notions of penalty, judgment, or consequence such as "law of the jungle" (*hukum rimba*). Within Islamic discourse the term refers to the legal value given to any action, from obligatory (*wajib*) to forbidden (*harâm*).[8] Hukum has a third Islamic-legal meaning as well, that of the valid consequences of an act. The hukum of a husband uttering certain words is divorce; the hukum of a man and a woman's guardian exchanging the words of a marriage formula is marriage, and so forth. Hukum in this sense is a "constitutive speech act" in the tradition of Oxford philosophers. Here, too, there is a scale of validity of such acts. The most important terms are those designating the end-points on this scale: "valid" (Ind. *sah*, Ar. *sahîh*) and "invalid" (Ind. *batal*, Ar. *bâtil*). From the perspective of Islamic law, what we may say is that hukum is most importantly about assigning certain values and certain binding consequences to specific acts.

What is at stake with the second "law" term, sharî'a (Arabic *sharî'a*), is far broader. Sharî'a is the path or the way that was pointed out by God and His Messengers for all humans. It is sharî'a that Muslims have in mind when they say that nothing in the world is outside Islam. But this path, even if it is all-encompassing, is not clearly set out in all its detail for humans. It must be discerned through correct interpretation of the specific directives and the general principles found in the Qur'ân, the *hadîth*, and the consensus of the Islamic community. Muslim scholars, in evaluating Indonesian laws, have had as their reference point not a fully codified, fully encompassing law, but a

---

[8] The continuum extends from obligatory (*wajib*, Ar. *wâjib*), through recommended (*sunna*), permissible or indifferent (*mubâh*), and reprehensible (*makrûh*), to all that is forbidden (*harâm*). The familiar term *halâl* refers to everything not forbidden, in other words, all acts falling under the four categories other than harâm. As the reader might already suspect, the terminology and the distinctions are more numerous than suggested here, and there is more than one continuum of valuation (see Schacht 1964:120–23). In particular, the term *fard*, which yields Indonesian *perlu*, also refers to obligatory acts but is used to distinguish between duties incumbent on each individual (*fard 'ayn*) and duties that fall on the community as a whole (*fard kifâya*).

general set of guidelines, sharî'a, and a much more narrowly focused set of valuations, hukum.

Linking hukum to sharî'a, specific consequences to general guidelines, is the act of jurisprudential interpretation, or fiqh. Fiqh refers to knowledge but in an active sense, as an interpretive process. Fiqh is another candidate for "law," but only in the sense of law as active engagement with texts and norms, not law as sacred rules. Fiqh is fallible; it is human knowledge of a divine law. Islamic jurisprudence also generally recognizes the state as a source of valid law, and specifically of "policy for religious law" or *siyasah sharî'a*. The state has the legitimate power to regulate how acts that have a particular religious-law status (hukum in the third, narrow sense described above) are to be carried out.

So far, fairly clear; but this sort of typology has a way of becoming muddled in practice, and different actors have different interests in representing "law" in particular ways. Each of these ideas of law brings in different ideas of legitimacy. "Sharî'a" can serve as an all-purpose term. In July 2000, the Governor of Aceh declared that henceforth his government would "develop, guide, and oversee the application of Islamic Sharî'a" in the province, but officials were hesitant to say what this measure would mean.[9] "Fiqh" is more specific, as an interpretive process that is inherently older and broader than the state. Legitimating a proposition in terms of fiqh involves citing decisions and positions taken in Islamic history in the Islamic world, with little place for specifying an Indonesian content. "Hukum" can refer to both of the above, or to state statutes, or to "law" in general.

Some of this semantic muddle is due to the efforts of colonial and postcolonial states to bring fiqh under state control. Islamic jurisprudence in much of the region that eventually became the Dutch East Indies was carried out by more or less trained jurists and judges, the former giving legal opinions (*fatâwa*) about Islamic law, the latter hearing disputes and rendering judgments, all of which was carried out in more or less informal settings (Lev 1972a). Dutch efforts to create Dutch-like Islamic tribunals were followed by a series of Indonesian state efforts to "regularize" Islamic law, culminating in a 1989 bill that established a national court structure with, among other things, parallel Islamic and civil courts at the district and provincial levels, all under the jurisprudential supervision of the Supreme Court (Cammack 1989). Despite this legal domestication of Islamic law, Islam as a discursive tradition continues to provide a world-wide universe of past and present interpretations of the Qur'ân and the Prophet's sayings, interpretations that need not make reference to state law.

[9] The order, technically a *Peraturan Daerah*, "regional order," was published in the legal journal of record, *Varia Peradilan* (184:113–22), in January 2001; the quoted phrase is Article 3 of the order. This step was authorized in 1999 by the Indonesian Parliament as part of the law allowing greater legal autonomy for Aceh, and it was later put into a statute of the Acehnese Parliament (*Lembaran Daerah Aceh* No. 30, 25 August 2000).

Sharî'a and adat share the feature of reaffirming worlds of law outside the state, indeed, worlds existing before the state, that do not require state sanction for their legitimacy. However, the two normative systems resonate across different domains. Throughout their colonial histories, in most Muslim-majority countries Islamic law was restricted to "family law," and the most widely felt demands for "applying sharî'a" have had to do with matters of marriage, divorce, inheritance, and male–female relationships more generally (and, in Indonesia, much less with matters of commerce, theft, and so forth). Adat plays on different normative registers. Despite New Order government efforts to limit adat to domains of marriage customs, kinship, and art (and thereby have it substitute for sharî'a), it has retained a sense of legitimacy as a basis for resolving disputes, regulating land use, and, more vaguely, regulating interethnic relationships.

The boundaries of state law

The idea of state law (*hukum negara*), or positive law, at first glance seems more clear-cut than do sharî'a and adat, because of the familiarity to Western readers of such institutions as the Parliament, the courts, and an Executive Branch, all the heirs of a Dutch colonial system modeled on the Roman-French-Dutch civil law tradition. Indonesia, today, has a judicial system in theory independent of the executive and consisting of a number of specialized courts, plus two nationwide hierarchies: first-instance civil courts and Islamic courts at the district (*kabupaten*) level, each with its own provincial appellate court; both subject to cassation by the Indonesian Supreme Court.

And yet some (e.g., Lindsey 1999) would say that the "rule of law" has not taken hold in contemporary Indonesia because the idea of a tripartite government is a sham: the legal system itself, starting from the 1945 Constitution, relieves the president of any obligation to account for his or her actions to Parliament or to the Supreme Court. The Constitution makes the president the chosen "mandatory" of the superparliament, the MPR (Majelis Permusyawaratan Rakyat, People's Consultative Assembly), which consists of parliamentarians plus additional appointed delegates. Indeed, it was this body that in July 2001 voted to remove President Abdurrahman Wahid from office, automatically elevating to that office his vice-president, Megawati Sukarnoputri.

But by the turn of the century the legitimacy of all state institutions had been severely weakened. Corrupt judges, delegates elected in fixed elections, a president who entered office under the banner of reform but quickly was tainted with old-style scandals: these, unfortunately, became the branches of the early "reform" state. In the search for legitimacy, international and transnational concepts were imported: a truth and reconciliation commission, human rights tribunals, "voting" in the legislature (rather than state-managed acclamations by consensus).

The tainted character of the new "new order" has been scandalous because it prevents Indonesians from blaming their problems entirely on Suharto. Institutional reform, strengthening the judiciary, will doubtless be part of any possible improvement in Indonesia's political condition. Constitutions can be reinterpreted, and jurists and judges have begun to propose a stronger notion of "judicial review" of statutes and of presidential orders (*Inpres, Instruksi Presiden*); indeed, a number of repressive orders delivered by Suharto have been challenged and are likely to become dead letter rules.

On another level, the basic interrelationships between separate sources of norms and laws are being rethought. Adat and sharî'a increasingly are invoked as new sources of hope for order and justice in the provinces. Refashioning what is understood by hukum, by adat, and by sharî'a is a task that will occupy the attention of many Indonesians over the coming years.

This task also requires understanding how they came to be intertwined with positive law, with hukum negara, in the first place. The actions of the colonial and postcolonial states to incorporate adat and Islam into substantive law, or "positivize" them, created new ambiguities. Some of the uncertainties stemmed from Dutch policies that segregated the legal systems, with "natives," "Europeans," and non-native "Asians" treated as legally different types of person, and within the category of "natives," differential treatment of Muslims and non-Muslims. This policy of state-law pluralism meant that, upon independence, some citizens of the new Indonesia were used to having their affairs judged under something other than the civil law tradition, and, indeed, many of them saw this compartmentalization of laws as granting them a small measure of autonomy, whether as Muslims, or as members of an ethnic group (Lev 1972b, 1978, 1985; Lindsey 1999).

As a result, creating a unified legal system after independence meant either replacing adat law and Islamic law with positive law, or developing a legal rationale for preserving separate spheres of judgment. What happened during the Sukarno and Suharto regimes was a combination of these two processes, replacement and compartmentalization, along with an intermittent attitude of *laissez-faire*, allowing local courts or other bodies to proceed as before, without a consistent rationale as to why they should do so (Lev 1973). Thus, the 1974 Marriage Law provided a set of positive law redefinitions of and constraints on Islamic procedures for marrying and divorcing, and the 1992 Compilation of Islamic Law, "enacted" only as an executive order, extended this "positivization" process to inheritance disputes. These laws replaced an older fiqh process, where judges drew on Arabic-language books of jurisprudence, with a more civil law process of applying a code.

At the same time as these efforts to replace fiqh with positive law, judges were left free to ratify agreements made among parties on the basis of local norms on any subject where doing so would not contravene positive law, a position which allowed judges to continue to apply a form of "adat law." And, finally, the Supreme Court has tended to look the other way when lower courts systematically enforce local patrilineal inheritance norms, despite the Court's rulings against these norms in a handful of cases from the early 1960s.

In some sense, in terms of the traditions of reasoning to which each refers and defers, these three sources of law – adat, sharî'a, and state law – may be seen, in Sally Falk Moore's (1978) words, as "semi-autonomous." To the extent that adat processes still resolve everyday disputes, adat has a delimited "semi-autonomy" in practice as well. Each Indonesian government has tried to shrink that sphere of autonomy, to create something like a juridical field in Pierre Bourdieu's (1987) sense, a political space defined by the variable access to legal resources, with a single hierarchy of adjudication. But the proper shape of such a field is precisely what is under debate in Indonesia today. Whose words *do* have the force of law? Which mechanisms convert simple social actions into legal ones? Which resources are "legal" and which merely "traditional" or "religious"?

Not only are the bases and boundaries of the legal field itself under debate, but two other elements of current Indonesian public life additionally mean that we cannot refer to "law" to predetermine the subject matter of this study. "Law" is never a primitive term. First, as we already have begun to see, the normativity of adat and Islam comes from outside the field of state-constituted law. It is not that the state gives the normative force of law to Islam and adat; it is rather than the state attempts to appropriate their specific normativities to its own institutions. Our subject is thus a multiply located sense of normative pluralism, which interacts with, and in some cases may even serve to define, the sphere of state law itself (see Assier-Andrieu 1987; Dupret 2000; Greenhouse 1982; Griffiths 1986).

Second, the complex of values and norms surrounding marriage, divorce, and inheritance cannot be predefined as mainly about "law." In Indonesia's villages, as we shall see in the next chapter, disputes about inheritance invoke relationships to the ancestors, religious obligations, land histories, and a sense of propriety. In courtrooms, the same disputes are narrowly couched in terms of law, but even in those confines judges invoke broader notions of normativity and tradition. In national debates, disputes about family and marriage evoke worries over Muslim–Christian relations; the legal issues become sites for these worries to be expressed.

Re-understanding Islam

Across the institutions and levels of society examined here – village meetings, judicial disputes, nationwide debates – we return continually to matters of family and gender. Marriage, divorce, and the transmission of goods across generations – the basic practices that constitute, divide, and reproduce family relations – are major sites for contemporary Islamic public reasoning throughout the Muslim world. It is with respect to these key family processes that rules deriving from the interpretation of Islamic texts most often pose challenges to local and transnational norms and values.

The whole of anthropology has pointed to the close interrelationships of family forms with local material and cultural forces: kinship, marriage, and inheritance regulate the way people work, feast, play, and die throughout the world. Land is passed down through lineages or in villages; rights of women and men are functions of the groups they join after marriage; the whole social group is responsible for easing transitions of humans in and out of this world. Here is where demands for uniformity, whether they come from Islam, Christianity, or modernizing individualism, run up most sharply against the reasoned persistence of local culture. Hard though it may be to give up pork, fast for one month in the year, and adopt new forms of worship, these practices can relatively easily be added on to social life. But approaching the family as the result of a contract among individuals rather than as part of an ongoing relationship among social groups, as demanded by the individualistic codes of Islamic and other modern legal systems, has posed acute and difficult challenges to local social life. All the more so as traditions and norms that first developed in the Arabian peninsula, in a specific cultural context, needed to be reasoned through, critiqued, and reinterpreted as they were introduced to peoples in Asia, Africa, Europe, and North America.

This book concerns those processes of reasoning about apparently incompatible ideas, toward workable arrangements to govern everyday social life. It points to the possibilities for reaching agreement as well as the obstacles in the way. I intend it as a refutation of all ideas that Islam (or any other collection of norms) consists of a fixed set of rules – as if a codebook called "shari'a" contained a timeless and repressive plan for abolishing rights and diversity. The history of Muslim societies proves otherwise, but learned people continue to offer broad generalizations about "Islamic civilization" and its supposed incompatibility with "the West." In a reality where Islam has become one of the major religions in North America and Europe, and where Muslim scholars and public figures play increasingly visible roles in public life, with all the demands for accountability and consistency that these roles demand, these broad civilizational contrasts look increasingly out of focus.

Indonesia offers a critical case in our efforts to reorient how we understand Islam. As the largest Muslim society, and at the same time the most distant, in space and in ways of life, from the Arabian heartland (or even from the broader Arabian-Persian-Turkish one), Indonesia is a site of particularly marked struggle to bring together norms and values derived from Islam, from local cultures, and from international public life. And yet the processes and the imperatives are the same as are found elsewhere, whether in Morocco, Iran, or Saudi Arabia. Nowhere is there an "Islamic society," if that phrase implies people simply applying a single set of texts to social life; everywhere there is one if that phrase implies people struggling to rethink those texts in the light of alternative cultural and legal norms.

Studying multilevel phenomena

How, then, does one carry out a study of normative pluralism, if the goal is to show how the issues themselves shift across levels of society? The methodology I have chosen, in the hope of remaining faithful to the questions and topics I pursue, is to combine studies of village life and legal processes in one part of Indonesia, the Gayo highlands of Aceh, Sumatra, with archival court study and broad analyses of national debates.[10] The Gayo cannot possibly be "representative" of Indonesian societies, but the processes and mechanisms found there illustrate the ways in which national legal and political institutions interact with local norms and values.

I have written extensively about the Gayo elsewhere (Bowen 1991, 1993b), where I also mention many of the friends and neighbors who helped me during fieldwork. I will introduce particulars as we go, but a series of snapshots of the "field sites" and working methods used in the book is appropriate here. I lived and worked in the five-village settlement of Isak for over two years in 1978–80, and then returned for frequent visits over the period 1980–82, when I lived in Banda Aceh and Jakarta, and then for two summer visits in 1989 and 1994. I visited Isak briefly in 2000, when random highway shootings made, in my friends' and family's opinions as well as my own, a prolonged stay inadvisable. My village fieldwork was traditional in many ways, including as it did surveys, textual studies, historical work, but above all long hours in conversations with people who became friends: in their houses, on treks over mountains, and while boiling palm sap into sugar in the forest. My continued strong friendships with a few families, those with whom I experience the passing of time most profoundly, include those with Ayah Tengku Asaluddin (since passed away), Abang Kerna, Ibu Inën Rat, Aman Dewi, Aman and Inën Samsu, and Abang Das.

I have at least equally strong personal ties in the main highlands town of Takèngën, where I have been a member of the family of Abang Evi (Zaini Wahab) since my initial visit to the region. I myself grew from late adolescence to "maturity" together with members of that family. Evi, the oldest child, studied English with me as a middle school student in Takèngën, and during her high school years lived in Jakarta, in a house I rented with one of her uncles. She

---

[10] See, regarding the issue of "place" in anthropological fieldwork, the essays collected in Gupta and Ferguson (1997).

since has made her permanent home in the United States, with her Egyptian husband, Ashraf, and has worked first as a successful executive, and then as a fashion designer and non-profit consultant. It was through the continuing relationship with this family that I first came to understand fieldwork as, among other things, a life-long conversation, with a special intimacy that serves as both the condition of possibility for the work and, in a sense that goes beyond professional considerations, the whole point of the enterprise.

My fieldwork in Takèngën initially was an extension of village work, to gain an idea of townspeople's religious and social practices in contrast to those I was studying in Isak. Later, however, town work came to center on the courts. I studied everyday life in the courts and, through work in their archives, their history, on various town visits, but especially in 1994 and again in 2000.

Jakarta is the third field site for the research reported on here, and like all other cities poses special methodological challenges (which I am facing again in new work on Paris). Jakarta is both a local place like any other, and a site for national debates that attract people from across the nation. The "field" appropriately includes social networks, large institutions and their leaders, public intellectuals and jurists, newspaper reports and the discussions people have about them, and so forth, from the highly personal to the most impersonal. In Jakarta I have visited legal aid offices and ministries, courts and judges' homes. I have also learned from friends and colleagues in Jakarta, some of whom themselves are key players in the debates discussed here; they include Gayo family members, especially Abang Gemboyah (Dr. Baharuddin Wahab), as well as friends and colleagues such as Nurcholis Madjid, Azumardi Azra, Taufik Abdullah, and Duane and Reti Gingerich.

In the next chapter, I begin the ethnographic account where my Indonesian fieldwork began, in Isak, with a dispute that raised the question of how, when faced with conflicting norms, people arrive at effective and legally valid resolutions. This case will bring us to an analysis of how norms are used as part of a repertoire, in this case how "adat" and "consensus" can be invoked as cultural categories in order to obtain certain desired ends. This look at local complexities and mechanisms will then lead us, in chapter 3, to a broader consideration of adat as a schema for the interrelation of people, places, and property in Indonesia today.

2   Adat's local inequalities

Isak is only one of Indonesia's thousands of rural villages, and it has its own particularities: Gayo-speaking, Sumatran, coffee-growing, and so forth. But if Isak does not represent Indonesia as a whole, it can illuminate one set of conflicts and deliberations that one would find in any village in the archipelago. Isak residents are engaged in an internal debate over how one can, and should, weight the competing demands of traditional social norms, state-enforced laws, new ideas about equality and mobility, and religious commands. In these debates the categories of "adat," "law," and "Islam," as well as those referring to broad values such as "consensus" and "fairness," serve as resources that speakers can mobilize in their efforts to elicit assent from their fellow villagers. Disputes are settled, or at least quelled, less by applying rules than by assembling persuasive tokens of legitimacy.

Technically, Isak is a grouping of five small villages, totaling about one thousand people. It lies in a valley through which flows the Isak, or Jambo Ayer river, right across the main mountain range of Sumatra, the Bukit Barisan, down to the eastern coast of Aceh province.[1] Most Gayo consider the Isak river valley to contain the oldest villages in the highlands. In the 1980s, Isak residents added coffee growing to their list of means of livelihood, a list which already included irrigated rice-farming, tending water buffalo, and cooking palm-sugar. Households began to plant coffee gardens in forested areas to the west and south of Isak. Some people moved north to clear coffee gardens close to the main town of Takèngën, the capital of the Central Aceh district (*kabupaten*) of Aceh. Improved roads have made it much easier to travel to Takèngën, and beyond to the cities of Banda Aceh, Medan, and Jakarta. Improvements in the southern road, which winds through Karo Batak country on its way to Medan, have made it easier for highlands residents to avoid traveling the roads of coastal Aceh, where attacks by Indonesian troops, Acehnese liberation fighters, and unidentified "third parties" claimed many lives during the 1990s and early 2000s.

---

[1] For details of the history, politics, social organization, and cultural forms of Isak see Bowen (1991).

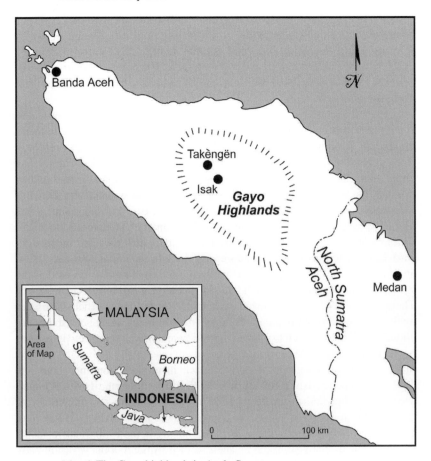

Map 1 The Gayo highlands in Aceh, Sumatra

Beginning in the early 1980s, hundreds of Javanese people entered the Isak area to take up residence in state-sponsored transmigration camps; these camps eventually became state-recognized villages. Most Gayo welcomed the Javanese. Many of the camps are located within a few kilometers of Isak, and the new roads made it possible for Isak residents to continue to live in Isak while working their coffee gardens. Many Gayo also found the Javanese provided good examples of how to prosper in agriculture. Some Isak residents moved permanently to the camp areas, and by 1994 one Gayo man who had learned Javanese had become headman of one of the new, majority-Javanese villages.

The new coffee crops bore fruit just in time to enable most Isak people to weather the Indonesian economic crisis of the late 1990s, and at the end of that decade most people probably were economically better off than they had been before the rise in coffee growing. A power generator now brings electricity to many of the homes in Isak, and satellite dishes (about forty of them by mid-2000) give access to international television. The past two *bupatis*, district heads of Central Aceh, have been sons of Isak, and have brought some of these improvements to the area.

In 1999, the relationship of peaceful coexistence among Gayo, Javanese, and Acehnese was brutally ruptured by a series of killings in Javanese settlements throughout the highlands. Resistance to rule by Jakarta had been present in Aceh, including the Central Aceh highlands, since the 1950s. The Darul Islam armed resistance lasted from 1952 through the late 1950s, officially ending in 1962, but some of the movement's leaders never abandoned the dream of independence from Jakarta. The DI's successor was GAM (Gerakan Acheh Merdeka, the Free Aceh Movement), called the Gang of Troublemakers (GPK, Gerombolan Pengacau Keamanan) by Jakarta until such pretense became absurd. GAM activities in Aceh rose steadily through the mid-1970s and 1980s, and flared up in 1990, largely in reaction to the brutal repression carried out by the Indonesian military, which included the torture and murder of villagers. These acts elicited a violent response from GAM, but the conflicts have been made worse by acts of provocation and by "people taking advantage of the situation," as friends so often explained night-time gunfire or shots fired at passing buses. In the early 1990s the violence largely by-passed the highlands, but later in the decade armed groups began to attack Javanese settlers near Isak and Takèngën. When I visited Isak in June 2000, friends told me that about a hundred unidentified bodies had been pulled from nearby rivers and ditches during the previous year. It was unclear to them who was killing whom. Hundred of bodies were found in settlements north of Takèngën in the first half of 2001. In the middle of that year, some Javanese, armed by the Indonesian army, were attacking Gayo and Acehnese in those northern settlements, and thousands of people fled to the northern coast.[2] The killing in the Gayo highlands subsided in late 2001 and early 2002, but has continued unabated elsewhere in Aceh.

Throughout these recent, violent years, which remind many of the violence of the Darul Islam period in the mid-1950s and the massacres of "communists" (often political or personal enemies) in the mid-1960s, the Gayo have found themselves poised precariously between the Acehnese and the Indonesian state. Although they, too, have suffered under military violence and New Order repression, on the whole the Gayo have maintained a strong sense of kin-mediated

---

[2] The origins and composition of "militias" in northern Central Aceh remain unclear; some Javanese have been quoted as seeking to defend themselves "against GAM," but the role of certain Gayo is unclear. Political rivalries between the current bupati and other Takèngën politicians and traders seem to play a role. In any case, the presence of such armed militias, reminiscent of the militias in East Timor, chills.

relationships to the country as a whole. Many "grandchildren" of Isak play major roles in education, law, and civil service in Jakarta and elsewhere in Indonesia. They do not regard with favor the idea of living under Acehnese domination in a separate country or in a highly autonomous special area of Aceh. On 28 July 2001, the majority of delegates to the Central Aceh Parliament supported a popular proposal to create a separate Indonesian province that would consist of the Central and Southeastern Aceh districts, and perhaps part of South Aceh.[3]

For the moment, Gayo remain very much part of Indonesia; most, I think, see themselves as continuing to be so, however the Indonesian state eventually may be reconfigured.

Disentangling norms in practice

The early years of the third millennium have been a particularly unstable period in highlands history. The political and legal institutions in the highlands are in disarray. The district attorney and most judges not native to the area fled in 1999, leading the civil court to shut down and the religious court to work with half its previous number of judges. Other non-native officials also left the region. Decentralization is promised for this as for other districts in Indonesia, but so is a new degree of autonomy for Aceh under which Muslims are to be governed by sharî'a.[4] The general state of violence has led many Gayo to move to Medan or Jakarta.

Whatever the future political and legal system shakes up to be, it will require Gayo men and women to continue doing what they have been doing, that is, to try and reconcile, or at least negotiate among, the conflicting norms and values that have local currency. Neither autonomy nor independence will put an end to the legitimacy of Gayo notions about their own adat, or that of decisions and judgments made in the name of Islam, or the changing cultural ideas about family and gender that grow out of, and shape, local social practices and social criticisms.

Convinced as I am that disputes are excellent starting points for understanding how such negotiations are carried out, I was quickly intrigued when, on a visit to

---

[3] As reported in *Waspada*, 30 July 2001. Three days earlier, 15,000 Central Acehnese residents, presumably mostly Gayo, had demonstrated outside the Parliament building in support of the proposal to create the new province.

[4] A 1999 bill (Law 25, 1999) set out the conditions for autonomy for Indonesia's provinces, and contained some special dispensations for Aceh, particularly the right to retain 70 percent of oil and gas revenues, a much larger percentage than that retained by other provinces. This bill made possible the subsequent "Laws for the State of Aceh Darussalam" (*Undang-undang Nanggroe Aceh Darussalam, NAD*), signed into law by President Megawati Sukarnoputri in July 2001; the bill, significantly, gives the province an Acehnese name (the *NAD*), but retains the common Indonesian spelling "Aceh" instead of the GAM-favored "Acheh."

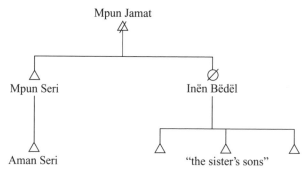

Figure 2.1 The descendants of Mpun Jamat, 1994

Isak in July 1994, I heard that a long-standing argument over a piece of property was coming to a head. At issue was land associated with Kramil village, the Isak village that I have followed most closely over the past two decades. The quarrel pitted Mpun Seri and his son, Aman Seri (Grandfather of Seri, and Father of Seri, respectively), against Mpun Seri's sister's sons and their children. The two sides each claimed a rather valuable one-half hectare parcel of land, on which stood six houses and the adjoining gardens.

The argument reached back to events occurring in the late colonial period, when Mpun Seri's father, Mpun Jamat, sought to marry off his children. To his son (later called Mpun Seri) he gave some riceland and his own house, both located in Isak. For his daughter he found a husband from the west coast. The boy married into the family under the type of marriage called *angkap nasab*, "uxorilocal for life," meaning that the couple was obliged to remain in the area to care for the wife's parents.[5] They became known as Aman and Inën Bëdël once their first child was born.[6]

Aman and Inën Bëdël lived in a house located about a kilometer from the center of Isak, but they worked the Isak ricefields together with Mpun Seri, and the two men became close friends. This arrangement came to an end in 1952, when the Acehnese Darul Islam rebellion broke out, and troops from Java occupied Isak. These troops began to search for rebel forces in the forest, and it became dangerous to live far away from the main concentration of people. Mpun Seri invited his sister's family to live on his own land in Isak. He built

---

[5] It has long been common to offer Acehnese from the west or north coasts positions as sons-in-law on these terms; for that reason this type of marriage is sometimes called *"angkap Aceh."* These men are quickly integrated into village life and no ethnic distinctions are made between their children and those of others.

[6] Gayo use teknonyms, meaning that after the birth of their first child, parents trade in their personal names for *Aman* ("father of ") [child's name] and *Inën* ("mother of ") [child's name]. Upon the birth of their first grandchild, they both become *Mpun* ("grandparent of ") [child's name].

six houses on the land: three for himself and for his own children, and three for her family, including her three sons.

In the 1990s, long after the death of their parents, these three sons and their children occupied the three houses given to Aman and Inën Bëdël. The sons spent most of their time cultivating coffee north of Takèngën. Suddenly, early in 1994, Mpun and Aman Seri summarily ordered the sons and their families to either vacate the houses or pay a market (high) price for them. Aman Seri insisted that the land had never been theirs, that it had only been loaned to the sister's family. He let it be known that he held a deed that gave him title to the entire land parcel. (As the village religious official, the *imëm* of Kramil, he had been able to obtain the deed directly from the land office in town rather than following the normal route through the village headman, who might not have approved of his action.) He had also paid the tax on this land for the previous three years, a clever step that strengthened his claim in the eyes of the state. He went so far as to have his own son-in-law begin laying a cement foundation on an unused portion of the disputed land.

For their part, the sister's sons argued that their mother had been given the land outright in 1952, and that they had a perfect right to remain on it. Unsettled by Aman Seri's legal actions, however, they demanded that they be given title to the property. They did offer to give Mpun Seri a token payment for the land, but no more than that. Others in the village took one or the other side. Some argued that to evict the sister's sons would be breaking their ties to their ancestor, Mpun Jamat. Others said that the land had only been loaned. Despite earlier efforts at mediation, the two sides had not been able to reach agreement, and each had lodged complaints with the police. The matter had threatened to get out of hand when Aman Kerna, the former head of Kramil village, called a meeting to try and resolve the dispute.

Aman Kerna had been a healer as well as a headman, and was now something of an elder statesman in the community. He was one of my main teachers in Gayo affairs. In 1998 he made the pilgrimage to Mecca. He was skilled at weaving together homilies, adat proverbs, carefully worded accounts of each side's actions, and directives of his own. The meeting he called was of a sort that would be called a *musyawarah desa* in Indonesian, a "village deliberative discussion." Isak people, less concerned than are state ideologues to find nouns for events, spoke of people "coming together" (*morum*) that evening, who would "come to a decision" (*mupakat*). Such meetings are emblematic of Indonesian ways of resolving disputes, especially as idealized by commentators on and in Indonesia: disputants meet and, through mellifluous verbal exchanges, reach a state of specific agreement and general harmony.

These village meetings are supposed to paint a formal word-portrait of a process of creating harmony. The parties should exchange some formalized phrases, which begin as statements of their initial positions, and then move towards statements of agreement and resolution. But norms are one thing and practices another, and these days many such events resemble the meeting called by Aman Kerna, in that one individual dominated the meeting, searched for new ways of framing events, and left many of those attending uncertain as to whether anything had been resolved at all.

Aman Seri and his close relatives were the first to arrive at the house designated for the meeting; the sister's sons straggled in late, having traveled directly from their coffee gardens north of Takèngën. Aman Kerna opened the meeting with prayers, and then held the floor for nearly an hour, allowing only brief responses to questions that he posed.

In the meeting, Aman Kerna tried to do something more than calm the two sides. He endeavored to create an agreement that would respect the legitimate claims of the ancestors on their descendants, and at the same time take into account future potential legal claims based either on Islamic family law or on the possession of land title. These three types of claims – those of the ancestors, Islam, and the state – are not perfectly reconcilable with each other, notably because ancestors' claims demand the sort of multiple and context-dependent relationships of persons to land that are at odds with the finalizing, context-independent concepts of sale, gift, or inheritance found in both Islamic law and Indonesian civil law.

In Aman Kerna's speech these incompatibilities gave rise to a discursive instability, as he shifted among different possible resolutions of the conflict, none of them completely satisfactory. He began by placing the dispute in the context of the norms of Gayo adat; specifically, the obligations that all hold to their ancestors. He reminded everyone of the reasons why one should follow adat, and recalled what had happened in the time of their grandfather, Mpun Jamat:

So, if these children fight, it must be resolved; that is the task of the parents, because for them as well, he [pointing to Mpun Seri] is the only parent here, and because the wish of grandfather [Mpun Jamat] at that time was as such. What was his wish, the wish spoken to our parent [Mpun Seri]? "Provision while alive, bury when dead"; that is why grandfather's wish came to be part of adat.[7]

---

[7] (070) "Keta ikë pelulu kekanak ni, harus idamèn. Ini tugës ni jema tuë, sebeb ni paké ini pé, oya wë jema tuë sara, karna niët ni awan sa'at né, oya. Sana niët ku jema tuë? Uripi murip, tanom maté, oya kati niët ni awan terjadi si masuk ku ëdët."
    Aman Kerna uses Malay-Indonesian words from time to time when speaking Gayo, as do many other people in Isak, often when referring to a political-legal fact, such as "masuk ku ëdët" instead of "mayo," signaling the social norms that will be relevant for the entire ensuing discussion. Semantic differences also motivate the choice of Indonesian words; in this case, for example, "masuk" has the idiomatic meaning of "is included in"; the Gayo word is less idiomatic when used in this way. (Numbers preceding Gayo transcriptions indicate tape recorder counter indications.)

Starting points are everything – he who writes the agenda rules the meeting – and Aman Kerna's starting point was the *niët* of their grandfather, Mpun Jamat, to bring a son-in-law into the family. A niët, an intention or a wish, or a *manat*, a request or a legacy, concerning something of this order – marriage, succession, or land use – is not a matter of a fleeting mental state, but is, rather, a directive for descendants to observe and carry out. These directives provide the main moral anchor for social continuity in the Gayo highlands. As Aman Kerna will later remark, a failure to respect a niët severs ties with the ancestors: our prayers no longer reach them, and their blessings – for health, fertility, or good crops – no longer reach us. In this case, grandfather's directive had been that the marriage of his daughter to a man from the west coast begin that perduring relationship of sons-in-law to parents that is labeled angkap nasab and that is routinely referred to by the maxim quoted above. Sometimes the maxim includes a third phrase, "using the broken needle" (*pemaké jarum patah*), that signals the son-in-law's continued use of the estate after the parents' death. Much of the dispute hinged on the obligations attached to that relationship, the extent to which such obligations had been inherited by the sister's sons, and what they had to do with rights to the disputed land.

"Legal pluralism" recognized

Aman Kerna pointed out that these obligations were quite apart from anything required by "hukum," by which, at *this* point in his speech, he meant the Islamic rules of marriage and inheritance. "These words are not found in hukum," he said. "With hukum, you marry off a child, and no matter where he/she wanders, the child gets the share [of the estate] determined in the Qur'ân." Rather, he explained, the obligations were a matter of "adat."

Gayo "adat" (*ëdët*) includes practices, norms, and claims about social life that draw their force not from scripture, nor from a positive-law-like process of enactment, but from their source in the Gayo past. Adat is a source of legitimate categories, practices, and understandings that, once enacted, carry a predictable and morally weighty set of obligations. Mpun Jamat's son-in-law had agreed to marry under the adat category of angkap nasab, and so had cut himself off from his past – his family, his village, his identity as an ethnic Acehnese. His new isolation, his condition of hanging in space until he should be taken into his new family, was expressed by Aman Kerna in the words of a common Gayo maxim: "Skyward there is no summit; earthward there are no roots."[8] The son-in-law's new identity was that of a man tied to his wife's parents, obliged to "provision while alive, bury when dead," and whose claims to property depended on his continuing relationship of service to and coresidence with his wife's family.

---

[8] "ikë ku langit gërë wé mupucak; ikë ku bumi gërë wé muuyët."

Having identified the grandfather's wishes, Aman Kerna urged all those attending the meeting to respect those wishes and to resolve their differences without interference from government officials, lest this "argument among kin" become a "formal dispute" (*perkara*, the word used for litigation). Not resolving differences is easy in today's climate, he added, because when people find themselves losing an argument, "they make appeal to three sorts of hukum: God's hukum in the Qur'ân, hukum adat, and hukum negara (the law of the state)."

At this point Aman Kerna began to use "hukum" in an expanded sense, to refer to the three types of norms insofar as they acquire legal force.

Now, when we consider disputes these days, we find that these three hukums conflict among themselves. If someone is called to give account according to adat, he runs to Islamic law; if he is called to account on the basis of Islamic law, he runs to the rules of the state. Now, choosing the rules of the state means appearing before a judge. If he does that, then the family breaks up, and our grandfather's niët, just mentioned, is annulled. And if we change [the niët] we all commit sins; father's brother here [Mpun Seri] sins too.[9]

When he declared that "these three laws fight among themselves," Aman Kerna decried not the existence of more than one set of rules and forums, but the consequences that ensue when people turn away from adat and towards the state. These negative consequences include not just the inherently conflictual nature of litigation, but also, and more centrally here, the inevitable outcome of litigation: no judge would recognize as legally relevant the obligations of his generation toward the grandfather. Courts would deny the validity of the adat arrangement, and would consider only a title or a bill of sale as proof of ownership. Even though adat and Islam are sources of law, and thus can be called hukum, the judge looks only at who has title to a plot of land, and does not consider more deeply the web of obligations surrounding it.

The case at hand illustrates law's refusal to recognize the complexities of adat. In his next statement Aman Kerna called to mind the moment when Mpun Seri extended an invitation to his sister. "Why did they build those houses? Because the brother and sister *mupakat* (reached an agreement)." Because times were dangerous, he continued, Mpun Seri invited his sister to live with him on his land. We may not annul that agreement, he said, "but that which is not valid (*sah*), let us make it valid, as children to parents."[10]

---

[9] (071) "tulu 'hukumën: hukum ollah wan Qur'ân, hukum ëdët, hukum negara. Jadi, si tulu ngë perebut, ikë kita èngon perkara besilo ni. Talu terëdët, mayo terukum; talu terukum, mayo terperaturën negara. Jadi ikë ku peraturën negara turah ku hakim; ikë ku hakim ceré-beré, niët ni awan sat né batal. Jadi ikë kite robah, dosa kitë, ngah pé dosa."

[10] [109] "enti né batalan, keta si gërë sah, isahan, sebagai anak ku jema tuë."

The original agreement was certainly valid under the norms of adat. Was not the land given to the sister at that moment? And yet, he continued, the transaction was not so clear as that:

if we consider his intentions toward his sister, they were good, [the land] was given. But what we do not understand clearly here concerns the two types of giving: one type is conditional giving (*osah mukait*); the other is definitive giving (*osah mutlak*). When I look into the matter, it seems that the land was given conditionally, so I hope that father's brother here clarifies this matter of conditions, so no one is driven away; this would make us all ashamed.

The land's status needs to be made "valid" and "clear," then, not because of something wrong in adat terms about the transfer, but because the land was given conditional on the continuing social relationship defined by the marriage. This gift was therefore not of the definitive (*mutlak*) sort that would resemble the absolute property right (*milik*) recognized by the state through its assignments of title deeds (and also recognized in Islamic law). The sister's children's claim cannot be rejected, because it is based on their ancestor's wishes, but neither can it be left as it is, because its form is recognized as valid neither by the state nor under the terms of Islamic law.

What, then, can be done? Aman Kerna proposed converting the conditional gift into a transaction that the state would acknowledge as a sale of land to the sister's sons, but that the parties involved would recognize as "clarifying," and not annulling, the conditional nature of the gift. Therein lay the tricky part – what would such a transaction be? Here is how Aman Kerna put it, by invoking a kind of moral double bookkeeping:

So father's brother [Mpun Seri] has the right as the parent, he validates the giving [of the land] to these children – and don't you raise claims to it anymore! The children ask his permission, give him something, however much they like, just so it is not a sale. Because in adat, it's like this: even if you sell something, if it is to someone else or if it is among your own relatives, the price is not the same. We can sell it only because we are willing to sign our names [to a deed].[11]

There will, then, be a sale, but all will agree that it is not a sale. Why the subterfuge? At stake is not a vague respect for tradition or a fussiness over terms, but some very practical problems in religious communication. When one sends prayers to ancestors, those prayers travel along a chain that depends on a very specific type of material support, namely, the handing down of ancestral land from parent to child. If the material chain is broken, the prayers can reach only

---

[11] (142) "Keta berhak ngah selaku jema tuë, ngah mengesahkan penosahan ku anak ni, enti né ungkit-ungkit, dan anak ni muniro izin ku ngah si këdër mudah, kë beta, gërë nguk juël-beli. Karna, iwan ëdët pé, beta kirë-kirë, ikë orum jema juël, ikë orum diri, walaupun ku juël, gërë dis rëgëë. Kati nguk pé juël karna nguk kitë mera tanda tangani."

the living, not the dead. If the land remains with the sister's sons, explains Aman Kerna, then:

When we recite prayers to our ancestors, to the inhabitants of the graves, it reaches father, grandfather, and grandmother. However, if [the land] goes to other people, then when we pray it only goes to father's brother here . . . That is why there arose adat that we should not sell to other people, because when we have a ritual meal, we call spirits of all Muslims of our ancestors, that's why, in my view, this adat is very good. But now the world has moved along and it is no longer like that, so let us fix things. So do not annul [the gift], and let's not have it be a conditional gift any longer; let's draw up a deed.

Aman Kerna then continued to remind them of the dire consequences that would ensue if they were to continue to argue, and urged them to do as follows:

So, father's brother, change what transpired between you and our aunt, and give them the land unconditionally, and, whether it is little or much that they offer you, you must accept it. But they then are obliged to care for you, that was the niët of our grandfather [Mpun Jamat], "supporting while alive, burying when dead, using the broken needle": that was grandfather's niët – and if they fail to do that we can come for them and demand that they do.

Aman Kerna went on to suggest how Mpun Seri could spend two nights with one of the sister's sons, then two nights with another – not because anyone desired such a mobile sleeping arrangement (least of all Mpun Seri), but because by spelling out these actions Aman Kerna gave tangible form to the idea of not breaking the affinal tie. The sister's children still bore their obligations to care for the mother's brother's side, and Mpun Seri had the right to live with any of them whenever he wanted.

When he had finished his monologue, Aman Kerna asked Mpun Seri for his opinion of the proposed solution.[12] The older man replied succinctly, "Just so they do not sell it off." At this, Aman Kerna turned to the sister's sons and reminded them that "it is not a sale, and you cannot sell it, only give it back to our father here, or to Aman Seri, because if you did [sell it] then where would be the tie to our grandfather? His wishes would be annulled if you did so."

At this point an apparent resolution was reached: Aman Seri and the sister's sons agreed to draw up a document attesting to a transfer of land to the sister's sons. But they disagreed over how the transfer was to be spoken of – there were no categories that had both the desired legal effects and the desired implications about marriages and ancestors. Aman Kerna proposed that the document say that the land was given as *hibah*, the Islamic law category of "gift," and thus

---

[12] Unlike ritual speaking, where a designated interlocutor frequently ratifies the speaker's words with words meaning "yes, truly," in this case and in other meetings with more fluid scripts the monologue was performed in silence, with responses only afterwards. I think no one was really sure what was to be the outcome; most preferred to see what others did or said over the ensuing days.

irrevocable, and without any explicit mention of recompense. Aman Seri (and others) objected to using the term "hibah," on grounds that it implied that the transfer broke the spiritual link to the ancestors and would prevent prayers from reaching the grandfather. Aman Seri suggested using the Gayo term for a gift, *penosan*, which has no clear legal meaning, no connection with the legal world of individuated private property, and it was with that suggestion that the discussion ended.

A necessary subterfuge

Consider the difficulties encountered by Aman Kerna in labeling the transaction. The land's status had to be converted into a sale so that the sister's sons' claims would be recognized by the state, and the dispute not resurface in the future. A clear advantage lay in making use of state-backed property rights to gain some certainty about future control of the land. But a sale could lead to danger if it broke the spiritual ties to the grandfather, so the sale must be really a gift. But the gift could not be the formal gift recognized by Islamic law, the hibah, because the idea of hibah also implies cutting off ties – except for gifts from parents to children, hibahs may not be taken back.

Therefore the sale had become an informal gift, to be matched by a gift from the sister's sons, who must then declare that they are still caught up in the web of reciprocities implied by the marriage, and express their willingness to act in the way sons-in-law are supposed to act by welcoming Mpun Seri to live with them. The fiction, played out at great length that evening, that he would live first with one of the brothers, then the other, was intended to dramatize the kinship character of the relationship sufficiently to counteract the impression of a sale.

The brothers pulled off a side deal towards the end of the meeting, managing to have additional lands divided into inheritance parcels, with the stipulation that whoever cared for Mpun Seri in his last days would receive his own parcel. Aman Seri was taken unawares by this request – he had hoped to end up with most or all of this property – but the logic that linked receiving property to "caring for our father" had been accepted and was hard to refute.

Over the next few days the consensus of others in the village was that the sister's sons had won a great deal. From once fearing total dispossession, they now had assured title to the land, at a "price" of their choosing, and they had obtained the promise of additional lands as well. Aman Seri was very discontented, insisting that Aman Kerna had sold off what he had no right to sell off, namely Aman Seri's claims to the land on the grounds of his possession of title. Aman Seri pinpointed the moment when the proceedings went the wrong way: when Aman Kerna started off his speech by recalling the agreement between Mpun Seri and his sister. "The agreement between father and aunt was annulled when I got title to the land. I'll sell it to them, but at market prices!" he insisted vehemently. For his part, Aman Kerna told me that he had had a dream after the meeting in which he was eating eight *lukup* fruit, which he took as a sign (I never found out why) that the agreement was going to fall through, because they had allowed Aman Seri to do precisely what he now threatened to do: set the price high, which would lead the brothers to denounce it as a sale and to repudiate the deal.

Several other people who had attended the meeting pointed out to me the significance of the posture adopted by the local police chief, who had been asked to attend, in part because of his own kin ties to the parties, and in part because he was perceived by some, certainly by Aman Kerna, as capable of helping to enforce the eventual agreement. He had signaled that he wanted no part of the agreement by remaining silent throughout the proceedings, and by wrapping himself in his sarung and at times nearly turning his back on the others. (I had perceived his actions but not understood their significance.) He himself said the next morning that "they did not need so much around and around talk; they should have just divided the land and set the price." The village headman, Aman Samsu (who did not attend), said that because Aman Seri had not been asked to speak at length, the decision taken at the meeting was not valid.[13]

In part the dispute had been about past events – including whether Mpun Seri had even owned the land in question – but it was intensified and peculiarly shaped by the tension between two kinds of claims: property rights and deeds that allow free use or sale of property, on the one hand; ties to spirits kept open by maintaining land in the family and keeping past promises, on the other. As suggested by Aman Kerna's successive backtrackings, from "sale" to "gift" to something still less formal, the conceptual terrain of the evening was uncharted. Although the dispute continued after the meeting, his words were a sophisticated attempt to find footing amidst the criss-crossing currents of deeply felt obligations toward ancestors, rules of Islamic law, and the powerful state-issued tokens of land titles and tax receipts. Aman Kerna knew that if the dispute ever went to the religious court the land might all be redivided, relatives long departed from Kramil might demand shares, and the grandfather's intent would be thwarted and his legacy renounced. What he sought was a way to keep faith with past promises by reinvigorating the adat relationship of sons-in-law to their parents-in-law, and at the same time forestalling court challenges by handing out clear titles to land shares, titles that would prevent challenges in either the religious court (because the division would have been accepted by all parties) or the civil court (because the ownership rights would be in writing).

Aman Kerna's efforts involved both legal actions (getting title), deliberative processes (this and many other nightly sessions), and discursive innovations

---

[13] Although in May 2000, Aman Samsu said to me that he thought that the conflict over the houses was now resolved.

(the "gift-that-is-not-a-gift"). They are among many such subtle shiftings in language, claims, and social ties that Gayo men and women are deploying in the face of a changing social and legal environment, one in which they find themselves often desperately bound up in conflicting sets of norms and laws, each of which claims to bear on the matter at hand.

His efforts to disentangle norms can be judged to have been successful. Two of the three brothers did indeed accept the offer, pay something to Mpun Seri, and continue to have their children live on part of the land. No case was ever brought to court and the dispute did not resurface. Aman Seri continued to occupy his share of the houses until his death in 2000.

Let me leave the case of the Kramil houses by noting three features of public reasoning in Indonesian disputes that we will see reappear throughout this book. First, Aman Kerna took as a given that the people of Kramil should not violate past agreements, agreements conducted according to a process understood as *musyawarah mupakat*, consulting and then agreeing on a solution. To violate these agreements would have disrupted the social, and potentially the cosmological order. Second, the central challenge faced by Aman Kerna was how to make the *status quo* valid, *sah*, both in the eyes of the ancestors and in the eyes of judges and other state officials. His reasoning was pragmatic, in that he experimented with possible compromises, formulations, and terms, all with an eye to how they would be understood by other people. In the language of the political economists, he reasoned "in the shadow of the law." Finally, Gayo adat did not dictate a solution; the situation of normative overlap in which Gayo people live required, and requires, that reasoning and innovation take place on a "metalevel" relative to adat, Islam, and state regulations, on a level of reasoning *about* the interrelationship of these various kinds of law and social norms.

As the following examples show, Isak villagers engage in metanormative reasoning even when the conflicting norms in question are *within* the category of adat. Adat then appears as a resource that may be called on to resolve a dispute in one way or another, but not one that can provide an automatic, algorithmic resolution of a conflict.

Engendered inequalities in Isak

Although the particular entanglements in which these Isak men and women found themselves were recent, one feature of the Kramil dispute would have been familiar to a Gayo person of a century ago, namely, that it was precipitated by efforts of a brother's son to seize land that had long been used by the sister's children. For, although formal statements about marriage and property suggest that Gayo rules allow an equal chance for daughters or sons to inherit from their parents, it is the sons remaining in the village who control most of the land. As the late Pierre Bourdieu (1990:39), citing Wittgenstein, often reminded us, the language of "following a rule" often disguises the processes of appropriation and misrecognition, *méconnaissance* (1990:140–41), by which a particular group or class reproduces its power over another. In this case, to be precise, men claiming long-standing membership in a village hold power over women, and over men who have moved into the village from elsewhere.

Gayo practices and understandings include two ideas of social continuity, one that highlights ties through men, and the other, ties through women. Both ideas refer to membership in a village, but are politically unequal. The village acts as a political body with respect to disputes, enforcing generally correct behavior through social suasion of the sort exemplified in the meeting just described. Villagers also try to maintain residual rights over the lands and rivers within the territorial boundaries of the village. But not all members have equal say over village affairs. Ties through men outweigh ties through women, so that a man whose pedigree in the village goes back through father and grandfather is in a stronger position to exercise leadership than one whose father or grandfather married into the village. These differences are sometimes expressed through the pan-Austronesian botanical metaphors of "trunk" versus "branch" lines.[14]

These different kinds of continuity are constituted through marriage, which also is, roughly speaking, of two kinds. Men who remain in the village, taking wives from elsewhere, reproduce the continuity of a "trunk" line, or (because genealogical memories rarely exceed five generations) they eventually elevate a "branch" line to "trunk" status. The wives may be from the village next door, but they abandon claims to land in that village when they marry. This renouncement is symbolized by a gift of "bride goods" to the daughter from her parents. These goods typically include kitchen utensils, bedding, and gold; they are thought of as a kind of capital for starting a new household as well as a sign that ties to the natal village have been cut: "the bridge is broken," as a maxim says. These "virilocal" marriages are sometimes referred to as *juëlën*, the wife having been "sold" to the husband's side, or as *ango*, because she is "brought in" from elsewhere.

A second kind of marriage allows for a different kind of social continuity, one based on ties through women. This type of continuity is expressed not in genealogical (or botanical) terms, but in terms of place: residing in the same village, working on the same land, caring for the parents. Marriages that bring husbands into the village for daughters are often intended to ensure that a daughter will remain to care for her parents, or to bring in a needed male

---

[14] The two sets of metaphors referred to here and found throughout the Indonesian world – plants and places – have been the topics of comparativist treatments in volumes edited by James J. Fox (1980, 1997). The importance of place as a reference for bilateral societies was noted by Shelly Errington (1989); for other Sumatran cases see F. von Benda-Beckman (1979) and Watson (1992).

laborer – as when Mpun Jamat sought a son-in-law to help him and his son farm. These husbands are sometimes from outside the immediate area; they will have lower status in the village as a result. In many cases, including the Kramil one, they come from coastal regions and are ethnically Acehnese. But even if the husband comes from a nearby village, he loses his claims to his own parents' lands by marrying out.[15]

These two ideas of continuity are accompanied by feelings, images, and practices that also serve as social resources. Continuity through men is often phrased in terms of the transmission of land over the generations, "one after the other," *turun-temurun*. Riceland then becomes an heirloom, something not to be sold, nor worked or owned by anyone other than the sons of the village. The crops are better, say Isak farmers, if men of the same village work together (Bowen 1993b:186–90). Even when men have married out of the village, they may later revive their ties to other men in their village of birth, by sitting with them at a marriage celebration or by taking up political office in that village. In Isak in the 1980s, four headmen did just that: although they had married out of their village of birth and into their wives' villages, they reestablished ties with their birth villages by becoming headmen in those villages, without renouncing their obligations to their wives' relatives (Bowen 1988).

The ties established through uxorilocal marriages, when daughters remain in the village after marriage, are more complex. Statements about their value may center on the cooperation and sharing between the sister and her husband as a unit with the brother, and on the economic advantage to be had from expanding the family as a work unit, "widening what is narrow, easing what is difficult" (*kati impit luës, nyanya temas*). Often continuity over the generations is foreseen as a chain of uxorilocal marriages, bringing in husbands to reproduce or broaden the means of support. My friends Aman Ipol and his sister Inën Dar thought about the future in this way when I first met them in the late 1970s. Inën Dar's husband had married into Kramil village, and worked well with his wife's brother (Aman Ipol). She planned to bring in "an Acehnese" for her own daughter, Dar. Indeed, Dar did bring a husband into the family productive unit, although he was a Gayo resident of Isak, and in 2000 they and their children were working Kramil land (see below, however, on the instability of the family land claims).

The power that sons have over daughters and over incoming husbands shapes the transmission of property not so much at the moments when parents designate heirs, but in the years after their death, when their wishes, their niët, may be

---

[15] Although these statements are valid renderings of local formulations of "marriage adat" for the Gayo highlands as a whole, the two types of marriage are more or less valued, and correspondingly more or less frequent, in different regions of the highlands, on which see Bowen (1984).

overridden by a son or son's son.[16] The parents may assign a parcel of land and a portion of their house to each son or daughter at the time when he/she marries, if the couple remains in the village. Usually one child, son or daughter, often the youngest, will be expected to stay in the house to care for the parents in their old age. In the case of "uxorilocal for life" marriages, the very label for the marriage – "provision while alive; bury when dead" – describes this expectation. But a son may also carry out this duty, as in the case of my own "elder brother" and closest Gayo friend, Abang Evi, who renounced higher education in order to take over a trade from his parents and then to care for them until their death. This child, the one who stays behind, will inherit land retained by the parents. Termed the *umë pematang*, the "border land" – land lying between main rice plots, suggesting its insignificance – this land is a form of bequest, but rarely is it formally given to the child. Instead, it is left as a future benefit, the receipt of which is conditional on service the child gives to the parents. This promise creates an incentive for good care from the intended recipient. (As we shall see in later chapters, court cases sometimes involve accusations that the eventual recipient did not in fact provide adequate care and thus did not deserve the land.)

Some land may be left undivided and not formally promised to a particular child when the parents die. The eldest son then becomes the guardian (*wali*) of that property. He is to supervise its division among the remaining siblings according to kinship norms and a variety of specific considerations: a sister is more likely to receive a house, but a brother receives larger shares of land; the youngest child often has cared for the parents and should receive a larger share as recompense. Siblings sometimes exchange these goods afterwards in accord with their respective needs (e.g., a house for a piece of land), farm the same plot in alternate years (as did Aman Ipol and Inën Dar), or agree that one sibling should work all the land without paying rent to the others.

The elder brother's power

At least, such are the norms, the way Isak people generally say things ought to happen, and sometimes the way things do happen. But the guardian sometimes delays the division of the estate for a generation or more, either to farm all the land himself or to permit informal use arrangements to continue. In some cases I learned of during my years of residence in Isak, the guardian's reputation for a strong temper, or his knowledge of sorcery, kept would-be heirs from complaining. These delays place women who have brought in husbands from

---

[16] Because I later discuss changes in property division, I should make clear that this account of norms and practices is consistent with property histories and interviews about property divisions gathered in Isak during the period 1978 to 1994.

elsewhere in a particularly disadvantageous position. If they are granted any use-rights over the estate at all, the portion they receive is smaller than that taken by the guardian and his brothers. Moreover, lands they thought they would receive as *umë pematang* may be seized by the brother, on grounds that the sister's family only had temporary rights to them, as Aman Seri tried to take land on grounds that it had been given only temporarily to the sister's children.

These delays in distributing wealth in one generation shape marriage decisions made in the next. Several members of Kramil village had married out of the village (thus, uxorilocally) because their own fathers had married into Kramil and still had not received land from their wives' estates that they might then distribute to their sons. These lands remained undivided until long after the grandsons had married – thus, into the third generation!

The overall data for Kramil village suggest that men who were born in the village have greater control over resources than men who married into it. First, let us look at the distribution of village resources in 1979. Of the fifty-two Kramil households who controlled land in that year (out of fifty-five total households), in twenty cases the wife had been born in the village (uxorilocal households), and in thirty-two cases it was the husband (virilocal households). The former were much less likely to have received a share of an estate (eight of twenty or 40 percent) than were the latter (twenty-seven of thirty-two or 84 percent). Five of the uxorilocally married men farmed land in their natal villages, but under adat rules they eventually would lose access to this land because they had married out of the villages.

This gender-based inequality (more precisely, an inequality by direction of marriage) shaped the subsequent decisions taken by these households. Fifteen years later, in 1994, those households with a husband who had married into the village were much more likely to have left the village: 50 percent of the uxorilocal couples had left by that year, compared with 19 percent of the virilocal households. These moves were almost always made because land was insufficient in the villages.[17]

The lesson here is that although rules of inheritance might look even-handed, the control of land at any one moment can be in the hands of men born in the village. The marital status of a household in a village is a good predictor both

---

[17] By "controlling land" I mean using land that is owned, or used pending an eventual distribution (or on a sharecropping basis). I collected data on land control in Kramil at four different periods – 1979, 1983, 1989, and 1994 – but here only refer to the two outside data points. As these figures show, in 1979 nearly all households in the village farmed; the important differences lay in the juridical relationship to the land, which would have important consequences in the future. A point of general methodological concern to be made here is that, because out-migration is much greater among some types of households than others (here, uxorilocal versus virilocal), cross-sectional analyses of land control will generally understate the degree of inequality between groups in a village, because they fail to take account of the unequal fortunes facing the two groups.

of current resources and of future movements. Moreover, a plot of land may be used without settling the matter of ownership. In some sense, the very idea of "ownership," milik, is a recent innovation; control of land was long thought of as a function of status in the village. "Before the Dutch came," explained Tengku Asaluddin, my teacher in many affairs, "there was no ownership in Isak; only use-rights." The community still acts to prevent the alienation of land to someone no longer affiliated with it, but long-term use of land is no guarantee that one will not be deprived of it by a superior power in the future.

Several cases of just this sort of land-grabbing were under heated discussion in 1994. One such case shows that conflicts cannot be resolved by "following the rules," both because conflict is built into the system, and because the rules themselves often conflict, with no clear village-level institutional mechanisms existing to resolve those conflicts.

Use-rights versus the army

For as long as I can remember, two sisters, Inën Mar and Inën Anwar, had alternated farming a sizable rice plot a bit to the south of Isak. They were born in Kramil and remained there after marriage, and both they and the village officials classified the land as their mother's property, to be inherited by them.

Then in 1990, Jul showed up. Aman Bani, a former headman, told me how, on the Feast of Sacrifice that year, a man appeared dressed in army fatigues and started asking for M. Yusuf (Aman Bani's proper name), "in tough-guy style Indonesian." He entered Aman Bani's house, and walked over to the place where his guests were eating, but refused all food and drink. "Oh, what sins have I committed in the eyes of the state," moaned Aman Bani to himself at that moment. Then the man identified himself as Jul, and demanded to know who had taken his land.

Aman Bani breathed a bit easier once he realized who it was. Jul was the son of Acim, the mother's brother's son of the two sisters, Inën Mar and Inën Anwar. As in the case of the Kramil houses, he was a brother's son who was now trying to wrest land away from the sister's children. Jul had been away for many years at school and then in the army. He demanded not only the land worked by the sisters but another plot as well, one that was currently farmed by another relative.

Now, was the land Jul's by right? The Gayo adat norms for according land rights did not clearly decide for or against him. On the one hand, the plot had first been cleared and planted by the father of the two sisters, Inën Mar and Inën Anwar, and this action gave the father the right to use the land. But on the other hand, before the land had ever been cleared, the grandfather of Acim and the sisters had planted a stake on its border to claim it, and staking, too, can be the

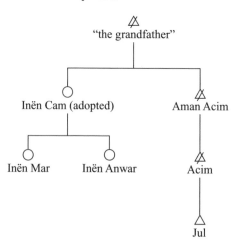

Figure 2.2 Jul's relatives

basis for adat claims to ownership. Some members of Kramil village said that it had been that grandfather's manat, his request or legacy, that Jul eventually receive the land. And, just as in the case of Mpun Seri, respecting the wishes of the ancestors was considered paramount.

If rules for determining land rights did not resolve the matter, some in Kramil village thought that Jul's patrilateral tie to the village tipped the scales in his favor. The village headman at the time, Aman Samsu, denied knowing precisely what the grandfather had intended, but he pointed out that Jul was his son's child, whereas the sisters were his daughter's children, and this difference gave Jul the definitive right to the land, the *hak mutlak*. To further complicate the kinship logic involved in the case, the grandfather's daughter (and thus the mother of the two sisters), Inën Cam, had been adopted by their grandfather. Jul himself had emphasized this fact when he had demanded the land, reportedly saying to Inën Cam, "You are only adopted, child of a dog; you have no rights here." (Aman Kerna commented in 1994 that someone probably had egged him on, that he would not have known about the adopted status on his own.)

Others in Kramil dared not oppose Jul because of his army connections, but some thought his claim was rather tenuous. Aman Bani added a further complicating factor: it turns out that Inën Cam had raised Jul's father, Acim, and his brother, Enam, after their father, Aman Acim, had been killed during the Darul Islam rebellion. For Aman Bani, her nurturing more than canceled out the fact that she had been adopted rather than born to the grandfather. As he told it, with a touch of self-aggrandizement (or perhaps self-exculpation), Acim, Jul's father, had tried to take the land back years earlier but Aman Bani, headman at the time, had refused to let him have it. " 'So be it; you may have it,' " he reported himself as having said, " 'but then you have to pay Inën Cam for each day she took care of you.' Acim backed down; but who can stand up to the army? They would shoot you if you said anything, so Inën Mar has to remain silent."

Aman Mar, husband of Inën Mar, had an entirely different story to tell: that Jul's father, Acim, had wanted to purchase some water buffalo from their grandfather but did not have the money. The grandfather suggested that Acim give the land to Inën Mar and Inën Anwar in exchange for one buffalo and some money, and he did so. Aman Mar said that he even had the deed to the land, signed by the headman at the time, but because he had no proof of the exchange he did not think he could do anything. "Better just to keep quiet; I asked Jul for the money back" but had not heard anything in over two years. Aman Mar was, of course, a man from another village who had married into Kramil, and he had little local clout.

No clear rules existed to resolve this dispute. How would one compare the relative claims generated by Aman Cam's having first cleared the land, the grandfather's act in staking it out (combined with the claim that the grandfather had intended that it go to his son Aman Acim), the decades of nurturing of Acim and Enam by (the adopted) Inën Cam, the patrilateral ties of Jul back to the grandfather, and the claim that Acim had given the land to the sisters? These claims are all valid in the conceptual scheme of Gayo adat, but there is no algorithm to compute their resolution.

To make matters much worse, the events and intentions embodied in some of these claims were each disputed by someone, and it would be very difficult to prove in court that the grandfather had intended such-and-such, or even that Aman Cam had first cleared the land. What carried the day in 1994 was not the higher normative value of one claim over another, nor the legal weight that a judge might grant to some specific set of proofs. (Indeed, given the regular role of bribery in determining the outcome of land disputes, the likelihood of winning would be rather difficult to compute in the abstract.) What counted in practice was the combination of two indisputable social facts: that one defied a member of the army at one's risk, and that Kramil villagers of "trunk" status, with patrilateral ties to the village whether they themselves were male or female, tended to support each other. One could, looking back, explain Jul's victory in terms of certain Gayo norms (as Kramil people did indeed do to me in the accounts mentioned above). For us to do so, however, would be to substitute a normative justification of a state of affairs for an adequate sociological account of a set of social processes.

Viewed in the village, then, adat exhibits two radically different faces. One face is that of norms and consensus. Norms of adat shape the ways in which one may marry, the ways one may transfer property to others, and the consequences of each. They limit outcomes; not just anyone could have made the claims that

Jul did, for example. Some ties of kinship had to be generally recognized by the community for Jul's claims to be even entertained. Adat norms also provide ways of settling conflicts, and, as the case of the Kramil houses shows, these ways can be quite innovative.

But one cannot deduce the outcomes of social conflict from the norms of adat, because they may be called on in different ways, and may suggest several different legitimate outcomes. Which outcome is realized can only be understood in terms of adat's second face, that of power and inequality. Sons and their families exert a greater control over resources than do daughters and their families, and this inequality can be represented as sanctioned by adat. Other sources of power, such as Jul's army connection, have no adat-based representation, but can lead someone else to opt for one adat-legitimate outcome over another. In Isak, then, the category of "adat" can best be seen not as a fixed set of rules on which all agree, but as an interpretive resource, recognized as legitimate by all, but open to multiple interpretations, and more easily mobilizeable by some people than others.

3 Remapping adat

The debates and conflicts over land in Isak show that village norms do not provide a rule book to be applied to each practical situation. The ideas, values, and phrases associated with adat are resources that can be mobilized to provide normative support for claims, but what I have called adat's second face, that of power and inequality, inflects the direction in which resolution is reached.

To point to the workings of power is not to say that adat's rules have no coherence. We may indeed contrast Gayo adat with alternatives ways of mapping people, places, and property, such as those to be found in other Indonesian societies, or in certain representations of Islamic law. At those moments when a local specialist such as Aman Kerna highlights the contrasts among institutions, the norms presented as "Gayo adat" cohere around certain ideas of collective social continuity, centered on the village and the descent line, that are to be distinguished from the rules of Islamic law, or the workings of the state. As they are represented and typified at such "metanormative" moments of contrast, adat norms highlight the value of maintaining links to the ancestors. In the case settled by Aman Kerna, maintaining these links required people to follow the distributive commands of the previous generation.[1]

In the way most Isak people see most things, collective agrarian life requires maintaining ties with the dead and ties among the living. Certain grave sites dispense fertility to the land and rid the crops of pests; each area of rice-farming has its own specific relationship to one of these grave sites, a relationship that is renewed at the start of each growing season (Bowen 1996a:173–201). Success at the harvest also requires harmonious relationships among the living, and is the most common explanation I heard for why one must reserve farming areas to the members of a single village. In the Gayo mapping of agriculture, social relations, and ritual, people are assigned to places by birth and marriage, and through those places to the ancestral anchors of the past. Practices and understandings of property follow from this social mapping: acquiring land

---

[1] These upwards links are also routinely followed whenever two people describe their degree of kin closeness. Ties to each other as kin are figured in terms of the distance they have to go to find a shared ancestor; they might be, for example, "cousins one-great grandfather."

requires belonging to the village and participating in its rituals.[2] But colonial and postcolonial regimes have reshaped the meanings attributable to "adat," both in terms of its forms and in terms of its scope, and it is to this history that we now turn.

Person, place, and property

We must distinguish between two distinct projects concerning "adat." One is describing and comparing social norms and practices identified with particular groups and regions in Indonesia, a project often described as studying "adat." A second project, distinct but in the end closely related to the first, involves describing the history and variation of how the *expression* "adat" has been used across the archipelago.

A good deal of work on Indonesia has been of the first sort. For example, Clifford Geertz (1983:201–14) organized his study of law and culture in Indonesia around the idea of adat. He argued that basic to Indonesian agrarian life is a particular sensibility and a set of discursive processes intended to restore things to a state more reflective of that sensibility once conflict has broken out. This sensibility and these practices are, for Geertz, the essence of adat as an Indonesian ideal type. Microsociological analyses of these processes, by, for example, Joel Kuipers (1990) for the Weyewa of Sumba, and Susan Rodgers Siregar (1983) for the Angkola Batak of northern Sumatra – and I would add my own (1991:139–68) study of Gayo ritual speaking – have provided one type of empirical foundation for comparative studies of social life in the region.

But these processes are not always called "adat." The Gayo word *ëdët* is used in this way, although the sense of social process the word indicates is far more grounded in the political role of the village and its head than are the Indonesian uses of *adat*. Many people living in the western part of the archipelago, including the Angkola Batak mentioned above, use a cognate of "adat" to refer to indigenous norms and practices. Elsewhere in the archipelago, however, other ways of talking about social practices are used, such as the "ways of the ancestors" or references to specific forms of ritual speaking. In these societies, "adat" is a word used by government officials to describe a state-recognized set of traditional art forms or social structural features. In Weyewa society, for example, the word shows up in displays of "traditional dancing" (*tarian adat*), but is not used to refer to older forms of ritual speak and dispute resolution (Kuipers 1998:4, 123).

---

[2] The elements combined to form a Gayo conception of social life and continuity are, of course, found throughout the Indonesian archipelago and beyond. Among the more important syntheses of these archipelagic commonalities are Atkinson and Errington (1990); Fox (1980, 1988, 1997); Macdonald (1987); Wolters (1999).

But even for the Gayo and other Sumatrans, contemporary uses of "adat" in many public settings have been shaped by the history of colonial rule. Dutch administrators, jurists, and anthropologists developed a science of Indies *adatrecht*, "adat law," for a variety of reasons: to systematize administration, to produce laws for the natives, to study local culture, and to keep Islamic law at bay.[3] This mapping of a finite set of sociolegal systems has a broad legacy in contemporary Indonesia, from the judicial to the bureaucratic to the cultural – for example, Indonesia as a finite set of cultures, embodied in the Jakarta cultural theme park called the "Beautiful Indonesia Garden" – but the impetus for the intellectual pursuit came from the world of governance and control.

The creation of "adat law"

As it developed in the course of the nineteenth century, the colonial system was based on, one might say defined by, legal pluralism: separate laws and distinct procedures for Europeans, natives, and others. Europeans had their disputes heard in a court system where proceedings were governed by civil and criminal codes incorporating the rights guaranteed in Holland. Native matters were heard in a separate set of courts, the highest of which, the Landraad, was presided over by a Dutch judge (although by the 1920s "natives" had begun to serve as chairmen). A separate procedural code, with fewer guarantees of rights, was used in these courts.[4]

Each of these systems had to have substantive law as well as procedural regulations. The Europeans were governed by the Civil Code (the Burgerlijk Wetboek), but what was the law for natives? At first colonial rulers had assumed that Muslim natives were governed by Muslim family law, and allowed local Islamic judges or officials (*qadi*s, *pengulu*s, or *imam*s) to handle disputes involving family law matters of marriage, divorce, and inheritance. On Sumatra, Sulawesi, Borneo, and smaller islands the Dutch generally allowed religious authorities to develop or stagnate on their own. On Java and Madura, however, they tried to regularize and regulate what they thought were native institutions, or rather what would become "appropriate" native institutions if given proper tutelage. In 1882 the colonial authorities created religious courts for Java and Madura, built along Dutch ideas of what a proper court would be, with a panel

---

[3] The political struggles over law and courts through the 1960s have been explored in detail by Daniel Lev (1972a, 1973, 1978). Clifford Geertz (1983) gives a more cultural reading of adat than that given here; M.B. Hooker (1978) a more lawyerly one. Roy Ellen (1983) provides a very useful analysis of intellectual and political currents in the Indies.

[4] After independence, Indonesia adopted the 1941 version of this code, the Revised Indies Regulation (H.I.R.) for its courts. Jurisdiction was in reality much more complicated; not only were there Chinese and Foreign Orientals to allocate, but the setting of a dispute and its nature could change the law deemed applicable, on which see Lev (1976, 1985:61–63).

of three to eight judges (precursors of today's tribunals). These courts had jurisdiction over family law matters, though they depended on the civil courts, as had their immediate predecessors, to issue an order of execution for a contested decision.

By the 1920s, colonial policy had taken a different course, one that moved away from accepting Islam as a basis for social life, and toward the substitute notion of "adat law" as the appropriate basis for hearing disputes among natives, even Muslim natives. Dutch scholars of adat law, especially Barend ter Haar and Cornelis van Vollenhoven, argued that each Indies society had its own set of concepts and rules, and that colonial policies of indirect rule ought to rely on these indigenous systems rather than on the foreign ones of Islam or the Civil Code (ter Haar 1948; Holleman 1981; Lev 1985).

Here entered the adat law scholars – Dutchmen and their Indies, particularly Javanese, students – who divided the colony into nineteen "adat law areas," each defined usually by the relative mixture of kinship and territoriality used to create social units – clans, villages, clan-villages, and so forth. The best-known version of this adat mapping was by C. van Vollenhoven (Holleman 1981:44–53), who provisionally distinguished nineteen law areas in the Indies, and then made further distinctions within each circle, by either place or ethnic group, in terms of the different rules followed by each. The Gayo, for example, were part of the "Gayo, Alas, and Batak lands," where, unlike what one finds in lowland Aceh, society was said to be organized around principles of common descent from ancestors, in some cases combined with organization on a territorial principle.

Dutch administrators had, of course, a particular interest in these mappings of native legal structures, for they were to furnish the base for the administrative structures of indirect rule. Social-structural anthropology fit well with the practical burdens of colonial life, and some of the best social anthropological studies of Indonesia – Vergouwen's (1964) analysis of Batak "customary law" comes to mind – grew out of this rather specific conception of "adat law." The outcome of these studies was a comprehensive map of the Indies, on which every person was assigned his or her "law area." In turn, each study of an area further mapped the "tribal areas" within each area, as did Vergouwen (1964: endpiece) for the Batak societies.

Some of the resulting studies – for example, ter Haar 1948 – did, as is so often charged (Geertz 1983:208–09), vastly oversimplify things, grouping together distinct societies and mistaking as "rules" what were variegated and context-dependent behaviors. And yet much adat law research sought less to group and extract than to transcribe and fill out; these more finely differentiated analyses stand, if one may make a comparison, to the "rule book" sort of adat law study as Malinowskian empiricism did to Radcliffe-Brownian typologies in social anthropology. The most compendious product of the adat law idea was the lengthy series of *Adatrechtbundels*, thick collections of court cases, colonial regulations, and field reports. Though organized into the "law areas" of adatrecht thinking, these volumes are endlessly detailed and innocent of the slightest conclusion.

As well known as ter Haar's thin book intending to cover the Indies is Supomo's monograph on West Java.[5] Supomo does organize his analysis of adat in this law area into general rules – 151 of them, in fact – but under each heading he amasses a variety of cases to describe a range of ways in which people handle their affairs. To offer one example, his section on dividing an estate (1967:94–97) lists as rule 79: "people with the same claims are to be treated in the same way." To fill out the discussion of this rule – more a principle of justice, one would think – he then lists cases (encountered in the field, not the courts) where children received differing shares of their parents' estate according to the particular histories and respective needs in each case. The general drift of the cases is that widows, sons, and daughters all have similar claims, and that *ceteris paribus* ought to receive equivalent shares. But the section, and the manual as a whole, is less a code for adat law than a jurisprudence, and a rather pluralistic one at that.

In any case, these books and new ways of thinking, the changing of adat into adatrecht, were the product of a new relationship between state authority and everyday life that law now underwrote. Older village-level ways of resolving disputes did and do emphasize conciliation and mediation, with third-party binding decisions considered a rather undesirable last resort (Geertz 1983). But the new "adat law" was meted out by third parties – Dutch third parties at that – after direct, often hostile, questioning of parties and witnesses. It is primarily in the new institutions that used it, rather than in its content, that adat law was, in Lev's words (1985:64), "fundamentally a Dutch creation."

Islam only when "received"

Colonial adat law was intended to be not just a set of administrable rules, but a specifically non-Islamic set of rules, and it is largely as "not-Islam" that it is remembered in Indonesia. Leading the charge against the very idea of a public role for Islam was C. Snouck Hurgronje, already a renowned Islamicist (famous for having surreptitiously entered Mecca) when called to the Dutch East Indies in 1891 to help win the war against the Acehnese. He urged the Dutch to ally themselves with the traditional rulers in Aceh and to oppose those rulers' rivals, the Islamic leaders. He then developed a sort of systematics out of this political advice, one based on a distinction between two kinds of Islam: Islam as

[5] Supomo (d. 1958) was a high-ranking noble who studied under van Vollenhoven, wrote in Dutch, and in the 1940s and 1950s became the leading proponent of a Javanese cultural view of law and national culture; see Lubis (1999).

worship, to be encouraged as a genuine source and means of piety; and Islam as politics, repellent to Snouck Hurgronje and to some other Europeans. Islam as politics contradicted European notions of what a liberal, civil society ought to be. It posed real (in Aceh) and potential dangers to colonial domination. And it seemed to them to be foreign, in contrast to the local or "native" norms of adat. This distinction between two Islams, one of worship, the other of politics, and their opposite valuations, continued in force long after the demise of colonial rule (and is not without its adherents today among Western social scientists).

Law was Snouck Hurgronje's prime example of how Islam had lost touch with the real world. Laws must be – and therefore are – bent when they conflict with practical necessity, especially with regard to government and trade, he wrote, but "the schools of religious learning" cannot recognize this as legitimate so they continue to develop legal codes independently of practice (1906, II:315). Throughout his writings Snouck Hurgronje contrasted "the law," or "the rules of *fiqh*" with "national custom, which gradually alters to suit changing needs" (1906, II:320). Islamic law was for him a set of fixed rules which, by virtue of their rigidity, could never be implemented.

Snouck Hurgronje neatly reversed prior assumptions about what came to be called the "reception" of law into society. If his predecessors had assumed that Muslims followed Islamic law unless proved otherwise, he argued that only when one could ascertain that an element of Islamic law had been "received" into local usage should it be enforced. Here, inheritance law proved the most compelling example for his Dutch audience. The Islamic rules for dividing estates clearly had not been received on Java, or in most other places, because they differed at base from Indonesian social ideas. Adopted children were recognized as having the same claims to wealth as other children in adat, but not in Islam. Javanese adat gave sons and daughters equal shares of an inheritance, but Islam favored the sons. On Java grandchildren could inherit if their parents had died before them, but not in Islam.

The logical conclusion of the reception doctrine plus such "facts" as these was to return the domain of inheritance to bodies that would apply adat law. And this was what happened in 1937, when the state removed jurisdiction on Java over inheritance from the Islamic courts and gave it to the civil courts.[6] Religious courts continued to informally resolve disputes but had no power to do so, a situation which continued in much of Indonesia until 1989.

---

[6] The regulation, which was passed six years earlier but not implemented until 1937, also created a single Islamic appeals court.

As Daniel Lev observes (1972a:24–27), the courts that now were to apply "adat law" to inheritance disputes, the Landraden, could not be assumed to be closer to Javanese social life than had been Islamic courts, both because the judges were not necessarily learned in adat, and because Javanese practices varied much more than was stated in the the codified Javanese adat, for example in the precise allocations of wealth between sons and daughters.

The adat law scholars won out against all unified legal concepts of the time, not just against Islam but also against proposals for a unified civil code for the colony. Such a code, argued its proponents, would bring natives into the modern age and facilitate the building of a more autonomous colonial structure. But Van Vollenhoven's conservative position worked to the benefit both of local rulers, whose powers were aggrandized through the indirect rule political system, and of the Dutch officials who ruled through adat institutions.

Furthermore, the pluralism of adat law was always motivated by fundamental political and economic considerations: how to best preserve political distinctions among groups of people, and how to ensure that Dutch prerogatives in the control of land and extraction of resources remained legally unchallenged (see Lev 1985). In the Gayo highlands, for example, the vast lands that were outside village agricultural systems had once been the prerogative of the district lord, the Kejurun, but had been open to anyone seeking new garden land; he or she only had to ask permission and pay a nominal fee to the ruler. The Dutch took over this authority from the Kejurun on the grounds that they were assuming his adat-based prerogatives. They then used that authority to close these areas to local cultivators, and to grant concessions to foreign enterprises seeking large areas to grow tea, coffee, and especially the dammar pines whose sap is processed to make turpentine and hard resin. The local Dutch authority, the Controleur, deemed these leases to be commercial matters and thus outside the reach of adat law and the local court, the Landraad (Bowen 1991:76–79). After independence the Indonesian state assumed this authority, and in many parts of Indonesia used it to grant concessions that infringed upon local patterns of land use.

Dutch colonial ideas about adat do indeed highlight the importance of place, and in that sense they bear a certain resemblance to Gayo (and other) ways of mapping adat; both stand in stark contrast to the Islamic legal mappings of social relationships to be considered in the next chapter. But the adat circle schema, which continues to inform much Indonesian state thinking about social difference, rests on two additional ideas about rules or norms that are not part of local ways of understanding adat, whether Gayo, Javanese, or some other.

First, the colonial system identified norms with spatial units. This identification has two important implications. One is that the practices and understandings that constitute adat are assumed to be distributed in such a way that within the smallest bounded unit the rules are the same, and that units lying within the same adat circle resemble each other more than they resemble units lying in other circles.[7] Thus, the Gayo and the Batak (the latter itself a grouping of many

---

[7] The logic is to a degree one of segmentation, and indeed one could develop a comparison with mid-century British social anthropological representations of territorial divisions as based on segmentary kinship structures.

distinct societies) are assumed to be more like each other than either is like any other ethnic group. Second, any native (thus, not Chinese or Europeans) living in a particular place could be assumed to follow the rules attached to that place. In other words, norms were held to be uniquely relative to space, and not to religion, or to social class. Most importantly for the case of the Indies, Islam was not located anywhere, and thus could be said to have no social or cultural existence. Having no place, it was not adat, but superficial to it.

The second, and somewhat more subtle, idea about social norms basic to the Dutch schema was that the codes of adat law described what people actually did as well as what they were supposed to do. Adat codes were equally descriptive and prescriptive; indeed their prescriptive force had no source other than practice or habit, and thus relied on their descriptive accuracy. Adat was, therefore, normatively in the present, rather than depending on the past for its normative value, or referring to an ideal future state of affairs. One legal consequence of this way of thinking has been that adat was and is eminently subject to empirical verification. Unlike the case with a statute or a tenet of Islamic law, if people no longer think that such and such should be done, then, under this conception of adat, a rule loses its normative force and its legal standing.

Together, these two ideas created a representation of "adat law" that monopolized space, and was restricted by it. Each corpus of adat law pretended to exhaustively characterize the norms and behavior to be found in a particular place in the Indies, and it only characterized norms and behavior found *there*. Class differences and urbanization, demographic movements and education, religion and conversion – none of these sources of differentiation within regions and of transportation across them was capable of being represented within the adat circle schema. You could not carry adat along with you and change it as you traveled. Nor could there be several different adats in one place, practiced by people speaking the same language. Nor could there be a different idea of social norms, something other than adat, because once anything else, including Islam, came to be conceived of as locally normative *and locally practiced* it was then seen as part of adat. Islamic law was caught in what could anachronistically be called a Catch 22: to become the general way of doing things, Islamic legal provisions would need to be enforced by the local courts, but unless they could be shown to be already practiced, they could not be deemed to have been "received into" adat and be made the basis for legal rulings.

Both of these Dutch ideas about adat have been of considerable consequence for the way Indonesians have come to understand "adat law" in relationship to its alternatives, and in particular in its contrast to Islamic law. Adat has retained a deep ambiguity: does it designate a specific set of "traditional" rules, which could be studied by looking at Dutch manuals, and which might disappear (but cannot change), or does it designate the social norms in fact followed in a particular place (or in the nation as a whole) at a given moment? Neither conception allows for multiple adats in any one region, but the first takes adat as a local name for one of several possible sets of norms, to be distinguished from, say, Islam, or "modernity," while the second takes adat as an analytical concept for whatever the current local norms might be, whether they are locally referred to as "adat," "Islam," or not given any name at all. As we shall see, judges have depended on a notion of "one place, one adat," but have wavered between these two more specific notions, preserving the legal ambiguity of the term.

Looking forward, we might also see the Dutch adat law mapping as at the root of New Order non-legal representations of Indonesian "unity in difference": adat as clothes, dances, house styles, and marriage customs, one for each province. During the New Order, the state insisted that one should speak only of the adat of a province, never the adat of an ethnic group. This insistence was supported by the colonial heritage, and it was also instrumental in state efforts to suppress discussion of ethnic, religious, racial, and intergroup differences, the topics given the acronym SARA (*suku, agama, ras, antargolongan*). Furthermore, although adat law continued to play a role in local court decisions, national representations of adat were in terms of narrowly conceived "culture" – dance, clothing, and so forth – but *not* adat law, and *a fortiori* not adat assemblies, deliberative bodies, or broader political traditions. This New Order duality of a trumpeted adat-as-culture and a quiet colonial legacy of adat-as-law was to be placed in question after Suharto's fall.

Adat, revolution, autonomy

Through the Japanese occupation (1942–45) and after independence, Indonesia retained most of the colonial-era legal structure, both the basic laws (the Civil Code and the H.I.R. procedural code) and the very pluralism that had been an instrument of colonial repression.[8] Lawyers and intellectuals generally favored replacing the old system with a unified legal code, in tune with European civil law, but administrators (and President Sukarno) generally favored retaining the separate adat law system as the legal basis for a new political and social nationalism. This second position was also the inertial one: in effect, leave the laws alone until we have time to rethink them. As a result, in the constitutions of 1945, 1949, and 1950, all previous law was explicitly stated to be in force unless abolished or superseded by a new statute.[9]

---

[8] Much of the Civil Code was superseded by subsequent statutes, particularly the 1974 Marriage Law; the criminal procedural code was revised in 1981 as the *Kitab Undang-undang Hukum Acara Pidana (KUHAP)*, which continues to be under attack for its retention of repressive articles, particularly regarding subversion and defamation.

[9] Lev notes (1985:70) that as a result "the law in force frequently contradicted constitutional provisions – e.g., with respect to human rights."

But the Civil Code applied mainly to Europeans and Chinese. For most Indonesians, in the early years of independence the relevant civil laws were those of adat. Or, rather, multiple adats – this multiplicity, within the already pluralist colonial legal structure (and a rapidly expanding network of Islamic courts), seemed to many to undermine the anti-colonial, revolutionary concept of the nation as consisting of one people (*bangsa*), and the modern ideal of a unified legal system (Lev 1973). In order to create a national law out of this confusion of pluralities, some political leaders realized that they would have to draw on local ideas of adat to gain support, but that they also would have to assert a set of new, supra-local principles.

A national adat?

In the 1950s and 1960s, the Supreme Court took on the task of reconstructing these local adat law systems to fit post-revolutionary national sensibilities. The Court sought to discover, not adat laws, but the changing "sense of justice" of the people (Lev 1972b:312–13). The judges "nationalized" adat by recasting the specific features of local societies (for example, lineage structure) as general features that would be applicable across Indonesia (for example, as gender distinctions), and then modifying them according to the new national priorities.

Already in a 1948 draft bill was introduced the concept of "the living law of society," a concept used to justify a continuing role by authorities outside of the new civil courts. Daniel Lev argues (1973:21–22) that this language was acceptable both to Islamic leaders, who thought that it was a wedge to be used against adat, and to adat advocates, who thought precisely the opposite. In any case, by the late 1950s the phrase had become a thorn in the side of both groups. The Supreme Court invoked it to render invalid specific local adat provisions, and Parliament included it in a 1957 statute to qualify the jurisdiction of Islamic courts.

The Court used this concept of "living law" to promote the bilateral inheritance of property. In the 1950s it made the modest stipulation that in any given society, men and women had equal rights to inherit unless otherwise specified by "the specific social structures concerned" (Subekti and Tamara 1965:126). But in 1961 the Court declared that bilateral inheritance was now "the living law throughout Indonesia" and that it superseded local adat in all cases (Subekti and Tamara 1965:85–88; see also Jaspan 1965:262–63).

As a vehicle for declaring a principle of national bilateral inheritance, the Court chose a case brought by a woman from Karo Batak society in northern Sumatra. The plaintiff had married out of her patrilineage and had been denied a share of her parents' estate. The defendants argued that, under Karo adat law, daughters always married out of the patrilineage and therefore had no claim to lineage land. Daughters became part of the category of "wife receivers" (*anakberu*) upon marriage, and no longer could claim inheritance from their lineage of origin (Slaats and Portier 1986). Their exclusion rested on the categorical opposition between lineage members and affines.

The court, here as in other such cases, did not engage the issues of lineage structure, but rather represented the issue in individualistic terms, as a claim by daughters to shares in an estate. The judges decided that the "living law" in the region had changed to accommodate the post-revolutionary equal rights of women, and that daughters now had the same rights as sons. The decision occasioned extensive protests and discussions in the Karo region. A book on Karo adat law published eighteen years later (Meliala and Peranginangin 1979) still felt it necessary to include summaries of the papers presented at a seminar held to debate the merits of the Court's decision. The authors conclude that the Court's decision was unfortunate, and, had it been followed locally, would have caused extensive social disruption.[10] (Intriguingly, the book has an approving foreword by Prof. Subekti, a noted jurist who became Supreme Court Chief Justice in 1967, in which he warns that changes in family law must be carried out slowly.)

But the local, first-instance court to which the Supreme Court sent the case for execution was able to reinterpret the ruling in such a way as to minimize its effect. The local judges ruled that the daughters (along with the sons) should receive goods acquired during the marriage, but that the more extensive ancestral ricelands would be reserved for the sons, as heirlooms (*pusaka*) rather than inheritance (*warisan*). Courts in the Karo area continued to apply the law in this way, and as a result they did not see a substantial rise on the number of cases brought for redivision (Slaats 1988:144).

None the less, the 1961 Karo case is generally mentioned as the landmark case in the Court's claims to have found a new, living law (see Harahap 1995b), and it continues to be cited as the jurisprudential basis for challenges against patrilineal adat. In 1994, for example, a Toba Batak woman successfully referred to the Karo case in suing her younger brother for a share of the family estate. (He, in turn, cited jurisprudence to the effect that inheritance was to be decided according to adat law.) The first-instance court, which happened to be in West Java, applied what it termed "national law," and sided with the daughter (*Forum Keadilan*, 26 May 1994, 107).

Nor has the jurisprudential value of the case been limited to Sumatran disputes. In a 1982 case in Lombok, eastern Indonesia, a daughter sued her brothers for a share of their parents' estate. The brothers argued that the adat of the area was patrilineal, but the lower court cited three distinct grounds for siding with

---

[10] Lev (1962:218–21) points out that before the 1961 decision it was the Medan appellate court that had spearheaded legal change, notably by upholding a widow's right to a share of community property.

the daughter: that adat norms had changed, as shown by a university survey
carried out in the area in 1979; that the jurisprudence of the Supreme Court, in
the 1961 Karo case and subsequently, had established that daughters and sons
had equal claims to an estate; and that law is a "tool of social engineering" (in
English) and a general sense of justice demanded that law be used to promote
gender equality. The Supreme Court affirmed the decision in 1985.[11]

Judges and justice

The reasoning used by the court in Lombok is typical of recent judicial decisions
that find against older adat notions, in that it combines the empirical claim that
local norms already have changed with the prescriptive statement that people
ought to change their adat practices. Lev (1962) describes a similar duality of
justification with respect to another gender issue, that of the rights of widows
to inherit their husbands' property. Adat law scholarship on Java and Sumatra
had generally indicated that widows were not heirs but they did have the right
to continued support from their husbands' wealth. On Java, moreover, they had
the right to either one-third or one-half of marital, or joint property. During the
1950s the Supreme Court chairman, Wirjono, argued that, in addition to what
adat scholars had found, widows in some parts of Java received a portion of the
wealth the husband had brought to the marriage that was equal to that received
by the children. The Court then found that in Central and East Java adat law
had changed, and that it now granted widows half the marital property. In 1960
the justices stated that widows were entitled to inherit a share of the husband's
property equal to the share received by each child.[12]

In these decisions the justices did refer to the "sense of justice" (*rasa keadilan*)
or to the "adat law" of a region as if they were making an empirical claim, but
they also drew on their own ideas about what was implied by the ideals of
a democratic, independent Indonesia. Judge Wirjono argued that the judge's
sense of justice should itself be a source of law (Lev 1972a:216–18). The style
of reasoning developed in colonial studies of adat law – that adat law was
merely a translation into legal form of what was already the common practice –
continued to be used, even as the legal and political project had become quite
different, namely, to change practice rather than freeze it (see Pompe 1999).

The concept of "judge-made law" implied here broke both with adat law
rhetoric and with the ideology of the civil law tradition, in which judges apply

---

[11] The case was MA [for *Makamah Agung*] 2662 Pdt [for *Perdata*, civil]/1984, as reported in the
authoritative report of Court cases, *Varia Peradilan* 24:59–71, 1987.

[12] Protests and pressure on the Court led it to pull back somewhat from this position (Harahap
1995b, 1995c), in part through granting shares to additional kin of the husband; for example, in
a 1975 case the Court awarded siblings shares of a man's personal property that were equal to
the widow's share.

law created by the legislature – not that such a tension is at all unusual in civil law tradition countries (Merryman 1985). In Indonesia, the Supreme Court in theory functions as a court of cassation, that is, serving only to quash cases where lower courts have mistakenly interpreted the law, but not examining the validity of the law or the nature of the evidence. Even with a broader mandate the Court would have difficulty trying to create uniformity of lower court actions through its decisions alone, as the aftermath of the 1961 Karo case shows. The Court could assert new principles by overturning, one by one, lower court decisions that were behind the times, but even if lower court judges were to wish to follow the Supreme Court's lead, in the 1960s they had difficulty even knowing what the Court had decided: libraries and law journals were hard to come by away from the major cities.

The conceptual weight of the civil law tradition and the weakness of the judiciary have led some scholars to propose new legal codes to supersede adat law and replace the older Dutch code (see Lev 1965). In the 1950s and 1960s, law professor Hazairin proposed that inheritance law for all Indonesians guarantee widows a share of their husband's estate, not only on the grounds that some adat systems were developing in this direction already, but also on grounds that Islamic law, which was already widely used, treated widows as heirs. More recently, Supreme Court Justice Yahya Harahap (1995a, 1995b, 1995c) proposed a "New Adat Inheritance Law" code that would guarantee the rights of (non-Muslim) women to equal shares of inheritance whether they inherit as widows or daughters.

Harahap argues that his New Law was already produced in the path-breaking decisions made by the Supreme Court in the years 1958–61, and in particular the 1961 Karo case. These cases created a precedent that now only needs to be made more explicit in a code, he states. The dominant style of the Court, however, is to let change happen with as little commentary as possible. Indeed, this is precisely the process that continues to follow precedent without explicitly referring to it, in, among other cases, appeals by widows. For example, in a 1993 decision by the Supreme Court, written by Justice Bismar Siregar, the court redivided an estate among the widow and her children to give them equal shares, but did so without referring to any law, case, or principle. It was left to the jurist who edited the case for the review of Supreme Court cases, *Varia Peradilan* (111:68, 1994) to note that the division was based on current interpretations of adat law under which a widow and children each take equal shares.

In similar fashion the Court relied on a technicality in a 1992 case from Central Java to avoid any sweeping pronouncements about the relative claims of widows and siblings. The Court held that a man's widow and son were his sole heirs, and that when the son died the widow inherited all the land, even though she had remarried. The husband's relatives had brought suit on grounds that the land was "ancestral," meaning that the man had inherited it from his parents, and that it should, therefore, be returned to them. The case could have been used to reaffirm the principle that widows and children have priority in inheritance, but instead the Court relied on the fact that the man's widow had registered the land in her name after he had died and so had "cleansed" it of its ancestral status, making it the clear property of the widow.[13]

Older sources for adat law also continue to be used by the lower courts, but they are highly subject to cassation. These sources include the Dutch adat law books. In a 1982 case from South Sulawesi, a husband had sold land held in common with his wife without her permission. (The suit was brought by the buyer who wished to take possession.) The lower court consulted the 1948 adat law compendium by ter Haar, available in Indonesian, and reported that according to the adat law of the area the husband could indeed sell marital property without his wife's approval. But in 1986 the Supreme Court reversed this decision, citing a Court decision from 1975, and the 1974 marriage law, to the effect that husbands and wives must concur on any sale of marital property.[14]

But it would be a mistake to think that judges have renounced the idea that existing local norms are a basis for adjudication. Judges on local courts continue to try and discover local "adat law," which they expect to find in the form of rules and regulations. Local notables continue to write lists of such rules and to testify about adat in courtrooms. In the Gayo highlands (and in most of Indonesia) there are no readily available "adat law manuals," and these piecemeal efforts by judges often are their only source of knowledge about local adat. Judges on the civil court interview men judged sufficiently old to have an authentic version of adat, and read the several lists of adat rules drawn up over the years by men with leisure and interest.

In the Gayo case, at least, what these judges find is an adat that consists of rules, an idea of adat that, as we have seen, does not accord well with the reasonings and debates that characterize village life. Thus in 1994, I found a civil court judge from Java, Ibnu, perusing a typescript written a decade earlier by the Islamic law professor Muhammad Daud Ali, called "Gayo Adat Law." Judge Ibnu had marked the passages in his copy that pertained to land sales and inheritance, where Daud Ali had provided rules. For example, according to Daud Ali, Gayo adat provides that wealth is to be divided before death, rather than afterwards as inheritance. Judge Ibnu concluded that such was Gayo adat, and he was not entirely wrong in so doing. This statement of a rule does have a relationship to social practices, namely, that men and women have generally

---

[13] The case was MA 975 Pdt/1988, reported in *Varia Peradilan* 84:69–74, 1992. This way of adjudicating cases, of looking for relatively noncontroversial grounds, is so far from being specific to the Indonesian case, that one can make of it a principle even of Anglo-American adjudication, as does Cass Sunstein (1996).

[14] Case MA Pdt 2690/1985, in *Varia Peradilan* 21:47–48, 1987.

tried to allocate wealth to children during their lifetime (although this practice is now shifting in the direction of post-mortem divisions). They saw an advantage in doing so, mainly in that these allocations allowed their children to attract spouses, raise children, and eventually support their parents. However, it does not appear ever to have been the case that it was a rule, with normative force, that all wealth be so divided. In addition, Isak people have seen a danger in dividing up all one's wealth, in that it left one open to neglect by one's children. (Aman Kerna delighted in telling a story about such a sad situation.) As we saw in the previous chapter, as often as not a couple died leaving a sizeable amount of land to be divided among the children, and it was precisely because of that situation that elder sons were able to exert power.

In subsequent chapters we will see just what judges in the Takèngën courts have done with these forms of knowledge about adat over the years since independence. The general picture across Indonesia has been that, while the sense of adat as a set of "traditional" norms and practices continues to be applied in court proceedings, in those cases when that idea conflicts with that of "living adat," the Supreme Court generally has found for the latter. From time to time, conflicts between these two ideas of adat rules reach the national spotlight, especially when large sums of money are involved. Someone with enough influence and money can always assemble an impressive body of adat experts to present his or her case.

Money was certainly not lacking to the sons of the millionaire Toba Batak hotelier Pardede when he died in 1991. In 1994, his three sons, hoping to claim all of the estate on the basis of Toba Batak patrilineal adat, called together an assembly of adat leaders from various Batak clans. The assembly, reportedly attended by over a thousand clan representatives, was referred to as a *Dalihan Na Tolu*, the "three hearth stones" of society – a clan, its wife-takers and wife-givers.[15] The hearth stone image functions as the most salient emblem of Toba Batak adat, and, not at all incidentally, signals a patrilineage-based conception of inheritance rights. The assembly concluded by declaring that the three sons of the deceased were the heirs to the Pardede fortune, and that the six daughters were not heirs and could only receive gifts as compensation, and not inheritance. Millions of dollars were at stake.

A delegation from the assembly then set out for Jakarta to meet, they hoped, the Supreme Court's Chief Justice. Another of the Court's justices, Bismar Siregar, a North Sumatran himself, received the delegation, and reportedly "validated" (*mengesahkan*) their assembly, stating that "this adat culture must be preserved." But later (after some commentary in the press) he clarified what he meant by adat: "They must use the Dalihan Na Tolu that gives the same rights to daughters as to sons," he stated: "the Dalihan Na Tolu that adapts to

---

[15] I draw from coverage in the newsweekly *Forum Keadilan*, 11 May 1994, p. 91.

the demands of the times, not adat that is sterile." The parties withdrew to North Sumatra and eventually settled among themselves.

The seemingly innocent idea of "local adat" thus has become the site for a contest over power and resources that involves notions of tradition, continuity, gender, and regional versus central control. These struggles play on the fundamental ambiguity of the concept of adat: between an image of traditional social norms, and a designation of current and possibly future norms. In deflecting the Toba Batak delegation's challenge, Bismar Siregar invoked the latter understanding, continuing the stance of the Supreme Court that has denied the validity of local property systems in the name of gender equality. This stance also was part of the New Order state's broader project of rendering law more uniform and control more centralized.

Adat as "not-the-state"

Even before the fall of Suharto's New Order regime in May 1998, new claims began to be made on the basis of regional adat and adat bodies. The West Sumatran Adat Assembly, recognized in 1983 by Jakarta as a legitimate political body, increasingly has represented its deliberations as resulting in "decisions" (*keputusan*) that had the force of law, much to the consternation of Jakarta judges.[16] These regional assertions of authority on the basis of "adat law" increased in the late 1990s as the state began to hold out promises of greater autonomy for districts and provinces.

Since 1998, adat has become an opaque, negative symbol of "not-the-state," as when in March 1999, 230 women, representing all Indonesia's provinces, gathered as Perempuan Adat, "adat women" or "women of adat," calling on the state to stop destroying the environment, give back autonomy to the regions, and renounce the use of force against women. In their environmental and political grievances they were echoed by a group of "indigenous peoples," acting in the name of 200 ethnic groups, who threatened separatist actions unless the victimization of these groups ceased.[17]

Regional alliances have begun to emerge around groups each claiming to represent a specific *masyarakat adat*, a phrase that means "adat community" but more exactly: "people who live according to adat." A recently created Aliansi Masyarakat Adat Nusantara (Alliance of Adat Communities in the Archipelago), the group behind the Perempuan Adat march, lobbied the national parliament for greater self-determination by such adat communities. One delegate put the alliance's claims in terms close to those used by Will Kymlicka (1995) to justify self-determination by indigenous groups: "Long before the

---

[16] *Varia Peradilan* 19:168–72, 1987.
[17] Coverage of the Perempuan Adat march was in *Detik*, 17 March 1999; protests in the name of "indigenous peoples," in *Agence France-Presse*, 22 March 1999.

state existed, adat communities in the archipelago already had succeeded in creating a way of life; the state must respect the sovereignty of the adat communities."[18]

The concept of "adat community" has provided a source of legitimacy for groups seeking to act in the name of society against the state. Their claims may amount to a recall petition, as when in West Kalimantan three such organizations, claiming to represent Malays, Dayaks, and Chinese, "the majority of residents" in the province, sent a petition to the regional parliament asking for the dismissal of the governor. The three groups said they acted in the name of "the people of West Kalimantan" and called their statement a "no-confidence motion" (*mosi tak percaya*), in other words, as if they were a shadow parliament.[19]

The claims made by such groups are based on the claim that their society is governed by adat, and that these adat norms predate 1945, the birthyear of the Indonesian state. "Adat" as used here includes most importantly the norms governing family life, methods of resolving disputes, and rights to resources. For many groups, the importance of highlighting adat has to do with resources and self-government, and in particular: (1) claims to *hak ulayat*, rights to land held in the name of the community as a whole, now brought to bear on agricultural estates and logging companies which had been authorized by the Suharto state; and (2) institutions of dispute resolution, weakened by the state, which might help ease current intercommunity tensions.

Groups actively claiming recognition in the name of adat communities make diverse claims regarding the bases for these communities – for example, with regard to the issue of whether they correspond to ethnic groups or rather to the population residing in a particular region. In Aceh, the calls for the sovereignty of the Acehnese people/nation (*bangsa*) alternate with a plea for all ethnic groups to consider themselves a welcome part of a future Acehnese state. In North and East Sumatra, rival groups claiming to represent ethnic Malays in land disputes have also tried to include other ethnic groups in the category "Malay adat community." One group speaks of the "adat community of Deli," referring to the territory once ruled by the Malay Sultan of Deli, and has declared: "Anyone, as long as he/she lives on Deli soil, is included in the Deli adat community." Indeed the group has Javanese, Bataks, and Malays on its rosters. This group's major struggle has been to regain control of communal (hak ulayat)

---

[18] As reported in *Kompas*, 22 March 1999. The English version of the event, as reported by *Agence France-Presse* for 22 March 1999, translated *masyarakat adat* as "indigenous peoples," replacing the specific sense of adat, with its notions of spatial distinctiveness and legally binding norms, with the international NGO term "indigenous," with its particular connotations of temporal priority and small-scale societies. However, the translation of the ILO phrase "indigenous peoples" in *Suar*, a newsletter of the National Commission on Human Rights, is *penduduk asli dan masyarakat pribumi*.

[19] In *Kompas*, 14 June 2000.

land currently controlled by a private company, and its self-definition around territory of residence fits its project. Another group defines its wider scope in terms of "Malay adat and culture" throughout eastern and northern Sumatra, but also highlights the fashion in which Malays have married with other groups and yet preserved Malay norms.[20]

As "adat" becomes a something that a group can represent, issues of the legitimacy of various forms of representation were bound to arise. The delegates to the Alliance of Adat Communities are generally affiliated with local councils; locally, debates are underway about representation and the very nature of the "people" concerned. For example, the Majelis Adat Dayak Kalimantan Barat, Dayak Adat Council of West Kalimantan, proposed in 1999 that one of its leaders, Drs. Ar. Mecer, be selected as a representative of the Dayaks to the national "superparliament," the MPR (Majelis Permusyawaratan Rakyat, People's Advisory Assembly), in the category of "group delegate" from an ethnic minority. But this very idea of an "ethnic minority" grates on others' ears: two other Dayak leaders – one a Council officer, the other described as an "informal leader" (*tokoh masyarakat*) – argued that Dayaks should not be represented as "ethnic minorities," both because on Kalimantan they are the majority, and because it is control of local resources, and not representation in national forums, that is important.[21]

Translating "local aspirations" on to the national and international stage has involved the efforts of NGOs, which make it possible for statements to circulate world-wide as representative of the opinion of an ethnic group. For example, the Drs. Ar. Mecer mentioned above wrote in an article in November 1999 that "the Dayak adat community" demanded that a federal system be put into place for Indonesia. His article was posted on a "civil society discussion" Web site run by PACT (Private Agencies Cooperating Together), which is headquartered in Washington, DC, funded by USAID, and involved in civil society, HIV/AIDS, and civil–military dialogue projects; it was then emailed by the site's editor to a free Indonesianist list serve headquartered in Maryland, USA, and in that way ended up on the computer screens of many Indonesians and Indonesianists throughout the world as well as in Indonesia.[22] Left unexamined in these postings were the relationships of his claims about federalism and Dayak "ethnic minority" status to the broader universe of Dayak opinions on these topics.

In the end, nationally and internationally as well as locally, "adat" is one of several resources that can be deployed in public debates about regional

---

[20] On the Deli adat community, *Forum Keadilan*, 18 June 2000; on Malay adat and culture, *Kompas*, 13 June 2000.

[21] In *Kompas*, 9 August 1999.

[22] The institutional underpinning of this communication is even more complicated: PACT asks regional offices of major Indonesian NGOs (most often offices of the environmental NGO, WALHI) to sponsor coffee shop discussions of major issues, which are then transcribed and sent to the Web site editor.

autonomy, debates that have become more pressing as districts and provinces have begun to exercise greater autonomy over internal affairs, and an increasing number of regions have petitioned for status as independent districts or provinces. In general, it seems that an expression such as "adat society" was heard in those provinces such as Riau or West Kalimantan, where indigenous peoples felt themselves displaced or deprived of older resources by immigrants. Elsewhere, such as in Aceh or South Sulawesi, a past, sometimes centuries-old history of enjoying sovereignty has led to a highlighting of Islamic law, sharî'a, as a symbol of (again) not-the-state, of an alternative, more authentic basis for self-rule. Still elsewhere, in Ambon and Central Kalimantan, adat emerged as a source of indigenous peace-making processes and, more generally, rules governing social life and the relationship of people to the environment.

One should note the dogs that did not bark in the conflictual years since Suharto's fall. From a comparative perspective, a striking feature of the debates about violence and separatism in Indonesia is the absence of a divisive politics of language. The use of adat to claim control over regions and resources resembles the way in which regional languages and language histories have been invoked in Spain, France, and elsewhere in Europe as signs of allegiance to a regionalist political cause and as evidence for the cultural and social foundations of that cause. In general, language plays a less critical role in Indonesian autonomy debates than it does in some other parts of the world – it is less frequently a sign of one's allegiance to either the center or the region. There may be a number of reasons for this difference; two come immediately to mind. First, in most parts of Indonesia, the numerically and politically dominant Javanese are not perceived as owning the national language. Although reassertions of linguistic distinctiveness may well arise, state control or exploitation is not *generally* associated with linguistic imperialism, as it often is in India, the Philippines, or Spain. It may be so associated in specific cases, however, such as that of East Timor, where the imperialism has been Indonesian *per se.*

Second, the major fault-lines in recent, violent local conflicts have not been linguistic, nor have they been part of a single nationwide cleavage. Most, rather, have pitted a specific, recent group of immigrants against other residents. Hostilities in both Kalimantan and Ambon in the late 1990s and early part of the twenty-first century had as their underlying causes resentments of the economic success of the immigrants, in some cases exacerbated by behavioral differences that grated on the sensibilities of the local population. In Kalimantan, Malays and Chinese joined forces with Dayaks against Madurese traders; later, Dayaks acted on their own. In the Moluccas, Ambonese fought against Bugis and Makasarese immigrants from South Sulawesi. In the latter case, but not the former, the cleavage was also along religious lines, pitting Ambonese Christians against Sulawesi Muslims. The churches and the mosques of the

Moluccas served as rallying points, and the larger national communities joined in, further inflaming the conflict.

A more general point about how we understand local phenomena is worth making here (Horowitz 2001). If we consider only cases of conflicts and struggles for local control within Indonesia, a variety of issues appear. However, once we compare Indonesian cases with those occurring in other countries, the specificity of Indonesian ways of arguing about autonomy and peoplehood emerges more clearly. When they cite "adat" as a normative reference point, Indonesians tend to downplay differences in language or claims to indigenousness, but generally highlight the control of territory and other resources, local norms of conflict resolution and rules of land management, and the glories of past sovereignty. Ways of mapping difference and normativity in terms of adat continue to shape the discourses of politics and representation in the uncertain (post-) Reform era; where they take Indonesia is yet to be seen.

Part 2

Reasoning legally through scripture

4   The contours of the courts

Islam, sharî'a, fiqh, hukum – these several ways of referring to God's path or law provide a second set of resources drawn on by Indonesian Muslims. Strikingly, the path along which Islam has been reformulated as a national legal resource in Indonesia parallels the path followed by adat: from a treasury of examples and sayings, brought to bear on a particular case, each has been transformed into a set of rules, an explicit code to be applied by judges. But this codification masks the ways in which Muslims draw on the Islamic discursive tradition to evaluate, justify, or critique specific events.

Over the next four chapters, I consider the ways in which judges, jurists, historians, and ordinary Muslims have sought ways to justify or critique social norms on the basis of Islamic tenets, and to reinterpret Islam on the basis of other social norms. This succession of analyses begins in the courts of Takèngën, with the reasoning processes of judges who live close to everyday Gayo social life. In succeeding chapters, I consider the relationship between social change and justificatory argumentation over a period of forty years in these courts, and the parallel national debates about how to understand Islamic history and law.

In these chapters, we shift our societal focus from village processes to the legal institutions situated in towns and cities. Village life does not disappear from our view, of course; it is conflicts over land and succession that drive people to court. But the analysis becomes centrally one located at town and city level, around how judges and jurists attempt to reason in legally relevant ways, often through specific legal cases, but sometimes through reflections on history and scripture, about the proper relationships of Islam, adat, and equality.

Islam as *dis*placement

Although (as I have been emphasizing in general) Islamic inheritance rules do not and cannot themselves produce decisions (judges do that), the overall character of those rules provides a set of discursive possibilities that both limits and facilitates certain kinds of public reasoning. That overall character provides a stark contrast to the ways of imagining social life provided by adat. If adat ties people to places, Islam juridically displaces them. If adats are fixed and restricted in space, Islam is to be expanded and carried across space. Adat and Islam contrast most starkly not with regard to specific rights or rules, but rather in the ways in which people and property are mapped on to places: the one produces a set of lines drawn on a map, the other a universalist grid of kinship and property.

Islam supersedes place in two major ways. First, it has an intrinsic affinity with movement. Its transmission to new cultural settings has been facilitated by the ease of conversion to Islam (by simply professing faith), by the relative portability of its required actions (one may worship anywhere), and by its emphasis on laws governing social and economic transactions (subjects of particular interest to travelers and traders). Second, Islamic law describes the juridical relationships among persons in a resolutely universalist fashion, based on ties of birth and marriage, and it gives persons absolute rights based on those relationships, rights that others can circumvent only in a limited fashion.

Islam's universalism is best understood in terms of the initial development of the religion and of its jurisprudence. Muhammad's call, or, in Islamic terms, God's message delivered through Muhammad's voice, was a reminder of the truth of monotheism that was intended for all people, including Jews, Christians, and polytheists. For Christians and, especially, for Jews, Muhammad's early allies in Medina, the call was to rediscover the lost truth of this shared single God; for polytheists, it was to renounce the wrongs of setting up "partners" of God. The goal was to overcome barriers of tribe or confession, not to create a new tribe or a new tribal faith.[1]

One way to unite diverse tribes and peoples was to develop a uniform legal structure that could be employed in a wide variety of cultural settings within the new Muslim region. Family law played a major role in these social transformations. Under Islamic law, a person's property is divided after death in accord with the fixed rules of division, the "science of shares" (*'ilm al-farâ'id*). These rules guarantee the rights of heirs, whose shares are explicitly set out in the Qur'ân.[2] One may say that the major innovation of Islamic law was its insistence on these fixed shares, in keeping with the saying attributed to the Prophet Muhammad that "the laws of inheritance (*farâ'id*) constitute one-half of all knowledge and are the first discipline to be forgotten."[3]

This "science" brought about a sharp shift in how wealth was transferred – students of Islamic law and history agree on this point if on no other. In the

---

[1] A good, recent introduction to early Islamic history is Peters (1994). On movement in Muslim history and Islamic doctrine, see Eickelman and Piscatori (1990). Powers (1986) offers an original argument about the early development of inheritance law. For much of the general discussion of inheritance law I rely on Schacht (1964) and Coulson (1964, 1971).

[2] For a detailed account of these rules, see Coulson (1971); and for an account of their social import, Mundy (1988).

[3] Quoted in Powers (1986:8); this is the usual interpretation of the saying, although Ibn Khaldun argued that by *farâ'id* was meant obligations in general (ibid.).

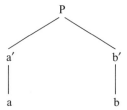

Figure 4.1 Inheritance shares in Islam (Thalib 1982:30)

societies of pre-Islamic, seventh-century Arabia, wealth was passed down from senior male to senior male as a fund for provisioning the group. By contrast, the Islamic rules awarded wealth in fixed proportions to individuals, women as well as men, in accord with their precise kin tie to the deceased. The power of Islam's new counter-mapping of rights lay not just in the fact that individuals now could make absolute claims on wealth by virtue of their birth or marriage, claims that did not depend on the good will of an elder or a chief, nor in that these claims were portable, i.e., did not depend on residing in the place of one's birth, but also in the fact that these claims derived their normative force from that which is farthest from being earthly, namely, the eternal word of God.

As Coulson (1971:31–32) points out, the law as it was eventually developed sets out rules of priority – at which stage in the division a particular heir's share is calculated – and also rules of apportionment – how the wealth that remains at each stage is divided. The Qur'ân stipulates that fixed proportions of an estate be given to a set of relatives, the "sharers," before the remainder, if there be any, passes to a second set of relatives, the "residuaries." The residuaries include most of the male agnates who, under pre-Islamic Arabian practice, were the sole heirs, whereas among the sharers are relatives who previously received nothing from the estate.[4]

Figure 4.1 is drawn after a diagram in one of many "how to" books on inheritance, Sajuti Thalib's *Islamic Inheritance Law in Indonesia* (1982), in its fourth printing in the mid-1990s. The diagram shows the deceased (P, for *pewaris*), a son (a′) and a daughter (b′), both of whom died before P, and their children in turn, a and b. The children of the deceased normally would be among the heirs; in the situation diagrammed, the grandchildren become the "substitute heirs" (*ahli waris pengganti*). This particular inheritance situation is that described in chapter 4, verse 33, of the Qur'ân, where God says that He has provided such heirs for the people.

---

[4] This correspondence between legal categories and temporal periods has led most commentators (i.e. Coulson 1971; Esposito 1982) to view the Qur'ânic rules as superimposing a new set of categories on top of the pre-Islamic patrilineal system. Powers (1986) challenges this view, arguing that the rules found in the Qur'ân and *hadîth* were greatly modified to create what is now thought of as Islamic inheritance law.

What is striking about this diagram is that we need know virtually nothing more about these people, other than that they are considered to be Muslims, in order to decide what the shares of each are to be. We do not need to know their intentions, the customs of their society, where they live, or what other arrangements they may have made.

Indeed, the inheritance laws dictate several measures intended to ensure that all sharers receive portions of the estate, and they are justified in these terms. One of them is a restriction on the capacity of a Muslim to bequeath his or her wealth. Although in theory one may give away all one's wealth during one's lifetime, and one may bequeath up to one-third of an estate, one may not leave bequests to heirs, in order that no heirs be favored over others. This emphasis on distributive fairness within Islamic law has been taken to be a general principle in Indonesian jurisprudence (see the chapter 5).

These Islamic norms regarding inheritance stand in striking contrast to all adat-based systems. Among Indonesian local systems that are tied to long-standing adat norms, some allocate a share to every child, others give shares of ancestral land either only to sons or only to daughters, and still others, such as the Gayo, allocate ancestral lands to whichever children remain affiliated with the ancestral village after marriage. Most local systems consider the local corporate group, usually a village or lineage, to have some residual claim on ancestral lands. A considerable amount of property may be transferred *inter vivos*, via direct gifts of land, or bequests, or transfers of use-rights that then become ownership rights at the parent's death. Bequests, in particular, are a favored mechanism, because they allow the parents to fine-tune the transfer but retain the property, and through that property exercise some control over their children.

Islamic jurisprudence knows nothing of village or lineage claims. Islamic law dictates that property be awarded in fixed ratios according to the gender of the claimants and their genealogical ties to the deceased, and it disallows any bequests to heirs and places limits on the giving of property. It is in deciding cases about family property that the conflict between these two schemas arises most often. How are these conflicts resolved in Indonesia? How do judges deal with the fact that such directly opposed schemas for resolving disputes, adat and Islam, both have legal validity? Just as we looked at the dynamics of property allocation in one village to perceive the mechanisms that may be clouded by explicit statements of "rules," so, too, can we look at processes and histories of judicial reasoning in court to ascertain the mechanisms leading judges to interpret the relationship of Islam to adat in particular ways.

A tale of two courts

Taking a case to court is a relatively new experience for the women and men of the Gayo highlands, as it is for most Indonesians. The Dutch took until the late 1920s to set up a civil administration, which was ended by the Japanese invasion of 1942. As part of his duties, the colonial administrator of the Takèngën district, the Controleur, presided over a native court called the Landraad, where he was advised by the local rulers and "adat experts." The Landraad dealt with those matters involving "natives" that the Controleur deemed injurious to the public interest – murder, attacks on colonial officers, nonpayment of the head tax, or local land disputes. Although inheritance disputes could also be brought to the court, seldom, say older Gayo, were they brought.[5] The court continued to function during Japanese rule, and after independence was declared it became the civil court, called the State Court (Pengadilan Negeri), and was charged with hearing a full range of civil and criminal cases.

The Islamic court grew out of village-level institutions. No courts as such predated the colonial period; village officials presided over marriages, circumcisions, and funerals. (As one Islamic court judge put it, in the jargon of his profession, there was, at that time, "religious justice" (*pengadilan agama*), but no "religious judiciary" (*peradilan agama*). In the late 1930s, Gayo men who recently had returned from schooling on Java (where they would have learned of the religious tribunals created there by the Dutch) established an Islamic court in each of the two political domains, Bukit and Ciq, in the immediate vicinity of Takèngën. The courts were without enforcement powers and had no official status in the colonial legal system. Each had for a judge a *tengku*, a man learned in religious matters, with one or more associates. Although these courts were willing to determine the correct division of an estate, people rarely petitioned them to do so.

In late 1945, shortly after Sukarno and Hatta declared Indonesia's independence, the new leaders of Aceh province sent out instructions for each district to set up an Islamic court, to be called the Mahkamah Syariah or Sharî'a Tribunal. In Takèngën the colonial-era religious tribunals took on this function, with an appeals court in Takèngën. In 1950 these three courts merged into a single Mahkamah Syariah, officially called the Religious Court (Pengadilan Agama).[6]

Only in 1989 were the many Islamic courts in Indonesia given a uniform status. Since that time, all such courts, now uniformly called Pengadilan Agama, handle matters of family law, mainly marriage, divorce, and inheritance, for Muslims. Judges are to apply Islamic law, since 1991 with a Compilation of Islamic Law in hand, but they often devise special exemptions for local practices they consider to be valuable, or at least to not openly contradict tenets of Islam. The civil courts, the Pengadilan Negeri, handle all other civil petitions (including, in most provinces, but not Aceh, inheritance cases from a Muslim

---

[5] Although the two courts have archives dating from 1945, and in 1989 I discovered a large quantity of colonial-era records in the attic of the former Controleur's office (which are now in the archives in Banda Aceh), I have yet to locate colonial-era accounts of Landraad or other legal hearings.
[6] I use the phrases "Islamic court" and "religious court" interchangeably throughout this discussion; both terms refer to the Mahkamah Syariah/Pengadilan Agama.

who prefers to take it to the court) and all criminal cases. Here judges apply statutory law and "adat law" – but whether "adat law" means the Supreme Court's notions or those of the local notables is in practice up to the judges to decide.

The settings

In Takèngën the Islamic court meets in a one-story wooden structure on a quiet residential street in the center of town. The court is near shops, primary schools, the mosque, and the district administrative offices. Two large buildings are joined by an open walkway. During court hours people mill about in the front courtyard, most of them relatives or supporters of someone appearing before the court that day. The scene is chatty and informal; people sit and openly discuss the cases at hand, with much less animosity between sides than I expected to find. Even in mid-2000, as violence was increasing in the highlands, the court was busy.

A man or woman coming to the court first visits the clerks' building, which holds about a dozen male and female court clerks. Some clerks already have their law degrees and are waiting for judicial appointments; others have only completed high school. A clerk will interview the petitioner, usually trying to persuade him or her to settle the matter privately. Failing that, the clerk will help with the paperwork, and often give advice about how best to present the case – suggesting which complaints are legitimate grounds for divorce, for example.

Clerks have an informal division of labor. Some do most of the front-line interviewing. One writes the day's cases on a large blackboard in front; others travel to villages to survey land under dispute. In the mid-1990s, three men shared duties as court reporter, sharing also a single dark sportcoat that they donned just before entering court. One clerk filed current cases, law books, and copies of the official journal, *Mimbar Hukum*; another trundled older cases into the archives – a small back room with dusty, nearly forgotten files dating back to the 1940s.

Next to the large, shared work area of the clerks is the office of the chief clerk, the Panitera, who supervises the stream of paperwork flowing between clerks and judges. There is also a small, one-judge courtroom. The second court building contains a larger courtoom, where all panel cases are heard, and two judges' offices: one for the chief judge, and one shared by the others. Each has a back door, allowing the judges to enter the larger courtroom directly.

Most clerks plan to continue their careers at the court; in 2000 only one had hopes for advanced schooling. (Judges, by contrast, are expected to rotate to a new posting within five years.) During my visit in June 2000, in one room two Gayo men and one Acehnese man, each at his own desk, were typing up documents on manual typewriters. One woman whom I had first met in the

Table 4.1. *Cases decided in the Takèngën Islamic court, 1992, 1993, and January–July 1999, by type*

Type of case	1992	1993	Jan.–July 1999
Marriage			
validation of marriage	28	25	0
approval of polygamy	11	4	1
petition for husband's support	3	2	0
Divorce			
husband's petition	110	99	80
wife's petition	95	102	91
child custody	2	0	0
Property division			
post-divorce property division	0	3	4
inheritance	12	5	3

Note: Divisions of marital property often are decided as part of a divorce settlement, and in those cases are not listed separately. These divisions thus are much more frequent than suggested by these figures.
Source: Court records.

early 1980s had become the informal leader among the clerks, and it was to her that most court visitors addressed themselves. Dressed in a white headscarf and a long print worn over trousers, she addressed everyone, judge, supplicant, or colleague, in the same friendly and direct manner. On one day in 2000 she was busy typing up divorce papers for a Javanese couple in their late teens, lamenting to all who could hear, "Oh, you're so young and you're divorcing! Well, I guess you're no longer meant to be together (*tidak jodoh lagi*)." She asked them if they had children, and if the wife was pregnant, carrying on conversation rather than speaking in an official capacity.

In another room a senior clerk was dealing with a large group that was involved in an inheritance dispute. A young man was visibly fuming about the fact that the other party was occupying the house and selling things from it even while the suit was in progress, and the clerk kept urging him not to take things into his own hands (*main hakim sendiri*), not to turn a civil suit into a criminal matter.[7]

The court's cases include such matters as a request for permission to take a second wife, a demand that a husband meet his obligations to support his wife, petitions for divorce from men or women, a request that the court formalize the (quite rare) reconciliation of a divorced couple, or a request to determine the proper division of an estate or settle a dispute over that division. Table 4.1

---

[7] Although, given that the civil court and the jail had shut down, and people were being arrested and released, the threat was more moral then real.

indicates the range of cases decided in the calendar years 1992 and 1993, and again during the first half of 1999.

Cases involving marriage occupy a small part of the court's time. Some are requests for marriage certificates from people who have lost the original or who had married before such certificates were routinely issued. These cases were numerous in periods of social upheaval, and again in the years after the passage of the 1974 marriage law, but few thereafter. A small number of requests to take a second wife are made each year. Divorce cases are the most numerous cases heard by the court, and the number doubled over the course of the 1990s. Inheritance cases are far fewer in number, but because they often require numerous witnesses (some of whom fail to appear), as well as trips to measure disputed plots of land, these cases usually stretch out over weeks or months. About half of the inheritance hearings I attended in June–August 1994 lasted less than a quarter of an hour because a witness had failed to appear or a document had not yet been produced.

The cases are spread evenly throughout the year (including the fasting month of Ramadan). The court hears cases each Monday through Thursday, from about 9:00 a.m. until about 2:00 p.m. A blackboard lists the cases scheduled for each day, along with the judges and clerk assigned to each. The court usually hears inheritance cases on Mondays, after each judge has finished hearing his assigned divorce cases and all three judges are free to make up the judicial panel. No hearings are held on Fridays, when the judges and staff spend a few hours catching up on paperwork, and then drift off to play badminton. Some set up ping-pong tables in the large courtoom and play until it is time to attend noontime congregational worship in the town mosque.

One judge suffices to hear a divorce case, or to legalize a marriage, although by 2000, with what in theory was a larger staff, the chief judge had decided to assign three judges to hear each divorce case. Three judges must sit as a panel to hear an inheritance case. In 1994, twenty to thirty people would show up for the inheritance cases, fewer for divorce cases. Farmers for the most part, they dress up for the occasion. The women wear long batik wrap-around skirts (rather than the everyday India-cloth kind), the dressy shirts called *kebayas*, and headscarves. The men wear good shirts, trousers, decent sandals, and black caps. One or two men don sportcoats.

The larger courtroom can hold forty people if they sit close together on the long wooden benches. Staff carry in chairs for witnesses, who sit in front of the benches and face the judges. The three judges sit in back of a table on a raised dais, with the court reporter to their right and slightly behind them. The judges wear robes with maroon fronts and black sleeves, with a white ascot tied around their necks. They wear the same black caps worn by all other local men. Although the court has a permanent chief judge, in the courtroom they take turns presiding.

As a case is ready to be heard, the presiding judge rings a bell, and a clerk calls for the parties to enter the courtroom. The judge calls the session to order by pronouncing the *Basmala* ("In the Name of God, the Merciful, the Compassionate"), and proceeds to business. When the session is over he says so, pounding his gavel once to emphasize closure. The inheritance hearings are entirely open to all visitors. So is the first part of divorce hearings, when the judge tries to reconcile the parties. But if the parties to a divorce insist on proceeding, the judge continues in closed session.

Plaintiffs always sit to the judges' right; defendants to their left; witnesses are asked to leave at the beginning of the session so as not to be influenced by others' testimony, and then are called in turn to testify. As the witness testifies, he or she sits on a folding chair in the front of the room, facing the judge. After giving testimony the witness joins the others on the long benches.

Between cases each judge sits in an office, reads new or pending cases, listens to the radio, and fields requests from petitioners. As I sat in the chief judge's office one day in 1994, a steady stream of people knocked and entered. One woman came to request a divorce. The judge posed some questions to determine the grounds for her claim (her husband had taken her to her parents and not returned for fourteen months) and then gave her the right form to fill out. Other people came with various pieces of paperwork to be dealt with.

The civil court, by contrast, is far removed from everyday bustle. The court-house, an imposing, new, two-story cement building, sits on a hill one kilometer from the center of town, and presents a stark face to the ordinary person arriv-ing with questions or petitions. People wait for hearings in a central courtyard, where they are surrounded by judges, staff, and the occasional policeman. They are much quieter than in the Islamic court. I spent considerable time at the court in 1994; in 2000 the judges, none of whom was Gayo, had fled the highlands and the court had temporarily closed.

The first story of the civil courthouse contains clerks' offices, a library, a small snack shop, and a large courtoom. On the second story are the judges' offices. A small jail is located in back for prisoners in criminal cases. The library is rather well stocked with books on a wide range of legal topics, arranged in four long, glass-fronted cases. A small room off the library contains the archives. As in the Islamic court, these archives reach back to 1945, even though the staff could legally toss out cases once they are thirty years old. Case files are contained in folders labeled by year and tied together with plastic twine.

The court hears all criminal cases (*pidana*), and those civil cases (*perdata*) not specifically reserved to the religious court. The most common criminal cases concern theft, assault, rape, traffic accidents, and narcotics, roughly in descending order. The civil cases are mostly about land rights, often in the form of a challenge to the validity of a land sale. Such challenges usually come from a close relative (a sibling, child, or cousin) of the seller, who argues that the seller did not have the right to sell because he or she did not own the land (it had not been divided among the heirs, for example) or did not inform all the heirs of the sale (to give them a chance to purchase the land). Other disputes over land are embedded in battles among heirs over the division of an estate. Some of these cases come first to the Islamic court and are referred to the civil court for a decision on the rightful owner of the land; others come first to the civil court and then are sent over to the Islamic court.

A person coming to file a petition will first see a clerk in one of the several large, shared offices. The chief clerk in early 1994, Gani Abdullah, had served since the mid-1960s (he died in July of that year). As with his counterpart at the Islamic court, he had attended law school but had never finished his degree. The culture-brokering role of the clerks is even more important here than at the Islamic court because they mediate between a largely Gayo community and an entirely non-Gayo judiciary.

The courtroom is a little larger than that at the Islamic court. The judges are also farther away from everyone else. They sit behind a high table, with the clerk a little to the side and in back of them. The table itself sits on a dais, and the plaintiffs, defendants, and witnesses sit just below and in front of them. There is a long, gated wooden fence separating this area from the area of general seating. The overall appearance is much like that of a small US courtroom. Three judges sit as a panel for every hearing, with one acting as chief judge and doing most of the talking and questioning.

The social movement of judges

The composition of the two courts has changed in similar ways but at different rates. Both courts began their lives staffed largely by local men. By the late 1970s, however, judges on the civil court increasingly came from outside the highlands, and after they had received law school educations. By the early 1990s, all the civil court judges had law degrees and came from outside the region, primarily from Java and West Sumatra. Islamic court judges were from the highlands or the nearby coastal areas until the end of the 1990s, when several judges from Java were appointed, took up residence, and shortly thereafter fled the highlands to escape the violence directed against Javanese settlers.

In 1994, only three judges were serving on the Islamic court; each had followed a distinct career route. Drs. Hasan Usman, a Gayo man from the nearby community of Bëbësën, had been the chief judge at the court since 1985. Early in his high school years (in a school for budding teachers) Judge Hasan knew he wished to become an Islamic judge. He spent two years at a school in Takèngën designed to prepare students for study at one of the State Islamic Institutes

(IAIN, Institut Agama Islam Negeri). In 1967, he entered the IAIN located in the provincial capital, Banda Aceh, but two years later moved to the more prestigious IAIN in Jogjakarta, in Central Java. He majored in Islamic law, and also took courses at a nearby law school. He was thereby able to earn two degrees: a BA in 1970 from the law school, and a higher *doctorandus* degree in 1975 from the IAIN. The latter degree qualified him to become a chief judge; other Islamic court judges need only the BA, either from an IAIN (with a major in Islamic law) or from a university law faculty. After terms as associate judge elsewhere, in 1985 he returned to his home town of Takèngën to become chief judge, and remained on the court until he retired in the late 1990s.

The second judge with university credentials was Drs. Salamuddin Ismail, an Acehnese man from the northern coast. Unlike Judge Hasan, Judge Salamuddin had never intended to go into law. He did attend the IAIN in Banda Aceh, but after receiving his undergraduate degree set out with friends to find work in whichever ministry would have them. They found it at the Ministry of Religion office in Medan, the largest city in Sumatra. He was assigned as a clerk to the religious court in Langsa, the capital of East Aceh district, and worked there for six years before returning to Banda Aceh to earn a law degree. (The Takèngën Islamic court's chief clerk in the 1990s, Drs. Zainal Bakry Rakam, was Judge Salamuddin's classmate.) A calm, pleasant person, Judge Salamuddin suffered quietly through long court sessions where witnesses and the other judges spoke in Gayo (which he did not understand). His wife worked as a schoolteacher on the coast, and he made the five-hour commute every weekend to spend time with her. He was transferred elsewhere in Aceh in the late 1990s.

The third judge was M. Kasim T.H., a Gayo man in his sixties who was born in Isak. Judge Kasim, known in Isak by his teknonym, Aman Arlis, had attended middle school in the 1940s – a relatively high level of education for that time and place – and the first chief judge, Tengku Mukhlis, appointed him as chief clerk in 1956. He soon learned how to fill out forms, and how to avoid censure by the court of appeals for sloppy or late paperwork. His role on the court was always as an extra hand and an expert in local affairs, and from time to time he served as judge to bring the court closer to full strength. Judge Kasim has a blunt, forthright style; people from Isak consider him to be a man of some influence, and he does not hesitate to chew out a witness who has given an implausible account of events. Like Judge Hasan, he was frequently called on to informally settle inheritance disputes. By 2000 he had retired.

In the courtroom each judge had his own way of dealing with witnesses, which he followed rather freely. Judge Hasan, though quiet and even-tempered, none the less would stop a witness quickly if he or she strayed from answering a question directly. Judge Kasim was folksy, referred to his own feelings, and was quick to question the integrity of witnesses. Judge Salamuddin was correct and proper, even a bit removed. Together they presented a united front before the parties and witnesses, broaching no departure from the procedures and the limits of the parties' roles.

The religious court always had suffered from a shortage of qualified judges. By the 1990s it should have had at least four qualified judges; it was able to assemble the three-judge panel required to hear major disputes only because Judge Kasim had been upgraded from clerk to judge. (A fourth judge had been assigned to Takèngën, a woman from West Java who had graduated from the Jakarta IAIN, but in mid-1993 she was assigned to another district.) By the late 1990s the court had finally reached full strength, just in time to lose all its Javanese judges in the anti-Javanese climate of the Aceh rebellion.

In mid-2000 the acting chief judge was a Gayo man, Drs. M. Anshary M.K., SH. He had been born near Takèngën, and attended both the State Islamic Institute and the Faculty of Law in Surabaya, on Java, before being appointed to the religious court in Surabaya. He served on other religious courts on Java for twenty years, then in 1993 was appointed to the court at Bireuen, on the northern coast of Aceh, from where he moved to Takèngën in 1998. He told me that he had decided to attend the law school as well as the Islamic one so as to have not just the religious point of view but also the legal. (It is also true that he would have needed the additional credential to become a Chief Justice.) A thoughtful, reflective person, he asked me questions about life in the United States that were probably the most thought-out of any I had been posed in Takèngën.

Anshary was acting as head of the court while the officially appointed chief judge, Drs. Muhammad Is, ethnically Acehnese, was away for further schooling. Two other Gayo men served at the court, and the three men spent much of their time together. Both Drs. Abdul Rahman Usman and Drs. Zakian were born in Takèngën, and both had served on the court in Blangkèjerèn, the second largest Gayo city, in southeastern Aceh, before moving here. The two other judges were an Acehnese, Drs. Alimurdin, and Drs. M. Ihsan, who was a Malay from Medan, but who had served for many years on the Aceh north coast. Three Javanese judges had been appointed to the court, but had left during the conflict.[8] The Panitera, chief clerk, was Drs. Hasanuddin Jumadil, a Gayo man.

Since the 1980s, the civil court judges have all been from outside the area. In 1994 the civil court had six judges, three from West Sumatra (including the chief judge, Nazifli Sofyan) and three from Java. All had completed law school and some had also completed special legal training programs, such as that designed to train prosecutors. Judges serve on any one court for a maximum of five years; most are transferred before that time. Judge Ibnu, from Central Java, had served since 1989 and was the longest-serving on the Takèngën court. In 1994

---

[8] These were Drs. Jumadi, Drs. Suharto, and Drs. Farisol Chadid.

he was about to be transferred. He explained the policy: "The government fears that if someone is here too long he will become close to the local people, and then his friendships will influence his decisions. He will no longer be able to apply the law impartially." Others said that the time limit was to prevent them from taking advantage of their position to make themselves rich. (Other civil servants, presumably in more lucrative posts, are on an even tighter rein: police chiefs, for example, are allowed only one year, and some are transferred after eight months.) One judge said that he thought the government feared that they would make common cause with the people against the state.

The general pattern of a judge's career takes him (or, much more rarely, her) from law school (either private or public), to three to four years as apprentice on a court near the law school (and often near home), and then to a judgeship in a small district capital. After that he will move every three to five years until retirement. Judge Ibnu graduated from law school in Java and served for four years as an apprentice judge (*hakim muda*) in his home town of Perwokerto before coming here. His office-mate, Judge Ridwan, came from West Sumatra, where he attended law school and had his first posting as apprentice. He served several years on the district court in West Aceh before being assigned to Takèngën. Takèngën was the first or second posting for all but the chief judge. The judges expected their next positions to be in cities larger than Takèngën.

The peripatetic life is hard on the judge's family, and makes it difficult to build up sideline sources of income to support the family in retirement (an overwhelming concern of every Indonesian civil servant). Judge Ridwan: "If I were to build a house here, what would I do after I moved? Or if I built a house back in West Sumatra, who would take care of it?" Civil court judges sometimes make local friends, but rely more on each other for companionship. They may run into each other in future postings, and will frequently serve with alumni of their law schools. They develop a stronger horizontal sense of professional camaraderie than a vertical sense of local community.[9]

Adding to the social isolation of many judges is their sense that local people fail to appreciate the positive role of courts and police. Judge Ridwan complained, "Most people know little about the law. Often the subdistrict head (*Camat*) thinks he can settle a case, and he calls forth people to take evidence. But even if he's trained to do so he has no authority to do so." Judge Ibnu added, "Often the village headman is annoyed when the police arrest someone without asking him first. Maybe they should let him know they are doing it, but

---

[9] I comment on corruption below, but here I should mention that, although it is a widespread problem in Indonesia (particularly on the new commercial court), most accusations that I heard regarding the civil court referred to cases that were heard in the 1970s and 1980s. I heard little more than vague rumors regarding corruption on the religious court. An earlier study by Lubis (1994) of courts in North Sumatra and Aceh reaches similar conclusions.

they need not ask him." Conflicting understandings about who ought to handle village-level problems – from land quarrels to fist fights – do indeed cause annoyance and resentment among villagers and officials. Judges and police see the problem as part of the bumpy road toward a society where law officers enforce the law. Many villagers and some local administrators see it as officials interfering in local disputes in hopes of payoffs and power.

The civil court's one large courtroom stood unused much of the time, and some of the judges thought they ought to have more work. "We have very few cases to try," said Judge Ridwan, "even though there are a lot of problems here." Indeed, although the number of criminal cases had been steady – forty-six in 1992, fifty-six in 1993, and twenty-five by mid-1994 – the number of civil cases had been declining: twenty-seven in 1991, fifteen in 1992, nine in 1993, and eight by mid-1994. One judge speculated that the decline was because people became a little more afraid of the court in the early 1990s, when some men accused of supporting GAM, the liberation movement, were tried in Takèngën in 1992. The trials received a great deal of attention, the courtroom was mobbed, and the judges had to set up loudspeakers, because the trials are supposed to be open to the public. Two men admitted being leaders – one claimed to be the information minister and the other the area commander for Free Aceh. They were convicted of subversion and sentenced to twelve to fifteen years (the sentences were later reduced on appeal). People may have been afraid of bringing cases after that. "They figured that cases could wait," said the judge.

Another reason for what judges perceive as a low number of cases is the low profile of lawyers here relative to other parts of Indonesia. In Takèngën, defendants in criminal cases are generally not represented by lawyers, although for serious cases the judges have certain responsibilities to provide them with legal advice. Judge Ibnu: "We must offer someone a lawyer if the charges against them could bring five years or more in jail. They must have a lawyer if the charges could bring fifteen years or more. If they sign a letter saying they are poor they get one free."

Lawyers have been involved more frequently in civil suits. Judge Ibnu estimated that about one-third of the people who appear before the civil court in civil cases, either as plaintiff or defendant, have a lawyer. "Two men work locally to provide legal help: Duski S.H., and Abdul Qaidir. Duski, who has a law degree, gets most of the business. Qaidir does not have a law degree but worked as staff member of the civil court, and then took a test from the Banda Aceh court to become a 'practicing lawyer' (*pengacara praktèk*). These were the old rules, now you have to have a law degree to practice in court."

Much, then, continues to distinguish Islamic court and civil court judges, in Takèngën and in Indonesia generally (Lubis 1994). Islamic court judges still are more likely to be from the community and to remain on the court for a long period of time, although this has begun to change; the regular rotation of civil court judges has been longer established. Civil court judges are much better paid and generally better educated. They hear a wide range of criminal as well as civil cases, and therefore more often find themselves fining, or jailing, or otherwise harming someone. They also hear cases involving greater sums of money, and the temptations and occasions for corruption are correspondingly greater. Islamic court judges often act as counselors or mediators, usually in informal settings away from the courtroom; civil court judges much more rarely do so.

But much else about the courts is strikingly similar. The two sets of judges may have different backgrounds (Islamic judges usually graduate from Islamic institutes, civil court judges from law schools), but some Islamic judges also have law degrees, and in any case both kinds of judges learn on the job how to separate truth from hearsay, how to write decisions using the same forms, inherited from the European civil law tradition, and how to appear natural in their identical judicial robes. Both courts must pay some attention to Supreme Court cases, especially to those enshrined in the books of case law entitled *Yuriprudensi*. Both rely for procedural guidance on the version of the civil law tradition practiced by the Dutch in the East Indies, although they differ in practice: the civil court makes heavy use of written arguments, counter-arguments, and summaries; the Islamic court relies much more on oral testimony. In both courtrooms, however, judges, usually sitting as a three-judge panel, hear petitions, interrogate witnesses, and issue decisions. Rules about witnesses, testimony, oath-taking, and burdens of proof are similar. The legal culture in the two courts is much the same as well. Judges on both courts share a number of assumptions about law and about how they are to determine facts. They share a language of individual property rights and positive law. They also share an epistemology that is quite distinct from that followed in everyday life. Although at first blush, then, the two sets of courts might seem to partake of two separate worlds, in fact much more unites than separates them.

The resemblance between the Islamic and civil courts is in part because judges have tended to look to their more prestigious counterparts on the civil courts. By the same token, the Islamic courts are quite unlike those contemporary Islamic judicial institutions in other majority-Muslim countries that draw inspiration from the institution of the Islamic judge, the *qâdî* (cf. Antoun 1980; Eickelman 1985; Hirsch 1998; Messick 1993; Vogel 1993).[10]

---

[10] Regarding the format of decisions, compare the similar records in Dupret (2000) for Egyptian judges. Unlike the judicial reforms that took place in Ottoman or post-Ottoman settings, those in Indonesia did not occur against the background of earlier broadly based judicial systems. Compare the study of courts in Egypt and the Gulf states by Brown (1997).

Jurisdiction and procedure

The jurisdiction of the religious court is limited to a very few types of cases. In principle it decides cases on the basis of Islamic law, and therefore only has jurisdiction over Muslims. However, a non-Muslim may be a party to a case; for example, if the heirs to an estate include people of more than one religion, or if a wife converted to Christianity and is sued for custody of her child. Such cases rarely if ever arise in Aceh but often become high-profile cases elsewhere in the nation (see chapter 9). The court decides cases regarding marriage or divorce, as well as matters directly related to marriage and divorce such as the reconciliation of a couple or the custody of children. Everywhere in Indonesia, marriage and divorces of Muslims may only be brought to the religious court. The court also determines the rightful heirs to an estate, adjudicates claims that property was given or bequeathed according to Islamic law, and divides marital property as part of (or following) a divorce. The relative frequency of different kinds of cases has shifted sharply through the years, for reasons given below: to put it generally, in its first few decades, the court heard a relatively small number of cases per year, often involving the registration of a marriage or a property dispute, whereas by the 1980s and 1990s the court was hearing a large number of divorce cases annually, and few cases in other categories. (Of 181 cases decided in the first half, of 1999, 171 were divorce cases.)

The civil court, by contrast, has a very broad jurisdiction. It hears all criminal cases and all civil cases not specifically reserved to the religious court.[11] Until 1970, disputes over inheritance anywhere in Aceh could be brought to either court, as was the case elsewhere in Indonesia. However, this "forum shopping" possibility always aroused some discontent. Indeed, decisions in inheritance cases by the civil court in Takèngën and by civil courts elsewhere in Aceh often were overturned by the Aceh appeals court on grounds that they had overstepped their jurisdiction. In 1970, public protests arose against decisions taken by a civil court judge in West Aceh that awarded property to a Christian heir. Subsequently, and consequently, the two appeals courts in Banda Aceh jointly declared that thereafter only the religious court could hear a case brought by a Muslim about how an estate ought to be divided. However, because many inheritance disputes involve side issues that continue to fall under civil court jurisdiction, such as the validity of a document or the ownership of a plot of land, even today some cases end up at both courts. (Several cases from Takèngën reached the Supreme Court twice during the 1990s, once from each of the two courts of first instance!)

---

[11] Three other courts play important roles but are not relevant to this study: the Military Court, the Administrative Court (which on several occasions during Suharto's rule stood up to both Suharto and the Supreme Court), and the very recent Commercial Court, created in 1998 to hear bankruptcy cases – but quickly "captured" by some clever defense attorneys with deep pockets.

National legislation enacted since 1970 has restructured how marriages can take place, what it takes to carry out a divorce, who gets what portion of the property after divorce, and how an estate is to be divided among heirs. All of these measures have had the effect of expanding the reach of Islamic courts into what had once been the domain of religious law but not of state control.

In both types of courts, procedure follows a colonial-era version of European civil law. Plaintiffs and defendants introduce written statements, replies, and counter-replies, which are handed to the judges and entered into the court record. Panels of three judges preside over inheritance disputes; a single judge may hear and decide other matters. Attorneys may or may not be present or involved in any way; in religious court proceedings they rarely are. After questioning the parties and their witnesses, judges write a decision in which they outline the arguments and testimony offered by each side, and present the legal considerations relevant to the case, followed by their decision. In all cases regarding the disposition of property, the proceedings are open to the public.

At times the judges speak in an everyday manner, tending to preach to the litigants at least as much as they convey formal decisions. But at other times the concern with formality gives to the proceedings a mind-numbing quality even for someone relatively acquainted with legal terminology. Thus in June 2000, I heard the final session in a divorce case, with three judges sitting in judgment. They granted the husband's divorce request (see chapter 9 for details on divorce proceedings). One of the three judges read out the details of the judgment, which included the value of all the objects that were to be divided between the ex-husband and ex-wife. The text was in dense legalese. There had been a countersuit (*recompensi*) to the initial litigation (*compensi*), such that each time the text identified one or the other of the two parties it labeled his or her position in each suit, as "penggugat compensi tergugat recompensi" or the other way around. The judge read the text very quickly, and I doubted whether anyone in the courtroom could have followed it entirely.[12] There was no plainspeak translation afterwards, only the explanation by the presiding judge, Anshary, of their options. Each party could choose to accept the decision, in which case the court would set a date for the husband to pronounce his divorce of his wife (the *ikrar talaq* utterance), or refuse it, in which case the refusing party would appeal to the appellate court in Banda Aceh, or they could take two weeks to think it over. They each said they wanted to think about it.

At the appellate level,[13] the judges reiterate lower-court proceedings and then issue a judgment. Generally they work only from the documents forwarded to

[12] The proceedings reminded me of the famous speech by Groucho Marx in *A Night at the Opera*, regarding "the party of the first part."
[13] Both religious and civil courts have district-level appellate courts, and the Supreme Court acts as court of cassation for both systems. For a detailed account of the Supreme Court, see Pompe (1996).

them. The appellate court might overturn, affirm, or send back the case for further evidentiary hearings at the first-instance level. More rarely, it might issue its own decision in the matter. The Supreme Court has the same options, but it generally restricts itself to the question of whether or not the lower court interpreted the law correctly, and avoids weighing claims about evidence, or considering arguments not already introduced at a lower level. A published account of a case that has been heard by the Supreme Court includes the decisions of the first-instance and appellate courts, and thus allows the reader to follow the arguments and legal reasoning presented at all stages.

Judges in Indonesia are notoriously corrupt, but one ought to qualify this claim. It is fairly predictable where one will find the most corruption, namely, when the most money is involved. In this respect judges differ little from other poorly paid Indonesian officials and bureaucrats. It follows that one will find more corruption in, say, disputes over valuable land holdings or bankruptcy proceedings than in a divorce court, and more corruption in regions and towns where there is more wealth. My own sense of things in Takèngën would confirm this rule. There, I found few accusations of corruption against Islamic court judges, and fewer than I expected against the judges serving on the civil court in the mid-1990s. It appears that corruption was more rampant when judges served for longer terms in the highlands.

Women against men in the courts

One might expect that if Islamic law, with its clear substantive and procedural biases in favor of men, is introduced into a society, women would see their rights and resources shrink. Of course, so goes the usual argument (e.g., Powers 1986), the introduction of Islamic law in Arabia benefited women because there, at that time, women were so bereft of rights that even a half share of inheritance, or half the standing as a witness, was much better than no rights at all.

But Southeast Asian societies exhibit a more gender-balanced approach to life. On the level of sheer demographics, women are about as likely to survive relative to men as is the case in the United States and Europe – in stark contrast, say, to South or East Asia, where unequal distributions of food and medicines ensure demographic ratios sharply biased toward men (Bowen 1983). In the domain of social structure as well, for example with respect to rights to property and to control money, women appear as relatively empowered. Therefore, one might expect Islamic law to have negative effects on women's rights in Southeast Asia if such were to be the case anywhere. What can the Gayo case tell us?

From what we learned about Isak in chapter 2, we would expect that the unfavorable position of women and of in-marrying men would be a major factor determining who in Gayo society brings litigation to court. I wanted to see whether this had been true, what kinds of cases came to the courts in

Takèngën, who tended to win them, and whether legal reasoning had changed over the course of the courts' existence. (The last question is addressed in the next chapter.) My sample of cases was drawn from the files of the two courts in the course of fieldwork carried out in July 1985, June–August 1994, and June 2000. For each court, I selected blocks of years, beginning in the late 1940s and including all available cases from the 1990s. For each sample block I read all cases with a bearing on issues of family property and tried to get an idea of the frequency of different types of case.

In the civil court, two types of family property cases predominate (with ten or more cases of each type appearing in the sample): first refusal and marital property. In first refusal cases, a villager challenges the right of a fellow villager, usually a close relative, to sell land without first offering the land to him or her. In marital property cases, the plaintiff is usually an ex-wife, and she argues that she was denied her share of marital property, wealth acquired during the time of the marriage but kept by the husband after a divorce. Usually she wins.

In the religious court, three types of family property cases showed up most frequently in the sample: two types of inheritance claim, and marital property suits. In one type of inheritance claim, the plaintiff asks the court to divide an estate along Islamic lines; the defendant is a sibling, cousin, or other close relative who has refused to divide the property. Little opposition is made to the request, and the court divides the property. In the second type of case the plaintiff makes the same request, but it is met with a counter-claim from the defendant that some wealth had already been given to the plaintiff as a gift (*hibah*). The court either accepts or rejects the counter-claim depending on how strict a burden of proof is required. Finally, in a third type of case, first heard in the 1970s, the plaintiff, an ex-wife, asks for her share of marital property.

For both courts, then, women are the more frequent plaintiffs in family property cases. However, to more precisely characterize the relationship of what happens in court to the village dynamics of property distribution we also want to know the kin relationships of plaintiffs and defendants to the property in question. For the civil court, I have sufficient information about these relationships for forty-seven cases, and for the religious court sample, forty-nine cases. Because, for this particular set of questions, I was interested less in the person who spoke in court about the case than in the kinship dynamics that led the plaintiffs to sue, in a small number of cases I recoded the gender identity of the parties to reflect the gender of the party in whose name the claim was entered.[14]

---

[14] For the civil court, in three cases the plaintiff was male but petitioned in the name of a female (in one case, his father's mother, in two cases, his wife), and I offer a recoded tabulation where these three cases are counted as female. For the religious court as well, I recoded four cases of a male plaintiff appearing in court as female, because in three cases he appeared in the name of his mother and in one case, his wife. (There are no reverse instances, of women bringing

Table 4.2. *Cases by gender of plaintiff (recoded) for case sample, Takèngën civil and religious courts*

	Women	Men	Mixed	Total
Civil court	30	12	5	47
Religious court	31	14	4	49
Total	61	26	9	96

Source: Court records.

Table 4.3. *Cases by gender of plaintiff and defendant, for case sample, Takèngën civil and religious courts*

	Women against			Men against			
	women	men	mixed	women	men	mixed	Total
Civil court	6	20	4	3	8	1	42
Religious court	9	17	5	3	9	2	45
Total	15	37	9	6	17	3	87

Note: Nine cases with mixed-gender plaintiff groups are not included here.
Source: Court records.

The information I offer here regards the gender of the party in whose name the suit is brought (usually also the party appearing in court). I would argue that it is the politics of gender – who sees herself or himself as able or unable to reach a satisfactory outcome without going to court – that is most telling in explaining the role of the courts. In other words, these numbers require a great degree of interpretation; they do not "speak for themselves." Table 4.2 shows the cases brought by men or women (recoded as described) to the two courts.

Clearly, women have brought most of the cases to both courts. We can further analyze the data into the gender pairings of plaintiff versus defendant, leaving out the nine cases where men and women are joint plaintiffs. Table 4.3 shows that most cases brought by women or men are brought against men.

As we saw in Isak, it is men who hold on to land and delay division of lands, and it is women and their own heirs who have an incentive to approach the courts for relief. These data show that they do indeed make use of the court; Table 4.4 shows that their experience provides some encouragement for the next potential litigant.

cases in the name of male relatives.) In some cases where a male plaintiff appeared in his own name, his relationship to the estate was by way of a female; the data thus could be even further recoded, and variable interpretations offered.

Table 4.4. *Cases won by plaintiff, by gender of plaintiff, for*
case sample, Takèngën civil and religious courts

	Women		Men		Mixed		
	won	lost	won	lost	won	lost	Total
Civil court	16	9	6	8	1	3	43
Religious court	14	3	5	6	4	0	32
Total	30	12	11	14	5	3	75

Note: Totals are smaller than in previous tables because some cases were withdrawn and some decisions were not recorded.
Source: Court records.

Table 4.4 shows that female plaintiffs win far more than they lose, while men
lose a little more frequently than they win. The pattern of decisions thus would
encourage women to bring suits much more than it would encourage men, and
this effect of the pattern of past decisions would tend to reproduce the difference
in the gender of plaintiffs.[15]

Both courts have served as institutions that work in favor of female plaintiffs.
They can grant shares of an estate promptly; indeed, about one-quarter of the
family property cases that are heard by the courts (and a larger percentage of the
cases ever brought to the attention of a judge or clerk) regard timing: daughters
or their children want brothers to divide an estate. It is also likely that the threat
of taking a case to the court strengthens the bargaining position of the party
with matrilateral ties to the property in question.

The court decisions tend to favor female plaintiffs for two additional reasons. One will be considered below: that the courts have become increasingly
skeptical of claims that some land was given or bequeathed to a child, or that
all parties had agreed to an earlier division of the estate. Since the 1980s, the
religious court has generally placed such property into the general estate pool,
and these measures seem on balance to favor daughters, in that they frequently
deny claims made by sons to have been given extra rights in land. The second
reason is that because more daughters marry out of a village than do sons, the
application of adat rules have favored sons over daughters; asking for the application of Islamic rules therefore overall gives daughters claims to land that
they did not have under adat.

The overall data indicate that the Islamic court has worked in the interest of
women, but not because the substantive rules applied by the court constituted an
improvement over those of adat. It is only when we compare the male–female

[15] These findings support those of Lev (1972a:178–82) for Islamic courts on Java in the early
1960s; see Peletz (1996) for a parallel study in Malaysia.

balances of power under the two regimes, "village adat" and "town courtroom," that the role of the Islamic court in promoting equality can be understood.[16]

But these data hide a sharp difference in how judges decided cases in earlier and later decades. Only by looking at the history of court decisions in Takèngën can we understand the way political changes in the highlands have reshaped judicial reasoning about Islam and adat.

---

[16] Similar results have been reported for Islamic courts elsewere (Hirsch 1998; Shaham 1997; Tucker 1998).

5   The judicial history of "consensus"

In this and the following chapter, I consider the history of decision-making in the two Takèngën courts. I draw on case dossiers, interviews with judges, and field research into the social history of the region. In this chapter, I focus on how judges weigh and evaluate claims that a social consensus has been reached *vis-à-vis* claims that one has overriding rights under Islamic inheritance law. The case shows the multiple ways in which judges can translate cultural ideas of fairness and agreement into publicly arguable rules of law. Because little change has occurred in the basic normative frameworks to which the judges refer, the study allows us to highlight the relationships between these legal changes and concomitant social changes. A microhistorical study of this sort has the methodological advantage of greater control over other elements than does a comparative study of courts.[1]

Judges on both Takèngën courts have shifted their approach to family property disputes. From independence through the 1960s, judges usually upheld Gayo adat norms in disputes about the proper distribution of family property. Local norms were at first assumed, later explicitly claimed, to provide sufficient legal grounds for dividing wealth. Beginning around 1970, however, the courts began to rule against these older divisions. Both courts now held that the only acceptable basis for dividing family property was Islamic law, either because those norms had become part of Gayo adat, or because, whatever adat might say, Islamic norms took priority in such matters.

This change meant that requests to overturn past divisions became much more frequently upheld than before. Table 5.1 compares outcomes for the period up through 1970 with outcomes after that year.[2]

Plaintiffs won much more often in recent than in earlier decades. Before asking why such changes took place, I first set out the institutional history of the courts, and then focus on the interpretive operations involved in looking

[1] Elsewhere (Bowen 1999b), I have set out my reasons for this claim in detail, drawing on a collaborative study by political scientists and anthropologists of comparative methods.
[2] In Aceh 1970 is a judicial watershed year, because after that year only the religious courts were allowed to divide property. The year of court reorganization, 1989, will provide another watershed year for future analysis.

Table 5.1. *Family property cases by outcome for plaintiff and year of decision, case sample, Takèngën civil and religious courts*

	Plaintiff wins	Plaintiff loses	Total
1945–70	20	36	56
1971–98	26	3	29
Total	46	39	85

Source: Court records.

at adat and Islam in one or another way. It turns out that the key operation is evaluating claims that a consensus or agreement was reached between the parties, and, on what we might call a metalevel of judgment, how judges weigh claims based on rights as opposed to claims based on prior consensus.

Delicate judicial politics, 1945–1960s

The two courts that were created in the highlands shortly after independence had very different histories but they shared two things: a subjective commitment to creating a more Islamic society, and an objective problem of being weak institutions in a social climate of turmoil and uncertainty. As we saw in chapter 4, the civil court succeeded a local colonial court, and continued to hear all criminal cases and to accept litigation on a wide variety of civil matters. For its first three decades it was dominated by men from the Gayo highlands or nearby northern Aceh, and its chief judges served for as long as ten years.

The Islamic or religious court (Pengadilan Agama), by contrast, was a new institution. During the colonial period no such courts had existed, and although in theory people could take inheritance cases to a religious official, they rarely did so. When the court was created in 1945, it was on provincial, not central government authority. For its first few decades, its legal basis remained unclear, it received little funding, and it had to rely on the civil court to enforce its decisions. Although its authority to handle marriage and divorce matters was popularly accepted, such was not the case with its authority over inheritance disputes. For staff and judges it depended on local talent, on those few Gayo men who had received training in Islamic law outside the region in the 1930s.

Remember that for the first twenty years after independence, the highlands were in near-constant turmoil. The battles fought in northern Sumatra in the late 1940s against the returning Dutch and their allies involved many men and women from the highlands, who sought to keep the colonists from re-taking Aceh. The Darul Islam rebellion erupted in 1952, two years after the anti-colonial struggle had been won. The rebellion set villagers against one another, and isolated the towns, largely controlled by Jakarta troops, from the villages, largely controlled by rebels. The rebellion faded in the late 1950s and was settled in 1962, although the cause of greater autonomy continued to fan flames throughout Aceh, until its more recent explosion in the 1990s.

During this period of political and social turmoil, highlanders argued among themselves about the relative status that Gayo adat and Islamic law were going to play in the new republic. No judge wished to invite retaliation from the rebels by coming out against Islamic law, or risk accusations of rebel sympathies by coming out against adat. Furthermore, most judges on both courts saw their tasks as incorporating norms of Islam and adat. Most considered their judicial roles to be part of a general effort to replace colonial-era institutions with new ones that better reflected the shared Islamic orientation of Gayo people. However, they also saw the norms of local adat as important safeguards of Islam – as the "fences guarding religion," in the words of one religious teacher. These perceptions made deciding cases in which Islamic norms stood counterposed to those of Gayo adat a task to avoid when possible, or to finesse when not.

Caught between norms

Judges on the two courts faced very different challenges. Those on the Islamic court thought they had a pretty good understanding of Islam, but knew they had little or no formal legal experience. A few of their counterparts on the civil court may have had such experience, but they had a more diffused idea of what law was, or should become. In the aftermath of the revolution, it seemed to include local adat (whatever that might be), the civil legal system (which had just become "postcolonial"), and whatever new social norms might have come out of the revolutionary struggle – ideally combined with elements of Islamic law.

The Islamic court had two clear advantages. It could draw on the talents and energies of local men who had recently returned from religious studies in prestigious places. It also stood for something positive, the postcolonial return of Islam to the rightful place that it had held before the coming of the Dutch. Its weaknesses were also formidable, however. The court had a weak legal base and no enforcement powers. Despite the high value placed on Islamic learning in the highlands, people were not used to having their property divided up by others, and certainly not along Islamic lines. The judges had no training in the procedures and terms of the civil law tradition, in which the Indonesian legal hierarchy conducted affairs. They often had no typewriters with which to write their decisions in the required triplicate forms.

Not that the Islamic judges put off the task of organizing the courts. Weeks after Indonesian independence was declared, the provincial government of Aceh ordered district officials to establish Islamic courts. In Takèngën it was a local religious teacher, Tengku Abdul Mutalib, known as Tengku Mukhlis, who was given this task. Religious judges in the two large villages near Takèngën, Kebayakan and Bëbësën, already had begun to hear cases during the colonial period, and they became courts of first instance. Tengku Mukhlis presided over an appeals court in Takèngën.

The judges in the new system either had served as religious officials under the Dutch, or, as was the case with Tengku Mukhlis, were younger men who had recently returned from religious studies. But none had been trained to work as judges in a hierarchical legal system. As Judge Kasim, who began working on the court staff in 1956, remarked,

> many more cases were brought to the court's office than were decided, because we lacked skilled people. People knew substantive law but not how to properly resolve cases. So we heard few of the cases brought to us. Tengku Mukhlis knew nothing of how to write documents or how to process cases. Indeed, people used to refer to the judges as "Pak kutèkèn" ("Mr. 'I'll sign it' ") because they would not even read the documents drawn up by the clerk, just sign them.

Judge Kasim had learned some clerical skills in middle school, and as a trainee for service on the civil court. Tengku Mukhlis convinced him to join the Islamic court instead, and secured him a civil service appointment three years later, the only such appointee at that time other than Mukhlis himself. He served as chief clerk. When Tengku Mukhlis needed a panel of three judges to hear an inheritance dispute, he drew on two other local men with religious training, Tengku Usin and Tengku Abdurrahim Daudy.[3] These men were acknowledged by the appellate court, but never were given official appointments; they were paid a small honorarium for each case heard. For all other cases, Tengku Mukhlis presided and decided; Kasim took care of the records.

Judge Muhklis was succeeded by another local religious teacher, Tengku Ebbës, in 1972; a third local man, representing the next generation of Gayo scholars, Tengku Abdul Jalil, served as temporary chief judge during 1983–84. During 1984–85 there was no judge – Kasim simply continued to take care of paperwork on his own as *de facto* chief judge until Judge Hasan was appointed in 1985. The court had no permanent building until it moved to its present location in 1975. The Islamic court was, literally, a storefront operation with a makeshift staff.

The earliest case documented in the archives illustrates the difficulties faced by a court with no enforcement powers. In late 1945, three brothers asked the Islamic court to divide land left to their father by his parents. The father had

---

[3] Tengku Usin was an older man with some religious law training; Tengku Daudy was of Mukhlis's cohort, and was best known for his role in developing the new Gayo religious poetry genre, *saèr* (Bowen 1993a). The appellation "Tengku" indicates some religious education or local acknowledgment of religious authority.

just died, and his brother, their uncle, refused to give them their share. The court managed to get two of the brothers and the uncle to sign a typed letter of agreement, stating that the uncle would get the land and one of the brothers would get some money. But a note dated 1947 records the refusal of the third brother to go along with the settlement, and in 1948 the matter was brought back to the court. No document survives as to its final settlement, if one took place.[4]

Most inheritance disputes brought to the court met similar fates: either they were informally settled, with a judge acting as mediator, or they ended in stalemate. In 1948, for example, the first-instance court in Bëbësën was asked to hear thirteen inheritance disputes, heard nine of them, but apparently did not render any formal decisions. The judge probably provided an informal finding (*penetapan*) to the parties as to the identity of the heirs and the appropriate division of the estate among them. A finding is a legal opinion, in practice equivalent to a *fatwa*, which the parties may follow or ignore, but which cannot be enforced. An Islamic court judge could render a decision (*keputusan*), but at that time he had no authority to enforce that either; a litigant who wished the decision enforced would have to file a separate appeal to the civil court, but rarely did litigants do so in the early decades.

The court did decide other cases, mostly concerning marriage and divorce. The small number of property cases decided by the court turned on questions of fact, usually whether the defendant had purchased, or had only borrowed, a plot of land. This type of case was decided on the basis of the testimony of witnesses, or by one party's willingness to swear an oath. Some of these cases were merely one more stage in multi-generational disputes reaching well back into the colonial period. For example, in a suit regarding the land of a man named Pang ("Warrior") Dama, land had been turned over to others when the Dutch invaded the region in 1904 and the owner had fled Takèngën; ownership of the land was then contested in the Dutch court in the late 1920s, relitigated in the Islamic court in 1951, and then appealed to the Islamic appellate court.[5]

When norms themselves were in dispute, the issues resembled those we saw in chapter 2 for Isak in the 1990s. In one 1948 case, a brother refused to divide land with his sisters "because they are all women," by which he probably meant (in addition to any general antipathy toward giving property to women) that some or all of them had married out of the village and foregone claims to the estate. A second case involved an elder sister who had stayed in the village after marriage to care for her parents. After their death she kept control of all

---

[4] These and other references come from the court archives; early cases sometimes were left unnumbered.

[5] The case is PA 29/1951. The outcome of the appeal is not mentioned in the file. Indicative of the working conditions of the day is a remark by Tengku Mukhlis, in his letter forwarding the appeal, that the appeal is late because he had great difficulty locating a typewriter.

their land, refusing to divide it with her sisters and younger brother. They took her to court and demanded an Islamic law division; under Gayo norms she had a valid claim to a larger share than that due her under Islam, because of her role caring for their parents (she would have claimed an *umë pematang*, a bequeathed extra share). In a third case, one brother refused to acknowledge that the parents had given a plot of land to the other brother and demanded that the entire estate be divided between them.

Some of these cases presented the judges with difficult factual questions – did the parents give one brother the land? Did the sister care properly for her parents? But still more vexing was the choice each case presented between Gayo adat and Islamic law. The plaintiffs had valid complaints on Islamic law grounds. The defendants had valid claims under Gayo norms, but not under Islamic ones. Unless factual findings foreshortened the judicial reasoning process, the court could not have rendered a decision without finding for one set of norms or the other without affirming the priority of Islamic norms, as one would expect from an Islamic court, or affirming the priority of local adat, as would have reflected the general normative state of affairs at the time. Neither choice was a happy one for these judges, who were Gayo men, fully appreciative of how things worked in the villages, but also Islamic scholars and advocates of a greater role for Islam in the highlands.[6]

As we shall see, in the 1960s the Islamic judges attempted to square this normative circle by claiming that the divisions had received the plaintiffs' agreement, but during their first decade the court seems to have generally tried to arrange an informal agreement among the parties and avoid posing the question in terms of adat versus Islam.

The struggle for recognition

Although the provincial government had charged the Islamic court with determining the heirs to an estate, Jakarta had never formally granted such authority. The judges felt themselves on shaky ground trying to change inheritance practices without proper political support. In 1953 the head of the Islamic appellate court in Aceh, Tengku M. Hanafiah, wrote the head of the provincial Office of Religious Affairs, with copies to all Islamic courts in Aceh, to complain about this situation. Although the courts do have jurisdiction over inheritance disputes, he wrote, trying to settle them "causes great trouble" (*sangat merumitkan*) because the court's status has not been clarified by the central government. "But we cannot just refuse to hear such cases," he complains, "so what should we do?"

---

[6] Tengku Mukhlis was one of the most outspoken proponents of a wholesale replacement of adat with Islam. In the late 1940s and early 1950s, the civil court included a slot for a religious authority among its judges, and other members were strong advocates of religious law.

The problem of legitimacy was limited to inheritance cases. As Judge Kasim explained to me in 1994:

Divorce and marriage had long been handled by the local religious officials and so the court's right was not in doubt. But from 1946 to 1957, the religious court was not recognized by the central government, and so some people considered it a mock court. It was very difficult to get people interested in working at it – this was the case until 1989 because we still did not have powers of execution. One of the reasons people supported the Darul Islam rebellion was so that we could have the religious court recognized.

After the outbreak of the Darul Islam rebellion in 1952, inheritance cases rarely reached the court. Judge Kasim commented: "conditions were terrible and people did not know about the court. Nothing was in good order then; it was worse than difficult."[7] The Darul Islam rebels, although usually termed separatists, in fact were seeking to redefine what place religion would have in Indonesian society. During the rebellion, many Gayo families joined rebel armies in their encampments in the hills. Darul Islam judges heard disputes of all kinds. As Aman Kerna of Isak explained:

The judge would try all cases brought to him, whether about inheritance, divorce, or fights. However, in serious matters, such as someone fooling around with another man's wife, the rebels would just shoot the suspect, as there was no jail. During the cease-fire period [1957–60], the judge set up an office in Isak, on the hill where the People's Hall was later built. People would bring inheritance disputes and divorce requests to him, and there were lots of both. In one case the judge decided an inheritance dispute in one man's favor, and the other man, the losing party, who lived in Isak, sought revenge by spreading it around that the man who won the case had been with the rebels. The Mobrig [government special forces] came and shot him. That land has never been productive since, because the loser got control in that way.

One of the fruits of the 1957 negotiations was an administrative regulation (PP 29/1957, later PP 45) that did recognize the legal authority of the religious court.

Fluid boundaries

Although the civil court had a much stronger legal basis than had its Islamic counterpart, it faced similar dilemmas. For its first twenty-five years, the judges included Gayo men of varying backgrounds, who usually served long tenures.

---

[7] The Takèngën court's report of cases decided during 1960 bears Judge Kasim out. In that year, the court decided eighteen cases where a woman demanded that her husband be ordered to provide her with sufficient provisions (cases called *nafkah*), seven requests for divorce brought by the wife and two brought by the husband, ten requests for marriage certificates for couples who had never obtained proper documentation (and, most often, now needed the certificates to enter civil service or demand pensions), two requests that hibah gifts be awarded, and only one inheritance dispute.

Local religious scholars often served on the court, together with men from the Gayo highlands or elsewhere who had received some legal training but not a law degree. They, too, wished to avoid making decisive choices between Islam and adat.

The civil court heard few inheritance cases. Nearly all the civil cases brought to it involved disputes over ownership of land or shops, and usually included a disagreement over the terms of a loan or sale. If they were asked to divide an estate, the court sent the litigation over to the Islamic court, or drew up a certificate of reconciliation (*akte perdamaian*) to be signed by both parties. Although in most cases they avoided rendering a decision, the court did decide some inheritance disputes; often the dispute festered, appearing in later years to be argued before different judges, following different norms.

We will follow one such case as it unfolded over the decades from early post-independence to the New Order. I call it the case of Aman Nurjati's lands; it surfaces in the court records under different numbers in different years. I first encountered it in the civil court file as Case PN 28/1969.[8] Reading the file sent me back in time through two other sets of records, dating from 1947 and from 1963.[9] The original case (PN 8/1947) concerned the estate of Aman Nurjati. He had owned about three hectares of well-irrigated riceland in the village of Telintang in the Peugasing area, a few miles from Takèngën. He had died around 1915, about thirteen years after his son, Aman Segërë. He also had a daughter, Inën Dingin, who in 1947 was the plaintiff. Inën Dingin had married uxorilocally, remaining in their village of Telintang. She had had one child, Inën Ismail, who had died in 1936. Aman Segërë also had remained in the village after marriage, and when he died he left four children: three daughters – Inën Garut, Inën Bakar, and Inën Daud – and one son, Rabil Aman Seriah, the 1947 defendant. The daughters had married out of the village; Rabil remained in it, and in 1947 farmed the entire three hectares of land.

The initial resolution of the case illustrates how the early civil court saw no sharp distinctions between adat and Islam. In February 1947, Inën Dingin submitted a written petition to the civil court asking for part of the land. In court, she was questioned by the chief judge, a local man named Abdussalam. She explained that Rabil was the youngest of four siblings. He was still in his mother's womb when his father, Aman Segërë, died, about 1902. His mother

---

[8] The case numbers indicate either Pengadilan Agama (PA), religious or Islamic court, or Pengadilan Negeri (PN), civil court, followed by the number and year when the case was first heard. Case designations for the Supreme Court begin with MA, for Mahkamah Agung. Because only civil cases are considered in this book, I have omitted the additional designation Pdt, for *perdata*, "civil."

[9] I also found in the 1969 files the transcript of the hearings from 1947 and 1969, the *berita acara*. These transcripts are rarely found in the files; in recent years the court has included only a summary of the arguments followed by their decision in the archives. The entire legal process in this type of case is, however, a matter of public record and so can be properly quoted here.

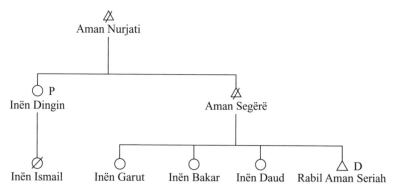

Figure 5.1 The case of Aman Nurjati's lands, 1947 (P and D indicate plaintiff and defendant)

soon remarried, and his three sisters brought him up. When, about eleven years later, her father was near death, he told her and Rabil that they should use the riceland. He did not divide it between them, she explained, and he gave four plots, amounting to a little over one hectare, just to her. The rest "descended to us as our ancestral wealth."[10] But ever since then all the land, including the plots given to her, had been farmed by Rabil.

The chief judge then questioned her. "Why did you not demand your share of the land earlier?" Inën Dingin replied: "Because I thought I would wait until Rabil had grown up and acquired reason (berakal), then perhaps he would become aware (insyaf), and as it happened I was cared for by my daughter, who has now died." Since then, she said, "I live by working on other people's fields, and they give me something as a daily wage." She said that when Rabil had seized the parcel of land her father given to her, she complained to the ruler of the area, the Rëjë Ciq of Peugasing, who said: "Just wait until Rabil is older and acquires reason." She went on to testify that additional wealth that had once belonged to the estate had previously been sold off by her father, Aman Nurjati, to pay for the upbringing of his grandchildren.[11]

The chief judge then asked Rabil for his version of the events. Rabil denounced everything the plaintiff had said as lies. Back when he was still in school, he reported, the Rëjë Ciq had told him that when he grew up he should take back the land held by Inën Dingin, because it was his heritage (pusaka) from his father. In 1914, the Rëjë Ciq had awarded him the land not held by Inën Dingin, and three men had witnessed the transaction, but all three since had died.

---

[10] "[J]atuh menjadi pusaka kepada kami."

[11] For a pertinent disquisition on "reason" and individual development in the ideas of Acehnese, see Siegel (1969).

Now, back in 1914, the Rëjë Ciq of Peugasing would have been an exceedingly powerful figure. The office existed before the Dutch came, but they gave it additional authority. The Rëjë Ciq could exact taxes, order men to report for corvée labor, and adjudicate disputes. Some of the men who occupied the office used their power to take land and to order people to work for them, with the threat of reporting them to the Dutch if they did not comply. One did not cross a Rëjë Ciq (see Bowen 1991:68–79).

The judge turned to the one witness called by Inën Dingin, a man who farmed the plot next to the disputed land. The witness said that the land had belonged to Aman Nurjati, and that he knew that such was the case because he had seen Inën Dingin work it annually over a period of twenty years, until about 1930, and because his mother had told him that the land had belonged to Aman Nurjati. His mother's words made sense to him, he added, because, after all, Aman Nurjati was Inën Dingin's father. (Each witness and litigant was asked if he or she would be willing to take an oath should that be called for, but none ever appears to have been sworn in.)

Assisting chief judge Abdussalam at the trial were the three other judges serving on the court: Joyodinoyo (ethnically Javanese but probably of long residence in Aceh), Tengku Abdurrahman (a religious scholar who at the same time was serving on one of the two first-instance Islamic courts that still existed), and Tengku M. Husin, who sometimes assisted Tengku Mukhlis on the Islamic appeals court. Tengku Husin occupied what seems to have been a religious slot on the civil court, and in the proceedings was referred to by Judge Abdussalam as "the Islamic scholar." During colonial days Tengku Husin had sat on the local Landraad court as the Islamic law expert, and he evidently continued to serve this function well into independence. He had also served as a subdistrict qadi, the religious official in charge of performing marriages and approving divorces.

Before issuing a decision in this case Judge Abdussalam first turned to Tengku Husin to ask him his opinion; he replied that the wealth in question was entirely the estate of Aman Nurjati. The other judges agreed. This simple statement annulled any gifts or transfers of the land, and started anew the process of dividing the estate. Although the court transcript includes no mention of how the land was to be divided, we know from later records that Judge Abdussalam ordered an equal division of the property between Inën Dingin and Rabil. The court's order was about what one would have expected under Gayo adat norms: the daughter who remained behind and cared for the parents split the estate evenly with her brother.

The court record shows little concern with the boundaries between judiciaries, or for distinguishing between "Islamic law" and "adat law." One judge, Abdurrahman, served simultaneously on the civil court and an Islamic court. An Islamic authority, serving in that official role, seems to have been given priority in reaching a decision. No explicit discussion occurred about which set of laws ought to be applied, nor whether the dispute should have been taken to the Islamic court instead. (Neither of the phrases "Gayo adat" or "Islamic law" appears in the proceedings.) Moreover, even though two of the four judges were recognized as Islamic authorities, the court divided the land in accordance with generally accepted Gayo adat practices and understandings.

Had the court followed the Islamic "science of shares" as it was generally understood at the time in Aceh (and elsewhere in Indonesia), they would have reached very different conclusions. The decision could have gone in two directions. The court would first have had to tackle the problem posed by the fact that Aman Segërë died before his father. Under the Islamic legal interpretations of the day, a grandchild could not inherit directly from his or her grandparent. Aman Segërë's death cut off his own children from receiving a share of their grandfather's estate. If the court had applied this rule, Rabil, Aman Segërë's son, would have received nothing, and Inën Dingin the entire estate, and the case would have been closed.

If, however, they had ignored this rule, they would have had to include Rabil's sisters in the award under standard interpretations of Islamic law, but the potential claims of these three women are never mentioned in the court transcript. Rabil and his sisters together would have received two-thirds of the estate; Inën Dingin, one-third. Rabil then would have received double the share awarded to each of his sisters, thus two-fifths times two-thirds of the total estate, or four-fifteenths of the total. Such is the inexorable logic of the Qur'ânic shares, but such was clearly not the norm followed by either court in the early post-independence years – nor did the plaintiff ask for such a division. However, rights to an estate share do not lapse in Islamic law, and the claims of the sisters were to resurface in later years, as we shall see.

Later the courts were to develop an explicit rationale for allowing adat norms to override Islamic ones, one that could be consistent with general support for Islamic law. But this rationale involved reconceptualizing adat in terms of individual rights alone, a shift that was to lead to a more activist judicial role by a new group of non-Gayo judges.

Affirming consensus in the 1960s

In the late 1950s and early 1960s, the waning years of the Darul Islam rebellion, both courts continued to feel politically weak. Truce and settlement did not mean trust and harmony. To the contrary, the rebellion ended by the sowing of new hatreds. Some rebels had been pointed out to the army by fellow villagers who often were members of the Nationalist or Communist parties. The rebels nursed their grudges through the 1960s, and some were to seek revenge during the long nights of massacre in 1965–66.

In this climate of brittle, tense relationships, and of an increasingly sharp polarization between Islamic and non-Islamic political parties, people watched their backs. Taking a strong position for Islamic family law was probably even less attractive an option for judges than it had been in the early 1950s. It seems likely that judges were searching for a rule that would allow them to avoid advocating Islam over adat; in any case, by the early 1960s they had found one. Both courts issued decisions stating that an earlier division of an estate was consensual and binding, and rendered null subsequent demands to have an estate divided according to Islam. Because the general idea of agreement, consensus, or contract can be given bases in adat, in Islamic law, and in civil law, these findings allowed the judges to avoid having to give priority to either Islam or adat.

Avoiding conflict over norms

By the 1960s, a handful of inheritance cases began to show up in the Islamic court each year, but even then most suits were withdrawn after the two parties reached a settlement.[12] When the parties failed to settle, the dispute usually involved a conflict between the Islamic norms cited by the plaintiff as the grounds for requesting a redivision of wealth, and the adat norms invoked by the defendant according to which the wealth had in fact been divided. It was precisely the stark opposition between the two sets of norms that made settlement in such cases difficult. As before, the judges tried to avoid siding explicitly with either Islamic law or adat, but instead searched for a standard that could be reconciled with both normative systems. Sometimes they found that a prior agreement between all parties nullified the plaintiff's claim.

In the public dossier for a case, the presiding judge must give the reasons for the decision in a deductive manner, in the format associated with the European civil law tradition (but not with those Islamic judiciaries not reorganized under civil codes; see Messick [1993] and Rosen [1989]). The judge's statement thus allows us to understand something of the public interpretive process at work.

Illustrative of the reasoning followed by the Islamic court judges in this period is the 1961 case, *Usman vs Serikulah* (PA 41/1961). The case pitted the child of a sister (Usman) against the child of a brother (Serikulah). Usman asked the court to redivide land once belonging to his mother's father, and to do so according to Islamic law. He admitted that two years earlier, in 1959, there had been an attempt to divide the ricefields by general agreement among

---

[12] I hesitate to give counts of kinds of cases based on all the files I have read for a given set of years, because I do not know whether the files are complete. For example, a record without a decision probably means that the case was withdrawn but it could, especially during the years of local armed struggle in the 1950s, simply mean that the decision is missing. Thus for a sense of the frequency of cases I rely on the few annual tallies provided in the archives.

the heirs, but said he no longer was satisfied with the results of this meeting. The defendant, Serikulah, was the daughter of the original owner's son, and thus was Usman's mother's brother's daughter. Her son Sahim controlled the land at the time of the suit, and had obtained title to it from the district Land Registration office (making a redivision of the land difficult).

Serikulah said that Usman's mother had married out of the village, and that, following Gayo adat, when she married out she had received bride goods (*tempah*) that were intended to cancel any future claims to a share of the estate. Thus, she said, according to Gayo norms the plaintiff's claim was without basis. Her claim that paying bride goods had signaled Usman's mother's renunciation of any further claim on the estate fits my own information about Gayo norms and practices prevailing at that time (and to a lesser extent today). Daughters or sons who married out of the village lost claim on village lands, affirming a cultural emphasis on maintaining social continuity by keeping all ancestral lands in the hands of members of the village. Land, village, and residence were of a piece.

But Usman's claim that Islamic law entitled him to a share of his grand-father's lands regardless of such payments or marriage type also agrees with the understandings of religious norms commonly held by scholars and judges at that time, as well as today. Therefore, no obvious error in logic or in the substantive claims about the norms of the time is to be found in either party's case.

The case thus presented the judges on the Islamic court, all Gayo men, with a clear choice between two sets of norms, Islam and adat. These norms were made all the clearer in that one side explicitly cited Islam and the other side, Gayo adat, as the respective bases for their claims. The judges could have taken either side, redividing the property in the name of Islam, as the plaintiff wished, or reaffirming the appropriateness of Gayo norms, in accordance with the defendant's rebuttal. But taking either side on these grounds would have been difficult. Affirming Gayo adat against Islamic law would have contradicted the judges' sense of their mission as Islamic judges, their very reason for having joined the court. Several of the judges, in particular Tengku Mukhlis, chief judge from 1945 until 1972, were vocal proponents of a greater Islamization of Gayo society.

Affirming Islamic law against adat would not, however, have been an attrac-tive alternative. Property divisions in the 1960s continued to follow the general logic of adat, and to oppose them would have required a great deal of authority, and the power and willingness to withstand sustained opposition. Such were not the characteristics of the Islamic court in 1961. Although overturning adat practices in the name of Islam might have been the policy preference of some judges, doing so at that time with respect to inheritance would have severely eroded the already thin legitimacy of the court. Taking a strong stand one way or the other also would have been personally dangerous during this period of rebellion by an Islam-based movement. No judge wished to invite retaliation from the rebels by coming out against Islamic law, or risk accusations of rebel sympathies by coming out against adat. Furthermore, most judges on both courts saw their own tasks as incorporating norms of Islam and adat.

The judges avoided framing the case as "Islam versus adat" by stating that in 1959 the two parties already had reached an agreement, a *penyelesaian secara perdamaian*, "bringing (the matter) to a close through reconciliation." The 1959 meeting had ended by awarding Sahim the ricefields. The judges noted that the plaintiff, Usman, was present at the meeting but he had remained silent, even after the meeting's presider had called out three times to all those present: "Don't anyone ever bring suit over these fields again." The judges concluded that Usman's silence had implied his consent to the agreement, and they rejected his suit.

Other cases were decided in similar ways. In a case heard the following year, *Inën Deraman vs Inën Nur* (PA 25/1962), the plaintiff, who had married out of the village, had received about one-half as much land as had her sister, who had remained in the village. The plaintiff requested a division according to Islamic law, which would have given the two sisters equal shares. The defendant replied that when the plaintiff had married out of the village she had received bride goods and thus abandoned her claim. At the hearing, a man who had been a judge on the Islamic court in the 1950s testified that he had attended the meeting where land had been divided, and that the plaintiff had been overjoyed to get anything, "because in those days women who married out of the village never inherited land." The court said "We should not keep redividing wealth," and again rejected the plaintiff's claim.

Inventing adat

During this period, judges at the nearby civil court were also hearing appeals to divide wealth. In the 1960s these judges resembled their counterparts on the religious court: they were mostly Gayo men, often from religious backgrounds and sometimes without law degrees, although all had some previous court experience. As with their counterparts on the Islamic court, they sought to avoid overturning past property divisions and argued that outcomes of village deliberations rested on consensus.

Principal among these judges was Abubakar Porang. Born in the southern region of Gayoland, Judge Porang was a strong proponent of Islamic law, but he was also reluctant to challenge older Gayo practices. He joined the court in 1961 and served until his death in 1970. By the 1960s, the civil court no longer avoided deciding inheritance cases; indeed, in 1961 alone it decided seven of them. Abubakar Porang wrote most of these decisions. He claimed that the court was enforcing adat, and that the "living adat" in the Gayo highlands was now Islamic law.[13] Accordingly, in cases where the plaintiff asked for a division of property, and the defendant did not make a reply based on adat, the judge generally found for the plaintiff, and ordered a division according to Islamic law. When these decisions were appealed the appellate court overturned them on grounds that the civil court did not have jurisdiction to determine the heirs or divide property.[14]

However, in those cases where the defendant did claim that general agreement based on adat norms had been reached when the property was divided, Judge Porang and his colleagues tended to support the defense. Indicative of his reasoning was a 1964 case, *Inën Saidah vs Aman Jemilah* (PN 47/1964), which presents facts similar to the religious court cases examined above. Two sisters, both of whom had married out of the village, sued their cousin, Aman Jemilah, who had remained in the village, for equal shares of lands once owned by their grandfather.[15] The defendant stated that he had received the land as a gift from his father and had farmed it ever since then. Several witnesses testified that prior to the litigation he had made no claims to the land.

The way the case was presented to the court differed in a crucial respect from the religious court cases, reflecting the different jurisdictions of the two courts. Because the civil court was supposed to decide according to adat, both parties couched their demands in terms of Gayo social norms and not Islam. The plaintiffs demanded their equal rights in the name of the "living adat," the phrase used by the Supreme Court in granting equal rights to an estate to all children (see chapter 3). The defendant based his claim to the land on the argument that the plaintiffs were silent during the period when he worked the land. Thus, the dispute involved a conflict between two ways of interpreting

---

[13] Indeed, the Supreme Court (MA 564/1975), in its comment on a case that had originated from Takèngën in 1969, made the same claim, stating that in Gayoland the adat law on inheritance was that division is according to Islamic law (*Yurisprudensi Aceh* 1979:7). The Court may have based its statement on a 1973 study by law students in the highlands, or on Judge Porang's decisions. As with most such statements, which are meant as prescriptions but masquerade as descriptions, this one in no way reflected local practices.

[14] Among such cases are PN 28/1961, PN 121/1963, PN 66/1964, and PN 110/1964. In these cases Judge Porang ordered that the estate be divided "according to *farâ'd* [Islamic shares]," and in each case the Aceh appellate court found that this instruction overstepped jurisdictional bounds. The appellate court's comment in overturning PN 110/1964 was typical: "It is the Religious Court that has the right to investigate and decide cases involving inheritance and inheritance disputes, according to the laws in force in this area." The appellate court acted in the same manner on appeals from first-instance civil courts elsewhere in Aceh. For example, in a 1964 inheritance case from Lhokseumawe, in North Aceh, the appellate court ruled that the first-instance civil court did not have jurisdiction to hear an inheritance dispute (*Mimbar Hukum* 2, 1990:97–98).

[15] The record is unclear as to the genealogical connection. The sisters had married out of their village; whether the tie to the original landowner, the grandfather, was through their mother or their father is not recorded, precisely because it is the form of their marriage that is the relevant fact, not the genealogy.

"Gayo adat," and not a conflict between adat and Islam. Neither party referred to Islamic legal concepts, nor did Judge Porang.[16]

In *Inën Saidah*, Judge Porang found for the defendant. He stated that the two sisters had received bride goods at marriage, and that "often among the bride goods is included a share of the estate, which sometimes is made official and sometimes not. Furthermore, from the time when the defendant's grandfather still lived, to the defendant's father, to the defendant, the plaintiffs never came forward to make a claim, such that the plaintiffs, according to adat law, are 'hanging, not quite reaching, having no wealth; with a broken bridge, having no inheritance,' *laman*."

The decision justified the prior division of wealth on the basis of what Judge Porang claimed were two norms of Gayo adat. One of these norms resembles the concept of "adverse possession" in Anglo-American law, that a claim elapses if the plaintiff has allowed the defendant to possess property without objecting to that possession. Judge Porang emphasized that a great deal of time had elapsed after the property settlement with no one objecting to it.[17] This norm had been invoked by the court in earlier cases concerning property that had been abandoned or lent out and then reclaimed; some of these decisions (e.g., PN 76/1959) quoted the same Gayo maxim. The other norm was the one that was cited by the Islamic court in the cases discussed above, that the plaintiff had already received a share of the estate at the time of marriage, and so expected to receive no further portion of the estate. This norm served to explain the plaintiff's silence. Justified in this way, the civil court's decision did not contradict the Supreme Court's ruling on the "living adat" because it did not affirm a principle of the unequal division of property; for this reason, it was upheld by the provincial appellate court in 1975.

The court's justification involved an extension of Gayo concepts into new domains. In its everyday use, the Gayo term *laman* refers not to the elapse of claims, but to the specific right of a ruler to withdraw use-rights to land if stipulated conditions for that use (such as improving the land) are not met.[18] The maxim quoted by Judge Porang is used in everyday social life to refer to the break that a daughter makes with her natal village when she marries into another village.[19] Understood in this way, the maxim did indeed apply to the

[16] Perhaps his experiences of being overruled by the appellate court had made him wary of mentioning Islam as a legal basis for his decisions.

[17] The colonial-era civil law code, the *Burgerlijk Wetboek* (Subekti and Tjitrosudibio 1961), which continues to be cited in court decisions, recognizes a version of "adverse possession," but the code was not cited in this case.

[18] Two surveys by the Ministry of Justice found that Gayo adat law did *not* recognize a concept of "elapsed claims" (Indonesian, *daluwarsa*) for any type of property (Departemen Kehakiman 1973, 1984).

[19] On the ways in which Gayo adat is embodied in general maxims, to which village headmen, religious officials, or others claiming authority then give contextual specificity, see Bowen (1991:139–68).

case at hand – the daughter who married out had thereby lost her claim on her parents' estate. However, that way of applying the maxim would have directly contradicted the new distributional norms proclaimed by the Supreme Court. Understood in another way, as about the plaintiff's implicit agreement to the property division (signaled by her inaction), the maxim invoked a general theory that a past consensus over how to distribute property ought to be respected. This understanding evidently was acceptable to the appellate court.

Thus, the Tak̀eng̀en civil court justified its conservative decisions regarding family property along the same lines as did the Islamic court, and elaborated the justification by incorporating a principle that had already been well established with regard to another class of cases.

Inspecting consensus: the assumptions behind the decisions

These decisions by the Islamic and the civil courts rested on two assumptions. The first was the empirical assumption that the village-level deliberations dividing the estates were consensual rather than coercive. The second assumption concerned the correct set of norms to apply: that the social norms understood and accepted by the parties to the original divisions at the time of those divisions are the correct legal norms on which to base a current decision. From these assumptions one could quickly infer the decisions themselves. Because the prior distributions of property did indeed comply with the norms of adat, and because they had been ratified at village assemblies attended by the plaintiffs, the plaintiffs lost their cases.

Both assumptions are open to question and, indeed, both were rejected in later years by judges on Islamic and civil courts. Let us consider each in turn. The first is that village meetings led to decisions by consensus. Such claims are ubiquitous in Indonesia; indeed, "consensus through deliberation" (*musyawarah mufakat*) is a key plank in the state ideology, Pancasila. It is invoked daily in national political life, often as cultural cover for efforts to suppress popular dissent.[20]

Any legitimacy attached to these national claims is at least partly due to their resonance with long-standing local norms in most Indonesian societies that decisions should be reached through consensus. In Gayo society, *mupakat* names the appropriate way of reaching all decisions through a consultation among village elders. Movement toward consensus is structurally part of the Gayo ritual speaking that resolves village-level disputes (Bowen 1991:139–68); this movement diagrams the putative social process of people changing their

---

[20] So accustomed are political actors to deciding by "consensus," with varying degrees of *de facto* underlying coercion, that when in the post-Suharto era the national Parliament made a decision by "voting" (English in the original, in scare quotes), it was the headline story of the day (*Kompas* online, 18 September 1998).

opinions from divergent to convergent. So widespread in the archipelago are such norms that Clifford Geertz (1983) took Indonesian ideas of arriving at consensus through harmonious speaking as the defining feature of archipelagic adat.[21]

Double-voiced claims

The frequency of claims that decisions were consensual does not make evalu-ating such claims any easier, however.[22] My own experience in Isak would lead me to say that not only do different participants in village meetings evaluate the outcomes differently, but that even in the words of a single participant one can find more than one type of evaluation. Consider how in 1994 Tengku Daud Arifin, a former Isak religious official (*qadi*) whom I knew well from 1978 until his death in 2000, explained, first, how these village deliberations produce a consensus and then, immediately afterwards, how in fact he and his siblings divided their own parents' lands.

When I was the qadi we never had a case go to the Islamic court, nor has there been one since. I have often been called to resolve cases. I always first specify the shares of the estate according to Islamic law. But then some of those present will say, "but that is not fair (*adil*)," because the daughters get less then the sons. Or some of the children say, "I don't really need that," or the sons ask the daughters to renounce (*ikhlasën*, "give sincerely") their shares, because they are already provided for in their husbands' villages. So they work out a better arrangement peacefully. That's then fair and sincere.

When my mother died [his father had died first] we all gathered together to divide the estate. One younger brother said if he did not find it fair he would not go along with what we did. Another suggested they divide it all up, and we worked out a division whereby I got the riceland way up in the weeds. But then I spoke, and as the eldest I could say: "No; let's try again," and we redid it, and now I got the lion's share of the riceland close to the village [here he breaks into chuckles]. The other siblings have not used their shares; I work all the land, and now my children and grandchildren, because they are all civil servants [rather than full-time farmers with their own lands].

Tengku Arifin's recounting of the process was complex. He initially described the village deliberations as moving from an application of the letter of the law toward an application of superior arrangements that responded to ideas of fairness. This movement was possible, he suggested, because some participants

---

[21] A distinct theory about consensus comes from Islamic jurisprudence, in which the consensus (*ijmâ'*) of jurists can be the basis for law. The validity of arguments from consensus is hotly debated within Islamic circles.

[22] The problem is a general one for theories of deliberative democracy as well as for studies of specific political processes. On what grounds can one claim "consensus," given that any deliberative process will involve people changing their minds (perhaps by definition), and such changes involve influence, probably authority, and perhaps power?

sincerely renounced their rights in order to respect the balance of needs. It is this sort of characterization of village deliberative processes that makes plausible a legal judgment (such as in *Usman*) that agreements proceeding from such meetings ought to be taken as evidence of the sincere wishes of all participants, particularly in the absence of any public objections. I also heard villagers, usually men, counterpose the mechanical application of Islamic law to the morally superior recourse to feelings, needs, and sincerity that they associate with adat. It is this type of claim that is drawn on by government officials to support state ideology.

But Tengku Arifin spoke in a different way later in this interview, when he chuckled over the way he, the eldest brother, could dictate which agreements would be acceptable and could also, even after the agreement, retain *de facto* control of most of the land, with the justification that his own children, with civil service occupations, did not have their own land. As we saw in chapter 2, it is precisely this power of eldest brothers to defer divisions and retain control that has driven some children, or even grandchildren, to sue for redivisions in the court.

As the qadi's "double-voiced" recollections illustrate, one can infer from these meetings either consensus or coercion, or some combination thereof. Judges in the 1960s tended to practice a "consensus" reading of such meetings. To support their reading in any particular case, they would point to evidence indicating that, despite the plaintiff's subsequent dissatisfaction, at the time of the original agreement she or he was part of this consensus. This evidence could include testimony that the plaintiff had been silent when the deliberations were read aloud for final approval, or that the plaintiff freely accepted the result, as in the former judge's testimony that the plaintiff had been happy with the outcome.

Of course, the plaintiff's satisfaction at the time may have been because the then-prevailing social norms did not offer any alternative. As the former judge said, that was how things were settled at that time; no one who married out ever inherited wealth. That the satisfaction of the plaintiff some years earlier should be decisive brings into play the second major assumption underlying decisions of the 1960s, namely, that it was the role of the judges to render decisions according to what was appropriate under the local social norms prevailing at the time, and not to challenge those norms on the basis of the plaintiff's rights under Islamic law or under a new interpretation of adat law.

As applied by the Islamic court judges, this assumption, which may or may not have been publicly articulated, resembles the so-called "reception doctrine" advanced by colonial administrators, under which Islam was considered to be the law of the land only insofar as it had already been accepted into local adat. (This doctrine has become emblematic of colonial anti-Islamic policy, and for that reason a religious court judge would be horrified at my comparison.)

The assumption justified the courts proceeding cautiously and conservatively at a time when that course may have seemed more prudent to the judges.

The decisions taken by the Islamic court judges in the 1950s and 1960s provide another example of how one cannot read from rules to outcomes. One might have expected to see the inheritance rules of Islam, the unambiguous "science of shares," enforced by the religious court judges and, to the extent possible, by the Islamic-minded civil court judges. But both sets of judges were able to construe village social life in such a way as to obviate the need to invoke these rules.

Aman Nurjati's lands once more

An early indication that the Takèngën courts were changing direction comes from a rehearing of the matter of Aman Nurjati's lands in the late 1960s. The dispute was heard by the civil court twice in the 1960s, with very different results. Recall that in the 1947 hearing, three grandchildren of Aman Nurjati were considered irrelevant to the decision. The three sisters of Rabil Aman Seriah, the defendant, all had married out of the village, and, following adat norms, had not been entitled to a share of the estate. Their potential claims under Islamic law were not raised by the judges, despite their Islamic training. Instead, the land was divided evenly between the plaintiff, Inën Dingin, and the defendant.

But when, sixteen years later, the division ordered by the court in 1947 was challenged, the suit was brought by descendants of those three married-out sisters. The 1947 division of the lands had been carried out. By 1963 the original principals had all died and the land had passed into new hands. Rabil's ricelands had been inherited by his daughter, his only child, Seriah (see Figure 5.2). Inën Dingin's daughter had died before her, raising the Islamic law barrier to inheritance by granchildren. Inën Dingin therefore had given her land as a gift, hibah, to her two grandsons, Ismail and M. Sarif. These transactions were perfectly acceptable to the heirs of Rabil and Inën Dingin, but not to the collateral relatives who had been left out of the 1947 settlement.

One such relative, Rachmatsyah, son of one of the three sisters, Inën Bakar, brought suit (PN 70/1963) for himself and in the names of his mother and her sister, Inën Garut (he brought signed powers of attorney to the court). The defendants were the three people who now controlled the land: Ismail, M. Sarif, and Seriah. The plaintiff asked that the land be divided "according to Islamic Law and Gayo Adat that is valid today." He claimed that adat law gave all children shares in an estate, however they had married.

The defendants replied in a straightforward manner, stating that the 1947 decision had settled the issue, and that there remained no land that had not already been divided. The court, with Abubakar Porang presiding, agreed that

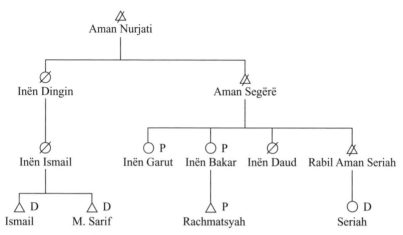

Figure 5.2 Aman Nurjati's heirs, 1963 (P and D indicate plaintiff and defendant)

the earlier decision closed the case, and found for the defendants. So far, the court had continued its 1947 stance.

But the court was in the process of changing. Seen from a later period, the 1960s appear as the time of transition, from a highly localized institution, on which local men, often with Islamic training, saw themselves as mainly mediating between highland social processes and Jakarta's dictates, and a more highly bureaucratized court, on which men from elsewhere saw themselves as mainly applying national law, here and wherever their next assignment would take them. Two new judges signaled the beginning of the transition. In the late 1960s the Abubakars were joined by a new judge, J.P. Sihaloho, a Karo Batak man from North Sumatra. Sihaloho may have been the first law school graduate to serve on the Takèngèn court, and his degree allowed him to join the court as Chief Justice. In 1969 another North Sumatra man and law degree holder, Kamar Sembiring, came to the court, where he served until the mid-1980s. Sembiring stood at the crux of the transition process. Although he came from elsewhere, he also used his long tenure on the court to amass an impressive knowledge of Gayo adat – and he was the last judge to do so. The court was still small in those days; sometimes illness left it with only one judge to hear a case (a defect that on at least one occasion [PN 28/1969] led a defendant to complain to the Supreme Court).

It was before this transitional court, with Judge Sihaloho presiding, and joined by Judges Sembiring and Abubakar I.B., that the Aman Nurjati case was heard for a third time, in 1969. (Judge Porang, who died shortly after this case was decided, did not participate.) Rachmatsyah had appealed the 1963 decision denying his petition. The appellate court (then in Medan) had heard the case in 1968 (PT Mdn 440/1965). The appellate court rejected the reasoning of the lower court, on grounds that the plaintiff had argued precisely that the land which had been divided in 1947 needed to be redivided, and that the court had not justified that earlier settlement. They remanded the case to the lower court (through a *keputusuan sela*, "decision [to create an] opening"), ordering it to rehear the plaintiff's arguments, which it then did in July 1969 (PN 28/1969).

It was essentially a new trial, although the positions argued by the two sides were the same. Rachmatsyah claimed that his mother and her sisters had repeatedly asked to receive their share of the original estate "according to Gayo Adat Law," but the defendants had refused their requests. He asked the court to "determine and validate who are the legal heirs to the deceased Aman Nurjati, and what is the Gayo adat that was valid at that time" and also to "divide the estate among the valid heirs." The defendants responded by underscoring the legal processeses by which they received the land they now held. Ismail rehearsed the story of the 1947 suit and the division of land between Rabil and Inën Dingin, and her gift of land to himself and his brother. He added that the gift had been witnessed by the village elders, although no document was drawn up. Seriah's husband, who represented her, told a similar story: that they had their land as inheritance from Seriah's father, and that this transaction was validated by the civil court in 1947. He denied even knowing Aman Nurjati and Aman Segërë, or the three sisters in whose names the suit was brought. (His point was that those persons and older transactions were irrelevant, because the inheritance transaction that awarded his wife her land had been upheld by the court.)

The judges questioned the defendants, and, interestingly, they asked each if any one of the three sisters had been part of the 1947 suit, to which each defendant replied in the negative. Judge Sihaloho then determined that what was to be divided were the plots of land held by the three defendants, which was to be considered in its entirety as Aman Nurjati's estate. This seemingly trivial finding in fact was extremely important: it restarted the process of dividing the land back at the beginning, at the moment of Aman Nurjati's death, in effect canceling all transactions made after Aman Nurjati's death. The judge mentioned the exclusion of the three sisters from the 1947 case as one of his considerations in making the decision.

Judge Sihaloho also specified that the heirs to Aman Nurjati's estate included all the children of the brothers and sisters, thus including the three sisters. He added that "according to Adat Law the son's share is bigger than the daughter's." The decision was for the plaintiff, for the land was ordered redivided among all the children. The division was to be on the basis of adat, but the judge's stipulation that sons receive more than daughters brought adat closer to Islam. He did not specify how the shares were to be determined.

Why did the judge void the earlier transactions? The very fact that he did not comment on them individually, but simply started anew the process of estate division, makes clear that he found the logic of Gayo adat that had been applied in 1947 to be legally invalid. The judge was working in an entirely different conceptual framework from that of his 1947 predecessors. At issue for him was not whether past settlements had been consensual or not, nor whether one should apply Islam or adat, but rather who were the genealogically entitled heirs to Aman Nurjati. His questions to the witnesses never concerned how someone married. They were intended to help the judge in constructing a genealogy: who was the child of whom? Inheritance, clearly, now was a matter of rights based on genealogical ties among individuals, not linked to village affiliations. In effect, Judge Sihaloho was following through the implications of the remapping already begun by Abubakar Porang. If adat property rights truly were a matter of the division of property among children, on some general basis, then all one needed to know was the identity of the children at each generation, and the basis for division.

To chart out adat in this way, to reestablish it on a new social basis, the judge needed no testimony from adat experts, or surveys of rural practices (although these have been used in other cases, for other purposes). The shift in the legal meaning of adat came about in less conscious ways. Judge Sihaloho and his colleagues were not Gayo men. They brought with them general ideas of what Indonesian people thought, with no practical basis in experience with Gayo social practices. But their conceptual framework would not have been judged alien by many of the Gayo men and women living in town. Islamic reformist attacks on older marriage practices had already made the terms *angkap* and *juëlën*, the terms for uxorilocal and virilocal marriages, into words of derision. Reform-oriented Gayo tried to see their marriages as Islamic and individually oriented, not involving long-term ties to villages.

The outcome of these and other cases depended on whether or not the judges reopened a past division. If they did, then the outcome was highly predictable; if they did not, then the past division stood. The decision to reopen seems to have been motivated by other grounds, however; it was hardly ever itself given a legal justification. Changes in these motivations surely involved the arrival of new judges, with new backgrounds and new ways of understanding "adat," but more fundamentally they came about as a result of broader changes in society and politics in the highlands.

Hierarchy and economy since the 1970s

Changes in highlands (and national) political and economic life that began in the 1970s presented the Islamic court with a new set of possibilities and constraints. The court's prestige and the volume of its tasks have risen since the mid-1970s, due in part to changes in the national legal environment.[23] The 1974 marriage

---

[23] Recall that after 1970 decisions on the proper division of an estate were reserved to the Islamic courts.

law required all Muslims, men and women, to declare their divorces in the Islamic court; no longer could men simply pronounce the divorce utterance, the *talaq*, in order to be recognized as divorced (see chapter 9). The 1989 bill creating a uniform system of Islamic courts throughout Indonesia gave the courts the power to enforce their own decisions. The Compilation of Islamic Law, given the force of a Presidential Decree in 1991, was intended to render the substance of religious court decisions uniform throughout Indonesia (see Cammack 1997).

At the same time that these measures gave greater powers to the Islamic judiciary, other measures were intended to increase the degree of hierarchy within that judiciary. The Ministry of Religion has required all courts to subscribe to its publication *Mimbar Hukum*, which presents critical reviews of decisions by Islamic courts. In Aceh, the provincial appellate court began to subject local judges to more scrutiny outside of the formal review process, through seminars and briefings held in the capital. Review itself became more likely, as litigants more often persisted in their attempts to redivide wealth, appealing to the court in Banda Aceh, requesting cassation in Jakarta, and then starting all over if they lost. Few cases in the 1960s were appealed; by the 1980s nearly all inheritance-related cases brought to either Takèngën court were appealed. In Aceh, the appellate court has increasingly demanded that gifts, bequests, and other transactions be carried out to the letter of the Islamic law, as they see it, and they do not hesitate to sharply rebuke the Takèngën judges when they err in this or in other regards. (I have witnessed rather sharp rebukes delivered in person by the appellate court head to his Takèngën subordinates.)

But the broader political environment also changed. The first decade of the New Order saw a gradually successful effort by the central government to suppress political dissent, to force local religious leaders into GOLKAR, the state party, and in general to penetrate civil society through state-run schools, mosques, foundations, and so forth. Interrogations of local religious leaders and the continual invoking of the "latent Communist threat" kept the level of fear high. Requiring civil court judges to move from one posting to another at frequent intervals was part of the strategy of greater central control, intended to prevent judges from developing sympathies with local movements and causes, and to emphasize their financial dependence on the central government.

Money and movement

The decades since independence also witnessed a movement in economic activity and social norms, away from a life focused on the village and on the ancestral land contained therein, and toward a life focused on new cash crops and trading activities. In the 1950s and 1960s, even in villages near Takèngën, farmland was usually ancestral riceland, tended by sons or daughters who had remained in the village after marriage. Households farming a group of contiguous plots shared the work of managing irrigation and performing rice rituals, and saw the occasional outsider who acquired one of their plots as bringing disharmony to the land. Children who left the village after marriage had no continuing claim on village lands.

By the late 1970s, more and more villagers had chosen to pursue cash cropping, particularly of coffee, as coffee prices soared, and improved roads lowered transportation costs. In Isak, by the late 1990s the vast new area of coffee gardens opened in earlier decades had begun to bear fruit. Prices soared during the economic crisis. In June 2000 coffee was bought from growers at 7,500–8,000 rupiah per kilogram, but at one point in 1999 the price had reached 35,000 Rp/kg, and "everyone was buying new trucks," said Aman Samsu in Isak. Coffee prices tended to rise and fall with the dollar; the prices of other crops, not themselves exported, such as rice and vegetables, tended to rise and fall with that of coffee, such that those who sold any of these products were doing relatively well.

Through the 1980s and 1990s, villagers left their home villages to open up new lands, some branching out from coffee into other crops such as patchouli or citronella. Sometimes they returned to their villages, but their movements had created a new sense of the relationship between village and land. Rather than something you inherited as part of your continuing membership in the village collectivity, land was more often than not something you obtained on your own. More people after marrying were living in neither the husband's nor the wife's village but somewhere else again where the resources were: the town of Takèngën, the coffee-growing villages to its north, or in a new area of settlement.

By the mid-1990s, quite a few Isak residents were growing crops on non-ancestral land, many of them had lived for some time away from Isak and returned, and many continued to live apart but remain Isak people. We can quantify these proportions for Kramil village, which officially (according to the register kept by the village secretary) contained fifty-five households in 1979 and had grown to seventy in 1994. But of those seventy households in 1994, only forty-seven had their main house in Kramil village or nearby along the main road through Isak where shops are located, an area belonging to no one village. The others lived in coffee-growing areas or in the transmigration camp – in the latter case, not as transmigrants but as camp followers, so to speak, who remained Kramil residents. Many of them had secondary houses in Isak and returned to work the ricefields, weed, and harvest. Eight of them had been part of the official transmigration program but then changed their status so as to return officially to Kramil but to retain an economic presence at the camp site. Thus, between 1979 and 1994, Kramil had grown in the number of affiliated households. This growth was almost entirely due to the addition of married children, who made their own new households in the village or in the coffee areas, and who otherwise would have migrated to Takèngën or beyond. But the village had diminished in the number of resident households, those living most of the time in Kramil or nearby in the general Isak area.[24]

Corresponding changes had occurred in the way villagers earned their living. Of the fifty-five households making up Kramil village in 1979, forty-six grew rice as their principal occupation. Six of these households had at least partially cleared a coffee garden, but none had ever harvested coffee. The remaining nine households either worked as laborers, engaged in trade, or held civil service positions. In 1994 the amount of rice-farming had remained exactly where it was: of the seventy households affiliated with Kramil, forty-seven grew rice. However, thirty-seven of the total were actively engaged in coffee growing, and twenty-nine were already harvesting beans from at least some of their garden land. Fifty-nine of the seventy households had at some time between 1979 and 1994 engaged in coffee growing, at least by clearing a half-hectare. Yields from these fields would be far greater than yields from ricefields. Isak ricefields only produce one crop a year, which made it possible for those who farmed both coffee and rice to stagger their work periods, to move back and forth between village and garden. The change in economic base is striking: in fifteen years, coffee had moved from being negligibly important to dominating the local economy. The new generation flocked to coffee, but so did many of those who were full-time rice-growers in 1979.

These movements in and out of Isak, and the increasing number of people who lived in more than one place, had contributed to what in 1994 I encountered as a new, and uncertain, way of talking about social units in Isak. When I asked Kramil officials about the current status of various households who had been resident in earlier years, they described a two-tier sense of village membership. They listed a core set of people who had a long ancestry of unbroken village ties – from grandparents down through grandchildren – and then they added a penumbra of on-and-off-again members, who might or might not have had a strong kin basis for their membership. (Those who do have such a basis do retain strong claims to property and to rights of reentry to the village.) In their discussions with me, Kramil women and men groped for new terms to describe whether a particular household was or was not "in" the village.

As movement among villages became more common, and land became more likely to have been purchased or cleared than inherited, norms about passing on land to children also changed. Awarding shares of an estate to children who had left the village came to be seen as less radical a move than it had been. This shift in the culture of land and home was reinforced by state laws,

---

[24] These figures are based on surveys taken in Kramil in 1979 and 1994; additional surveys were taken in 1983 and 1989. In each year, I also consulted with the village secretary to determine how they reasoned in counting people as members or not of the village; as this section makes clear (and as is an anthropological commonplace), residence is not a simple fact of location.

which recognized villages only as residential and administrative units, and recognized only ownership of land by individuals, with title or other written evidence of ownership outweighing any other kind of claim (recall from chapter 2 the difficulties this recognition posed to resolving the dispute over the Kramil houses).

Moreover, as the commercial value of some land increased, so did the stakes of battles over inheritance. Land litigation today concerns coffee plots or areas located near the expanding commercial section of town. Whatever the social cost of suing for such lands might be, the potential economic benefits have risen dramatically. Land suitable for coffee (and also land near the expanding town) rose in value from the 1970s onward, leading to, if not more lawsuits over land, at least more doggedly pursued ones. And as the Islamic court gradually began to overturn past settlements, villagers could begin to make use of this possibility in their own arguments. Although no cases from Isak were formally heard by the Islamic court, from time to time someone would approach Judge Kasim, born in Isak and known there by his teknonym Aman Arlis, to ask for an unofficial ruling. Sometimes the intent was to sue, and Aman Arlis would successfully discourage the suit by giving his informal opinion. These occasional sorties into town, which cost some amount of time and money, created a new resource to be used when bargaining over how to divide an estate: the threat of going to court.

In the early 1980s, for example, Aman Das, my neighbor in Isak, was able to keep dissident half-siblings from challenging the way he divided up their family property by threatening to take the matter up with Aman Arlis. He knew that his siblings believed that his own position would be upheld by the court. As he explained it to me in July 1994:

Well, it was like this. According to religion, sons are the ones who receive the most from an estate, because daughters can get wealth from their husbands. We [he and his siblings] are two mothers, one father: from our first mother came Inën Rohana, then me; from our second mother came Inën Ipol, then Aman Jul, then Arno Inën Yus, then Mansu Aman Idah, then Ucak Aman Yan, then Itëm – and I don't even remember her teknonym (*perinëné*). We all assembled and I divided up the land. I gave Aman Jul, Mansu, and Ucak each one and one-half *tèm* measures of riceland and I took the 3 tèm plot. Remember, that all the riceland was from a joint effort between *my* mother and our father; *their* mother did not farm any of the land. Her children can always ask to use the riceland and they never have to give me a share; but I said that if they opposed this division I would never let them use it.

Aman Jul at first said it was not fair, so I said, OK, rethink it, but I have the book [meaning Qur'ân, divisions according to Islam] and be careful before you challenge me. If you wish to, there is the pathway [at this point he pointed toward Takèngën], you can take it to the Islamic court. Inën Ipol reminded Aman Jul that there were two mothers, and that he had better think about that. So he went along. Inën Rohana kept quiet because she had asked me for a lot before. She had asked our father for water buffalo, and he said she should ask me, and I gave her five and loaned her another that she never paid back. So she had to keep quiet, she had her share already. As long as the division is good, you don't need to use *farâ'id* [the Islamic shares].

A "good" division meant a silent one, in which some combination of fairness and threat kept siblings from objecting to the outcome. Now that threat incorporated a sense of how the Islamic court might divide land if it were to get the chance.

An Islamic critique of marriage

These changes had broad religious aspects to them. A town Islamic culture had developed in Takèngën that defined itself against village life as much as it did in terms of universalistic Islamic values and practices. When speaking about how they marry, pray, or divide their wealth, reform-oriented Gayo in town emphasize universal Islamic concepts, but they do so with village practices in mind, as the silent interlocutor and point of reference against which "reform" has meaning. Elsewhere (Bowen 1993a) I have discussed this process of diacritically creating a reformist identity in regard to religious ritual – feasting, praying, sacrificing, and so forth. Equally important have been the self-conscious changes wrought in marriage and the transmission of property, in the name of individual choice and rights.

Dominating reformist discourse about marriage has been a refusal of the Gayo categories of marriage and the payments attached to those categories, on grounds that such practices downplay what is really at stake in a marriage, namely the free agency of a man and a woman. To call a marriage where the woman leaves her village for her husband's village by the term *juëlën*, "sold," implies to some that we can sell people, an implication that just shows the moral bankruptcy of the entire marriage system.[25] Similarly, paying bridewealth, the *teniron* or "requested" goods that the bride's family asks for, and of which most is passed on to the bride (thus as "indirect dowry"), reinforces the idea of buying people. Much, therefore, is made of marriages between children of self-styled reformist Muslims (*kaum mudë*) in which only a *mahar*, the gift made directly from the groom to the bride, is exchanged (underlining the idea that the marriage involves two individuals) and in which that mahar consists of a Qur'ân, rather than gold (underlining the idea that the mahar is a sign of a relationship rather than part of an economic transaction).

In this sense a specific kind of individualism has been the product of the process of remaking oneself around a reformist ideology. This individualism

---

[25] Others, seeking to validate their ancestry even while advocating reform, offered an alternative etymology: for them, *juëlën* would be a mispronunciation of *julën*, "escorted," as is, indeed, the bride to her new village.

has been celebrated as bringing with it the freedom to move physically in the world without the encumbrances of graves and land, and the freedom to marry across ethnic lines, as in the novels of the leading reformist preacher, Hamka, where an Islamic reformist ideology of choice, movement, and religious over ethnic solidarity plays out over the canvas of the Indies, or, later, Indonesia. The colony or the nation-state serves merely as the not-local, an imaginable version of the universalistic world of Islam, an unbounded space for self-discovery and liberation through religion. Two processes go hand in hand: overcoming the particularities of ethnic ties in favor of a broader sociability among Muslims, and refusing certain elements of adat in favor of a true understanding of Islam. It becomes easier to see why speaking any language other than the local language became valued: Arabic, for obvious reasons, but also Indonesian, as a non-local language rather than as an emblem of nationalism, and English, for the same reasons.

The reformist refusal of village marriage practices is accompanied by a valuation of Islamic inheritance divisions as a sign of religiosity, rather than for their material superiority, or even for the rights they confer on daughters (probably because of the unequal ratio of daughters' shares to sons', which nullifies this potential line of argument). In the 1930s and the 1940s, when they were arguing strongly for changes in religious ritual, village reformists did not press the case for changing village inheritance practices, just as judges serving on the Islamic court in town did not do so. It was one thing to urge someone to pray in a slightly different manner, but quite another to deny him or her a plot of riceland. But when the broader set of transformations in economy and demography took place, the religious value of individualistic ideas about marriage and inheritance more easily won acceptance.

In Isak the first major, public challenge to older norms came in 1979, as a challenge to the basic postulate of the society that land stayed in the village. The challenge was met in a way consistent with the postulate, and the event illustrates how social structures do not "break down," but are reshaped in distinctive ways (Sahlins 1985). The case concerned Aman Suri, a somewhat silly but decent man, whose sister, a real busybody, ran one of the two rice mills in town and a general store, and whose maternal uncle was Tengku Mukhlis, the well-known religious scholar and jurist in Takèngën. Aman Suri was a member of Kramil village, but he worked land in Kutë Ryëm, another of the five Isak villages. He worked this land because his mother came from that village and had married into Kramil, and her father had received the land from his father. Her father passed it on to his two children, Tengku Mukhlis and Aman Suri's mother, without dividing it up. Aman Suri had worked all the land, paying what most people considered a very high rent to Tengku Mukhlis. ("He is a sister's child, so he can only keep quiet," commented a relative.) But he did not own it; Kutë Ryëm

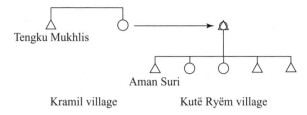

Figure 5.3 Tengku Mukhlis's land claim

villagers considered it their land, not to pass out of the village collectivity – a claim that in practice meant that they expected to exercise the right of first refusal to buy it.

In October 1979, the maternal uncle, Tengku Mukhlis (who was, recall, the first chief judge of the Takèngën Islamic court), came to Isak to announce that the land was now to be divided. Tengku Mukhlis was known as one of the sharper-tongued advocates of Islamization in the highlands. Against the background of general Gayo soft-spoken indirectness, he typically berated others – in the mosque, in the coffee shop, in the street – about their moral laxity, employing a mountingly high screech that threatened to pass beyond the frequency of human hearing. He was one of the most admired, yet most annoying, Gayo religious scholars.

The division was to be according to Islamic law, he declared. He would take two shares (about half a hectare), and the rest would be divided among Aman Suri and his four siblings (whom he would then ask to give him their shares, perhaps in return for some money or perhaps not). The problem was that this division would send some land (about a quarter-hectare) out of the control of one village, Kutë Ryëm, into that of another, Kramil, where Aman Suri now resided. (Because Tengku Mukhlis lived in town, his share would be thought of as remaining in the village, and he would have a Kutë Ryëm household farm it.) In November, the elders of Kutë Ryëm met and decided they would refuse to let Aman Suri take ownership unless he joined their village. Aman Suri wanted land, not monetary compensation. Tengku Mukhlis threatened to remain in Isak until the matter was properly resolved. Something had to give.

It turned out to be the system, and not Tengku Mukhlis, who gave in. Aman Suri retained his obligations by marriage, but changed his village affiliation, which meant just signing up in the new village register and informing the members of both villages. To cement his new ties, he was made the new village headman as well! People had not often changed villages before. Marriage determined where you lived and where your children lived, and you only changed if you converted a uxorilocal marriage into a virilocal one by paying bridewealth and then moving to the husband's village. But Aman Suri's move had nothing to do with marriage. He just shifted affiliation: he now sat with the other men of that village at weddings and on any other festive occasion – indeed, as headman he presided over these occasions.

But other Isak men had desired to change villages, including some who had married into their wife's village and had obligations to care for her parents and other close relatives. After Aman Suri's move, several of them shifted back to their natal village. In all cases they lived in the Isak shop area, which meant that their houses were not physically associated with one village or another, and so their move involved no physical change. In some cases they now claimed lands in their natal village, citing their rights under Islamic law. In at least two cases the men were chosen as village headman at the moment they changed affiliation, such that, at one point in the early 1980s, four of the five headmen in Isak were men who had married out of their village and returned, not by changing their marriage form but simply by signing the new book. Throughout the 1980s, members of the wives' villages grumbled loudly that they had been cheated, that they had been deprived of labor and loyalty in those matters where villages take sides (marriages, allocations of funds, poetry contests), and that the ingrates probably intended to acquire lands in both villages (which some eventually did).

Suspecting consensus: the Islamic court in the 1990s

These changes occurring at national and local levels – toward greater religious court autonomy locally but more supervision from above, toward more effective central governmental control of local affairs, toward movement and cash-cropping, and toward a more individualistic idea of residence and property – meant that judges in the 1990s faced a very different set of possibilities, values, and constraints than did their predecessors in the 1960s. In the early period, judges, especially Islamic court judges, found themselves with a weak political base and a relatively strong set of local norms. Judges on both courts operated in an environment of legal unclarity, both about which laws were to be applied and about who had the power to decide whether the court was operating correctly or not. By the 1980s and 1990s, Islamic court judges were expected to apply religious law, spelled out for them in the new Islamic law code, in appellate decisions, and in ministerial publications. They could do so in a social environment where older Gayo norms about the transmission and division of property were no longer clear to many actors, much less thought to be generally applicable. The overall legitimacy of the Islamic court in Takèngën had increased, and judges had less fear of retaliation for unpopular decisions.

By the 1990s judges considered themselves obliged to redivide an estate when the plaintiff had a valid case. In discussions with me in 1994, they explicitly denied that there was any temporal limitation on the right to bring suit. At the civil court, I asked a judge from Java about a hypothetical case where an estate had long ago been divided, and where a plaintiff had never raised the matter, and then ten or twenty or more years later brought suit to the court for a redivision. "Does the delay weaken her case?" The judge's reply was: "No, there is no statute of limitations in such civil cases. Furthermore, that she was silent would not signal that she had accepted the earlier division of wealth; she would have had to acknowledge that she agreed with that division." A judge at the Islamic court explained: "There is no statute of limitations in the religious court. In rights to land there is: for example if you and I work some land, and I let mine go and after a while you start working it and twenty years later I demand it back, that's too late. But if the case is clear a division made a long time ago can be successfully challenged." [What if the plaintiff was silent at a public meeting and sues much later?] "Well may be she was silent because she was embarrassed (*kemèl*) about opposing her parents' wishes."

Following this logic, the Islamic court judges in recent years have divided estates when asked to do so, declaring that the plaintiffs have the right to demand an Islamic redistribution of the property even if prior agreements had been made. When defendants protested that they had received portions of the estate as bequests (*wasiat*) or gifts (*hibah*), the judges usually have declared that the consent of all the heirs would have been required for those transfers to have been legitimate, and they have voiced suspicion about claims that consensus among the heirs was reached, even when a document to that effect was produced.

Contributing to such suspicions is a greater litigiousness in Takèngën. Today even an agreement reached in court may be challenged in subsequent litigation. Judges continue to urge parties to reach agreements on their own, however. The head of the Islamic court, Judge Hasan, explained in 1994 that

when people come to us, they usually begin by asking what the law is, to see if they have a claim. Of course, the people who come are those who feel they have not received their due, men or women. We explain that heirs have a right to a share of the wealth, and they also have the duty to pay off debts. We urge them to work out something by searching for consensus in their village. Even if they make a formal request for a finding we send them off for two weeks or sometimes one week to try and work it out first, and only then let them come back. Sometimes they come and ask me to divide the estate before them in a familial manner (*secara kekeluargaan*), not in the form of a lawsuit, and then I do that in the Islamic way.

If the heirs reach an agreement outside the court (usually with the help of a legal scholar) they usually write down the result and have it witnessed by their village headman. The document attesting to the agreement (a *surat penetapan*) then has legal standing: it is, for example, recognized by the Office of Land Registration as the basis for a valid claim to own a plot of land.

The following case illustrates the court's willingness to validate such agreements and also the difficulty of making them stick. *Sulaiman vs M. Ali* (PA 60/1973) was first heard in 1973, and ostensibly settled in that year, but it was resolved only in 1994. The dispute concerned a small amount of riceland once owned by Inën Lebah, who had had three children. Her son had inherited all the land, and had passed it on to his own children; these two grandchildren of Inën Lebah were the defendants. The three plaintiffs were the children of Inën Lebah's eldest daughter, who themselves had inherited no land from their grandmother.

In February 1973 the plaintiffs and defendants approached the Islamic court, and were told to settle the dispute among themselves. They informed the court that they had agreed to divide the land into three equal portions, one for each of Inën Lebah's children (each portion then to be subdivided among the children's children). The court agreed to divide the wealth in this way, "equally among all parties, given that this musyawarah mufakat does not conflict with the rules of Islamic law, and so it is proper to accept and ratify their agreement." The court cited as justification the letter signed by all parties.[26]

One might have thought the matter would be over, but the defendants refused to give up any of the land. Judge Hasan, in discussing the case with me, speculated that another relative had intervened, and told the principal defendant that he was being stupid: why should he give up his greater right as a son's child under Islamic law for the merely equal share to which he was entitled under the agreement? At that time the Islamic court did not have the power to enforce the agreement, and the plaintiffs turned to the civil court for help. The civil court put them off until 1984, when a judge ordered a marshal to put the land under court seal. The appellate court in Aceh overturned this order, however, on technical grounds. (The defendants also countersued in the civil court but lost.) Finally, in 1994 the original plaintiffs returned to the Islamic court and asked it to divide the land itself, an action which since 1989 the court had been empowered to carry out. In May 1994 the Islamic court marshal took possession of the land and divided it into thirds, laying out new boundaries in front of the village headman.[27]

This sort of behavior by litigants has led the judges to look with suspicion on any claims to have reached consensus. But the judges also seem to hold different theories about the prevailing social norms and about how to differentiate consensus from coercion than did their counterparts in the 1960s. In

---

[26] The court also cited verse 11 of the Qur'ân chapter An-Nisa', which stipulates that sons receive twice the share of daughters! The court's citation was probably a slip; but shows how any agreement among the parties is held to be proper despite the ratio of Qur'ânic shares.

[27] In most cases decided in the 1990s the court has set new boundaries, or at least specified the new amounts due each party in square meters, rather than, as was the previous practice, merely setting out fractions of the estate. The change was due to a demand by the appellate court that the lower courts divide, and not just determine shares, in line with their new powers under the 1989 Courts Bill. In this and most other cases, even though the land was divided the parties were expected to buy each other out – a portion of a hectare divided into six or eight parts is hardly enough to farm – but there was no compulsion to do so from the court.

the 1960s the judges on both courts stated that people followed the norms of adat, and that agreements based on adat norms involved true consensus. By the mid-1990s, Islamic court judges had adopted a different theory, namely, that Muslim women and men know the estate shares to which they are entitled under Islamic law, and they would not freely agree to a consensus that deprived them of those shares. They began to demand additional proof that an agreement had been freely agreed to by all parties before recognizing it as valid. They still stated that Gayo adat norms of distribution were legitimate, but they qualified that statement with the stipulation that the party relying on adat prove that all relevant parties had agreed to the division. In the absence of such proof, they rejected in practice nearly all litigation based on adat norms.

Judges, then, have reasoned and justified their decisions in terms of their own social theories about the distribution of religious knowledge in society, and about the likelihood that men or women would have acted in certain ways in certain periods. Part of what I have highlighted has been the change in these justifications, in order to show the non-necessary relationship between laws or doctrines and decisions. But these changes need to be explained, and to do so I have referred to the shifts in attitudes toward Gayo adat and Islamic alternatives, in sources of economic livelihood, and in the social and political conditions of legal life.

6   The poisoned gift

These shifts in how judges and jurists perceive fairness and agreement in local conflicts in turn have shaped legal decisions and scholarly writings on the national level. In this chapter I argue that local-level debates in various parts of Muslim Indonesia have shaped what is otherwise a surprising turn in interpretations of Islamic law by the Supreme Court and by Indonesian jurists. In the next chapter I examine the ways in which historians and jurists have drawn on everyday social life to reinterpret how women and men ought to divide property under Islamic law. These analyses suggest that arguments pitched at a universalistic level in fact are part of a multilevel network of reflection, argumentation, and debate – public reasoning across levels of society.

Legal conflicts in Takèngën and elsewhere often concern the legitimacy of gifts (hibah) and bequests (wasiat) made before death. Recall how, in Isak, at the heart of many disputes has been a claim that a grandparent or parent once gave some land, or assured a child that after death land would go to her or him. Claims to this effect are often central to efforts at resisting the division of an estate among heirs, and if the land is in or near Takèngën the parties are much more likely to come to court to contest the division. I make the case here that these struggles over gifts have prompted a nationwide effort to limit gift-giving in the name of fairness, and I refer to a parallel debate in West Sumatra as additional evidence for my claim.

Gifts *contra* fairness

I will begin with a conversation I had with Muhammad Nuh in Takèngën, August 1994. In a suit then before the religious court, M. Nuh was charged by his sisters with having refused to allow the division of their parents' riceland near the village of Kebayakan. The sisters' case seemed clear-cut, and indeed they won the case. I went to his house to hear his side of the story.

As he saw things, he and his brother Lahoda had acted as the brothers should in a sibling set: they kept the ancestral land for themselves, and they offered their sisters something in return, depending on what the sisters needed and deserved. He gave me the details of his conversations with each of their sisters.

Fatimah had come to ask for a division of the land. Lahoda and I said that for her and her two sisters there was a house, right here in Blangkolak, and a coffee garden, which had been the source of money for all of our school expenses, and there was our mother's riceland in Tan. She just went away and gave us no reply to that, but later on left at our house the keys to that house and to another house, located near the coffee garden. Up to that time she had been living in the garden house and harvesting the coffee. She probably was angry and wanted to just throw it all back at us.

Nurhayati acted differently; she just said: "Whatever you wish to give me is fine; I'm so far away anyway, in West Aceh." So I gave her 5 million rupiah and she said that was fine. Sofiah ran away with her first husband, then divorced and later reconciled with Father and things were settled, but then she ran away again! So we all threw her out of the family because she had betrayed Father, and of course she does not get any of the estate. She will burn in hell, so why should she get anything now? We did say that if she came back and apologized then we would let her have some of the wealth, but she has not wanted to. She lives in Balé [a nearby section of Takèngën], but has nothing to do with us.

Fatimah had gotten along just fine with us before this; I think that a cousin put her up to the lawsuit, gave her the idea of saying that Father had given the Tan riceland to her to use when she had married. She was the last to be married, and Father had found her a Javanese man as a husband, and he said he'd need some land and a house. Father refused, but the marriage worked out anyway. But she claims the land had been promised to them – probably the cousin said so in the hope that he would get some of that land – and she also wants a portion of the other wealth. She seems to want part of the Kebayakan riceland, not just money.

What would it mean to divide that land up in that way? The Kebayakan riceland is blood wealth (*harta rayoh*), passed down with the blood, which means it goes to sons, not to daughters; they cannot inherit it, but they can get other wealth, *poh roh* (marital property). This is how it is done here; I would not interfere in my wife's brothers' dividing up of their land, I'd be embarrassed to do so.

JB [to his wife, sitting over with the kids watching TV]: What do you think about this case, elder sister?
He: Oh it's none of her business.
She: We're not to say anything in it, but we can keep watch . . .

Once, when Sofiah was still in good standing with us, she came to me and said that Father had said it was all right to sell the coffee garden. I said, no, we all own it together and have all been fed from it and cannot sell that, and that if we needed to sell anything we should sell the Kebayakan riceland because we have not been working that. She went to Father and he blew up at that: "How could we sell the riceland? It is blood riceland; it cannot leave the line of blood!" That was his directive (*manat*) to us; he took Lahoda and I aside one day and said the riceland there was for us, not for the daughters, that since the time of our ancestors it had been like that. The proof is that he had three sisters, my aunts, and he had two aunts himself, and no one out of all those women got shares of that land.

In the suit then under appeal, it was Muhammad Nuh and his brother who were resisting a division of the extremely valuable riceland, valuable largely because its location meant that it could be turned into shops or multistory houses. But years before, one of his father's elder brother's sons had brought suit regarding the same land, and this time it was Muhammad Nuh who was on the receiving end, so to speak, of a claim that land had been handed down directly from father to son. As he told it:

This cousin had been given the right to work the riceland for a while by his grandfather [father's father to both of them], so long as he had not yet married, but not as property (hak mutlak). But he then said that it had been given (hibah) to him. One day he brought five men to the riceland and started to break open the dikes in order to turn it into a coffee garden. Father saw this and called me, and I took a picture of the men and went to the police and paid them 50,000 rupiah, a lot of money then, back in the 1970s, and the policemen went and arrested him and threw him into a cell for a week after beating him up.

Then the cousin's son sued to get the land, in 1978. He lost because he could provide no witnesses to the supposed hibah. However, he won at the appeals court in 1979 on grounds that his working the land "began a process of making the hibah," as the court put it. But then he lost at the Supreme Court. The Supreme Court said that Gayo adat law does not recognize this notion of a "process of making a hibah," as does Western law, but rather says that a hibah must be clear and observed (terang dan nyata), and this one was not; there were no witnesses.[1]

Now, in the current suit Muhammad Nuh had no witnesses either; his notion of proof was that never before had women received ownership of this riceland. He lost because there were no witnesses to the supposed act of giving. At the time of our conversation he and his brother had appealed to the Aceh appeals court, and intended to appeal to the Supreme Court if he lost again. And, after all, during a process of appeal and re-appeal that could take years, "in any case we have the land so we don't have to worry over it." The elder brother's village strategy of delaying division now was replayed through the courts.

As we saw in the preceding chapter, the Takèngën Islamic court increasingly has looked with suspicion at claims that property was divided with the consent of all parties. Claims such as those made by Muhammad Nuh, that parents already had given or bequeathed land, often ended up depriving daughters of productive land, and here too, judges have reviewed these claims with suspicion.

In standard interpretations of Islamic law, Muslims may leave a bequest (wasîyya, Ind. wasiat), make a gift or donation (hiba[h]) during their lifetime, or establish an endowment or trust (waqf) to be managed by designated persons. Each of these three mechanisms has its own attractions and limitations as a means of transmitting wealth outside the contours of the fixed rules.[2]

---

[1] The original case brought to the Takèngën civil court was *Karim Aman Lïes vs Aman Lahoda*, Case No. 4, 1978; the Supreme Court heard the request for cassation as Case No. 377, 1979.

[2] I do not consider trusts further here; for examples of their operation, see Layish (1983) and Powers (1993).

Bequests are initiated by the donor, or testator, during life, but only take effect after death. The total of all bequests may not exceed one-third of the estate, nor, according to long-standing interpretations of a prophetic hadîth, may they be made to heirs, unless all the heirs consent to such a bequest (Coulson 1971:213–58). Thus, although they allow the original owner to retain control of property during his or her life, bequests have limited value for strategies of heirship that seek to circumvent the rules of farâ'id. Modern jurisprudence, however, has weakened these restrictions. For instance, some Middle Eastern parliaments have passed statutes to allow bequests to be made to heirs (Coulson 1971:143–50, 255–57; Esposito 1982:53–57, 65–67, 94–96).

Gifts must be completed during the life of the donor, and indeed must be completed before he or she enters a terminal illness (*mard al-maut*). Under a generally accepted interpretation, one may dispose of all one's wealth to anyone through gifts. A person could, for example, give away all of an estate to one daughter or to one son, leaving other children and other heirs without any inheritance. Giving a gift is a kind of contract, in which the donor must explicitly offer the property (*îjâb*), and the recipient must explicitly accept it (*kabûl*). The property must be transferred immediately or soon thereafter. Once given, the donor loses all rights over the property – a drawback if one wishes to retain control over property as a means of ensuring that one's heirs continue to offer material support or affections. Gifts may be used to benefit one heir at the expense of others, although the Prophet Muhammad is quoted as condemning parents who apportion gifts so as to favor some children over the rest (Coulson 1971:239).

Suspected coercion

In the Takèngën Islamic court in the 1990s, judges frequently refused to recognize some gifts as valid because they suspected that the gifts had been made at the urging of one party, and resulted in another party receiving less than his or her rightful share. Hibah, gift-giving, was seen as a suspect departure from a farâ'id system of rights. Like a "suspect category" in US jurisprudence, gifts deserve close scrutiny.

Islamic law and Gayo practices in fact come into conflict on several levels, even if gifts are given in all sincerity. Recall that long-standing Gayo ways of passing on wealth were shaped by patterns of marriage and affiliation – only those remaining in the village receive wealth – and have allowed total discretion to the owner of the wealth in distributing it. If we translate these norms into Islamic legal terms, we can say that distributions have been mainly by hibah, as when land is given to a child upon marriage, or bequest, as in the case of the "support land" (*pematang*), left for the person who cares for the parents. Gayo people sometimes refer to the latter as a *hibah wasiat*, a "bequest gift."

None of these older Gayo ways of transmitting property precisely matches the way jurists see Islamic law. In Islam, bequests to heirs are only valid if all the heirs agree to allow them. Now, under long-standing Gayo adat norms, siblings usually respected bequests made by their parents, but their consent to the bequest was not necessary for it to be considered valid. In the Takèngën courts, when siblings contest the claim that there was a bequest, judges often disallow the bequests on Islamic law grounds, *even if* considerable evidence existed that indicated agreement among the heirs. Agreement has come to be presumptively suspected, whereas it had once been presumptively accepted.

Consider *Samadiah vs Hasan Ali* (PA 381/1987), with additional defendants Amiruddin, Hadijah, and Tawariyah. The case involves the estate of Wahab and Maryam, who had five children: Egem, Muhammad, Hadijah, Samadiah, and Tawariyah. Muhammad had died before his parents. The case pitted one of Wahab's daughters, Samadiah, against two other daughters (Hadijah and Tawariyah) and sons of his two other children (Hasan Ali, son of Egem, a daughter, and Amiruddin, son of Muhammad). Wahab and Maryam had left a good deal of wealth, including a house, and about four hectares planted in rice or coffee. Samadiah had received none of it, and she asked for the wealth to be divided among the heirs.[3]

Of the four defendants, the two men responded in one way and the two women in another. Hasan Ali and Amiruddin stated that Wahab already had divided the land except for some bequeathed (pematang) lands consisting of a quarter-hectare garden, about one-half hectare of riceland, and a house plot. The children had quarreled over the disposition of these lands in 1969, but had settled the dispute in a large village meeting that year, they claimed. Wahab had left a bequest that whoever took care of him would get these lands, and, according to the two men, it was Egem, Hasan Ali's mother, and her husband who had done so. They also stated that the bequest and the transfer of these lands to Egem was made publicly at a meeting, and approved of by all the children. They produced a document attesting to the bequest, a document that had been declared valid by the civil court in 1970.

These two men were in a strong position to control the family wealth. Both Hasan Ali's mother and Amiruddin's father had remained in the village after marriage, and they had taken control of family affairs. The two other defendants, the daughters Hadijah and Tawariyah, had married out of the village. They appeared as defendants only because they each had received a small amount of property at the 1969 village meeting, and Samadiah wanted this land redivided along with the larger portions controlled by the men. Under the judges' questioning, Hadijah and Tawariyah contradicted the men's story, stating that they

---

[3] Not to be included in the distribution were Muhammad's children, who under the jurisprudence of the time were kept from inheriting when their father died before their grandfather. This rule has since changed.

knew nothing about a bequest, and that the estate had simply been turned over to the village headman, who had divided part of it but left the rest in the men's hands. They, too, thought that the rest of the land should be redivided.

Now, two aspects of the case probably would have led the Islamic court of the 1960s to refrain from redividing the land. First, the village headman had already presided over a process of dividing the land that eventuated in an agreement, Second, although two defendants denied that all the land had been included in the agreement, the written agreement did include all the lands, and it had been signed by the defendants as well as the plaintiff, and subsequently upheld as a valid document by the civil court.

But the Islamic court judges ruled otherwise, stating that, despite the document, the very fact that some heirs now contested the case showed the absence of consensus. (Although they made no mention of this to me, they may have disregarded the civil court's finding as having been tainted by bribery.) Furthermore, the judges argued that, according to adat, bequests must be agreed to by all the heirs: "Pematang, according to the Gayo adat that is still held to and approved of by the people, is only considered valid if all Wahab's children accept and approve of the declaration (of the pematang agreement)," explained Judge Kasim to me. Because the plaintiff and two of the defendants said they knew of no such declaration, continued the court, the pematang bequest could not be approved.

The judges ordered all the wealth divided. They awarded two-thirds of the wealth to the four daughters to divide equally among themselves (following the text of Qur'ân, an-Nisa' 11) and the remaining third to the six children of Muhammad (as "residual heirs"). Hasan Ali and Amiruddin appealed the case. The Aceh appellate court heard the case in 1990, and returned the case to the Takèngën court, ordering them to take a second look at the document attesting to the 1969 settlement. The lower court did as they were told ("we still thought the daughters were pressured, but we followed instructions," said Judge Kasim), and sent the results back up to Aceh in 1992. Based on the civil court's ratification of that original document, the appellate court overturned the decision and decided the case itself, in favor of the plaintiffs.[4]

---

[4] For the record, here is how the case stood in 2000: the appellate court judges stated that the defendants had admitted that the continuing dispute was about the lands that were not part of the pematang, and that the pematang lands had been properly awarded already. They then specified that the estate consisted of one and a half hectares of riceland, a house, and a two-hectare garden. Hasan Ali and Amiruddin asked the Supreme Court to quash the ruling, pointing out (correctly) that the appellate court had included the pematang lands in the estate, and that these lands had been disposed of by the 1969 agreement that the court declared as valid. (They also claimed that all the rest of the land had also been divided, either in 1969 or as separate gifts from Wahab dating back to the 1950s, and they listed the lands received by each.) As of mid-2000 the case was still before the Supreme Court; one can safely predict that the Court will refuse to consider the new substantive arguments and information as inappropriate to cassation, but that the

As I mentioned earlier, the way the Islamic court currently interprets Gayo adat on bequests is inconsistent with village norms and practices, in the past and in most places today. A parent's bequest is *ipso facto* valid under adat; its authority comes from the right of the owner to dispose of the wealth, not the consent of the other children. The rule enunciated by the court is, however, an accepted part of Islamic jurisprudence; what the judges did was to recategorize the Islamic rule as "local custom." They did not need to do so in order to rule as they did, because the Islamic law on the matter is clear. But their invention made it possible for them to base their ruling not only on an Islamic rule, but on an agreed-upon local social norm. This claim made the decision a matter not of adat versus Islam, but of enforcing a rule found in both adat and Islam.

But on what grounds did the judges find that consensus had not been reached despite the existence of a document attesting to the contrary? Judges Hasan and Kasim explained to me in 1994 that the other heirs, principally the two daughters, could only have sincerely accepted the 1969 agreement if it had been in accord with their Islamic rights. But that agreement was clearly in contradiction of the contents of scripture, because it did not award them their rightful share, so it could not have been the product of consensus. Judge Kasim stated that he and the other judges had felt that the two daughters had been pressured into signing the 1969 document, even though such pressure could not be proved. Because no one would freely sign such an agreement if it were so clearly against her interests, he reasoned, there must have been pressure.

In 1994, Judge Kasim recalled a similar case that was awaiting review by the Supreme Court:

A father had a son and four daughters. He gave a lot of his riceland to the son and the son's wife; the son also received a large bequest. He gave very little to the daughters. In the 1970s, he drew up a document and had everyone sign. He even sent one of his grandchildren to persuade a daughter who had been reluctant to sign, and she signed. She was not satisfied, though. Later there was a second document, probably drawn up by the son, but written as if it were from the father, in which the bequest was made officially to the son, and the son's portion of the remaining lands was increased! Each daughter should have received 2.5 tem measures of land [under a hectare], but only got 0.5 tem!

This was going too far, it deviated too far from justice. There is a hadîth that says that, although gifts should be given fairly, they can still be valid even if they are not fair. But this is going too far. Finally, after the father had died, the daughter petitioned the court. She was joined by his other daughters, but at least one daughter sided with the son. The defendant based his case on the first document, but we said it was going too far. They appealed and lost, and the case is now with the Supreme Court.

confusion caused by the appellate court, in validating the 1969 agreement but redividing the lands disposed of in that agreement, will encourage the disputants to continue their arguments for years to come.

We are very interested in seeing whether the Court can support our judgment, because it introduces a sense of justice into the court. Now, no one is totally fair – just look at the fingers on one hand: they work together but are all different lengths. And so it is with children: some will taste sweet, some rich, some bitter. But there are limits.

Observe in this case how easy it would have been for the judge to say that the agreement was valid. After all, the letter of agreement had been signed by all the parties concerned, and no proof was offered of coercion. But the judges said that they disbelieved these documents. They contrasted sincere (*ikhlas*) agreement, which could only be obtained if the division had been fair, with mere procedural correctness.

In 2000 I was able to see the case, which indeed had been appealed to the Supreme Court but had been rejected by the Court.[5] The father's document stipulated that the daughters could not sell the land they did receive to anyone but their brother, the defendant, because the land was *tanah pusaka*, "heirloom land"; this was their father's "final wasiat" to them.[6] The land was divided at a meeting held in the presence of the village headman, but at that meeting the headman announced that the division was on the condition that "if you sell the riceland then one-half of your land will go to the defendant." In their written decision the court, presided over by Judge Kasim, stated that they doubted the validity of the letter, and added that "the division is far from being just, and is tied [*mukhait*, referring to the restrictions on selling the land], leaving the rights of the heirs unclear, and therefore this exhibit [the document] is not accepted."

The apple of discord

Giving gifts is sometimes seen as creating discord as well as creating an unfair distribution. Takèngën's most notorious recent case, *in re Sairar*, turns on the requirements for making a valid gift.[7] I summarize the various steps taken in the case in order to illustrate the complexities created by the coexistence of several norms concerning gift-giving.

The case began in 1977, when Sairar, the mother of seven daughters and one son, and the owner of considerable land and several shops, called a local

---

[5] *Syamsiah binti Mudali vs M. Aji Aman Sarana*, Case No. 180, 1991, heard and rejected by the Supreme Court in 1995. Aman Sarana then had asked for a judicial review of the case (*peninjauan kembali*) and engaged a lawyer, itself rare, but increasing, in Takèngën cases. As of June 2000 the file ended at that point.

[6] The document was signed in ways that shed light on the probable participation of the various parties in its drafting: the father, Aman Aji, signed "Aman Aji" in Arabic script; his wife, Inën Aji, just made a thumb print. Aji, the defendant in this case, signed in Latin script. Two sisters also signed: Jemilad made a thumb print, and Inën Lukman painfully printed IL. All documents are in Latin script, and by that time, the late 1980s, Arabic-script signatures were rare in the Takèngën area.

[7] *In re Sairar*, Pengadilan Agama Takèngën, 60/1977, in court archives. This summary is based on conversations with the religious court judges and with Tengku Ali Jadun.

religious scholar, Tengku Ali Jadun, to help her divide her wealth. She and her late husband had already given land to each child (and houses to two). One daughter, Aisyah, had purchased some of the property from her siblings. Sairar now asked Tengku Jadun to advise her on the division of the remaining lands. He suggested they ask the Islamic court to render an official opinion (*penetapan*).[8] He then represented her in court.

Although the hearing was to concern only wealth that had never been allocated or divided, in effect it opened up for reconsideration the entire property history of the family. The children argued among themselves in court about the original gifts. Sairar's son complained that the earlier division was unfair. (He undoubtedly hoped that the court would redivide all the wealth along Islamic lines, giving him an extra share.) The court sent the children away to work out a solution among themselves. They met in the house of one of the daughters, and produced an agreement that preserved the gifts but made some adjustments to resolve differences. The court then declared the agreement, including all the altered gifts, to be valid and ordered that the wealth be divided.

In the eyes of the Islamic court, any arrangement agreed on and ratified by the court is religiously valid. The court also held that the agreement was required in this case, that for a gift to heirs to be valid it must be agreed to, not just known by, all the other heirs (whereas if it were to a non-heir it only would need to be witnessed).[9] The court therefore was sympathetic to the son's complaint about the fairness of the earlier division, and attempted to rework the terms of the gift so as to arrive at a consensus.

The Islamic court's actions contradicted another interpretation of the law on gifts, however, namely, that they are contracts between givers and receivers, and are not subject to later adjustments. One of the daughters, Bona, appealed on precisely the grounds that a court cannot change a gift made by an individual, but only declare it valid or invalid. The appellate Islamic court in Banda Aceh accepted her argument, and overturned the initial agreement. The same daughter (together with the son and three other daughters) then sued in the civil court to prevent their siblings from using the land or shops. They claimed that the gifts were invalid, both because two of the children had not attended the session at which the agreement was ratified, and because that court's alteration of the gifts was invalid. The civil court agreed with the plaintiffs and annulled the gifts. Both the appellate court and the Supreme Court upheld the ruling.

This first round of the proceedings left undivided the original property, which was of considerable and increasing value. By this time, Sairar had died, and it was the children, without Aisyah, who approached the Takèngën Islamic court, asking it to redivide the entire estate. The court did so according to the "science of shares," a result that deprived Aisyah of the shops she had

---

[8] This request is considered by jurists to be akin to requesting a fatwa from the court.
[9] This argument is set out in a letter from the court reporter to the parties, in court archives.

purchased from her siblings. Aisyah successfully appealed the division to the appellate Islamic court, which stated that the lower court should have ruled on the validity of the original gifts. The siblings in turn brought the case to the Supreme Court, which ordered the Takèngën Islamic court to reopen the question of the gifts. The judges reheard the case in 1993, and simply re-stated their earlier position, that because the civil court had found that there were no gifts (because not all heirs had agreed to them), they were free to divide all the wealth into inheritance shares. They did so, for the second time.

Aisyah had by this time died, and Halimah, her sister (who after Aisyah's death married Aisyah's husband and took over control of the shops), continued the series of suits, this time appealing the Islamic court's division to its appellate court, and after losing, to the Supreme Court, again on grounds that the gifts had not been adequately considered. As of mid-1994 this appeal was waiting to be heard by the Supreme Court. According to the chief clerk at the Islamic court, even while she was awaiting the result of this appeal, Halimah had started new proceedings before the civil court, regarding the same land but now claiming that the sale of one of the parcels of land had been invalid. The aim was to give the case a slightly different twist, with the aim, said the clerk, of prolong-ing the process and retaining control of, and rents from, the land as long as possible.

By June 2000, the appeal via the religious court had been rejected and the land divided (the religious court clerk had participated in the division), but Halimah had not accepted the division; her litigation via the civil court was still pending: it had been heard at the civil court and at the appeals level, and was awaiting cassation (although there was no longer a first-instance court to which the Supreme Court could send its verdict).

This case is unusual for the persistence of both sides, and for its three separate appeals to the Supreme Court (possibly a record for Takèngën). It does, however, illustrate the legal legitimacy of a norm that gifts to heirs should be agreed to by the other heirs. Reinforcing this norm of agreement is a concern over the discord that gifts introduce into family life. Tengku Ali Jadun, the jurist who originally represented the mother, evinced uneasiness at the use of the gift even as he emphasized the right to give away what you own:

"After all," he told me in a 1994 interview, "the guardian of a child is the father; the guardian of wealth is the owner (*wali n'anak amaé, wali ni erta mpuwé*). If I want to give you this orange, here! [he picks up an orange from the bowl in front of us and hands it to me]. I don't need witnesses. If I want to give someone this chair, I just give it to him, I don't need to ask my children if they agree with me. I own it."

I pointed out that some people argued that if you gave wealth to your children, all other heirs must agree before it was valid.

Really, you should not give wealth to your heirs. Gifts are for cases like this: if one of my children dies, then his children get no part of the estate. So I might give something to them so they get something.[10] If you give a gift to your heirs that means that you are favoring some of your children over others. But they are all your children and you should not do that. It also just leads to arguments. I tell people who come and ask my opinion that if they wish to favor one child, they should buy some gold and give it to them, or open a bank account or the like. If you give land to one child, the land is out there in the open and will lead to quarrels later on. Gold you can hide.

For Ali Jadun, giving wealth is a right, but giving to heirs causes disagreement and should only be done in a non-disruptive way. (Indeed, by 2000, he told me that he was no longer willing to appear in court or consult privately on the *Sairar* case; he had been too hurt by their behavior and had now washed his hands of it.) Ideas about the conditions under which people freely agree to divisions are based on ideas about current social norms of fairness. For example, in the dispute over bequests described by Judge Kasim, the judges in Takèngën presumed that a daughter would not have agreed freely and sincerely to an "unfair" distribution. The judges do not have a strict rule that divides the fair from unfair – remember that the fingers of the hand are not equal – but some cases evoke a strong response that, being clearly unfair, they must have involved coercion. Conversely, in the *Sairar* case the same judges presumed that a set of gifts that were subsequently contested in court could not have been fair, or they would not have led to the legal action.

Echoes of these decisions can be heard in Isak. Most people agree that there has been a general shift away from dividing an estate during one's lifetime to leaving it to be divided up after death. Tengku Asaluddin went so far as to say (in 1994) that "in the past there was no wealth to distribute; people gave it away before they died; 'when you sweep, leave nothing behind; when you cut weeds, leave no shoots.'" Surely an overstatement, but something of the change may be seen in comparing how one of my close companions and teachers, the venerable Aman Kerna, spoke of his own plans to distribute his wealth in 1989, and again in 1994. In 1989 he said he hoped to divide up his land in equal fashion among all his children while still alive, and would rely on his daughters to care for him; he would require, however, that if any of his children sold land they would buy other land to replace it – this so that the daughter's husband (none of his daughters was then married) would not sell the land off and then divorce her.

Five years later he had become more cynical about the whole process, asserting several times that it was much better to let the land be divided later on, after

---

[10] The Compilation now stipulates that the grandchildren receive their parents' share. Ali Jadun was aware of this clause but he was not convinced that the code was correct, and for the moment was staying with the older fiqh interpretations. The Takèngën Islamic court was following this rule before the code was adopted, however. In *Samadiah vs Hasan Ali*, decided in 1987, the court ruled (even when not asked to do so) that the children of a son who predeceased his father has a right to that son's share of the estate.

death, according to Islamic law, so that he and his wife would have something to live on. Twice in the space of a month I heard him tell a story about a man who kept his children from abandoning him only by pretending that he had gold hidden away that would go to the one who cared for him. These concerns came up time and again with respect to the dispute between Aman Seri and his cousins, in terms of how best to ensure that Mpun Seri would be cared for in his old age. After telling the story at the night meeting over the controversy, he even invented an Islamic rule to express his sentiment, saying, "That's why the book [Qur'ân] says we can hibah wealth as much as one-eighth, but no more, and this is why we have the pematang for father's brother set aside!"

The concern for retaining some control over one's own children dictates more use of the bequest, but this is precisely what the local Islamic court seems to want to discourage. In the case of gifts, it may indeed be that local perceptions and ideas have driven national jurisprudence.

Limiting the gift: a step backwards?

If the conflicts and the mechanisms found in the Gayo highlands are also found in other Indonesian Islamic societies (and I will argue below that this is the case), then we can more easily understand a recently introduced national jurisprudential and quasi-statutory rule that limits gifts to one-third of an estate.

In most matters of Islamic thinking, Indonesian jurists have sought to bring Islamic law closer to Indonesian practices and understandings. But recent jurisprudence on gifts moves in the opposite direction. The 1991 Compilation of Islamic Law in Indonesia (*Kompilasi Hukum Islam di Indonesia*) forbids Muslims to give away more than one-third of their wealth during their lifetime.[11] The rule is a clear departure from standard Islamic jurisprudence, including long-standing forms followed in Indonesia, under which Muslims may donate all their property (as long as that donation occurred before the onset of a terminal illness).[12] It reduces the capacity of parents to transmit wealth in accord with local norms, for example, to give their wealth in equal portions to their children.

Why this sharp reversal in the general tendencies of Indonesian Islamic legal thinking? I believe it is because giving and bequeathing of wealth are viewed as

---

[11] Article 210 of the Compilation. Other articles add further provisos. In keeping with standard jurisprudence, article 213 states that if the giver of the gift is sick and near death, then the gift must have the consent of the heirs. Article 211 stipulates that a gift to an heir may be counted towards that heir's share of the estate – thus preventing one of three sons, for example, from receiving one-third of the estate as a gift and then an additional share as heir. Compare Coulson (1971:235–43).

[12] See, for example, the stipulations in one standard manual written in Indonesian: Rasjid (1954:311–14).

ways of departing from a system of fixed rights that open the way to persuasion, coercion, and manipulation.

Narrative structure and the Supreme Court's justification

In 1992, the year after the Compilation of Islamic Law was promulgated by the president, the first-instance religious court in Tasikmalaya, in West Java, issued a decision on the matter of a gift exceeding one-third of the estate. The decision was appealed and heard by the Supreme Court. In this case, *Mrs. Warsih vs Mrs. Iim*,[13] the plaintiffs asked the court to annul a gift made by their sister, Mrs. Ending, to her adopted daughter, the defendant Mrs. Iim.[14] Mrs. Ending and her husband had adopted Mrs. Iim; subsequently Mr. Ending had died and, in 1981, Mrs. Ending had given all her property to her adopted daughter. Mrs. Ending died ten years later, in 1991. That same year, the deceased woman's two sisters brought suit. They stated that, first, they were never told of the gift and, second, that the gift was for more than one-third of the wealth and thus violated the law.

A published account of a case that has been heard by the Supreme Court includes the decisions of the first-instance and appellate courts, and thus allows the reader to follow the arguments and legal reasoning presented at all stages. In the case of *Mrs. Warsih*, the Supreme Court affirmed the lower court's interpretation of the law. The Court's ruling was written by Justice H. Busthanul Arifin, who also had directed the development of the Compilation. The case is, therefore, particularly useful in understanding the reasoning behind the rule on gifts contained in the Compilation.

Mrs. Iim rejected the plaintiff's request that the gift to her be annulled. She stated that there were no legal limits on the amount one could give as a gift and that, in any case, the gift to her had been made according to adat law, rather than Islamic law, and that the religious court did not have jurisdiction in the matter. (The official document attesting to the gift is a standard form issued by the subdistrict administrative offices; the document attests that the gift was made and identifies the witnesses, without indicating whether the gift was carried out according to norms of Islam or adat.) Mrs. Iim also argued that because Mrs. Ending had made the gift long before her death, there were as yet no heirs or inheritance at the time of the giving, because these categories come into existence only at death (or just prior to death). Nor, she concluded, was the permission of the heirs needed for a gift to be valid.

The plaintiffs produced several witnesses, one of whom was their brother-in-law, a man who had been a village policeman in 1981, when the gift was

---

[13] *Varia Peradilan* 136, 1997:36–63.
[14] Adoption is recognized in both customary and state law in Indonesia.

made. He testified that he had urged the village headman to annul the gift on the grounds that it was in conflict with the law (he did not say which law). He had held a meeting that included Mrs. Iim at which he urged her to accept only one-third of the estate as her gift. He claimed that the initiative for the gift had come from Mrs. Iim and not Mrs. Ending and, furthermore, that it could not have been the "free act" of the deceased to give away all her estate in this way, or surely she would have informed the heirs, her sisters, about it. Other witnesses testified that the gift had been made, that the proper words had been said in offer and in receipt (the court chose to quote these words, in the local language, Sundanese), and that the plaintiffs had not been present.

The three judges hearing the case decided that the gift indeed had been carried out according to the legal procedures, as Mrs. Iim had claimed (and that they did have jurisdiction). There remained the plaintiffs' charges that they had not been informed of the transaction and that the gift exceeded the limit on gifts. It is at this point in the published decision that the judges presumably crafted their argument in such a way as to render it as convincing as possible – to the litigants, to any future appellate judges, and to any potential readers of these public decisions. We might, then, expect to find clues as to the norms supporting their decision in the narrative structure of the judgment.

The judges began by affirming that the plaintiffs were indeed heirs of the deceased. They cited as their support Qur'ân 4:176, which reads:

when they ask you for a decision, say: God decrees for you in the case of *al-kalâla*: If a man dies without a child, and he has a sister, then she is entitled to half of what he leaves. He is her heir if she does not have a child. If they [female] are two, then they are entitled to two-thirds of what he leaves. If they are brothers and sisters, then a male is entitled to the share of two females. God makes clear for you [lest] you go astray. God is all-knowing.[15]

Much has been written about this verse, and in particular about the appropriate translation of the term *al-kalâla*, which, in this passage, means either someone who dies without children, or all those except parent and child (Powers 1986:21–49, 99–109). The verse stipulates the shares to be awarded to sisters when the deceased has left no children. These shares are reaffirmed in the Indonesian Compilation (article 176).

Note that the judges decided to lead off their argument by citing a verse about heirs, rather than a verse about gifts. Although this narrative decision may seem strange, in that the case is about gifts, it does highlight the rights of the plaintiffs as heirs. Their situation is precisely that described in the verse – two sisters, no brothers, no biological child. With no need for additional commentary, the verse makes clear that, as heirs, the plaintiffs had the right to two-thirds of the

---

[15] Translation in Powers (1986:100), whose historical argument rests on this passage.

estate. Because she was adopted, Mrs. Iim is not an heir according to Islamic
law, which does not recognize heirship rights of adoptees (although she does
have other rights as an adoptee under the terms of the Compilation, which are
discussed below). The narrative precedence the judges gave to the definition
of heirs, then, supports the plaintiffs' complaint that they were not consulted
about the gift, as they ought to have been, given their status as heirs. It also
readies us for subsequent statements about the needs of heirs in general.

The judges then declared that the current "Islamic law that applies in
Indonesia" limits the defendant's share to one-third of the estate. They presented four legal sources to support this proposition. They began with the article of the Compilation that limits a gift to one-third of an estate. They then
quoted a portion of a hadîth in which the Prophet Muhammad limited bequests
to one-third of the total estate ("A third, and a third is much. It is better that
you leave your heirs rich than you should leave them destitute, begging from
their neighbors").[16] Although the court specified that the passage concerned
bequests, they chose to quote the portion that could be read as stating a general rationale for limiting the amount of wealth that can be kept from heirs by
whatever means, namely, that without the limitation, heirs could be left without
any wealth and be forced to beg from their neighbors. The court inferred from
the hadîth that "one may not exceed one-third and if one does, then anything
over one-third is void," but without adding that the prophetic dictum was uttered in response to a question about bequests. Next, the judges cited the liberal
Pakistani Islamic scholar Fazlur Rahman to the effect that if the heirs do not
agree to the excess, then the excess is void, but that the one-third of the estate
that can be given remains valid. Here again, the quoted portion does not make
explicit that Rahman was discussing bequests, not gifts.

The court's selection of passages emphasizes two aspects of standard Islamic
jurisprudence, probably acceptable to all readers of the decision, namely, that
the limitation on bequests is based on a concern for the heirs, and that one-third
of an estate is an appropriate limit to ensure the heirs' welfare. In other words,
the passages highlight not the specific rule about bequests, but the legitimate
needs of heirs that gave rise to the rule. (The passages also portray "begging" in
a negative light.) These carefully selected quotations lend an air of plausibility
to the new rule limiting the amount that may be given, suggesting that it does
in fact correspond with general norms of Islamic jurisprudence. The reasoning
process involves an analogy, a form of *qiyâs*, even though the term "*qiyâs*" is
never used, nor an explicit analogy ever drawn.[17]

Finally, the judges quoted a passage from a book of Shâfi'î jurisprudence as
follows: "Whosoever begs from another because he or she is in need, one may

[16] As translated in Coulson (1971:214).
[17] On forms of *qiyâs*, see the discussion in Hallaq (1997:101–07).

not give the person all one's wealth, nor most of it." This final source of law presumably is relevant in that Iim was accused of having initiated the gift by asking for it (or "begging") from her adoptive mother. The quote also nicely complements the hadîth quoted earlier in the decision: taken together, the two statements urge Muslims to treat begging for a share of an estate as a negative action, which should be hindered by ensuring that all heirs get something and also by not excessively rewarding beggars.

Having established the law upon which they would base their decision, the judges ruled that the gift was void because it exceeded the one-third limit on gifts, but that the defendant should retain the one-third of the total wealth that fell within the limit. The remainder became the right of the plaintiffs. The court assigned specific parcels of land to defendant and plaintiffs, but did not apportion the wealth between the plaintiffs.

Mrs. Iim appealed this decision, and, although the district appellate court refused to hear the appeal (on the grounds that it was made after the time limit), the Supreme Court did hear her subsequent request for cassation. The Supreme Court affirmed the lower court's decision, stating that the lower religious court had not misapplied the law. Their decision was then published, together with the two lower court decisions, in the country's case record of note, the *Varia Peradilan*, cases for which are selected by judges belonging to the Indonesian Association of Judges, IKAHI.[18]

One can see why the Supreme Court chose to decide this case rather than others in which presumably similar claims had been raised, and why judges selected it for inclusion in the case record: their intent no doubt was to present a compelling case for the new rule. The case involved a secretive defendant, who did follow established procedures to ensure that the gift would be recognized as valid, but who kept her parent's siblings out of the picture entirely. She was an adopted, not a biological child, and so was not an heir. Her adoptive status added normative support to the rule, both because the gift deprived the legitimate heirs of any share in the estate, and because the new rule allowed her precisely what she would have received had no gift been made. Her rights as an adopted child are stipulated by the new Compilation (article 209): she has the right to an obligatory bequest, a *wasîyya wâjibah*, of a maximum of one-third of the estate – the same fraction of the gift that the court allowed her to retain. The convergence of the two rules on the same fraction gave added credibility to the one-third limit on the gift in this case. Had the Court heard a different type of case – say, one in which a biological son was given one-half the estate despite the presence of several other siblings, but could advance an argument as to why he deserved the share – the result might not have been as convincing.

---

[18] Pompe (1996:377–79) describes the selection process; judges select cases for their "news value."

The use of obligatory bequests to supplement the shares allotted to heirs is found in other Muslim countries as well. The device is used mainly to allocate wealth to orphaned grandchildren, i.e., grandchildren whose linking relative to a wealth-holding grandparent pre-deceased the grandparent, thus, according to the science of shares, cutting off their path to inheritance (Anderson 1976:155–56; Coulson 1971:143–46). The maximum share of the estate that can be allocated as an obligatory bequest is one-third. (Other rules limit the proportion of an estate that can be allocated as an endowment: Egyptian law limits to one-third of the total estate the amount placed in an endowment of which non-heirs are to be guardians.)[19]

Not only does the existence of these specific rules in other Muslim societies give added legitimacy to the Indonesian rule concerning gifts, but the rules in turn have been justified by authoritative texts that urge Muslims to treat each child fairly. More specifically, certain Followers of the Prophet (the generation after the Companions) stated that no more than one-third of an estate should be alienated through any mechanism other than inheritance (Anderson 1976:166). The specific rule innovation made in Indonesia can, therefore, be justified by referring to a general principle that heirs should not be deprived of the majority of their estate. Finally, the ubiquity of one-third as a limit makes it an obvious "focal point" for determining limits on other types of allocations.[20]

Even before reaching their conclusion, then, the judges were able to create an implicit sociolegal argument by selecting and juxtaposing passages. I would characterize their argument as follows. Heirs should not be reduced to begging. Limiting bequests or gifts to one-third of an estate is motivated by this general concern, and the positive law limiting gifts is thus religiously well-grounded. Heirs also should be consulted about the division of an estate, and the fact that they were not consulted in this case made the gift improper, albeit not illegal. The defendant inappropriately asked for the gift; as an adopted child she was not even an heir, making this request even more inappropriate.

This reasoning process, which I infer from the narrative structure of the decision and from the several statements made by the judges, was far from being an automatic application of a legal rule. The rule, from the Compilation, was of course cited, and it is clear that it was applicable here because the entire estate was given away after the Compilation took effect. But most of the narrative work carried out by the judges was directed toward justifying the rule, not showing that it applies. The judges justified the rule both directly and indirectly: directly when they argued that limiting gifts preserves the welfare of

---

[19] Often the provision of shares to orphaned grandchildren represented a major departure from the normal reliance on one legal school. For example, in Egypt the obligatory bequest to orphaned grandchildren is contained in Articles 76–79 of Egyptian Law No. 71 of 1946, which otherwise generally codified Hanafi law on testamentary dispositions (Shaham 1997:200–01).

[20] On "focal points" as mechanisms for convergence, see Schelling (1960:111–18).

the heirs and benefits society by reducing begging; indirectly when they argued that the type of acts that led to the gift were socially inappropriate – an adopted daughter "begging" for the gift and then keeping the heirs in the dark.

Most of the legal argument presented was thus about norms, not legal rules. The norms have Islamic sources, but they do not themselves compel the judges to act in any particular way. They are important here because they give to the rule a moral and social grounding that its inclusion in the Compilation does not provide.

Fairness and agreement as social norms

How can we explain the rule limiting gifts? One way to do so is to see whether the norms used to justify the decision in *Mrs. Warsih vs Mrs. Iim* are referred to in other contexts as well. Such contexts could include other decisions and commentaries by judges and jurists, but also local social processes of transmitting wealth, such as those we have been studying in Gayo society. If ordinary people invoke certain social norms in these social processes, then it is reasonable to expect that those norms also would shape decisions taken by judges, whose interests, perceptions, and norms derive from their own backgrounds in particular locales as well as from their education in legal and religious traditions.

Little has been written to date about how this rule came to be included in the Compilation. Two of the officials working in the Supreme Court's Islamic division told me in June 2000 that the Compilation differed on this point from fiqh, by limiting gifts as well as bequests. "Perhaps it is because of a development of the sense of justice; if someone gives away all his/her wealth, exhausts the portion of the heirs, they suffer, and it is unfair to be rich based on someone else's suffering."[21]

One of the judges responsible for developing the code, Supreme Court Justice M. Yahya Harahap (1994:192), has written an extensive commentary on the Compilation, and mentions the rule briefly. He states that prior to the Compilation, some jurists and judges considered it legitimate to give away all one's wealth, while others thought that this was not allowed by Islamic law, and some of these people considered the proper limit to be one-third of the estate. The result of this difference of judicial opinion was that court decisions varied, and society was "confused," a confusion rectified by the Compilation.

The argument that codification has reduced legal uncertainty is made frequently by apologists for the code. But Harahap attempts to justify the content of *this* rule as well as the need for *some* rule. He argues that the rule limiting

---

[21] Interview with H. Achmad Djunaeni, SH, Director of Religious Civil Law, Indonesian Supreme Court, and Edi Riadi, Assistant Judge in the same division. Both had been working judges prior to joining the Court.

gifts brings Islamic law close to adat and European laws, by which he means closer to the general norms of fairness towards all children that are contained in adat and in European civil law.[22] That social norms can have Islamic legal force is explicitly stated in the final article of the Compilation (article 229), which urges judges to "take careful account of the living legal values in society, so that decisions are in accord with a sense of justice."

Alongside *fairness* as a candidate for explaining the rule is a second social norm of *agreement among heirs*. That this second norm is a non-legal social norm is shown by inspecting a case decided the year prior to *Mrs. Warsih vs Mrs. Iim*. In a 1996 ruling on the case *Endang Suarna vs H. Endang Sutisna*, the Supreme Court stated that notifying the heirs was not required for a gift to be valid.[23] As long as the gift was made with a pronouncement of giving and receiving, the fact that the giver's children were neither present nor notified did not detract from its validity. In the published version of the case, this conclusion was emphasized by being included in the boxed "legal abstract" preceding the text of the case. The Supreme Court's affirmation of this rule, which was written by the same judge who presided over *Mrs. Warsih vs Mrs. Iim*, makes clear that the basis for the 1997 decision was not the failure of the defendant to notify the heirs, but the one-third rule.

Why, then, was the failure to notify the heirs given such a prominent place in the court's narrative in *Mrs. Warsih vs Mrs. Iim*? Although not required for a gift to be legally valid, the agreement of heirs receives strong normative backing from the code and from lower court judges. As with all other rules in the Compilation that affect the inheritance system, the one-third maximum applies only if the heirs do not agree to a division. Article 183 of the code says that "the heirs may come to an agreement through consultation regarding the division of the estate, as long as they are aware of their rightful shares."

There is some evidence that lower courts give such agreements precedence over other legally valid acts, including gifts and prior divisions of wealth. As we saw in the first part of this chapter, judges on the Takèngën Islamic court may consider an agreement reached in court to override all previous gifts and bequests, and to prevent the parties from later bringing suit for their inheritance share. Thus Mrs. Iim's failure to even attempt to reach consensus may have been viewed as an aggravating factor, which, when combined with her asking for the gift, made her actions seem additionally inappropriate.

---

[22] His claim could not, of course, be that the new rule resembles local adat-based practices, because those practices frequently include giving or bequeathing most or all of one's wealth before death, practices rendered more difficult by the code.

[23] As reported in *Varia Peradilan* 134, 1996:40–65. In the request for cassation, the plaintiff put forth the claim that the gift exceeded one-third of the estate, but because this claim regarded a matter of proof, involving evaluation of the wealth (to determine the one-third limit), it was outside the bounds of issues considered in cassation.

The reasoning followed by the Takèngën judges, if followed in other Indonesian courts as well, might help to explain both the legitimacy of a rule that limits the power to give away one's wealth, and the references to agreement of heirs that, although apparently without legal force, were made in *Mrs. Warsih vs Mrs. Iim*. The close association of gifts and bequests, suggested by the Gayo use of a composite term *hibah wasiat*, is further clarified by these cases, because suspicion of coercion and unfairness arises for the same reasons with respect to both methods of transmitting property to heirs. Gifts and bequests are viewed as ways of departing from a system of fixed rights, and these departures open the way to persuasion, coercion, and manipulation.

Inheritance and Islam in Minangkabau society

I now consider the parallel dynamics in another society, to see if the Takèngën-type reasoning has been found elsewhere, and if it is reasonable to suppose that local processes and deliberations have at least partially shaped the change in national jurisprudence. Here we look again at village-level processes in order to make claims about national-level processes of reasoning and adjudication. Whereas in Gayo society explicit distributional norms are not strongly marked by gender, in some other Indonesian societies they are. In those societies, disputes over how to transmit property to the next generation may have generated additional support for the rule limiting gifts. The clearest example of this relationship between local disputes and a limit on hibah comes from Minangkabau society in West Sumatra, where ancestral ricelands, called *pusako tinggi*, literally "high heirlooms," have long been passed down intact from mothers' brothers to sisters' sons. This unbroken continuity of land acts both as the material underpinning and as the cultural sign of a particular norm of social continuity, itself the key to Minangkabau matrilineal tradition, adat.[24]

At least by the late eighteenth century, some groups in the region had begun to emphasize their Muslim identity by practicing and advocating the transmission of property according to Islamic law rather than Minangkabau adat. These groups included coastal traders and highlands cash-crop farmers, two populations whose newly created wealth stood apart from the "high heirloom" complex of older Minangkabau regions (Dobbin 1983:119, 128). The Islam-versus-adat way of conceptualizing economic and political differences contributed to the open hostilities that followed, and the so-called "Padri wars" (1803–19) in the region were fought over, among other issues, the matrilineal succession of rights and statuses.

---

[24] In what follows I rely mainly on the account in Benda-Beckmann (1979), and, for historical background, Dobbin (1983).

By the early years of the twentieth century, debates among reformist and traditionalist jurists threatened to lead to new hostilities in the region. A series of *fatwas* (legal opinions) and conferences over the succeeding decades led to a regional jurisprudential consensus about inheritance. The "Minangkabau consensus" involved *waqf* (endowments or trusts), bequests, and gifts. In the early 1920s, several highly respected jurists, among them Dr. Syech Abdulkarim Amrullah, delivered fatwas stating that the ancestral ricelands were in effect a form of endowment, held in trust by the sub-lineage heads in each generation, for which reason they were not to be divided according to the "science of shares."[25] This argument continues to be generally accepted by jurists in the region.

Left in dispute was the proper method of transmitting non-ancestral property, a category including land that had been cleared or purchased by the owner, and wealth obtained from ancestral lands and used to buy shops or other forms of immovable wealth (Benda-Beckmann 1979:324). Advocates of adat argued that these lands, too, should be included in the package to be transmitted to the control of their sisters' children. They pointed out that persons who created new wealth did so through the support of the ancestral lands – for example, by living off rice grown on ancestral lands while clearing new land or building up a business. Advocates of applying Islamic law argued that these lands clearly fell under the rules of farâ'id, and should be divided or given to children.

These disputes were sharply polarized between the rights of one's own children and the claims of one's lineage members, principally one's sisters' children. As Franz von Benda-Beckmann points out (1979:303), discussions about the division of an estate in this region have always concerned the relative rights of one's own children *vis-à-vis* one's sister's children, and never the rights of other potential heirs. Nor do these debates concern norms of division among children (such division was and is most often equal).

Furthermore, Minangkabau parents (like Gayo parents) have used gifts and bequests, not division into shares after death, to transmit property to their children. Hibah came to mean what most Islamic jurists elsewhere would have called a bequest, namely, a contract that only became effective after the donor's death. These locally named hibahs were revocable and restricted to one-third of the estate and to non-ancestral wealth. In effect, the hibah merged into the category of bequest.[26]

Minangkabau men and women have preferred to use this mechanism because it gives them control over property before their deaths and because it allows them

---

[25] See the account of his father's role in achieving this agreement in HAMKA (1984:103).

[26] Benda-Beckmann (1979:324). In Islamic jurisprudence elsewhere, for certain purposes gifts have been thought of as analogous to bequests, for example, in considering whether a murderer may accept a gift in Shâfi'î law, the legal school traditionally followed in Indonesia; see Coulson (1971:229–30).

to designate the persons to receive the property. As is the case in Gayo society, many Minangkabau find that this mechanism creates the right combination of incentives for the intended recipient: the gift will be theirs, but it can be taken back if they failed to take good care of the parents. The "gift bequest" thus served as a quite rational way of leaving property to designated children while ensuring their continued care and attention. These transfers also were preferred by many Minangkabau because they reduced the danger of conflicts between children and sisters' children. In addition, writes Benda-Beckmann, some Minangkabau may have found making such transfers to be an enjoyable assertion of autonomy, and to be preferred even when similar results could be obtained under the rubric of farâ'id – and even though Islamic law as understood elsewhere would have voided most of these transfers as illegitimate "bequests to heirs." As in Gayo society, these transfers sometimes were referred to as *hibah wasîyya*, and it may be that designating them as a type of hibah made them more acceptable to jurists (Benda-Beckmann 1979:277–79).

In any case, no objections appear to have been made to these transfers on Islamic law grounds; opposition has been entirely from advocates of adat. As early as the 1850s, lineage members sued in the colonial courts to prevent donations of lands to children. By the 1930s the legal principle had been established that one could give away "pure" non-ancestral wealth, that is, wealth not purchased with money derived from working ancestral lands, without the consent of the matrilineal relatives. Adat leaders continued to oppose these practices, and a formal compromise was reached after independence. In 1952 a conference of Islamic jurists and adat experts resulted in a proposal that landowners give one-third of their non-ancestral property to their sisters' children, dividing the remaining two-thirds according to the rules of farâ'id. This plan was reaffirmed at a 1968 conference, attended by members of the Indonesian Judges' Association, the IKAHI (Benda-Beckmann 1979:324–31). The latter conference also ratified the earlier fatwas identifying ancestral property as a waqf, and gave to those decisions an Indonesian legal language. The court decisions over this same period recognized the right of parents to donate non-ancestral lands to children, stipulating only that the donation had to be made with the knowledge and witnessing of both party's sisters' children.[27]

By the late 1960s, then, a formal consensus of jurists coexisted with a wide array of social and legal practices in West Sumatra. In practice, many Minangkabau people donated all their non-ancestral property to their children, and were supported in the courts in the rare instances when such donations were challenged. However, the jurists' consensus involved a rule that use of the hibah or hibah wasîyya ought to be limited to one-third of the estate. The idea of a one-third limit, the same limit that appeared later in the Compilation, thus had

---

[27] See the account of a 1969 case in Benda-Beckmann (1979:344–50).

achieved a general legal acceptance as a public compromise that could avoid social conflict.

This short conjectural history of the rule on gifts has revealed a complex set of historical processes that have given rise to a set of social norms. These norms have, I argue, given social and moral force both to the rule as stated in the Indonesian Compilation of Islamic Law and to the court decisions regarding the limits on giving away one's estate.[28]

Let me try to recapitulate. In at least some local ways of speaking about transmitting wealth, the Islamic terms hibah and wasîyya are closely linked, and both refer to mechanisms used by parents to ensure that their land goes to whom they wish it to go, when they wish it, and only if the recipients properly provision them in their old age. These mechanisms have been attacked, however, on a number of different grounds. From an Islamic legal perspective, this use of bequests violates well-established jurisprudence, and it is consistently disallowed in the courts when challenged. The reasons originally given for disallowing bequests to heirs were first articulated by the Prophet Muhammad. These reasons are cited as grounds for limiting gifts as well as bequests. The fact that bequests and gifts are sometimes merged in local ways of speaking gives added plausibility to this line of reasoning. In addition, jurists and judges argue that gifts or bequests made without the consent of the heirs produce quarrels, and provide an incentive for potential gift recipients to "beg" for extra shares.

The link between begging and gifts, via a hadîth of the Prophet, was also made to me by Ali Jadun, the Takèngën Muhammadiyah leader, who quoted the same hadîth as did the Supreme Court, and drew the same conclusions. Clearly, whatever the precise path of communication, a new set of legal ideas has come to have some local currency as well as being national jurisprudence.

Given these criticisms, placing limits on both hibah and wasîyya is seen as multiply advantageous. These limits preserve the rights of heirs, they ensure fair divisions of estates, and they minimize quarrels among siblings. In the Minangkabau case, these limits are also viewed as minimizing quarrels between proponents of adat (the advocates of sisters' children) and the proponents of Islam (the advocates of one's own children). In the end, what appeared as a rule that flew in the face of local social norms now looks like it may have been generated by local concerns. Local debates gave rise to a social norm in various parts of the country, which jurists and judges then turned into a quasi-statutory

---

[28] We might also ask what a more complete explanation of this gift-limiting rule would look like. It could include local disputes and histories from additional societies, as well as the stories of those "law brokers" who may have transmitted these local concerns to jurists involved in developing the Compilation. It would also include jurists' accounts of writing the Compilation and judges' accounts of applying its provisions in court.

rule (in the Compilation) and for which only afterwards did they construct an Islamic justification.

The Islamic justification created by judges departs from the usual reasoning of fiqh; it weaves together general moral principles, implicit analogies, and reports of statements by the Prophet Muhammad. Social norms and religious reasoning generated a law-like norm, which subsequently received legal justification. Here is a clear instance of the breadth of Islamic sociolegal reasoning.

7   Historicizing scripture, justifying equality

I now turn to a second set of channels and communications between local and national processes of reasoning and deliberation. Whereas in the last chapter we looked at the effects of events judged negative in towns and villages (unfair use of gifts to restrict women's access to resources) on Supreme Court decisions and on the development of rules in the Compilation, here I consider the degree to which participants in national Islamic scholarship consider local patterns to be of positive value. Some Indonesian Muslim scholars have drawn on their knowledge of gender-equal patterns of work and sharing in villages and towns to develop a critique of Islamic law. Others insist on the priority of the textual evidence found in scripture.

At issue in these arguments is the relationship between text and what in the Indonesian case is called "context." The very fact of revelation that is the proof of Islam's universal message contains a critical ambiguity. Revelation must be made in specific cultural, linguistic, and political surroundings, and the message must be one that can be understood, if not always accepted, in those surroundings. The revelations of Islam were made in Arabic, to people who lived and worked in an urban society, within a broader tribal, and patrilineal, social context. To what extent did the revelations "take account of" that context? What are the implications of the idea that the messages were in part shaped with time and place in mind, for Muslims living in far different times and places – say, in the late twentieth century at the other end of the world? Was the granting of what were new rights for women – for example, a fixed share of their parents' wealth, one-half that given to their brothers – the declaration of an absolutely just distribution, or the best that one could do in that time and place? Did the way in which pious women and men chose to clothe themselves represent a culturally specific (and, in the hot, dry desert, environmentally specific) response to God's call for women to conceal their beauty, or were these particular clothes a divinely directed preference by Muhammad?[1]

---

[1] This general issue of the status to be given to features of Meccan life or of Muhammad's own life is broader than these issues, of course, extending to the status of the Arabic language, the nature of Muhammad's experiences, and the religious value, if any, to be given Muhammad's personal preferences, e.g., for the color green.

This ambiguity is the critical point of entry for those Indonesian jurists and historians who wish to establish, if not an Indonesian legal school or tradition (*madhhab*) in the formal sense, at least a set of new interpretations of scripture. In doing so, they are asserting the importance of engaging in the individual struggle to interpret and reinterpret scripture, *ijtihâd*.

The term ijtihâd has a range of meanings, and must be understood in a larger conceptual matrix, especially *vis-à-vis* the term that often serves as its complement, *taqlîd*, the following of a madhhab. In Southeast Asia, Islamic legal education and scholarship has traditionally worked within the Shâfi'î school, one of the four major Sunnî schools. To the extent that scholars and jurists consulted books of jurisprudence, and did not attempt to reinterpret Qur'ân or hadîth, they were engaged in taqlîd. However, when there was no clear textual statement on a matter to be decided, a jurist would engage in what we may call ijtihâd. The two terms have taken on highly charged and varying meanings, especially (but not only) in the twentieth century: taqlîd can be seen as following a long-standing scholarly tradition, or as blindly imitating ignorant forebears (Hallaq 1997). Although both practices are legitimate aspects of fiqh reasoning, one can say that beginning in the late nineteenth century, scholars in the Muslim world, including Southeast Asia, began to engage more actively in the pursuit of and reflection on ijtihâd (Bowen 1999a; van Bruinessen 1990; Feener 1999). The range of proper ijtihâd was a central issue in the debates between "traditionalists" (*kaum tua*) and "modernists" (*kaum muda*) that developed in Southeast Asia, and that drew on new reformist movements in the Middle East (Hourani 1983). The several reformist movements called Salafiyyah, and the writings of Muhammad 'Abduh and Rasyid Rida, served to legitimate a return to direct inspection of scripture, as a step in arriving at a core of Islamic principles that could unite all Muslims (Noer 1973).

Fairness across gender and generations

One strategy of reinterpreting scripture is to consider the history of scripture itself. Why should the history of religion figure centrally in current debates about law? History can matter for two reasons: because the history of revelation may be taken as having a bearing on the contemporary interpretation of scripture, and because the legal practices of early religious leaders may be taken as a model for today's reform efforts. Both claims are hotly disputed, however. If scripture is clear it needs no further interpretation, say some jurists. Other jurists and historians argue that the early leaders of the Islamic community may have been as misguided as are their philosophical descendants today. These debates have defined both the capacity and the limits of Islamic scholarship to develop a gender-equal Islamic jurisprudence.

The first argument, about the history of revelation itself, centers on the claim that at least some of the Qur'ân and hadîth were intended to apply only for a certain period, or under certain conditions, or to convey only a general meaning through admittedly misleadingly specific rhetoric. Under this conception, each generation is supposed to provide socially appropriate specifications, or rules of application, for scripture.

In Indonesia, the historian of religion Nurcholis Madjid has been one of the more visible advocates of this argument. Madjid argues that the Qur'ân and hadîth contain two basic kinds of statements: eternal religious truths (some of which are also found in other religious traditions) and historically specific directives. The latter kind of directive or rule has a reason for its revelation, an *'illa*. As conditions change some of these reasons may evaporate, removing the obligation to follow the scriptural command.[2]

Indeed, argues Madjid (repeating an argument already made in the first century of Islam), God even took back some of his commands. Certain passages in the Qur'ân and in the hadîth are revoked or "abrogated" by later passages or by inspired statements by the Prophet Muhammad. Some of these changes concern central elements of religious life. For example, Muslims worshiped in the direction of Jerusalem during their first six months in Medina, after which a new verse ordered them to change the direction of worship, the *qiblat*, to Mecca. Inheritance practices underwent several stages of scriptural prescription: an early verse of the Qur'ân urged Muslims to make bequests to their wives and children; later revelations created a system based on mandatory shares to these and other heirs; finally, a statement by Muhammad specifically forbade making bequests to heirs. The abrogations (*naskh*) indicate a "historical consciousness" at the very center of Islamic textual authority, says Madjid.[3]

For additional support, Madjid turns to decisions made by the first caliphs, the successors to Muhammad as leaders of the Muslim spiritual and political community. Presumably they were as close as one gets to grasping the meaning of the verses at their source, he argues, and yet even they had to suspend or change scriptural directives. For example, the second caliph, 'Umar, urged a

[2] Madjid (1992, 1994a, b) has been a leader, along with Djohan Effendi, Dawan Rahardjo, and others, of a movement for "renewal in Islamic thinking" in Indonesia. His scholarship has drawn importantly from that of the Pakistani modernist scholar Fazlur Rahman (1965), under whose supervision he wrote his 1984 dissertation at the University of Chicago on Ibn Taymiya, a scholar often cited as a model for reinterpreting scripture. One can see Rahman's mark on many ideas examined here, including the distinction between eternal and historically specific Qur'ânic verses, and the status of scripture as "quasi-law" requiring further contextual specification. For a more detailed analysis of modern Indonesian contributions to fiqh, see Feener (1999).
[3] See Madjid (1994a:35). For a recent and controversial argument about the history of the bequest verses see Powers (1986). The jurist Ali Yafie (1994) compares these and other abrogations to Indonesia's revoking of Dutch laws, as historical developments internal to the legal tradition. The Sudanese Islamic law scholar Abdullahi Ahmed an-Na'im (1990) had made abrogation the central mechanism in his plan for legal reform.

Muslim man not to marry a Jewish woman even though such marriages were ex-plicitly permitted by the Qur'ân. 'Umar's reason was that if others followed this man's example, some Muslim women would be left unmarried. 'Umar thereby established the principle that something permitted by the Qur'ân none the less could be forbidden because of "the demands of place and time," and this basic idea has become a precedent in Islamic jurisprudence, writes Madjid. Later on the reason for forbidding such marriages disappeared as more women became Muslim, and so the prohibition itself was dropped. In this and many other acts 'Umar applied the principle that "every religious law contains its own reason (illah, *ratio legis*), which must be taken into account in applying the law, in accord with the general interest (*al-mashlahat al-ammah*) and with the respon-sibility of those in power and those charged with applying the law" (Madjid 1994:30–34).

The argument from historical contextualization has taken on wide currency in Indonesia, influencing both the direction of postgraduate training and public pronouncements by religious leaders. This argument is a more fiqh-friendly way of accommodating one's position to a wide variety of political impera-tives than is the argument from the separation of religion from state (or Islam from Pancasila, the Indonesian state ideology). An example of current political importance concerns the possibility of electing a woman as president. When he was the chairman of Nadhlatul Ulama, the largest Muslim organization in Indonesia, Abdurrahman Wahid met with the then Prime Minister of Pak-istan, Benazir Bhutto, and remarked that "Islamic jurists need not fear women leaders." Some scholars had quoted the Prophet Muhammad as saying that dis-aster would befall a state headed by a woman. "I answered that in Indonesia it is different," said Wahid. That hadîth was formulated by the Prophet for the warlike conditions of his time, he continued, when leaders led in battle as well as in holding court and issuing everyday orders. So the hadîth was appropriate. "Imagine, a woman couldn't be in the front ranks of battle. But today the gen-erals are in the command posts and the soldiers up front. Therefore, this hadîth could be said to be valid no longer."[4]

The weakness of this line of argument lies in its *ad hoc* character: "other times, other hadîth." Even generally sympathetic scholars sound alarm bells by following out the logic of the argument to what would be, for their colleagues, shocking conclusions. For example, Jalaluddin Rakhmat (1994), known for his writings on comparative Islamic traditions, objects to the idea that historical context can set aside sacred texts. Take, he says, the command that women should conceal their beauty from those not related to them. What was the purpose of this command? Surely it was to protect women on the grounds that revealing themselves to men would tempt men to commit improper acts. The

---

[4] As quoted in the *Surbaya Post*, 18 March 1996.

desire (*nafs*) of men is notably uncontrollable. But what if women were to become adept at not tempting men even as they let their beauty go uncovered, would the command then be set aside and women permitted to dress in any manner? Surely not. Or take alms: a major purpose of requiring us to give alms is to help the poor. If we lived in a truly egalitarian society would we then set aside the command to give alms because this purpose had been fulfilled? Were we to act along these lines, he continues, religious law would become only a "supplement" to the existing situation, dependent on it, and not, as it should be, an alternative to things as they are, the basis for critiquing society.

The debates continue. Most Indonesian religious scholars do agree that in interpreting the Qur'ân one must distinguish between general messages and specific rules, but they disagree on which are which. At a June 1997 conference on the subject, the jurist Ibrahim Hosen said that jurists fell into three categories: those who would reinterpret the entire Qur'ân, those who would allow no reinterpretation, and those, among whom he listed himself, who make a firm distinction between Qur'ânic passages that are clear and certain (*qat'i*) as written, admitting of no reinterpretation, and those that may be given new readings.[5] Hosen has strongly criticized jurists who would rework family laws with Indonesian culture in mind. No further interpretation is valid of those texts of Qur'ân or hadîth that provide clear, explicit directives, he argues. "This principle," he writes, "counters the current aspirations of that group who wish to destroy Islamic laws that are certain, such as the Qur'ânic inheritance laws" (a reference to Nurcholis Madjid). Individual interpretation (ijtihâd) can never have the status of certainty but only that of legal opinion, *zhann*, and can only be exercised on unclear passages.[6]

And yet in an article for the official religious law journal *Mimbar Hukum*, intended to be read by jurists and judges, Hosen (1995) found himself arguing from the other direction. He pleads for a highly contextualized reading of Islamic criminal law, on grounds that anything less will leave Islam out in the cold as Indonesia reforms its laws. Should we urge governments to implement the criminal penalties as written in the Qur'ân? he asks. His answer is entirely pragmatic: were we to so urge, we would endanger "the very existence of Islamic law": no government has been able to implement much of Islamic criminal law, and insisting on it would endanger our efforts to contribute Islamic law to our own national legal system. Henceforth, he adds, "we would be haunted by the feeling of having sinned."

---

[5] At the same conference, another participant, the scholar Ali Yafie, stated that he was among those jurists who would reinterpret the entire Qur'ân, as long as all jurists could agree on the '*illa* of a verse.

[6] Ibrahim Hosen's 1997 remarks were quoted in the online version of the Jakarta periodical *Gatra*, 14 June 1997. His criticism of inheritance reinterpretation was voiced in Hosen (1994:322). Hosen has been an important contributor to opinions of the Majelis Ulama Indonesia.

Better to look for the function, intention, and "the spirit of making something part of sharî'a (*jiwa pensyariatannya*)" and enact that intention. Thus, the Qur'ânic verse (Qur'ân 5:38) that directs the hands of thieves to be cut off can be read for its general intent, which is to prevent people from stealing. The meaning of the verse (again, the 'illa) is really "keep their two hands from stealing in an obvious and exemplary way." Further evidence that this kind of reading is necessary to understanding scripture comes from two incidents in which a petitioner approached the prophet Muhammad, and his directive to his followers was "cut off his [the petitioner's] tongue," a directive which his followers took to mean "fulfill his request." To cut off thus must have served as a way of speaking that meant "stop someone from doing something" by acceding to his demands.

Hosen's position is thus rather complex. He would have us take those scriptural passages that are to be considered as clear and certain at face value, but work to discover the intent behind all other passages, taking into account the rhetoric of Muhammad's day. (Note Hosen's assumption that at least these portions of the Qur'ân were delivered according to the rhetorical rules of the time.) We would then devise suitable positive laws that accomplish those same goals. The content of these enacted laws is not itself to be found within fiqh, but within the realm of "sharî'a policy" (*siyasah sharî'a*), which implies that "all types of laws and rules are to be valued as Islamic (or Muslim) laws as long as they are not in opposition to the intent and spirit of sharî'a, even if contradictory to the surface (*harfiah*) meaning" (1995:28).[7]

Is it then the case that, fortuitously, none of the verses most difficult to implement (criminal penalties) are clear and certain? Or, rather, that some may be clear and certain, but that the greater goal of Islamizing Indonesian law supersedes the goal of applying these verses?[8] Is the ultimate basis for creating law to be qualities of the scriptural text (clear versus unclear), or independent values (equity, justice), or the pragmatic criterion of advancing Islamization? We are left unsure.

The fiqh of 'Umar

One source of evidence for those engaged in these arguments is the decisions taken by the early leaders of the Muslim community, who presumably were

---

[7] The concept of siyasa (Ar. *siyâsa*) is of the state's right to regulate how sharî'a is implemented, even if it cannot legislate sharî'a itself. It has been used in particular to regulate the jurisdiction of various courts and the particular selection from among legal traditions that courts will apply. It is thus ideally suited to validate, from an Islamic perspective, positive law and executive decrees (such as the Compilation of Islamic Law). See Coulson (1971:137).

[8] An alternative way to avoid applying certain of these criminal *hadd* punishments is to invoke the prophetic hadîth, "Avoid the hadd punishments in cases of uncertainty (*shubha*)," a saying that was applied elsewhere (Powers 1994:339).

inspired by their close association with Muhammad. Of particular importance are decisions taken by the second caliph, 'Umar. With surprising regularity, scholars who argue for more reinterpretation of the Qur'ân support 'Umar's innovations; those who urge remaining closer to the Qur'ân criticize the caliph.

Former Supreme Court Justice Bismar Siregar, a leading proponent of Islamizing Indonesian law by reinterpreting scripture, finds in 'Umar's actions a principle of justice that ought to animate contemporary jurisprudence. Siregar wrote the foreword to an Indonesian translation of a book on 'Umar's fiqh, and he hands out copies of the book to visitors. The book consists of analyses of criminal decisions made by 'Umar, and stresses his use of individual interpretation based on the consensus of scholars as well as on scripture. Siregar himself interprets 'Umar's career as constituting the first stage in an admirable separation of executive and judicial branches, and 'Umar as an Islamic reformer who drew not just on theories but on "the demands and needs of the times." Siregar quotes Qur'ân 4:58: "When you set out laws for the people, do so with justice," and then urges that 'Umar's example be used for developing Indonesian laws based on "the legal values found in society," values that include "Islamic law in general, and the fiqh of Umar in particular" (1994b). 'Umar's jurisprudence is here interpreted not as an original model, true to the letter of scripture, that should be followed by Muslims today, but as precisely the opposite: an example of how, even then, the caliph had to reinterpret scriptural passages in light of ideals of justice and new social circumstances.

If the fiqh of 'Umar is used as a model for context-driven departures from the letter of scripture, the period after the first four caliphs, the period of the *Tabi'in*, or "followers," is used to depict advocates and opponents of ijtihâd in varying lights. In Nurcholis Madjid's (1994b:239–45) version, the authority to lead the Islamic community was hotly contested within about forty years after Muhammad's death. A coalition arose between the Mu 'awiyah caliphate in Damascus and the claimants to original authority in Mecca and Medina, who urged a return to the letter of the hadîth and to "Tradition with a capital 'T.' " Contesting these claims was a second school centered in Iraq, particularly in the cities of Kufah and Basrah, that claimed the right to use one's individual discretion (*ra'y*) to interpret scripture. These labels point to the general emphasis in each region, and to the fact that intellectuals in each place also drew on the methods of those in the other.

These two schools are variously labeled as Hijaz versus Iraq, or those who use hadîth versus those who use ra'y, or the advocates of the text versus the advocates of analogy (*qiyas*). Madjid and his allies see themselves as Islamic liberals and as inheritors of the Iraq school, the *Ahl al-Ra'y*, the "People of Reason," as against the Hijaz school, the *Ahl al-Riwayah*, the "People of Stories." Jalaluddin Rakhmat and others who caution against overreliance on analogy and ijtihâd refer to the Hijaz school in slightly different terms, as the *Ahl al-Hadîth*, the

"People of Hadîth," the scholars who, in Rakhmat's words, "based their fiqh on the Qur'ân, Sunnah, and the apostles' ijtihâd." In his account, in which this school clearly comes out better than in the version told by Madjid, the Hadîth jurists served to guard against the manipulation of hadîth, while the reasoning school played fast and careless with the texts. Rakhmat (1988, 1994: 269, 291–94) attributes the very rise of the School of Reason to 'Umar's failure to write down the hadîth, despite the urgings of Aisyah and 'Ali, the wife and son-in-law of the Prophet, that he do so. Rakhmat catalogues all the ways in which 'Umar was wrong: he did not know the Sunna; he reinterpreted verses that were out of bounds for ijtihâd because they were clear and certain (qat'i); he often simply erred in his reasoning.

Rakhmat (1994:296) sees the four Sunnî Islamic legal schools or traditions (madhhabs) as better than either of the two earlier positions, in that the legal schools combined both reasoning and texts. By contrast, he sees Islamic liberalism (the position of Nurcholis Madjid) as an unwelcome return to the extreme reasoning position. In his criticism Rakhmat targets Fazlur Rahman, Madjid's teacher (whose writings are widely known in Indonesia). Rakhmat denigrates Fazlur Rahman's ideas as nothing more than 'Umar's approach as it became embodied in the Hanafi madhhab. Claims to Rahman's originality, he writes, "can only be made by someone who has no foundations in traditional Islamic thinking" – a direct slap at Nurcholis Madjid, whose scholarly reputation is based precisely on his study of early Islamic thinking.

Epistemology and narrative style

One might seriously misinterpret this continued attention to the first Islamic century as the sign of a longing to return to a golden age. Quite to the contrary: for the partisans of contextualized reinterpretation and ijtihâd, 'Umar's decisions and the arguments of the Iraq school show how even those "close to the source" had to radically review scripture. For those less sanguine about ijtihâd, early history provides a way to show that current claims to be modern and liberal are in fact nothing more than the resurfacing of an ancient extremism.

But underneath these debates one also notices that the more humdrum sort of article – short instructional pieces in the legal journal *Mimbar Hukum* that are written for provincial judges, articles in general books on religious law, or chapters in textbooks – invariably embed their argument in the history of fiqh when they seek to champion jurisprudential reform, and choose an entirely different rhetorical form, that of close textual analysis, when they oppose such reform. Many of the pro-reform articles are little more than a rehash of well-known historical tropes: either 'Umar, the two schools, and the four madhhabs; or, in a local variant, precolonial Islam, colonial suppression, and independent self-determination.

Why this constant repetition of a historical narrative? For the more creative writers, Islamic history provides a familiar matrix in which to place a particular interpretive argument. But for most writers the historical narrative form gives to the very acts of law-making, institution-building, and journal-publishing a religious underwriting. If jurisprudence has a plot, then its main players – often the very authors – are making a kind of religious merit. The merit in question comes in various flavors. For the vigorously pro-government writers, including ex-ministers and senior judges, history from late colonial rule through the Compilation shows how government institution-building has finally given Islam its legal due. For scholars and jurists, history from 'Umar's time on shows how learned Muslims must continually engage in reinterpreting the law to fit the times. For Ministry of Religion staff who edit the journal *Mimbar Hukum* and oversee the religious courts, modern political history shows how the state sets the policy for religious law (siyasah sharî'a) and necessarily informs judges of the right decisions.

A historical way of writing has thus been harnessed to a point of view largely in favor of contextualizing scripture and of significant intervention by the government. Strikingly, a writer who adopts the historical mode for supporting reinterpretation in one area may switch into a text-positivist mode for resisting innovation in another. When Ibrahim Hosen urges that Indonesians contextualize criminal law in order to implement it, he begins with 'Umar and his refusal to cut off hands. But when he opposes reinterpreting the Qur'ân's stipulation of inheritance shares, he does so through a perfectly ahistorical typology: of the persons competent and incompetent to perform ijtihâd, of the kinds of cases legitimately subject to ijtihâd or not, and so forth.

Fairness as God's asymptote

I have already remarked that a telling weakness of the argument from history is its apparent *ad hoc* character. One cannot simply say that with changing times we throw out particular verses of the Qur'ân or valid reports of Muhammad's Sunna. On what set of norms then are jurists to base their decisions to implement, abrogate, or reinterpret scripture? In their otherwise strikingly different evaluations of recent Islamic law reform, Abdullahi an-Na'im (1990) and John Esposito (1982) agree that failure to specify this normative base vitiates all efforts to reinterpret scripture.

The major Indonesian attempt to develop such a normative base rests on an argument that Indonesians share ideas about justice and equity that differ from the ideas found in Arab society, but that are consistent with the general, eternal values found in the Qur'ân. (We saw allusions to such an argument in the quotations from Justice Bismar Siregar above.) Differences or changes in social practices and institutions are merely effects of this difference of what we might call local political philosophy. Furthermore, these scholars argue that Indonesian institutions are gradually shedding those social norms that somewhat resemble those in Arab societies, such as a patrilineal bias, and increasingly approximating the Qur'ânic ideal of equal treatment for all Muslims, men and women.

The argument about an Indonesian "sense of justice" (*rasa keadilan*) has been developed most fully with respect to gender biases in the transmission of property, beginning with a series of writings in the 1950s and 1960s by Professor Hazairin of the University of Indonesia Law School. Hazairin had been trained as a scholar of adat law, but taught Islamic and adat law, and in the 1960s turned his attention increasingly to Islamic law. He urged his fellow jurists to develop an "Indonesian madhhab" based on the bilateral principle that rights to property extend through sons and daughters. He argued that Islamic inheritance law contains general and universal principles, notably the principle that both women and men inherit property, and also specific rules. The rules derive from the Arab culture within which early jurists wrote, and in a different time and place they may be discarded.[9]

Notice, states Hazairin (1950:13–15), that in classical fiqh, after certain fixed shares of an estate have been awarded, the remainder of the estate is divided in such a way that agnatic relatives (related through males) take priority over uterine relatives (related through females). Arab jurists decided on this priority because Arab society is patriarchal, he continues, an analysis he finds confirmed by the fact that Iran-based Shî'î jurisprudence does not favor agnatic over uterine relatives. Both legal traditions are right for the society concerned:

The Sunnî approach is correct because it is in accord with their Arab society and so is the Shî'î one because it fits their society's needs...I believe that had there been a Minangkabau [West Sumatran] person among the Messenger's apostles, that person would have constructed a fiqh for his group that would have met the demands of the Qur'ân and Sunna but then would have favored not the agnates but to the contrary the uterine relatives according to the maternal adat of the Minangkabau. (Hazairin 1950:13–15)

Hazairin was aware of the slipperiness of his argument: he had to argue from specific Indonesian values to a normative sense of justice without letting his

---

[9] Hazairin (1962:4). Note the parallel structure of his argument about cultural differences, and Madjid's later argument about historical differences. Both resemble Fazlur Rahman's claim of eternal versus specific rules in the Qur'ân; Madjid's writings clearly developed from those of Rahman, his teacher, but may have been shaped by Hazairin's writings as well. An interesting feature of current writing is the convergence of religious historical scholarship, largely following Madjid's direction, with religious jurisprudence, largely following Hazairin's direction. The proponents of each are not entirely aware of the convergence; Madjid views the jurists as somewhat too concerned with Islamic law, while many of the jurists see Madjid as too little concerned with the legal status of scripture. For an extended analysis of the contributions of Hazairin, ash-Shiddieqy, and others, see Feener 1999.

position rest on mere empirical description. His approach also left him open to the charge that he was parroting the Dutch colonial "reception doctrine," which held that only those elements of Islamic law that had been received into local practice could be enforced in court – and he was careful to denounce reception theory as "the Devil's theory" (1962:5). Hazairin (1964:1) did retain a role for adat in his account, but only a very limited one, namely, as a general, evolving set of principles that attest to the shared Indonesian sense of justice. Normative value rests with this sense of justice, then, not with the specific rules of Indonesian adat. In his scheme, these rules, like their Arab counterparts, are subordinate to basic Islamic principles, and can be criticized on the basis of those principles. In particular: "I am certain that the Qur'ân only blesses societies that are bilateral" (1964:1).

I think that Hazairin saw the development of Indonesian societies as guided by Providence, and that this divinely guided change, this movement toward bilateral social systems, constituted both the empirical basis for a new madhhab and a transcendental grounding for it. The telos of adat law, as it develops, is the set of eternal values put forth in the Qur'ân. Seen developmentally, then, Indonesian society and Islam are not in conflict; the real conflict is between this shared bilateral conception of society and patriarchal Sunnî jurisprudence, "the fiqh of Arab culture" (1964:2).

Of course, Hazairin still faced the problem that certain passages in the Qur'ân do appear to advocate something less than a gender-equal social system (for example, the allotment of half shares of an estate to daughters). Rather than trying to reinterpret such passages (the strategy followed by current advocates of contextualization), Hazairin focuses on rules more easily interpretable under the bilateral rubric. Much of his detailed analysis of fiqh is devoted to the status of "replacement heirs," people whose linking relative to an estate dies before they do. In Indonesian societies, he wrote, the general rule is that when those who would have been heirs have already died, their descendants step into their shoes to receive their share. He argued that this rule is based on a pan-Indonesian principle, that in inheritance all descendants should have priority over other relatives, such as siblings or parents. The Qur'ân also allows this, he argues (in a highly tendentious semantic analysis best foregone here), although Arab jurisprudence did not, but in this instance it is the Qur'ân and Indonesian practice that ought to be followed.[10]

Hazairin's students became the leading architects of fiqh reform in the 1980s and 1990s. They include many in today's older generation of law professors and Supreme Court justices, who draw on Hazairin's argument in advocating current reforms. Consider how law professor Muhammad Daud Ali (1993), himself from Takèngën, describes the way the formulators of the Compilation of Islamic

---

[10] Hazairin (1962:2). On the "replacement heirs" doctrine generally, see Coulson (1971:143–58).

Law drew on history and culture in determining the new rule that orphaned grandchildren should inherit the share their parents would have received:

We took as our primary sources the text of the Qur'ân and Sunnah. But in practice we were flexible because the Qur'ân, as we all know, is not a law book, nor is the hadîth. They are the "mother books" containing fundamental messages for people everywhere and throughout time . . . The formulating committee [for the Compilation] always considered the conditions under which verses were revealed and hadîth pronounced. In this way the general principles contained in these two sources could be developed according to the changing conditions of time and place.

However, in this process the committee was limited by the fixed nature (*ke-qat'ian*) of certain texts. If a text was certain in its form (*qat'i dilalah*), such as the comparison of a son's and a daughter's shares set out in the chapter an-Nisa, verse 11, we did not change it: a son's share is twice that of a daughter. But if something was not fixed in the text of Qur'ân and hadîth but was felt to be among the needs of Muslim society today, we developed a "new line of law," such as the right of a child to take over the heirship status of a predeceased parent when an estate is divided.

The committee also used the fiqh principle of *al-'adatu muhakkamat*, adat that is good can be made into (Islamic) law – for community property, for example, which is not regulated in the Qur'ân or hadîth, nor in the jurists' books, but is to be found in the adat of Muslim Indonesians and lives in the legal consciousness of Muslim society in our country.

Historians of religion also recognize this "fiqh principle." Nurcholis Madjid (1992:550) puts it this way: "The possibility of reciprocal acculturation between Islam and local culture is recognized in a basic tenet of religious jurisprudence, that 'adat is made into law' (*al-'âdah muhakkamah*), or, more completely, that 'adat is syarî'ah that is made into law' (*al-'âdah syarî'ah muhakkamah*), meaning that adat and a society's customary practices, in other words local culture, are a source of law in Islam." Jurists, however, qualify this principle, perhaps because as jurists they are more directly vulnerable to charges of resuscitating the colonial legal "reception doctrine." In expanding on his argument about community or marital property in a 1994 interview, Daud Ali justified the Compilation's rule of equal division by drawing on a general Islamic principle of equity plus the social practices in Indonesia that underlie a local sense of justice. This Hazairin-style argument combines empirical reality with Islamic values.

We differ from classical jurisprudence on common property. The fiqh texts say that the wife takes care of the house and of her husband's wealth, and if she divorces she leaves with nothing. Well maybe in Arabia the wife does not do anything, but in Indonesia it is not like that. If a man takes up a machete to go out to the fields, his wife comes with him, carrying a bundle on her back. So she has contributed to the wealth, either by working on the fields or by taking care of the family, and she should receive some of the inheritance – and then we set specific amounts. Here we differ from fiqh, we take account of culture.

Note the way in which Daud Ali recognizes that Islamic law as transmitted in fiqh books already included Arab-world customary law and customary practices, and for that reason can be further modified to converge with Indonesian norms. This understanding of the place of custom in fiqh allows him to admit the Indonesian practices (men and women working together), indicative of a general sense of gender equity (equal work means equal rewards), into an argument for a particular interpretation of Islamic law.[11]

Other jurists, too, are careful to distinguish between principles of justice, whether they are conceived of as primarily embodied in local social practices or as primarily contained in the Qur'ân or both, and merely customary norms, adat, because of the latter's colonial taint. Bismar Siregar argues that it is "local values of justice" and not adat that have legal standing today. His response when I asked him in 1994 about adat's status today recalls the immediacy of the "reception doctrine" as a trap that one must avoid:

Too often judges are tied to adat, and that is dangerous. If you are a Muslim you should not use adat as legitimation for dividing an estate, you should use farâ'id [Islamic shares]. But today's judges studied van Vollenhoven and ter Haar [Dutch adat authorities], and they made gods of adat. This does harm to society. They used to say that Islam was in force only if it is part of adat, and now it is the case that adat is in force only if it does not contradict Islam.

Must women receive half?

On no issue of substantive Islamic law has there been more controversy than on the relative shares of an estate to be awarded sons and daughters. Professor Hazairin retained the 2:1 ratio in his proposals, but some of his successors have sought to substitute an equal division of wealth between brothers and sisters. Yahya Harahap (1995a, 1995b, 1995c), a Supreme Court justice and a formulator of the 1991 Compilation, deploys both the argument about eternal and specific elements in the Qur'ân cited earlier, and Hazairin's claim that adat regimes are already developing toward a bilateral set of Indonesian norms that best realize the eternal values of the Qur'ân. Harahap's writings thus bring together the two lines of reasoning we have examined, one from the history of religions and one from the study of Indonesian jurisprudence.

Harahap notes that Indonesian ulama, although ready to accept other changes, are uniformly unwilling to change the 2:1 formula. Their reason is that the

---

[11] As applied in the Takèngën courts, all property acquired by husband and wife becomes their common property, and is divided equally between them at death or divorce. Prior to this time, a women who had married into her husband's village and who was then divorced or widowed had no claim to any land in her husband's village. The change is of great material importance, because cases that come before the religious court often include claims by widows to their share: of an estate that has been taken over by a child or child's husband (see chapter 9).

formula is a certain and clear text. Yet one could weigh against this considerations of the reason for the revelation and the general principle that one finds in the Qur'ân of equal rights for men and women. The answer then must lie in psychology, he says: what does it mean when the verse in question (Qur'ân 4:11) ends with "it is an injunction from God"? What if the purpose of the injunction was to allow women as well as men to inherit, and to ensure that a daughter received a minimum of one-half the share given to a son? Under this interpretation, he argues, should the society so wish it could raise her share to equal the son's share. The norm that daughters should inherit is eternal, writes Harahap, but the ratio of two to one is contingent and "elastic."

In an interview (1995), he expanded on this argument.

Most people in Indonesia think that all directives in the Qur'ân are eternal and universal. But I agree with those thinkers who question which directives in the Qur'ân are eternal and universal, because many of them are "quasi-law" [in English], not yet a law ready for use, because each generation has to reformulate the directive to be effective and positive. What is eternal is the norm, for example that you shall not kill: from Adam on it has been a *mala in se*, eternal law. But matters of criminal penalties, for example, are not eternal; we can adapt them to changing conditions. Many ulama consider anything in the Qur'ân to be eternal and universal, and they say, "anyone who does not fit law to what Allah has said is wrong." But if we look into history, 'Umar did not cut off hands, because matters of sentencing are matters of specific rules, *hudud*.

Harahap offers a somewhat more satisfactory theory of jurisprudence than does Hosen. His advantage lies in adopting the reasoning developed by Hazairin, in which Indonesian social change is attributed to an Unseen Hand. In Harahap's writings the argument takes on a more feminist coloring. In patrilineal societies, he writes, "the role of a women is solely as a mother functioning as a container for a man's sperm, as a place to grow and give birth to the child." The low status of women is most striking in the older Arab world, where women had no rights to property, but the remains of this system "can still be seen in Batak, Bugis, Toraja, Bima, and Balinese societies." But Harahap sees a "New Adat Inheritance Law" already implicit in Indonesian judicial decisions that gave daughters equal rights with sons, and widows the right to property brought to the marriage by her husband (1995a:91).

Hazairin and Harahap constructed comparisons of Islamic and adat law in order to critique both of these rule systems as they were practiced in Indonesia. Hazairin's efforts in the 1950s and early 1960s were aimed at reforming both systems. He drew on the principles underlying all Indonesian regimes to urge a new understanding of the Qur'ân, and he drew on the rights of widows as heirs in the Qur'ân to urge a reform of adat. Harahap sets out to create a new code for adat, but one feels that his real target is Islamic jurisprudence: his three-part article is in a professional journal devoted to Islamic law topics and read mainly by religious court judges, and his adat law code focuses on the equal status of men and women, which, he implies, the Compilation just missed adopting.

The argument for contextual jurisprudence converges here with the argument for a new adat law: both involve critiques of patriarchy and a progressive view of sociolegal history. Arab society occupies the place in the cultural critique of fiqh that patrilineal Indonesian societies occupy in the cultural critique of adat: as the dying exemplars of a premodern system.

The hypocrisy of the ulama

From the New Order government itself came a call for reforming fiqh, in the form of a series of speeches, notable for their sharp-edged quality, delivered in the 1980s by the then Minister of Religion, Munawir Szadjali. Szadjali was a career diplomat rather than a jurist, served as minister during 1983–93, and during that time urged jurists to support a change in Indonesian fiqh such that it would divide wealth equally among sons and daughters. His argument begins in much the same way as did Hazairin's, with the specific Arab culture in which scripture was revealed and the need to adapt fiqh to other cultures and times. Remarkable, though, was the nature of the evidence Szadjali amassed against the 2:1 ratio: the hypocrisy of Indonesian jurists, the ulama, who, he said, in private find the unequal ratio unjust but publicly urge others to follow the letter of the Qur'ân.

Szadjali's (1993) sharpest version of this argument was delivered to the State Islamic Institute near Jakarta, the IAIN Syarif Hidayatullah, at their 1987 graduation ceremonies. The title of the address, "Signs of a Crisis of Intellectual Integrity among Muslim Intellectuals," suggests his line of attack. He points out hypocrisy on many issues. On bank interest, for example, he remarks: "Most of us, including those who declare bank interest to be forbidden, not only live on interest but in everyday life often use bank services." On inheritance, he notes that even the most learned of Islamic ulama will divide his wealth in equal portions among his children. "Indirectly, this signals that he does not believe in the justice of farâ'id [fixed shares]." He concludes: "Would not it be possible to search for a way out that is more honest toward religion and more honorable, for example by studying whether it is possible to modify or adjust the application of these Qur'ânic directives" (1993:4).

The reactions to these ideas, which had been launched first in the early 1980s, were by and large hostile, as Szadjali notes in his 1987 speech. Among the most frequently cited responses was that of the jurist Ibrahim Hosen, quoted above, that in the Qur'ân the ratios of shares of farâ'id are explicit and thus certain and not to be tampered with. Indeed, this response could be said to be the general one from most Indonesian Muslims who attended to the controversy. It was the most common response I heard from men and women, some of whom regretted that the ratio was explicit and certain, but also accepted the fact that it was so.

Szadjali's reply mirrors the arguments made by Nurcholis Madjid, namely, that 'Umar and other caliphs would not enforce all the commands found in the Qur'ân because times were already changing, and why should we do any less? The key terms used by Szadjali (1993:23–24) as his foundational concepts are the sense of justice (*keadilan*) and propriety (*peradaban*) found in a society. For example, he writes that despite the fact that the Qur'ân stipulates the proper conditions for having sex with slaves, as it does at four points, today we must set those rules aside as out of step with modern principles of justice and equality.

Szadjali's argument is thus one of the subservience of religious texts to the culturally accepted ideas about justice and proper ways of living. It is not that Islam has not been accepted, rather that, in the practices of precisely those people who are "strongly" Muslim, in his words, "including leaders of Islamic organizations," several specific Qur'ânic directives already are set aside. This setting aside in practice ought to be attended to, because it provides evidence that the text has been by-passed by history (1993:18).

To strengthen this argument he relates in several speeches and articles his experience as Minister of Religion, when he received reports from judges in strongly Islamic provinces – South Sulawesi, South Kalimantan, Aceh – that Muslim families, after receiving a legal opinion, a fatwa, about inheritance from the local religious court, would choose to go instead to the civil court so that a different division could be carried out. He also cites a study conducted in Aceh showing that 81 percent of inheritance cases in the sample were brought to the civil court and not settled according to farâ'id (1993:3, 17–19).

In a 1994 interview with me, Szadjali described his personal search for a resolution to this "crisis of the ulama":

People have abandoned the idea of two shares for a man and one for a woman, and this includes the ulama. I once asked the man who was then Chair of the Majelis Ulama Indonesia [Indonesian Council of Scholars] the following question. "I have three sons and three daughters," I told him, "and I have sent them all overseas to school. Only, the daughters all chose vocational schools, which are much cheaper, so when I die there will be this inequality in what they have received. What should I do with the rest of my wealth?" He answered that what he had done in his own case was to give all his wealth to his children in equal portions, in the legal form of a hibah. I then said: "That must mean that you are 'preempting' [in English] Islamic law because you wish to protect your daughters so they will not be victims of an unjust division." He answered: "Yes, that's right."

Hasan Basri [then head of the Majelis Ulama Indonesia] and Abdurrahman Wahid both say that in their villages the division is in equal amounts to sons and daughters, and Wahid said that his own father had given wealth to his children in that way. So the ulama say one thing and yet do quite another.

I asked Munawir Szadjali at that point, "And yet the 2:1 ratio is in the Qur'ân, is it not?" He responded:

But the Qur'ân was revealed in a certain society and in a certain culture. Back then, in Arabia, women received nothing, in fact they were disinherited. Then the Prophet Muhammad said that girls and boys were the same. But back then, and even today, in Arab societies only the man goes out to the market and buys things; his burden is greater and so it is fitting there, even today, that the division is 2:1.

But here it is different. In Solo [the central Javanese city of Surakarta], for example, in my family we run a batik industry, and it is the women who run everything, buy everything, are managers, while the men are just assistants. The Head of the Majelis Ulama for Solo said: "The 2:1 ratio is not fitting for Solo." The Qur'ân says that we must be just and good. Just! So 2:1 is fitting only when the man really leads the woman... Law is for people; religion is for us! The Qur'ân is not dead, it has a temporal quality.

The textual limit to reinterpretation

Szadjali's argument failed to carry the day, and the 1991 Compilation of Islamic Law contains the 2:1 ratio. Szadjali himself shrugged it off by adding that the Compilation "also says that the judge must take into account the values and the living law among the people – it was [Supreme Court justice and director of the Compilation project] Busthanil Arifin who put this part in."

The failure of the arguments against unequal inheritance shares for sons and daughters has to be understood in terms of how the Qur'ân itself is viewed. Advocating an explicit formula that differs from that contained in the Qur'ân is seen by many as a direct refusal to follow the Qur'ân. Ignoring the rule is much easier than rewriting it. Among the most developed rebuttals of Szadjali's position in recent writings is by Al Yasa Abubakar (1991), who proceeds, as my earlier observations on the use of historical and typological rhetorics would suggest, by constructing a typology of certainties.[12] Texts of Qur'ân and hadîth can be certain (qat'i) or only probable (zhanni), and each category is further divided into wurud, certain or likely because of their source, and dilalah, certain or likely in their form. Thus, in a passage from the Qur'ân a number is qat'i dilalah because it really cannot be interpreted to mean something else – twenty cannot be reinterpreted as thirty-five – whereas most of the rest is qat'i wurud and subject to interpretation. The passage in an-Nur:2 that fornicators shall be beaten a hundred times clearly involves a hundred somethings, but how the beating shall be administered, what counts as fornication, and so forth, requires further interpretation.

Abubakar's argument does admit future reinterpretations that might in effect create a condition of equity between sons and daughters. That a son shall receive

---

[12] Abubakar is from Takèngën, and by the early 2000s had become the leading scholar of sharî'a at the IAIN in Banda Aceh.

twice the share of a daughter contains a "certain in its form" element – the ratio of
2:1 – but also the categories "son" and "daughter," which could be reinterpreted.
Does a daughter who becomes head of household thereby take on the functions
of a son and merit the double share? Perhaps so, concludes Abubakar. Thus, he
continues, the argument by Yahya Harahap that measures to limit polygamy,
allow grandchildren to claim their parents' shares, and so forth, are correct,
because these matters, while set out in the Qur'ân, are only of the qat'i wurud
variety. Conversely, the resistance of scholars to measures to implement an
inheritance ratio of 1:1 is also correct, because the ratio is qat'i dilalah and
unchangeable. Until some different theory of scriptural interpretation is derived,
he continues, "efforts to reinterpret qat'i texts will always be seen as making
something up" (1991:176–77). It's not enough to say – here he attacks directly
Munawir Szadjali's argument – that people's legal consciousness differs from
that contained in scripture; law is an instrument that often is used to change
legal consciousness.

Abubakar underscores the jurist's need to find a legal principle to justify
reinterpretation, one that can add to a general norm such as "bilateralism" the
canons of interpretation that will justify a new way of reading and applying each
verse in question. His argument emphasizes the difference between a general
claim of cultural or historical difference, one which leaves the mechanism for
reinterpretation unspecified, and an argument that does specify that mechanism,
whether a sociologically based reinterpretation of the role of sons and daughters
(an argument also advanced by Szadjali), a claim that verses revealed in a certain
period were meant to be superseded by other verses (the argument made by
Abdullahi an-Na'im [1990]), or, to return to the line of reasoning pursued by
Nurcholis Madjid and Ibrahim Hosen, an argument from the specific intent or
reason behind a particular verse.

Viewed from within, the Indonesian debates span the spectrum of Islamic jurisprudence, from upholding an immutable sacred text, to reasoning from eternal
values and current social needs – and, indeed, these debates *are* old ones.[13]
But seen from outside, one can detect a common ground, even a convergence,
that marks out a new direction in jurisprudential reasoning. Hazairin may be
credited with laying the legal framework, into which the later historical arguments, developed by way of Fazlur Rahman's teaching at Chicago, were to be
fitted.

The argument begins with a belief that Indonesia is converging on the Qur'ân.
The development of Indonesian society reveals a bilateral telos, one that accords
well with the fundamental message of the Qur'ân that women have rights. Then
why does the Qur'ân contain some specific directives that are not gender equal?

[13] See Brown (1996) on such debates in earlier periods.

Here enters the history of religions argument, not yet developed in Hazairin's day: the Qur'ânic verses each have their specific reason, and in many instances that reason was limited to a specific time and place. 'Umar's statesmanship demonstrates this proposition. That a particular verse is limited in this way rather than eternal can be seen in its poor fit with the general values found in the Qur'ân – and with the providential drift of Indonesian society itself. We are now back at the beginning of the argument, one in which the values of modernity, the revolution, the Qur'ân and hadîth, the underlying sense of justice held by Indonesians, and historical scholarship can converge on a single set of social norms, themselves divinely inspired though still, as of now, imperfectly realized.

Contextualizing in practice

The most sustained efforts to bring this sort of "contextualizing" thinking to bear on social life have been carried out by activists working to improve the position of Indonesian women, through ongoing discussions about religion, interventions at religious schools, or legal advocacy in courtrooms, but above all through their many "networks" (*jaringan*), each focused on a particular problem or topic. Many of these women have been influenced by the writings of Nurcholis Madjid, but their goals are quite different: the practical improvement in women's lives through legal, social, and psychological as well as religious means.

To illustrate the range of their work I will profile several of their arguments here. Musdah Mulia is an active member of the Indonesian Commission on Human Rights, teaches in an advanced studies program at the State Islamic Institute (IAIN) in Jakarta, and participates in a critical Islamic discussion circle, Fiqun Nisah, which also involved Ibu Nuriyah Abdul Wahid, the wife of Abdurrahman Wahid. In 2000 the circle was developing a critique of a conservative book that remains required reading at pesantrens (Islamic schools on Java), the *Uqudulijain*, or "marriage ethics" by the Banten scholar Imam Nawawi (1995), widely available in Indonesian translation.[14]

We collected over 200 hadîth that were very gender biased. After we examined their genealogies, we found that they rested on weak hadîth (*dlaif*). These hadîth are very popular, and preachers use them in sermons. There is a mosque right here behind my house and I can hear their discussions, and they refer to these hadîth. They have been taught from the early days of Islam in Indonesia right to now. For example, that "if a husband asks to have sex and she refuses then the angels will curse her all her life." Now, this hadîth is reliable (*sahih*), but we have to look through the lens of gender, and

---

[14] For more on this book and the importance of "deconstructing" its argument in order to "reconstruct" it, see Munawar-Rachman (1996).

we have to understand "refuse": refuse for what reasons? The hadîth does not say; it could be because she is sick or tired, and of course then she cannot be punished.[15]

Other women work on specific legal ways to turn these reinterpretations of scripture into the bases for changed practices. For example, Ratna Batara Munti, recently graduated in sharî'a from the Jakarta IAIN, works at the legal aid society APIK (Asosiasi Perempuan Indonesia Untuk Keadilan, Indonesian Women's Association for Justice), and with the Koalisi Perempuan Indonesia (Indonesian Women's Coalition). The APIK main office is on a small side street in south Jakarta, near many of the poorer women who would seek and qualify for its assistance. APIK lawyers and counselors receive clients in a front room, and provide working space for most of the twenty-two (in June 2000) staff people in back rooms. The office handles individual cases and also formulates proposals for changing laws; in 2000 their priorities included labor law, domestic servant regulations, marriage law, and proposed changes in the criminal code. "APIK is the only institution that does these things from a women's perspective," explained Munti, adding that they work through branches in other large cities and work with Indonesia's pioneer Women's Crisis Center, Rifkah An-Nisa, in Jogyiakarta.

Ratna Munti's own work has focused on reinterpreting religious sources to change the idea that the husband is always the head of the household, an idea embodied in the 1974 Marriage Law (article 31).

Labor discrimination is promoted by this clause; for example, wives do not get the same social assistance (*tunjungan nafkah*) as do husbands, because they are assumed to have a working husband. Nor do they receive tax identification numbers (*nomor wajib pajak*), for the same reason. Without that number, a businesswoman must work through her husband to borrow money, for example; divorced or widowed women need to get a letter from their village head that says that they have no husbands. The woman is not seen as standing by herself.

In her book (Munti 1999) on the idea of women as household heads (published in a series of short handbooks designed to be made available to NGOs and used in arguing for legal changes), Munti argues that this idea also leads to gender-biased laws and to gender-biased decisions by judges even when the letter of the law is gender-neutral. She mentions (1999:18–26) the problem that the Indonesian penal code does not allow for "marital rape," prohibiting forced sexual intercourse only between unmarried persons, and that judges sometimes view a working woman as neglecting her duties toward her husband, an attitude based on gender biases. Some search for religious grounds for this discrimination, she notes, pointing to the hadîth mentioned by Musdah Mulia,

---

[15] Unless stated otherwise, the quotations in this section were based on interviews carried out in Jakarta in June 2000.

in which the Prophet prohibits a woman from refusing her husband's sexual advances, and to the verse of the Qur'ân (4:34) which describes the husband as *qawwâm* in the household, usually translated as leader, protector, head.

Munti argues that there is a discernible "moral message" of "universal values" to be found in the Qur'ân that must be the standard against which particular readings are tested for their plausibility. In this case the Qur'ân is replete with messages of equality and respect between men and women, and between husbands and wives in particular. When a surface reading of a verse or hadîth conflicts with these messages, then one must search for a new way of reading, and in particular one must consider the historical circumstances in which the scriptural utterance was revealed and delivered. Because in the Arab society of the time women had very few rights, it was "God's mission of justice" (1999:46) to impose those changes that were then possible, and gradually improve the status of women. The specifics of the rules imposed by God may no longer be just and fair today. It would have been impossible to change the fact that men were the heads of households; it was enough to restrain husbands in their treatment of women. Furthermore (1999:52), the same verse that mentions the status of men as leaders justifies their status in terms of the fact, true at the time but no longer true today, that it is they who provision their households. God was explaining to Muhammad why it was that men had to remain in their privileged domestic position.

Munti opens the scriptural door for the empirical facts that, today, women often are the bread-winners, and that a large number of households are in fact headed by women. The claim that scripture was shaped by the sociology of the day makes the sociology of today religiously relevant. Munti, working with Mulia and others, is currently trying to convince jurists and politicians that these arguments would make a revision of the Marriage Law Islamically acceptable.

The director of APIK, Nursyabani Katjasungkana, SH, complains of the difficulty of persuading these jurists and politicans, for example, that introduction of the concept of "marital rape" ought to be sanctioned. She showed me her scrapbook of opinions from leaders of Nahdlatul Ulama (NU) and Muhammadiyah on this topic. "They all reject the concept of marital rape, saying it is not in accord with Islam, that it is a Western concept." She admitted that "in the criminal code there is a clause that prevents people from physically harming others, but in practice this is not enforced or supported by society, because of Islamic teachings that the husband must beat his wife if she is not obedient. We bring these cases to court, and publicize the cases, for 'public awareness.' "

Indeed, the concept of "marital rape" has drawn a lot of Muslim fire. One frequent public critic of the concept is Busthanul Arifin, the retired Supreme Court justice and architect of the Compilation of Islamic Law. When I asked him about the issue in 2000, he called it a "sad joke," using the English phrase.

Because I am a judge I understand the issue. Indonesians are really proud if they use a terminology that Americans use, like "marital rape" or "ombudsman," but they don't know what they mean. Marital rape is violence. Not only Muslims, but everyone forbids it. There is already a law that says I may not harm someone else. The Prophet also was very angry when there was violence. But there really is not this specific problem. There have been one or two cases, with violence. The term has become political, Christians saying yes, yes they are for new laws, in order to confuse the Islamic scholars.

Nursyabani Katjasungkana links the "politicization" of Islam on this issue to a general tendency in the early 2000s to backtrack on women's issues,

for example on the issue of whether women can become leaders. In a 1994 congress, the NU said that of course they could, but then when Megawati became a presidential candidate, a larger gathering, the Congress of Muslims, said women could not become leaders, and Islamic parties followed suit, all of them, including the NU Party, and so Islam became politicized, there, and regarding other issues such as abortion and marital rape.[16]

A second kind of "applied contextualization" is exemplified by the work of Ciciek Farha Assegaf, a younger Muslim feminist, who works at the Perhimpunan Pengembangan Pesantren dan Masyarakat (Association for Developing Pesantrens and Society), generally known as P3M, directed by Masdar Mas'udi. As she explained it, P3M works for change in the legal realm in three domains: the content of statutes, the way law is carried out by judges, police, and prosecutors, and the culture of law, particularly as it is infused by Islamic ideas. The organization publishes a variety of newsletters and small books; its participants contribute to other publications and speak in public forums.

Engaged in activities of writing and lobbying similar to those of Ratna Batara Munti, Farha also works as a "trainer" on legal culture, carrying out discussions with ordinary women about problems related to violence, polygamy, and so forth, and also with jurists and Nahdlatul Ulama leaders.

For example, regarding polygamy, we start by "theorizing practice," starting from their experience, "oh yes, my elder sister, my neighbor experienced polygamy." "OK, was there a problem?" "Oh yes, problems with inheritance, the first wife was abandoned, she was struck..." So, we look at polygamy from all these aspects, but through the lens of religion, because that is their language. Then we ask them how we can overcome these problems as preachers and teachers. What we are doing here is *fiqh siyasa*, how to look at political issues from a religious point of view, and taking into account the religious heritage but with *reaktualisasi*, fitting it to the times. As times change, the results of ijtihâd have to be reconsidered.

---

[16] One of the outspoken opponents of a woman becoming president was Hamzah Haz, the head of the Islamic Party Persatuan Pembangunan Indonesia (PPP). Shortly after being named as her vice-president, Haz said he now had no objection to Megawati Sukarnoputri or another woman as president (*Tempo* online, 16 July 2001).

Farha's activist groups encounter opposition from the older religious figures within NU, the *kiyayis*.

Even when we work on secular issues, such as income-generating projects for women, the kiyayis say "but the man is the leader," so we have to work through a religious interpretation. So, all these aspects of gender are related: the husband hits the wife because she is involved in income-generating efforts, and the husband leaves to look for work, and attracts a sexual disease, and then passes it on to his wife; she does not know anything.

The Indonesian case illustrates the potential and the limitations of efforts to reach a gender-equal version of fiqh within the context of fiqh reasoning itself. Nothing about these arguments or their partial legal realizations guarantees their long-term acceptance – one recalls the exuberance of Middle Eastern law reform followed by the subsequent negative reaction. Neither the history of religions argument, nor the jurisprudential one, nor current positive law, calls for completely gender-neutral norms. But against the historical background of the failure of the secular reforms earlier in the century, in other countries, this direction, of changing fiqh through fiqh, may hold out the greatest promise.

Part 3

Governing Muslims through family

8   Whose word is law?

The debates examined in the previous chapter have taken place within the terms of Islamic jurisprudence, turning on how one may rethink fiqh in historical terms. Discussions about fiqh take place in a larger framework, however, one that concerns the very legitimacy of state involvement in Islamic affairs. Upon what authority do state-empowered actors make pronouncements about Islamic law? What role should state institutions play in regulating the life of the family, or the conduct of religious affairs?

If disputes over dividing and transmitting property fuel debates about adat and Islam in villages and towns (and in the courts called on to resolve these disputes), it is marriage and divorce that loom large in national-level debates about the role of the state in Islamic affairs. In the remaining chapters of this book we add those issues to the matters of inheritance and property division that have occupied us so far. The two sets of issues have different sorts of practical implications, ideological resonances, and legal ramifications. Inheritance and property divisions raise issues about equality and fairness across generations and among members of the same generation: what kind of contracts should be honored in transmitting wealth, what inequalities are proper and which are not, which set of norms ought to be relied on? These issues usually arise within a community, among relatives.

Marriage and divorce invoke a different temporality, that of the portion of the life-cycle stretching from marriage through divorce and death. They raise issues of equality of agency between men and women as much as they invoke distributional issues. They also raise basic questions of sociability across community lines. In Indonesia, marriage rules highlight the possibility of transgressing boundaries between religious communities – a prospect that, for some, harkens the end of the *umma*.

Islam and/in the state?

We begin by revisiting the courts, but now with a different set of questions in mind: how can the state legislate Islamic law or control an Islamic judiciary? Recall that each of the key terms used to discuss Islamic law has its own social and political associations. "Sharī'a" tends to be used as an all-purpose way of indexing an Islamic way of life, whereas "fiqh" is used to refer to more specific practices of interpreting texts. The inherent ambiguity of "hukum" gives the state a semantic opening for representing positive law (statutes, court decisions, executive orders) as if it were Islamic law. Finally, the recognition within Islamic legal writing of the state's right to regulate social life, as siyasah sharī'a, provides the state a different strategic possibility: claiming that its requirements merely set out conditions for the state to recognize marriage, divorce, or inheritance as legal; that they do not infringe on the autonomous processes of fiqh.

Indonesian state institutions have variously tried to combine these two strategies for legitimating their dicta: representing state law as itself Islamic law, or denying that statutes infringe on the rights of Muslims to engage in, or live by, fiqh. These strategies have not gone without challenges. In question are both the conditions for valid Islamic acts (can a Muslim marry or divorce without the state?) and the legitimating discourse underwriting law (whose interpretation of scripture counts as definitive?). Supremely at issue is the question that is the title of the chapter: Whose word is law?

The Jakarta Charter

Historians debate when it was that political and religious authority became separate in Muslim societies (Eickelman and Piscatori 1996:46–79). However, it is clear that not long after the death of Muhammad, debate began over the relationship between the two. The historian Ira Lapidus (1975:383) argues that it was in the early ninth century that a clear differentiation arose between the 'ulama, religious authorities, and the rulers, the caliphs. Colonial domination added a sense of privation to this distinction, a withdrawal from Muslims of their right to control their own affairs. In Indonesia, Dutch policies of separating Islam as politics from Islam as religion, and the withdrawal of state support for Islamic law in the 1930s, lent an additional element of nationalism and anti-colonialism to calls for incorporating Islam into the political and legal structure.

Contemporary debates about Islam and law frequently invoke the "Jakarta Charter" (*Piagam Jakarta*), a draft preamble to the 1945 Constitution written by nine of the authors of the Constitution. The charter characterizes the state as based on the belief in God "with the obligation to carry out the Sharī'a of Islam for its adherents." These "seven words" (in Indonesian), as they have come to be known, were already vague – who is to enforce this obligation? – but Vice-President Hatta and others decided that even this clause might threaten the cooperation of Christian regions in the national project, and many Muslims were opposed to what they saw as the beginning of state enforcement of Islam. In August 1945 the "seven words" were dropped from the preamble.

The deletion of these words – whether perceived as a founding moment of national consensus that must not be betrayed, or a stab in the back to the nation and Islam – is the charged starting-point for most discussions about religion and state. The resentment by some Muslim groups at the deletion may have been what led the drafting group to reverse an earlier decision and agree to establish a Ministry of Religion that would administer Islamic affairs – and the affairs of the four other recognized religions – under one roof (Noer 1978:8–13).[1] Muslim groups saw having "our own" ministry – it was assumed, correctly, that it would be run by a Muslim and primarily deal with Islamic issues – as a positive step toward constructing an Islamic society, if not an Islamic state.

By the late 1940s the ministry had established a strongly centralized system of religious administration, with an Office of Religious Affairs (Kantor Urusan Agama, KUA) at each administrative level, from Jakarta to the village. This hierarchy paved the way for the eventual creation of a unified court system. Even today, KUA village officials continue to act as the real first-instance institution with respect to marriage and divorce, where they try to reconcile couples before they reach the courts. (Their role with respect to inheritance seems to be minimal, however.)

The ministry also set out to organize religious courts, and a separate Directorate of Religious Justice was eventually established for this task. And in the absence of either a unified national religious court system (a High Islamic Court, the Mahkamah Islam Tinggi, acted as appellate court only for Java and Madura) or an Islamic chamber in the Supreme Court, the directorate took on functions of checking lower court decisions for consistency, creating a rudimentary system of jurisprudence, and circulating noteworthy decisions to other courts. The office even assumed a *de facto* function of judicial review (Lev 1972a:92–101), which the office has continued to covet well after the Supreme Court began to assume a review function in the 1970s.

Courts out of balance

Courts, meanwhile, were developing from below, as we saw in the case of Takèngën. The Japanese had let Islamic court matters stand as they were, but shortly after independence the government moved to exert greater control over these widely varying institutions. The Dutch-created courts on Java and Madura were brought under Ministry of Religion control in 1946. Emergency Law 1/1951 abolished all forms of adat courts (except for courts where religious

---

[1] The other recognized religions were Catholicism, Protestantism, Hinduism, and Buddhism. Some other religions are defined as "Hindu," Balinese being the major example; other collections of beliefs and practices are called "beliefs" (*kepercayaan*). In 2000, President Wahid supported the idea of recognizing Confucianism as a "religion" as well, but also advocated removing the state from the business of recognizing religions and certifying theological correctness.

justice was applied as part of the "living law" [Lev 1972a:79]), but did not give authority to Islamic courts.

This law left a legal and political vacuum: how was religious justice to be administered? In some parts of the new nation, including Aceh, religious courts continued to operate despite the lack of official sanction from Jakarta. The felt absence of support from the national government added fuel to anti-Jakarta sentiment in several provinces. In most of Sumatra, courts were few and far between. An alliance of traditional adat authorities, government officials, and civil court judges was able to prevent religious courts from functioning. In Aceh ("which, as always, caused the most difficulty for nearly everybody concerned" [Lev 1972a:80]), district authorities had created religious courts, Mahkamah Shariah, in each district by late 1946. In January 1947 the governor of Sumatra, Tengku Moehammad Hasan, ordered residents throughout Sumatra to do the same. Hasan stipulated that these courts and not the civil courts would hear inheritance cases. (As was the case in Takèngën, some civil court judges considered themselves to be competent to accept such cases none the less [Lev 1972a:82].)

Only in 1957, well after the outbreak of secessionist movements acting in the name of Islam in Aceh, West Java, and South Sulawesi, were courts on the Outer Islands given national legal standing.[2] New laws gave the religious courts outside Java, Madura, and South Kalimantan jurisdiction over family law matters, but only to the extent that "according to the living law they are resolved according to the law of Islam" (article 4(1)(2)). This clause in effect made the "reception theory" of colonial days the law of the independent land. Local courts consulted the easily available colonial-era studies of local adat law as a way of determining which court had the right to hear cases in which districts (Hooker 1978:103). To further complicate matters on the ground, although the law gave the religious courts jurisdiction over inheritance matters, it did not give them *exclusive* jurisdiction. A first-instance civil court might accept an inheritance case even if it thought that Islam was the local living law, and indeed the Supreme Court stated that they could do so (Lev 1972a:68–69). And because the civil court alone could execute decisions, order a bailiff to carry them out, it could declare its religious counterpart's decision null and void on "living law" grounds and retry the case. It was precisely such a nullification in the late 1960s in Aceh that led to mass protests and the provincial decision to forbid civil courts from hearing inheritance cases.

Nor were the judges on the Islamic courts necessarily supportive of Islamic political movements. On Java and Madura the judges were by and large government officials who had come up through the ranks in colonial or postcolonial

---

[2] Government regulation No. 29/1957 recognized the courts in Aceh. It was shortly thereafter replaced by a new regulation, No. 45/1957, promulgated under mounting pressure from several parts of Sumatra and Sulawesi. On the history of the Islamic courts generally, see Lev (1972a) and Lubis (1994).

administrations. Their loyalties and learning had less to do with Islam than with government administration. Their religious education usually led them to be traditionalists, meaning that they considered the correct way to decide a case to be to consult fiqh books that lay within the Shâfi'î legal tradition (*madhhab*), and not to engage in direct, individual interpretation of scripture.

Modernist Muslim jurists, those who did advocate the liberal use of such interpretation, avoided the courts, and took up positions in religious and political organizations. Those Indonesians who had formal training in civil law during the colonial period or thereafter generally thought little of the legal knowledge held by the religious judges – so much so that those law professors best trained in religious law, Professor Hazairin most notably among them, opposed the creation of Islamic courts on the grounds that the judges would be unwilling and unqualified to properly interpret Islamic law in the context of a changing Indonesian sense of justice (Lev 1972a:86–88).

The staffing of the religious courts gradually began to change with the creation of Islamic institutions of higher learning, the IAIN (Institut Agama Islam Negeri, State Islamic Institute), beginning in 1960. One of the main career paths for graduates of the law (sharî'a) faculty of an IAIN has been to become a judge on an Islamic court. And yet careers that pass through law faculties in the better universities have always been far more appealing and better paid. By the 1970s, Islamic courts had been created in most districts of Indonesia (except those with mainly Christian populations), and appellate courts existed on the larger islands (Lev 1972a:112–17). A 1970 law had given the Supreme Court authority to hear cases from the religious court system, and more judges, with more advanced educations, were being appointed.[3]

But the religious courts were not on an equal procedural footing with the civil courts. A religious court still had to ask the local civil court to execute a decision. The 1974 Marriage Law preserved the dependent relation between the two courts on grounds that the religious courts did not have bailiffs (*juru sita*) to execute decisions. On Java and Madura, colonial rules still applied that restricted the religious courts to issuing opinions, rather than enforceable decisions, in inheritance cases, even though people preferred to take disputes to the religious courts.[4] Elsewhere the "living law" clause of the 1957 statute

---

[3] The Supreme Court's authority to hear Islamic court cases was granted by Law 14/1970 (Ch. 2, Art. 10 (3)), but was not entirely welcome to Islamic judges and jurists, who feared that Supreme Court judges without religious legal education might give priority to civil law. The Court only made explicit its authority in a November 1977 regulation. The Directorate of Religious Justice in the Ministry of Religion then called a meeting of Islamic appellate court judges from throughout Indonesia to protest Supreme Court review of their decisions. The Court accepted the challenge, immediately reviewing two Islamic court cases, and in 1979 creating an Islamic chamber. To this chamber it appointed six justices (including one woman), none of whom was a religious jurist, although two had been trained in Islamic schools. The directorate then backed down (Cammack 1989:66–67).

[4] Habibah Daud (1982) reports that in 1976, in the Jakarta area, 1,034 cases were brought to the religious courts, and only 47 to the civil courts; and see Lev (1972a:199–205).

meant that the religious court's jurisdiction could always be challenged on grounds that Islamic law was not locally "living."

Controlling marriage

In this situation of an imbalance between the two judicial systems, and an uncertain legal basis for the religious courts, the government introduced a marriage bill that would have even further weighted the balance toward the civil courts. In 1973 marriage and divorce became the major issues for national debates about Islam and the state, and they have continued to be so ever since that time.

Marrying (and divorcing) according to "one's own laws" may be among the most strongly felt signs for Muslim minorities everywhere that they have control of their own affairs. Many Indonesian Muslims have seen maintaining marriage as a religious act, to be arranged – and if necessary dissolved – by the institutions of the Muslim community. Other Muslims disagree, considering marriage and divorce as practiced in Muslim communities to be areas of particularly sharp gender inequality. Many in this second category consider state legal intervention to be the only way to rectify these injustices. Self-governance according to religious norms conflicts with equality before the law.[5]

At the same time, the central Ministry of Religion has considered it to be in its own interest to regulate marriage and divorce. In 1946, one year after independence, the newly created ministry shepherded a law (No. 22/1946) through Parliament requiring that all Muslims register their marriages and divorces with the ministry's local office. A new post was created for this task, the Registrar of Marriage, Divorce, and Reconciliation (Pegawai Pencatat Nikah, talaq, Rujuk, NTR). Neither these religious registrars nor the courts were given the substantive law to accompany this procedural statute. What counted as a legitimate marriage? How could a woman obtain a divorce? Did a wife need to be consulted before a man took a second wife?

In lieu of positive law, religious registrars and judges followed local understandings of Islamic law, but, unsurprisingly, these differed from one place to the next. In 1953 the ministry tried to introduce some degree of uniformity by listing thirteen legal texts that were to be consulted, all from the Shâfi'î school. But variation still was to be found in these texts, and in any case the technical Arabic of many judges was far from adequate to study these books (Mudzhar 1993:37–38).

Did variation among judges matter? Aside from the usual government nervousness that matters were not under their control, jurists thought that within Indonesia, Muslims ought to operate with a common set of norms and concepts

---

[5] Compare the parallel debates in India over the status of separate laws for Muslims regarding marriage and divorce, a situation formally not unlike Indonesia's, but against a very different political background, which exploded with the "Shah Bano" case (see Das 1994).

concerning marriage and divorce. People ought to be governed by well-thought out uniform rules, not subject to the whim of local, possible poorly educated, officials. Jurists often will cite the case of Sukarno's daughter Megawati (later to become president) as a famous example of the problems caused by this legal vacuum (see Noer 1978:49–50). Megawati was married to an Air Force lieutenant whose plane crashed in Irian Jaya in 1971. His remains were never found and he was declared missing in action. Over a year later Megawati remarried, this time to an Egyptian, in a ceremony conducted by the chief religious judge of Sukabumi, on Java. Now, under Islamic law a widow is permitted to remarry after waiting a fixed period of four months and ten days, but Sukindro had not been declared dead. Megawati's brother, Guntur, claiming status as her guardian, then sued in the Jakarta religious court to have her new marriage annulled. The judge, who reportedly had been asked to summon the court by the Minister of Religion, annulled the marriage and declared that Megawati would have to wait another four years before Sukindro could be pronounced dead.

Religious scholars took sides in the case, with the best known among them, Hamka, siding with the Sukabumi judge. The affair was highly political, both because of Megawati's lineage and because, coming at a low point in relations between the government and the religious scholars, the case was seen by many as an improper government manipulation of the religious court. Different legal opinions and traditions were cited by each side, epitomizing the problems posed in a legal system where no single set of rules guides all judges. And if this amount of discord was possible within the Muslim community, marriage and divorce across all the religious communities was of course still more varied.

Even as jurists found these legal inconsistencies worrisome, women's groups had been struggling for substantive reform in how Muslim marriages and divorces were carried out. Since long before independence they had argued for restrictions on a husband's right to take a second wife. They had also tried to end his unilateral capacity to declare a divorce, his power to effect a divorce by declaring "I divorce you," with no judicial sanction and no recourse for the wife. These groups had achieved one success when, in 1955, the Ministry of Religion agreed to put on the back of its printed marriage contract, signed at the time the marriage is registered, the list of acts by the husband which give the wife grounds for a divorce (including desertion, maltreatment, and insufficient material support). This *sighat ta'lik talaq* made it easier for a woman to obtain a divorce in the Islamic court (see the next chapter).

Is marriage religious or secular?

However, it proved difficult to create a marriage law on which women's groups, Christians, and Muslim organizations could agree. Draft marriage laws were written in the 1950s and introduced in Parliament in 1958–59, but without result. A second round of bills and discussions, also without result, occurred in 1967–70. And in July 1973 a third round of debates began when a new marriage bill was submitted to Parliament.

The draft bill of 1973 created a greater uproar than nearly any other bill submitted in the New Order. During hearings in September, Muslim youths entered the parliament building and seized the floor. Students leaped on to desks, and one gave a lecture from the Speaker's podium. All told, the event was an unusually sharp demonstration of popular dissatisfaction. "Even before the turn came for the Minister of Justice, Oemar Seno Adjie, to speak, young men entered the Hall of Parliament with cries of 'God is Great, God is Great, God is Great,' " described a lawyer and champion of women's rights who was present in the hall. "They occupied the seats of the parliamentary leaders, who left the hall with members and other visitors. Outside the building gathered from all directions, in orderly fashion, groups of girls dressed in white, with green sarungs and white head coverings, forming 'silent masses' [English] in protest" (Subadio 1981:19).

Why such heat from Muslims? The timing was far from imperfect, in that the Islamic parties had fared poorly in the 1971 elections, and the government had just announced plans to merge them into a new party without Islam in its title, the United Development Party. Fears of Christian missionary activity in Muslim areas were at one of their periodic peaks. And the way for Muslim acceptance of the bill was poorly prepared: no Muslim groups had been involved in drafting it, and rumors flew that Catholic members of Golkar had been its architects. But Muslims also objected for substantive reasons, citing what they saw as three major defects of the bill (along with a number of lesser ones).[6]

First, the draft bill gave heretofore unheard of powers to the civil court. It would now be the civil court, rather than the religious court or the individual Muslim, that would regulate marriage and divorce. A man or a woman would initiate divorce proceedings in the civil court. It would be the judges, at the moment they declared a marriage ended, and not the husband, who would effect the divorce. A husband also had to seek the civil court's permission before taking a second wife.

Second, the bill took from religious officials the right to define what marriage is and what follows from it. It said that religious differences were no barrier to marriage. It recognized engagement as akin to marriage, and said that a child born during the engagement period would be legitimate if the parents then married. It stipulated that an adopted child had the same status as a natural child, and that his or her relationship to the birth parents was severed by adoption. These provisions contradicted widely agreed-on Islamic definitions of marriage and paternity: that only marriages performed according to Islam were valid, that

[6] As reported in *Tempo*, 8 September 1973.

marriage alone (not engagement) confers legitimacy on a pregnancy, and that only biological children have the social and religious status of children. (These issues have continued to be disputed ever since.)

Finally, and perhaps most objectionable, the draft bill tampered with religious law concerning the validity of a marriage. For Muslims, a valid marriage, a *nikah*, was an agreement between a man and a woman carried out according to certain rules: the bride has a guardian who acts for her in the public marriage ritual; certain binding words of agreement are spoken; a *mahr* payment is made by the groom to the bride. Indonesian law prior to 1973 recognized such an event as a valid marriage, and only added a civil requirement that the marriage be registered. The new bill, however, would have declared as invalid any unregistered marriage.[7] In other words, marriage would be *defined* as that which occurred under the supervision of the state.

The bill thus threatened many Muslims with loss of control over the one portion of Islamic law that had remained under Islamic jurisdiction after the many years of colonial disparagement and assault. In 1937 Islamic courts had lost jurisdiction over inheritance in Java and Madura. In 1945 those who advocated the enforcement of Islamic law for Muslims had failed to get that clause inserted into the Constitution. Islamic courts still had no nationwide legal foundation. For some, then, it was a last stand. And it was successful. After the unusually visible protests against the bill, which included the threat of a walkout by the Islamic faction in Parliament, the bill was changed radically. The offending provisions were dropped from the new bill, which was quickly passed and signed into law in 1974.[8] Jurisdiction over marriage and divorce was restored to the religious courts. Furthermore, these courts were given new tasks, a greater role in Islamic social life than they had ever enjoyed. They now had sole authority to settle disputes over the validity of a marriage and to grant permission to take a second wife. Only they could grant a divorce; the husband could no longer pronounce his "I divorce you" out of court and have it legally recognized. The religious courts now could settle common property disputes, a task formerly reserved to the civil courts. They were given clear authority to hear cases regarding child custody, alimony, and maintenance payments.

What makes a marriage valid?

The bill also stated that marriage is religious in character; specifically, that (Elucidation, article 2) "there is no marriage outside of the laws of the respective religions and beliefs." What did this clause mean? Would a civil marriage

---

[7] The draft also lengthened the *'idda* waiting period before a woman can remarry from three months for a divorcee and four months plus ten days for a widow, to 306 days.

[8] Law No. 1 of 1974, usually referred to as the Marriage Law of 1974.

be invalid? Could two people of different religions marry? I take up the first question in this chapter; it goes to the heart of the debates over whose word is law. I turn to the second question in chapter 10; it is critical to understanding the role of legal debates in Muslim–Christian relations.

The proposed bill and that which was enacted differed most fundamentally on this question. The draft bill would have changed the definition of a valid marriage, stipulating that it must be registered with the state to be a marriage at all. The final statute preserved the religious definition of validity; it states that a marriage is valid if performed "according to the religious law of the parties" (article 2.1). However, it also required, as state policy, that certain conditions be met. For example, under the final law, if one violates the minimum age require-ments for marrying, the marriage is still valid, but the parties have broken the law. Hukum in the Islamic-legal sense was preserved in that performative force remained attached to the utterances of the marrying parties or their guardians; the state merely attached its own penalties to certain actions or failures to act.

The same distinction applied to portions of the two bills concerning divorce. The draft law stated that the court would pronounce the divorce. The judge's utterance would replace the husband's utterance of the talaq as the speech act that effects a divorce. Put in Islamic terms, the husband's utterance would no longer have the hukum of divorce, but the court's declaration would have that effect. Religious law would have been changed, and in the eyes of many Muslims, violated. The revised statute places the court in the position of witnessing, not replacing, the husband's talaq utterance (though only if the judges have found sufficient reasons for the divorce). The utterance remains the act that constitutes the divorce; the law only regulates where and when it is performed. The bill's designers also represented the restrictions imposed by the law as motivated on religious grounds, by the fact that the Qur'ân itself considers divorce to be reprehensible except under stipulated conditions.

Katz and Katz (1978:316) report that Muslims generally interpreted the bill as preserving the substance of Islamic law while providing new proce-dures for implementing it. Cammack et al. (1996) agree, arguing that ordinary Indonesians interpret the 1974 statute as not affecting the religious validity of marriages, and that the religious courts have by and large taken the same view, and have been willing to waive certain requirements of the bill as not essential to creating a valid marriage. For example, courts have been willing to exempt would-be spouses from the legal requirements that they be of a minimum age, and that proof of consent be presented.[9]

---

[9] The law set the minimum age for marriage at nineteen for a man and sixteen for a woman, probably higher than the average ages of marriage. But the parents of an underage couple could ask the court to waive the requirement (article 6 (2)), and this clause may contribute somewhat to the apparent lack of any sharp drop in underage marriage (Cammack et al. 1996).

And yet the text of the 1974 law is ambiguous on this point, leaving room for conflicting legal interpretations. Article 2 of the law states: "Marriage is valid if it is carried out according to the laws of the parties' religion and belief." The following clause adds: "Each marriage is registered according to the rules of current statutes." (Implementing regulations then specify where the couple must register; for Muslims it is with the religious registrar.)

What is the relationship between these two clauses of article 2? Does clause 2 modify clause 1, such that an unregistered marriage is invalid? Or does clause 1 leave the issue of validity entirely up to religious authorities? This distinction may seem overly refined, but in the logical and legal space between these two interpretations lie the disagreements that led Muslims to occupy Parliament in 1973, and jurists to debate the sense of the act ever since.

In 1995, for example, two jurists writing lead articles in the same issue of the Ministry of Religion's publication *Mimbar Hukum* took opposite sides on this question. One of the writers (Mardjono 1995) argues strenuously that registering the marriage has nothing to do with a marriage's validity: validity is entirely a matter of religious law, and the confusion in society on this point is the fault of the compromising Parliament, which had adopted confusing language in order to appease secularists. A second jurist, who once worked in the Directorate of Religious Justice (Abdullah 1995), agrees that validity and legality are distinct. But he argues that only if registered is a marriage recognized by law – and of course the word here is "hukum." The author invokes the dual meaning of "hukum" that we have already discussed – hukum as a matter of religious validity, or hukum as a matter of national law – to try and persuade the reader that law requires registering even if religious law does not.[10] He repeats the opposition between a phrase featured in the article's title, "underhanded marriage" (*perkawinan di bawah tangan*), and its opposite, "marriage carried out according to law" (*perkawinan yang dilakukan menurut hukum*), such that in their minds readers may begin to merge "hukum" in the sense of religious validity with "hukum" in the sense of the state's requirements.

Which view one takes on this issue has immediate legal consequences, as we can see by considering two recent Supreme Court decisions (in Hanan 1995). Over a period of only two years the Court took contradictory positions about what "valid" and "legal" meant in the 1974 law (see also Butt 1999). First, in a 1988 decision, the religious court of first instance in Bandung (West Java) held that a man who had taken a second wife in a marriage ceremony that was valid from an Islamic perspective but had not been registered had none the less married, because clause 1 of the law defines marriage. However, because he

---

[10] The author adds, somewhat beside the point, that the 1991 Compilation of Islamic Law effectively makes registering the marriage a requirement of validity because it stipulates that only with a certificate of registration can the marriage be proved to have taken place according to Islam.

had not asked the court's permission to take a second wife he had committed a crime, and was sentenced to five months in jail. The appellate court reversed the decision, saying that only a registered marriage was valid, that both clauses of article 2 of the marriage law had to be met for there to be "marriage." Therefore he was only living together with, not married to, the second woman, and was not guilty of the crime of unapproved polygamy. The judges ordered him freed. But then in 1991 the Supreme Court quashed the appellate decision, saying that the lower court had indeed correctly read the marriage law and that the man was to be kept in jail. Marriage is valid even if not registered, concluded the Court (thereby agreeing with the position taken by various Muslim organizations).[11]

But only two years later the Court took the opposite view. The case originated in 1990 from a lower court in Aceh. It presented precisely the same set of facts as in the first case. A man married twice but never registered the first marriage, and the first wife took him to court. In its 1993 cassation, and without mentioning the earlier case, the Supreme Court said that "marriage" means marriage that is registered, and since no record of registration could be produced there had been no second marriage, and thus no crime. The man was freed.[12] Finally, in a 1995 decision the Court did indeed rule that even an unregistered marriage was valid.[13] But the debate continues, and it further complicates the debates over mixed marriages, debates that sum up a host of fears inside and outside the Muslim community (see chapter 10).[14]

The current legal situation leaves a wife in such a circumstance with only limited recourse. The best known of these unregistered marriage cases involves a popular television star, Mandra. The star of *Si Doel Anak Betawi*, probably the longest-running popular television series in Indonesia, had married three times, twice without registering the marriage. In 1998 his third wife, Rina, took him to the civil court in Depok, West Java, to force him to register the marriage. Only a registration could give a legal civil status to their child, born two years earlier and still without a birth certificate.

The Depok court ruled that the marriage was valid, because the *ijab-kabul*, the words that are "given and received" between the bride's representative and

---

[11] The Supreme Court's decision was as Case 2147/1988, decided 1991 and reported in *Varia Peradilan* 77, 1992:53–76.

[12] In his commentary, published in the journal *Mimbar Hukum*, a religious court judge (Hanan 1995) urged the Court to follow its first decision, a predictable recommendation as it preserves the Islamic view that a marriage according to religious rules is valid even without registration.

[13] Case 1073/1994, published in the journal of record *Varia Peradilan* 123, 1995:25–49.

[14] Butt (1999) points out that in the 1980s, many religious court judges continued to follow older interpretations of Islamic law concerning the validity of marriages, and especially polygamous marriages. He argues that, with increased subjection of religious court judges to state scrutiny, and increased education of such judges in law faculties, the trend is probably toward increased compliance with the Supreme Court's position. These observations are well founded, but the Court is not of one mind on the matter. Put another way, the problem is not simply one of more attention to existing jurisprudence; rather, the ambivalence expressed through the Court's decisions reflects a real conflict over the relationship between scriptural and positive sources of law.

the groom, were pronounced in the presence of witnesses. Mandra had violated the law by not registering the marriage with the local religious office (KUA). He was ordered to pay damages to Rina (of Rp 100 million) for that failure. But the court did not order the marriage registered; registering depended on the joint decision of the couple, said the judge, and could not be compelled by the court. The decision (which replicated an equally celebrated case from the late 1980s involving a member of Parliament, Nugraha Besoes) thus left the wife without recourse, without "marital agency," and completely dependent on her husband's decision to make legal the status of their marriage and their child.

Two views of legal uniformity

The shadow of the Jakarta Charter fell over the government's efforts in 1989 to create a nationally uniform religious judiciary exactly parallel to the general judiciary. The government had wanted to regularize and regulate the judiciary and saw the bill as a part of its continuing top-down effort to create uniform legal institutions. It also was trying to seek greater support from the growing middle-class Muslim population, and to deflect criticism of its domestic policies from certain Islamic groups.

The 1989 Religious Judiciary Act created uniform religious courts throughout Indonesia with jurisdiction over marriage, divorce, and inheritance; it gave these courts the right to execute their own decisions (both measures seen as finally reversing Dutch restrictions on Islamic jurisprudence); it stipulated that judges have college degrees either in Islamic law or in general law with an Islamic specialization; and it made divorce procedures nearly the same for men and women.

Little of the bill's substance was objectionable, and most jurists strongly favored the idea of reducing differences in jurisdiction from one province to the next. And yet there was public opposition to the idea of creating a separate Islamic judiciary. In the parliamentary debates and the newspapers, nationalists and non-Muslims argued that to create a separate system of justice for one segment of the population was to weaken the principle of the equality of citizens before the law, and smuggle the Jakarta Charter into law. To underscore the importance of legal uniformity for all citizens, they cited the Pancasila (always a good idea in such debates), along with a concept that had come to be its spatial equivalent, the "archipelagic idea" (*wawasan nusantara*), the idea that "all the islands of the Archipelago form one legal body with one National Law devoted to the national interest." As *Mimbar Hukum* editor Zuffran Sabrie (1990:27), who also edited a collection of the debates and articles, remarks, much of the debate turned on opposed interpretations of the Archipelagic Concept. Advocates of the bill argued that creating parallel religious and secular courts throughout the country would at last give the country a uniform structure to replace the off-Java/on-Java dualism created by the Dutch. The bill's opponents countered by saying that separating religious and secular courts would rigidify an already too-present legal dualism, and would be based on the mistaken idea that all Muslims preferred religious to civil courts.

Underlying these positions taken towards the religious courts bill were long-standing fears about religion and politics: that the law would lead toward a theocracy; that those opposed to the law sought to weaken Islam and strengthen Christianity; that the "extreme right wing" of Islam would be encouraged to step up their efforts; that if the bill failed that same "right wing" would be more difficult to manage.

A scandal erupted when strong opposition to the bill developed within the government's own parliamentary faction, Golkar (FKP), a rare occurrence in the flourishing period of New Order control of Parliament. A working paper drafted by one of the faction's vice-chairmen argued that the bill would revive the Jakarta Charter and would create legal dualism in Indonesia. The paper was excerpted in the national magazine *Tempo* (24 June 1989), and circulated as far as South Sulawesi and Aceh. But, because publicly opposing its own government's bill was unheard of for the faction, its chairman later stated that the document "was considered to have never existed."[15] And yet the vice-chairman of the People's Consultative Assembly (MPR), the larger group that selects the president, R. Soeprapto (also a former Governor of Jakarta) declared the draft bill to be unconstitutional because it discriminated against non-Muslims; a former Minister of the Interior and then Speaker of the House, Amir Machmud, agreed.

The nationalist faction (FDI), which tended to represent Christian interests, opposed the bill, as did the Indonesian Association of Churches. Although it eventually supported it, the Islamic party faction was at first rather quiet on the bill, out of ambivalence over the increasing control of the courts the bill gave to the government. The fourth faction, that of the military, strongly supported it, for the same reason. Some commentators saw the draft law as the foot in the door of radical legal pluralism: might we not see Hindu courts, Buddhist courts, and more adat courts? Indeed, the Hindu community took the opportunity to call for its own court system.

Of the many cautionary articles written in the Christian-controlled press, that by the Catholic writer Franz Magnis-Suseno (*Kompas*, 16 June 1989) was the most controversial, in part because it brought to the surface the latent conflict over the Jakarta Charter. The Jesuit priest of German birth argued that religion and the state ought to be maximally separate. Religious courts administering religious law are properly an outgrowth of a community, but to make such courts part of the state legal structure abdicates a portion of state sovereignty to religious groups, and also encourages divided loyalties. A state must have a

---

[15] In *Tempo*, 3 June 1989; see also Sabrie (1990:28); Syamsuddin (1995:59).

unified legal system based on shared, universal norms. For Indonesia, he argued, giving state sanctions to a religious judiciary would reverse the wise decision made by such Muslim leaders as Muhammad Hatta, the first vice-president, to strike from the Constitution the "seven words" that would have made the state the enforcer of religious law for Muslims. This national consensus, made to ensure the unity of law, must be preserved.

This article kicked up a flurry of protests. An article in the Islamic newspaper *Pelita* (27 June 1989) covered the main points. Far from surrendering sovereignty, wrote the constitutional law expert (later Minister of Justice, and head of the Islamic Bulan Bintang party) Yusril Ihza Mahendra, the proposed law takes it back from the Dutch. In any case, unification of the law is not supposed to transform all subject matters. In some areas the law already contains subsystems, with statutes and judicial decisions that are based on adat, religion, and even European laws. Does the judge who relies on the Dutch Civil Code thereby abdicate the state's sovereignty? And, finally, Hatta himself wrote that erasing the "seven words" did not prevent the government from subsequently passing laws for Muslims based on scripture.

Other articles for Islamic dailies emphasized that Magnis-Suseno was a Jesuit, whose order has promoted the expansion of Catholicism in the archipelago. The debate warmed up after this, with a more heated exchange between religious spokesmen. The Jesuit writer S. Wijoyo worried in the Catholic magazine *Hidup* (5 March 1989) that the law would bring Indonesia closer to a theocracy. Muhammad Natsir, the former chairman of Masyumi, complained in the Islamic publication *Serial Media Dakwah* (August 1989) that the Christians, having won in 1945 by delivering an ultimatum to Hatta – drop the seven words or we're out – have always tried to keep the Muslim community from having laws to better govern their religious lives.

The debate also took place on the higher, nearly indecipherable plane also common in Indonesian politics. The Minister of Justice, Ismael Saleh, in a series of articles in *Kompas* (1–2, 3 June 1989) argued for legal unification based on the "archipelagic idea," but also noted the importance of the "unity-in-diversity idea" (*Wawasan Kebhinekatunggalikaan*), that promotes pluralism. He expressed hope that a "common denominator" (using the English words) among religious, adat, and other sources of law could be found.

Suitably vague for a contribution from a minister, the article was cited by the Minister of Religion as favoring the draft law, but taken as cautionary toward the draft law by the human rights lawyer T. Mulya Lubis (*Kompas*, 23–24 June 1989). Lubis agreed that any legal system in Indonesia's near future must recognize a plurality of laws, but denied that this implied that the nation needed a plurality of legal systems. Doing so would replicate the divisive colonial *adatrechtpolitik*, he warned. The problem had begun when Law 14/1970 stipulated four judiciaries – general, military, administrative, and religious – leading to the current draft law on the religious courts. A special danger of the draft law, he wrote, was that it mingled executive and judicial powers by giving control over court administration to the Ministry of Religion. If we cannot have the best solution, a single first-instance court for all matters, then at least, pleaded Lubis, let us strengthen the judicial branch, giving it, for example, the right to review the legality of statutory laws (an attitude generally shared by the nationalist faction in the debates).

But others wanted to make the two court systems even more sharply separated than envisaged in the bill. The Indonesian Council of Islamic Scholars (Majelis Ulama Indonesia, MUI), whose chair, Hasan Basri, repeatedly denied that the law had anything to do with the Jakarta Charter, urged that "legal choice" (*pilihan hukum*), which in this case meant the right to take an inheritance dispute to either the religious or civil court, be removed from the statute in the name of "legal certainty" (*kepastian hukum*) (Sabrie 1990:179). The government reaffirmed the principle of legal choice in its reply (Szadjali 1991a:57–58, 63), and emphasized legal choice in the bill's appended clarification, which limits the religious court's jurisdiction over inheritance cases to those where the plaintiffs wish that the division be done according to Islamic law.[16] The argument that the 1989 law threatened the unity of law clearly touched a nerve. Long after the bill had passed, as it did that year, jurists writing in government publications have continued to emphasize the "legal-unity-in-diversity" theme that underwrote the state's case in 1989.

The executive and judicial branches continue to overlap in their control of the religious courts. The Ministry of Religion continues to compile and send to the courts collections of cases called *Himpunan Yurisprudensi*, and to feel justified in doing so, but somewhat defensive, as in comments by Wahyu Widiana, the head of the Directorate of Religious Justice, in a conversation with me in 2000.[17] Wahyu Widiana explained the tasks carried out by his office, and that they included compiling these decisions.

We began in 1978 because the Supreme Court was not doing it, but if they start to do it some day then we will stop and let them proceed. We also compile laws; it is the task of the Court, but if we waited for them . . . We also hold training sessions for judges, but we use people from the Court, especially as now there are three judges on the Court who used to work here. We do not meddle in jurisprudence when we talk to people in the regions, but talk about organizational matters.

Wahyu kept the same tone when I asked him about the case analyses in his office's publication, *Mimbar Hukum*.

[16] In the bill as enacted, what had been a clarification to the article on inheritance, article 49 (1), was moved up to become a head note to the clarification as a whole. It directs heirs to decide which law they wish applied before they approach a court.

[17] His official title is Direktur Pembinaan Badan Peradilan Agama, Departemen Agama; his office oversees the administrative side of the religious court system.

We do not analyze cases; we choose them and then it is academics who analyze them, such as Satriya Effendi. So what if they have a different opinion from the Supreme Court? Of course, others might also conclude that the Court's opinion was not right, but we never influence the Court's decisions; we only take cases that are completed and give a scientific perspective (*wacananya secara ilmiah*).

The Court's perspective is reflected by comments made in an interview in 2000 by Achmad Djunaeni, the Director of Religious Civil Law at the Supreme Court, and thus Wahyu's counterpart. "Frankly, when the Department does not agree about a case they discuss it in *Mimbar Hukum*, basing their argument on shariat, on this or that madhhab. The Supreme Court judges read these case analyses; they serve as material for reflection (*wawasan berpikir*), but the judges stick to the Compilation. Usually Satriya Effendi analyzes the cases, from a fiqh point of view, adding other elements, that is good, [it makes for] an opposition party."

Positivizing sharî'a

Several years after succeeding with its 1989 courts bill, the government set out to add content to the legal machinery it had created. This step threatened to be much more controversial, in that it recalled the parallel effort in 1973, and threatened to produce vigorous objections from Muslim groups.

In 1973 the New Order government had encountered stiff resistance because it was perceived as arrogating to itself the right to define what counts as a valid marriage or divorce, a right that some felt belonged to God, not the state. To avoid similar potential disruptions, the government decided not to risk presenting a bill to Parliament, but instead introduced its Indonesian Compilation of Islamic Law to the public as a presidential instruction.[18] As its chief architect, Justice Busthanul Arifin, remarked to me in 2000: "At that time it was all we could do; a lot of civil servants, Muslims, and army were afraid." In the Indonesian legal system, a presidential instruction has lower standing than a statute, but is enforced by the courts. Its precise legal standing came under dispute after Suharto's fall, because it had been used to promulgate a number of oppressive measures. But this particular instruction had been issued at the peak of Suharto's efforts to attract Muslim support, indeed, just before he left on the pilgrimage to Mecca, an action hailed at the time as a sign of the government's new positive attitude toward Islam.

The Compilation did contain a number of significant innovations, which only gradually became apparent (and to which I turn below). It contains clauses that formalize practices already accepted among jurists (such as the equal division of common marital property) and other clauses that were intended to change

---

[18] *Instruksi Presiden*, Inpres, No. 1/1991.

local practices (such as the treatment of orphaned grandchildren). But it also constituted a claim to have squared the circle of state control and ulama independence, in a fashion typical of the New Order. The commentators and proponents of the Compilation have presented it as both the result of a consensus among Indonesian ulama, and positive, state-issued law. As the consensus (*ijma'*) of Indonesian Muslim jurists, it is supposed to represent the "living law" of Indonesia. But its state-legal force derives from its promulgation as a presidential decree. The presentation of the code has thus come to signify both a particular way of ordering Islamic law and a particular process of legitimizing that ordering.

The Compilation is published as a small-format handbook containing the code, which resembles a civil law code with its short paragraphs and sections, followed by a history of Islam in Indonesia. The historical section culminates in a lengthy, detailed account of how jurists came to a consensus regarding the Compilation.[19] To summarize: in 1985, a drafting committee of Supreme Court justices and Ministry of Religion officials, headed by Justice Busthanul Arifin, chose forty-one Islamic legal texts to be studied, and distributed them to the seven State Islamic Institutes, located in various parts of the country, for their commentaries. The committee then interviewed 166 ulama, in ten cities, on the "living fiqh" in their region (Abdurrahman 1992:43), a concept that extended the Supreme Court's "living adat law" idea into the realm of fiqh. They also read cases from the Indonesian Islamic courts, compared laws in other Muslim countries, and held a massive workshop of jurists in a Jakarta auditorium in 1988, which prepared and, as a body, accepted a draft code. The handbook lists the name of every jurist involved at each stage of the process. And, in case anyone were to feel left out, participants who wrote about the process (for example, Daud Ali 1993; Abdullah 1994) said that they also consulted the opinions of the Council of Ulama, Muhammadiyah, Nahdlatul Ulama, "and others."

Top-down "consensus"

The particular form taken by this widely circulated history reveals its purpose: to publicize the involvement of these jurists in an "Indonesian consensus (ijma')," publicity that is clearly intended to preempt future disagreements by any of these jurists. In Islamic legal terms, ijma' (Arabic *ijmâ'*) is the "consensus" or "agreement" of the learned community on a legal matter, and it is recognized in treatises on the foundations of jurisprudence (*usul al-fiqh*) that constitute the

---

[19] See, for example, the account of the process in the 1997 edition of the handbook (Departemen Agama 1996/97:117–74). A virtually identical account has been published in a number of official and semi-official journals and books (for example, Abdurrahman 1992).

four major Sunnî schools of law as one of the sources of law that follows after the Qur'ân and hadîth.[20]

Soon after its promulgation, the Compilation began to be cited as the basis for decisions, supplementing or replacing citations from books of classic fiqh and sometimes overriding local social norms. In an October 1991 decision, for example, the Aceh appellate Islamic court cited the Compilation when it ruled that joint, or marital property should be divided equally between husband and wife (or their heirs) in the event of divorce or death of one of the parties. This decision reversed a 1990 lower court ruling that had affirmed local practices of unequal property division in favor of the husband or his heirs (Aulawi 1994).

Despite its quick application by judges, the legal status of the Compilation remains unclear. It contains something that looks like a statute, although it is not one, and it claims to contain all the Islamic law that the judge or other state employee needs to know to carry out his or her appointed task. But is it a law? The Ministry of Religion ordered all government employees to rely on it "to the extent possible" and proclaimed it to be the law of the land, designed to bring "unification and certainty to the law, especially among the people."[21] But others disagree. Former Supreme Court justice Bismar Siregar commented that the Compilation was not a law book, and judges should not hesitate to interpret on their own (through ijtihâd; *Pelita*, 8 January 1992). Yet Busthanul Arifin claimed that "an Inpres is a legislative product, along with statutes and so forth. So we all consider the Compilation to be *undang-undang* (laws, statutes); if there is a case before a court, it applied; it is positive law (*hukum positip*)" (interview, 2000).

H. Wahyu Widiana, the official in charge of religious justice at the Ministry of Religion, admitted that "experts, even within the Religious Justice section, differ on whether an Inpres can be a basis for law. Some judges use it, others do not, and their reason is because it is still only an Inpres; they say that they are not required to follow an Inpres, only a statute. The Inpres only ordered the Minister of Religion to distribute the Compilation, and it is part of the executive branch" (interview, 2000).

The state's case for the *Islamic* validity of the Compilation, a different matter altogether from its legality, is based on the idea that it merely codifies what was already present as a popular consensus. Here, for example, is the editorial opinion of the journal *Mimbar Hukum*, the official organ of the Ministry of Religion's Directorate of Religious Justice, in a special issue (No. 24, 1996) on the Compilation, which recalls for the reader the idea of "living law" that already had been applied to adat:

---

[20] For a more detailed analysis of the justifications of consensus put forth for the Compilation, see Bowen (1999a), and for an examination of the place of ijmâ' in jurisprudence see Hallaq (1997) and Vogel (1993).

[21] *Keputusan Departemen Agama*, 22 July 1991; Departemen Agama 1996/7:iii.

In its essence the Compilation is the *living law* [English] that has been voluntarily applied for centuries and that has satisfied those who carried it out. It is not going too far to say that the Compilation is the legitimation of legal practices carried out by the Muslim community since Islam itself entered Indonesia. The Muslim community can be proud that a portion of Islamic law has become positive law in their own country. (Sabrie 1996:5)

In other words, Islam has become the adat of Muslims, and has been rendered positive, that is, enacted in codified form, by the state. This living law is unified, even if the fiqh, the jurisprudential utterances of diverse jurists, has been disparate:

In contrast to Islamic jurisprudence that remains abstract and full of contradictions of opinion – because that is in the end the characteristic of any fiqh – the Compilation is concrete, codifying, unifying, and shielded from doctrinal contraditions. The Compilation may be spoken of as the result of ijtihâd, in the fiqh sense, but it is better described as the result of the Indonesian people's *ijtihâd jama'i* (collective reasoning) based on legal practices and on the culture of the Muslim community (*umma*) that is enspirited by Islamic law and faith. (Sabrie 1996:6)

Elsewhere the contributors make clear that by "Indonesian people's collective reasoning" they also mean that the Compilation represents a legal consensus, an "*ijma' ulama Indonesia'*" (consensus of Indonesian jurists) (Matardi 1996:34). If the idea of "living law" taps into the nationalist strain of legal-cultural thinking, then that of ijma' provides the code with an Islamic-law foundation.

What is meant by "consensus" is left unanswered, except insofar as the process that is laboriously detailed in the handbook is supposed to exemplify it. One could ask whether consensus was achieved, and whether participants' preferences changed as a result of deliberation, whether minority views could have been publicly admitted, and whether the greater participation of women would have changed the outcome. Consensus as ijma' is limited to the learned community, and thus the structures that control who receives the education and credentials of a jurist preselect those who get to participate. Yet many jurists are themselves engaged in local deliberative processes in which women freely participate and people do change their minds, and that do seem deliberative in the modern political sense. One can anticipate that the principle implicit in the compiling process, that sampling a wide range of opinions from each of the many historical communities of the country is good, may be cited in the future for other political or religious purposes.

Contesting ijma'?

How are we to consider the claims to ijma'? Probably most jurists find the Compilation acceptable, as Andrée Feillard (1995:293) found in Java, and I have found in Jakarta and in the Gayo highlands. Some of the major innovations in family law already had been made by statute; the measures that equalized divorce proceedings and stipulated shares of common property already were contained in the 1974 Marriage Law. In general, the Compilation took a conservative line – retaining the unequal ratio of estate shares, distinguishing between biological and adopted children, and disallowing the sale of waqf property – and thereby satisfied jurists belonging to the socially conservative (and largest) Muslim organization Nahdlatul Ulama (Feillard 1995:291–93). These clauses in the Compilation also accord well with positions taken by jurists who emphasize the importance of staying close to scripture, and who in other contexts are labeled "radical," such as writers for the journal *Media Dakwah*. True, some jurists, lawyers, and feminists would have liked the Compilation to go further in advocating religious change, for example in equalizing the ratio of inheritance shares. But the energies of many women's legal advocacy groups are focused on securing the rights already won, especially women's property rights. Most consider the absence of additional reform measures in the Compilation as relatively unimportant, except insofar as its publication pushes social practices away from more gender-equal inheritance regimes and towards fiqh itself (Feillard 1997:93–98).

Even in the celebratory *Mimbar Hukum* volume, however, there are signs of dissent regarding some of the innovations found in the Compilation. "Some traditional jurists," writes one legal scholar (Ilmie 1996:24), consider elements of the Compilation "not in accord with teachings to be found in books of fiqh." These disputes, as I have had heard them in Jakarta and elsewhere, are not about an arrogation of authority by the state via the Compilation. Judges have grown used to working in a system where their decisions may be overruled on appeal, and where the Ministry of Religious assumes a fiqh oversight role. Nor is the cultural form of the Compilation, that of codified law, in dispute. Religious judges have long couched their decisions in a civil code format that compels them to provide specific rule-like citations as the basis for their reasoning. The history of cultural and legal practices that preceded publication of the Compilation makes its cultural form and the source of its authority less at issue than might have been the case had it appeared fifty years earlier, or than has been the case in certain other countries.[22]

What dissent there is surrounds the extent to which the Compilation gives explicit rules on controversial matters. It is here where one sees most clearly the

---

[22] It is in the sequences of legal and cultural innovations that the experiences of Muslim societies differ. It may be that codification had the greatest impact when it was introduced against a backdrop of less Europeanized judicial practices, as in nineteenth-century Ottoman societies or even contemporary Yemen (Messick 1993). A more subtle shift involves colonial misunderstandings of the Moroccan *'amal* collections of judicial decisions as a sort of precedential jurisprudence (Buskens 1993; Rosen 1989:46–47). These examples suggest that one cannot read directly from the cultural form (here, "code") to the social effect without knowledge of these historical contexts.

tension between two ideas advanced by its apologists: the "expressivist" view that the Compilation merely makes explicit the living law, and the "positivist" view that the Compilation enacts new law. Indeed, the very idea of ijma' contains this contradiction, for if one jurist dissents, does one have consensus? This tension produced a shift in state rhetoric about the Compilation over the course of the 1990s, from claiming that it reproduced widespread Indonesian interpretations of Islamic law, to emphasizing that it brought in elements from adat, and from the prescriptive, bilateral notion of adat championed by Hazairin.

The plight of orphaned grandchildren

Two substantive matters have raised controversy among jurists: the fate of orphaned grandchildren, and whether daughters may inherit the entire estate in the absence of sons. The first issue concerns grandchildren whose linking parent died before the grandparent. Classical jurisprudence, including Indonesian practice, stated that in this case the parent's death blocked the grandchildren's access to a share of the grandparent's estate. The Compilation (article 185) gives them the shares their parent(s) would have received; they act as the substitutes for the deceased parent(s). Jurists defend this change in the name of equality: why should some descendants inherit and others not? (Daud Ali 1993; Harahap 1995a, b, c). However, before the Compilation took effect Indonesian judges had followed classical jurisprudence, and it would, therefore, be difficult to declare this provision to be part of a jurisprudential consensus. Nor could it be said to enact "living law" except in the very general sense of enacting general Indonesian values.

Consequently, in deciding cases, judges have ruled that this provision of the Compilation *only* has the status of positive law, with legal force only after 1991, the year the Compilation took effect. Indeed, in a 1993 case analyzed in the very issue of *Mimbar Hukum* that celebrates the Compilation, the Jakarta religious appeals court overturned a lower court decision awarding an estate share on the basis of the Compilation's replacement heir clause. The appeals court ruled that because the deceased died in 1985, six years before the Compilation took effect, the law to be applied was the older understanding of fiqh, under which orphaned grandchildren did not inherit. The jurist analyzing the case agreed with this decision on grounds that "it was the Compilation of Islamic Law that 'Islamicized' the concept of the predeceased heir" (Zein 1996:112). This quasi-official reading of the Compilation conflicts sharply with the editorial position described above.[23]

---

[23] For a discussion of the means by which predeceased heirs have been awarded shares in other Muslim societies, see Coulson (1971:143–58).

While I do not know how representative this case is, I did talk to one of the most independent-minded and well-read ulama in Takèngën about this specific issue in 1994 and again in 2000. In 1994, Tengku Ali Jadun had not yet read the Compilation, but his friend Muhammad Daud Ali had been one of the ulama working to produce it in Jakarta. At that point he still relied on his reading of fiqh books in resolving the many inheritance disputes that came to him, as a private religious scholar. In the course of a conversation in 1994 about the Bona case already discussed he mentioned the difficulties of giving wealth to one child.

Hibah should be for cases like this: if one of my children dies, then his children get no part of the warisan. So I might hibah something to them so they get something.

JB: But the Compilation talks about the "replacement heirs."

Yes, I haven't read the Compilation yet; I know that Daud Ali and Ismael Suny worked very hard on it. But according to the fiqh books I have read, the children don't receive any warisan if the parent dies first.

In 2000, however, when I asked about the Compilation, he responded that "I often speak to people about it. They accept it because it's the law. For example, *patah titi* (the bridge is broken) used to be Gayo adat, too.[24] The ulama had said that orphaned grandchildren could not inherit because you inherited from your parents. But now the whole approach is different; it is in terms of humanitarianism (*prikemanusiaan*); those who are orphaned especially need the inheritance." This change in Tengku Ali Jadun's way of speaking about orphaned grandchildren suggests a change in legal culture that may have been brought about in part by promulgation of the Compilation through the courts and the local Majelis Ulama organizations. Of course, Ali Jadun's friendship with Muhammad Daud Ali also may have led to a greater acceptance of the new rule. But it reminds us that "local" and "national" are not sharply separated levels of reasoning, that each shapes the other.

May daughters inherit all?

One innovation of the Compilation that took several years to make itself felt was the provision that even a single daughter will inherit the entire estate if both her parents have died. Other heirs, for example the brothers and sisters of the deceased, are "blocked" (*terhijab*) by her from receiving any share. This change was motivated by the Indonesian cultural model of bilateral kinship that lies beneath the Compilation, but the Supreme Court and supporters of the

---

[24] Recall the importance of this phrase in the legal reasoning developed in the 1960s by the Takèngën civil court judge Abubakar Porang.

Compilation have tried to justify it in fiqh terms, as an acceptable interpretation of the Qur'ân.

This provision ran against established Indonesian practice and generally accepted interpretations of the relevant fiqh books. Debates over this section turn on a passage in the Qur'ân (4:176), which declares that: "God ordains concerning collateral relatives that if a man dies without a child (*walad*) and leaves a sister, she takes half of the inheritance; and he will be her heir if she dies without a child. If there are two sisters, they take two-thirds of the inheritance. If the collaterals include both males and females, then the male takes a share equivalent to that of two females."

Early Muslim jurists interpreted this passage to mean that brothers and sisters inherit from each other: half the estate if there is only one sibling, or two-thirds, collectively, if there are two or more. And the internal division of that two-thirds is to be two portions for each brother and one for each sister. But this all occurred only if the deceased left behind no children. (If there were children then the siblings could inherit as residuaries.)

And yet Muhammad evidently did not follow this rule. In deciding cases brought to him, he allowed brothers or sisters to inherit as sharers when there was a daughter surviving the deceased.[25] This practice appears to be in confict with the Qur'ânic text. Now, Sunnî jurists did and do recognize the principle that the practice of the Prophet Muhammad, his Sunna, could abrogate a text of the Qur'ân, but this is highly undesirable, and so jurists have always tried to reconcile conflicting texts, often through creative reinterpretations of a word's meaning.

In this case a reconciliation was found by translating the word "walad," which in all other Qur'ânic uses refers to a child, male or female, as "male child" in this and only this verse.[26] The resultant set of rules is as follows: if the deceased left a son or a father then sisters, like brothers, are entirely excluded from inheriting. If the deceased left no children and no brothers then full sisters inherit as "sharers," one sister taking one-half the estate, two or more sharing two-thirds. If the deceased left daughters, sisters, and brothers, then the sisters inherit as "residuaries by another," together with ("by") their brothers.[27] This

---

[25] Muhammad allowed a sister to inherit when there was a daughter and granddaughter: the daughter received her one-half as sharer, the granddaughter was given one-sixth – she was considered as like a daughter and her one-sixth completed the two-thirds that several daughters share – and the sister received the residue of one-third. On this history see Coulson (1971:65–73).

[26] Early jurists also had to interpret "collateral" here as referring to agnatic or full siblings but not uterine ones. This way of reading the word was motivated by the demands of creating a consistent system of rules, because a different verse, Qur'ân 4:12, appeared to contradict the verse at hand unless the word interpreted *here* to refer to agnatic or full siblings was interpreted *there* to mean uterine siblings.

[27] However, if the deceased left daughters and sisters, but no brothers, then the sisters cannot sit in that category so they move into still another category, the truly residual one of "accompanying residuaries."

set of rather complicated rules appears to be historically based on decisions made by the Prophet Muhammad. Jurists then "back-translated" the Qur'ân to match the Prophet's practice (see Coulson 1971:65–66). But there continued to be disagreement about this translation of walad, and the disagreement among early jurists provided some room for subsequent reinterpretations of the rules within the confines of fiqh.

Such has been the strategy taken by backers of the Compilation and by the Supreme Court. The judges and jurists have argued that their innovation is entirely due to the correct reading of the single word walad in the Qur'ânic verse quoted above. The word once was thought to refer only to sons, goes the argument, such that even if there were daughters, the siblings would inherit. The correct reading, however, is that walad refers to children, daughters as well as sons, and thus if there are daughters, they "block" the siblings.

On a number of occasions during the second half of the 1990s the Supreme Court affirmed the new rule.[28] In its first major decision on this issue in 1995, the Supreme Court overruled the appeals court from Mataram which had followed established Indonesian jurisprudence. The Supreme Court did not cite the Compilation, only gave as its opinion that "as long as there still are children, whether male or female, then the right to inherit of those who have relationships by blood to the deceased, except for parents, husband, and wife are closed off (terhijab)." They then stated that this opinion "is in accord with the opinion of Ibnu Abbas, an expert in *tafsir* (commentary on the Qur'ân) among the Prophet's *sahabat* (companions), when he rendered the term 'walad' in ayat 176 of an-Nisa, saying that it was to be understood as including sons and daughters."[29]

Mimbar Hukum's regular case analyst, Satria Effendi M. Zein (1997:112), pointed out that although the Court's argument was acceptable, it "does not definitively refute the decision of the Mataram appeals court, which itself is in accord with the majority of the Prophet's companions." Two judges writing articles in the same journal two years later (Baidlowi 1999; Syafe'i 1999) disagreed even with Dr. Satria's qualified acceptance of the Supreme Court's reasoning. They each argued that Ibn Abbas did not intend that the deceased's brothers be blocked from inheriting by a daughter, only his or her sisters. Syafe'i (1999) goes on to argue that in Ibn Abbas's view, even when there are daughters and sisters but no brothers, other heirs, the *ashabah* category or "residual heirs," would inherit one-half the estate, and the daughter only one-half. The majority of jurists held that the brothers should not be blocked, and, continues Syafe'i, no one took walad to mean only sons. To rub salt in the wound, Syafe'i added (1999:8) that it is only Shi'ites who advanced the opinion later embraced by the Court.

---

[28] Among such Supreme Court cases are MA 86/1994 (decided July 1995), MA 184/1995 (decided September 1996), and MA 327/1997 (decided February 1998).

[29] Text of decision 86/1994, as found in *Mimbar Hukum* 30, 1997:150.

In the opinions of officials at the Supreme Court and in the Ministry of Religion, many first-instance judges have continued to judge cases based on the older jurisprudence, allowing brothers and sisters of the deceased to share the estate with a daughter. Judges in Aceh have told me that many judges and ulama in that province also oppose the change. H. Achmad Djunaeni, the director of the religious justice section at the Supreme Court, had the 1995 Supreme Court decision placed into the journal of record, *Varia Peradilan*; all the judges thus should know of the Court's decision. "All the judges subscribe to the publication, but perhaps they have followed sharî'a law instead" (interview, 2000).

This admission makes clear that the Court and the formulators of the Compilation were motivated by considerations other than those of fiqh, despite the efforts to revive Ibn Abbas as a source of law. By 1999, contributors to *Mimbar Hukum* were beginning to make more explicit the importance of Hazairin's model of gender-equal, bilateral kinship in moulding the Compilation. In an issue (vol. 44) partially devoted to the matter of the daughter's share, several first-instance religious court judges (Baidlowi 1999, Kasrori 1999, Nuzul 1999) contributed articles showing how both Hazairin and the Compilation diverged from the majority of ulama, in Indonesia and elsewhere, and that these divergences were always intended to privilege the direct descendants, male and female, over collateral relatives.

In Takèngën, in 2000, Tengku Ali Jadun spoke up in favor of the change.

Now that we are in the age of women's rights, we can't deny all the inheritance to daughters. People can be made to see that it is right to be fair. A woman came to me who was the only child, and so now could claim all the inheritance, but her mother's brother's son claimed some, under the older rule. I just told her what the law was and let her decide. She went away and came back sometime later and I asked her what she had done. She said she had given him some, that this felt right.

This analysis of jurisprudence thus returns us to the theories of the law scholar Hazairin, whose teachings shaped the positive law version of Islam, and to ideas of gender equality, which, as Ali Jadun's reference to "the age of women's rights" suggests, are gaining in acceptance as a normative base for reformulating fiqh. The culture of Islamic jurisprudence requires that jurists continue to present, albeit haltingly and partially, a fiqh-type justification for the radical reshaping of law. Indeed, if one looks at the law books consulted in formulating the Compilation one notes that, although they cover several legal schools, not just the Shâfi'î school dominant in Indonesia, they do not include the works of Hazairin nor those of Hasbi ash-Shiddieqy, the authors who proposed developing an "Indonesian madhhab." This omission plausibly was intended to reassure religious scholars that the end product would not diverge from traditional fiqh, *even as* the model of kinship formulated by Hazairin was providing the basis for the final version of the code.

The state has attempted to create a schema of Islamic law that contains within it the conditions of its own legitimacy – a bootstrapped fiqh. Both the form taken by Islamic law, a unique set of rules to be applied throughout the nation, and its proclaimed basis of legitimacy, that it merely renders explicit a popular legal consciousness, parallel the form and legitimacy claims associated with the Supreme Court's idea of a "living adat law." Neither corresponds to local perceptions of adat or fiqh, which are based on independent judgments. Adat draws its legitimacy, its normativity, from the experience or memory of practices specific to a place or to an ethnic group. Fiqh is legitimate only insofar as it is proclaimed by persons considered to be learned in the law, religious scholars and local *ulama*. The Islamic legitimacy of this bootstrapped fiqh continues to depend on the acquiescence of those scholars, but the increasingly recognized idea of international norms of "women's rights" continues to shape their responses.

9   Gender equality in the family?

When couples separate, the moral and material issues of gender equality receive their hardest test. Even under conditions of legal equality, a broad range of *de facto* inequalities can operate, including inequalities in access to legal resources, unequal distribution of marital wealth, unequal rights to initiate divorce proceedings, and inequalities in the finding of fault or moral responsibility. Islamic law would seem to be most severely tested here, because it formulates different categories of divorce or annulment for men and women. But, as others have shown in other Muslim settings (Hirsch 1998; Mir-Hosseini 1993; Moors 1995), knowledge of women's and men's outcomes in divorce disputes requires a study of how law is formulated, interpreted, and applied. As we saw in chapter 4, Islamic courts have generally acted to restore to women the shares of inheritance denied them in village settlement processes, *even though* on the surface the Islamic legal principles appear to be less favorable to women than do the principles of Gayo adat. Is the result comparable in the case of divorce and divorce settlements? To answer the question we return to the Takèngën courts, before ending the chapter with current national debates over polygamy.

Towards equal agency in divorce

Long-standing norms of divorce in Muslim Indonesia were recognizably part of the classical Islamic legal tradition. These norms made divorce a very one-sided affair. A man could "repudiate" (*talaq*) his wife without providing any reasons. He did so under any circumstance he might choose, and did not need to communicate the event to a judge or other official. He owed little to her thereafter, beyond three months of support, and he retained custody of their older children. He could repudiate his wife and reconcile afterward with her twice; after the third such event, she had to remarry and divorce before a third reconciliation could take place.

A wife seeking divorce, by contrast, had to convince a judge that her husband had committed one of several acts that qualified as grounds for an annulment (*fasakh*). These grounds included cruelty, failure to provide material support, or prolonged absence from the home. Islamic law also provided for divorce by mutual consent, referred to as *khul* or as *mubarâh*, if the wife was willing to pay a sum of money to her husband.

The 1974 Marriage Law was intended to give greater power to wives by placing the institution of divorce under the supervision of the religious courts. Under the law, only a judge can authorize a divorce. Technically, the judge deems the talaq to have been pronounced on behalf of a woman claimant, or permits the husband to pronounce the talaq if he is the claimant. The judge may grant this permission either because of long-standing conflict between the couple (*syiqoq*), or because either party has committed one of five things: adultery or addiction; desertion for two years or longer; imprisonment for five years or longer; treating the other cruelly; or becoming unable to fulfill marital duties because of a disability or disease. Katz and Katz (1978:310) claim that four years after the 1974 law went into effect the divorce rate among Muslims had dropped by 70 percent, although some number of husbands may have carried out divorces on their own without reporting them to courts or the local religious officials.

We should exercise caution in drawing conclusions about changes in marriage or divorce patterns. One would expect that the *reported* divorce rate would decline even if *actual* rates of divorce remained the same, because at least some men would have continued to divorce in the traditional manner without reporting their action. On the other hand, making divorces more difficult would tend to decrease their incidence. One suspects that the number of "completed" or definitive divorces would have been relatively unaffected by the legal change, perhaps rising or falling for other reasons, whereas the number of "one talaq" divorces that later lead to reconciliation would have dropped.

Impressions gained in Takèngën confirm this model. In 2000, Judge Anshary of the Takèngën religious court said that overall there were increases in divorces after the 1974 Marriage Law and again after the 1989 bill, and that this was not because of a breakdown in social life, but because of greater legal awareness.

People are coming to court more often, rather than just declaring divorce in the village.

JB: Yes, but are there people doing that, pronouncing the talaq in the village and not coming to court?

One or two, yes. Sometimes the man will come here after having pronounced the talaq three times in the village, and he will ask for a divorce in court to try and make the divorce legal, saying that his wife did this or that. But we refuse the lawsuit, on grounds that the husband already pronounced the talaq. But of course the couple still is not divorced legally, so often the wife later comes to us and asks to be divorced and then we accept her request. We do this to raise legal awareness, so that people stop doing this. (Interview, 2000)

(See Table 9.1 for confirmation of the claim of a rise in divorce rates.)

In any case, divorce rates are notoriously sensitive to economic changes, in ways that are not generally predictable. In Takèngën in the 1980s, judges said that divorces increased as incomes rose from coffee trading, because more men were traveling to trade, and were more often unfaithful. But in the late 1990s, divorce rates were said to soar in those parts of the country hardest hit by the economic crisis. The head of the religious court in Tegal, Central Java, claimed that the divorce rate had risen ten-fold in the period 1997–99, for much the same reason given in Takèngën for the rise during prosperous times: more men traveled to find work, and some stayed away for long periods (*Agence France-Presse* online, 26 February 1999).

The 1974 law also restricted polygamy. The law stipulates that a man has to prove one of three grounds for taking a second wife: that the first wife cannot carry out her conjugal duties, suffers from an incurable disease, or cannot bear a child (in which last case her permission must be obtained). Her views must be sought whatever the reason given, and he has to show that he has the means to provide in just fashion for both wives. Seeking this permission is costly and time-consuming. Furthermore, 1983 regulations (PP 10/1983) require that all civil servants obtain the written approval of their superiors to marry or divorce, and submit that approval to the religious court.

Polygamy accounted for only 5 percent of marriages before the law; Katz and Katz (1978:311–12) argue that the law reduced its frequency still further. They also suggest that the bargaining power of the wife may have increased because the husband can no longer so easily threaten to divorce his wife or take another. In the long term the greatest effect of the law may be that it guarantees women the right to sue for divorce or marriage annulment.

The law also allowed the religious courts to divide joint property, defined as all property acquired during a marriage, and said that both parties have the right to dispose of joint property but only with the consent of the other. Classical Islamic law did not recognize joint property, or alimony, only requiring that a man provide maintenance to a divorced women for the three-month waiting (*idda*) period, or during up to two years of a nursing period. The provision's supporters (e.g. Aulawi 1994) excuse the omission as understandable given the social conditions at the time of the early Islamic jurists, but argue that today women are in the workforce, and that Islamic law should draw on these new ways of life.

These new tasks greatly increased the case load of the religious courts – about four times between 1974 and 1976 – and led to a doubling of the number of judges and clerks during the same period (Katz and Katz 1978:317). However, the government tried to take back via the implementing regulations some of what it had passed in the statute. In Indonesian legal practice, a statute is a dead letter until the executive branch issues implementing regulations. When President Suharto did issue the regulations for the Marriage Law in 1975, he left out regulations to implement the statutory rules giving the religious courts jurisdiction over child custody and support, or the division of joint property, and the Supreme Court ruled that these areas therefore remained in the jurisdiction of the civil courts (Cammack 1989:65–66). However, in practice Islamic courts rule on all settlement issues arising from divorce.

Equivalent categories

The divorce reforms stipulated the conditions under which men and women could initiate those divorce actions provided for in Islamic law. For this reason, men continue to divorce by their action of pronouncing the talaq utterance, and women continue to divorce by asking a judge to declare that the divorce has occurred. And yet, to be recognized by the state, men and women alike must have judicial approval for a divorce to take place; they must provide the same degree of proof that the divorce is justified; and the divorce must occur in court, in the presence of the judge and the two parties. Thus, major changes in the letter of the law, at least, have occurred in the practice of divorce through state legislation, but within the compass of Islamic jurisprudence and the Islamic courts.

In his petition for *izin talaq* ("permission to divorce"), a husband must state his grounds for requesting a divorce, which are specified in the 1974 Marriage Law (and again in the 1992 Islamic Law Compilation).[1] The permissible grounds are the same for men and women, and include an absence of over two years without permission or a "valid reason"; committing bodily harm to the other party; infidelity, drunkenness, or gambling; converting from Islam to another religion; incurring a jail term of five years or more; or, the most frequently invoked reason, long-standing disputes and quarrels that prove the couple to have what in US courts would be called "irreconcilable differences." If, after the court hearing, the judge approves the husband's petition, then a date is set for him to pronounce the talaq. The date must be at least fourteen days after the initial hearings to give the wife the maximum permitted time to begin an appeal. Both the husband and wife must attend the second hearing, at which the husband, in the presence of the judge, pronounces the divorce utterance. If it is the wife who requests the divorce, the procedures are the same, except that on the post-hearing date set by the judge, it is he who pronounces the divorce.

In Takèngën, as elsewhere, the religious court was given an entirely new role by the 1974 law. In the early 1990s, the court decided about 200 divorce cases per year; by the end of the decade that number had doubled. Table 9.1 shows the divorce cases decided by the Takèngën religious court in 1993, and in the

---

[1] The permissible grounds for divorce are listed first in the government regulations accompanying the 1974 Marriage Law (article 19, PP 9/1975) and again in the Islamic Law Compilation of 1992 (article 116). The latter adds, significantly for Jakarta and some other areas but not for Aceh, conversion from Islam to another religion as grounds for divorce.

Table 9.1. *Divorces granted by the Takèngën religious court, by type, in 1993 and January–June 1999*

Type of case	Number of cases		
	1993		January–June 1999
husband's petition (talaq):		99	80
wife's petition, total for all categories:		102	91
breakdown for 1993	(ta'lik talaq	66)	
	(fasakh	34)	
	(syiqoq	2)	

Note: There were no reconciliation cases.
Source: Court records.

first half of 1999. The table shows the three categories of decisions in cases initiated by the wife and gives the total for those cases.

By 1994, the terms used to designate types of divorce had been replaced in the practice of the Takèngën court by terms that suggest the equivalence of divorce suits brought by men and women: cases initiated by the husband are now known as *cerai talaq*; those brought by the wife as *cerai gugat* (divorce by litigation). In the first half (January to July) of 1999, eighty cases of cerai talaq had been decided by the court, and ninety-one cases of cerai gugat – in other words, about twice the annual rate as that of 1992 and 1993 (and despite the unrest in Aceh at this time).

Despite the equivalence of grounds for divorce, these legal changes have not erased the gender-based difference in procedure stipulated by fiqh. The court continues to grant a woman a petition but permits a man to utter words that constitute the event of divorce. Indeed, those words remain legally crucial to establishing that a divorce has taken place. A court may not infer the intent to divorce from a man's actions, as Judge Kasim of the Takèngën court discovered:

I can only think of one case where we lost before the Supreme Court in recent times, and that was a divorce case. The husband sometimes lost control of himself, and at those times he might hit his wife, but when he came to himself he was very good to her. Well, on one occasion when he was in control of himself he took her to her brothers and said: "Here, once I took her away from you and now I return her to you." And this is just how it should be done according to Gayo adat. But he did not actually say, "I divorce you" as the *ikrar* (divorce utterance) should state.

The wife petitioned us for a divorce. We said that his actions in returning her were the same as an ikrar and declared the first talaq to have been declared by the husband's action. But he challenged us. He lost in the appellate court, but won in cassation, because he had not pronounced the exact words of the pronouncement. At issue was not whether we could grant her a fasakh divorce, but whether we were correct in claiming that in effect he had uttered the pronouncement, had himself initiated the divorce. (Interview, 1994)

Divorce initiated by women

Even though the categories are now reduced to two, the cerai talaq and cerai gugat, if the wife initiates the divorce there remain three legal pathways she can follow. She may argue that the husband committed an act that activates a talaq (*ta'lik talaq*); she may ask the judge to grant an annulment (fasakh); or she may argue that the couple has irreconcilable differences (the *syiqoq* procedure).

An extension of a general Islamic contractual understanding of marriage, the ta'lik talaq is a kind of "automatic talaq" agreed to before the marriage.[2] In Indonesia today, when a Muslim couple marries, the bride's guardian may ask the groom to read aloud a statement printed on the reverse side (or an additional page) of the marriage contract stipulating that the husband shall be considered to have divorced his wife (through a talaq) if he leaves or neglects her for six months consecutively, fails to provide maintenance for three months consecutively, or physically abuses her. The conditions were made uniform throughout Indonesia by decree of the Minister of Religion in 1955, but wives sometimes have added conditions of their own, in particular that the husband's taking of a second wife without permission from the first shall be grounds for divorce (Lev 1972a:138, 143–45; Manan 1995). After the wedding, the local Religious Affairs Officer (*Kuakec, Kantor Urusan Agama Kecamatan*) has the couple sign the book, and thereafter it serves as a marriage certificate. By signing, the groom signifies that he did indeed recite the list of conditions at the wedding and that he understands the written text. The book specifies that if he commits one of these acts his wife can go to court and pay a symbolic sum, stipulated in the book as Rp 50, which serves as a token of the groom (his *'iwadl*). At that moment the first talaq automatically occurs.

The frequency of reciting the ta'lik talaq varies in Indonesia: Takèngën religious court staff who also had served on the Acehnese northern coast reported that grooms there rarely recited the list of conditions. I was told that they were unwilling to do so because many of the men spend long periods of time away from their villages pursuing trade, and these long absences could be invoked as invoking the ta'lik. But "saying the ta'lik" is nearly universal in the Gayo highlands, and the Takèngën judges routinely find for the wife in such cases.

A wife may also file for divorce on the grounds of fasakh, which since 1974 invokes the very same list of offenses that give the husband grounds for divorce. These offenses also overlap with the specific provisions of the ta'lik; furthermore, often more than one of them applies. The judge, or a member of the staff, usually counsels the wife as to which legal pathway will be the easier

---

[2] Called *tafwîd al-talâq* in Hanafî doctrine, "delegated divorce" was recognized throughout Ottoman lands. In Egypt, in the early twentieth century, the formulations registered in the marriage contract were very general, without the specific stipulations found in Indonesia; for Libya see Layish (1991:35–40).

one to follow. Here, as in the ta'lik case, the husband need not even be present for the divorce to be effected.

Finally, if one party opts for a *syiqoq* argument, she or he claims that the couple has been fighting and cannot be reconciled. The judge then attempts to reconcile them before passing judgment on the divorce request. He does so by asking one or more relatives on each side to act as mediators, *hakam*, charged to try and bring the two together. If they report they have failed, then he may appoint a second set of mediators, this time not from among the couple's relatives, but from among older people or officials in the village. These second-level mediators usually can act in a sterner way with the couple, but if they, too, report no luck, then the judge will grant the divorce request.

Takèngën court staff told me that if it gets to the second set of mediators then the case is almost certain to lead to divorce, since by this time the parties have hardened in their positions. The procedure has been used throughout the court's history, indeed it seems to have been more formal before the 1974 law – a 1965 case, for example, involved the court issuing a separate document appointing a hakam for each side. Judges also sometimes appoint mediators in cases that have been brought as talaq; in the mid-1990s, Judge Hasan used the procedure as a last-ditch effort to get the parties to reconcile, failing which he granted the divorce.

Syiqoq only came to be used in Indonesia in the 1930s, and increasingly since the 1960s, particularly in Aceh (Lev 1972a:174). H. Abdullah Fattah, chief judge of the religious court for Banda Aceh from 1960 to 1968, mentioned it as one of the main innovations by the court during that period. He found his main challenge was "to change the mentality of the people working at the court and also of others in the society, to accept procedures that were known to jurists and judges but that had not been practiced, such as the syiqoq."

Male judges in Aceh assumed that using the syiqoq procedure would give wives too much power, explained Abdullah Fattah.

Before the Aceh appellate court changed its procedures, a wife could only obtain annull-ments on the stipulated grounds. If, say, a wife left her husband, returned to her village, and then asked for a divorce because they could not reconcile, the court would refuse her request, saying that it was she who had left her husband. This legal situation changed in 1957, when a provincial regulation, PP 45, said that if the conditions for fasakh were not met, a divorce could still be granted under the category of syiqoq. The two mediators were given the power to declare the talaq, to which the court then could give the force of law. At first judges in Aceh were reluctant to accept the procedure, as they feared that it would give wives the opportunity to revolt against their husbands. But the procedure was spelled out in detail in the regulation so they had to follow it. (Interview, 1994)

National legal changes thus appear to have compelled some judges simply to make use of Islamic legal categories that long had been recognized as valid, but which conflicted with their own gender biases. In other words, in at least this case the legal changes have made legal practice more Islamic and less culturally shaped.

The changes in categories used to classify divorce petitions have also been culturally important.[3] By reducing the number of legal categories to two – husbands' or wives' petitions – the reforms have both reduced the amount of attention paid to legalistic matters of classification, and underscored the basically equal footing on which men's and women's interests and claims should be placed. One result is that a judge's own norms about the relative seriousness of various offenses may play a greater role in shaping his decision, along with his sense of the burden of proof and the reasonableness of both parties' requests.

Any case that reaches the court has already resisted efforts to dissuade the plaintiff from continuing his or her legal suit. A husband or wife who wishes to divorce must approach the village headman first (even towns and cities are divided into "villages"). Before 1989 he or she also had to consult with the local Religious Affairs Officer, the Kuakec; since 1989 they can go right to court if the headman fails to dissuade them, but most continue to consult the local officer.

The Kuakec for Isak in the early and mid-1990s was Jamaluddin. In 1994, he thought the number of petitioners was declining, but in any case far more wives than husbands had always come to him.

Usually she complains that her husband has not provided for her. Often the headman does get them to reconcile, and I never hear about the case. If not, they still come to me, even after 1989. Of every ten cases that come to me, I figure four end in divorce and six in reconciliation. The headman always has a way of letting me know in his letter to me if he thinks there is a way of settling the dispute. If I think there is a possibility I send them back to think it over, as much as three times. If they won't talk about it, then I send them off to the court. (Interview, 1994)

Although my own knowledge of divorce proceedings in Takèngën suggests that women are treated in an equal manner to men, this is not necessarily the case elsewhere. Even when a divorce is granted because of irreconcilable differences, which is the most common result, the judge may write a decision so as to side more with one party than with the other; Ratna Batara Munti of the APIK legal aid organization writes (based on cases from Jakarta and West Java) that in the decision the judge may rely on biased notions about a woman's place being in the home and not working away from home (Munti 1999:8–33). Irawati Dasaad, SH, in 1995 the director of one of Jakarta's major women's legal aid organizations, the Lembaga Konsultasi dan Bantuan Hukum Indonesia untuk

---

[3] Other legal grounds for divorce existed; in Takèngën they were listed each year but were almost never used. A *li'an* suit, for example, is a claim by one party that the other party committed fornication. The plantiff needs two witnesses, and one never has two witnesses to fornication, so people rely on one of the other categories instead (usually "irreconcilable differences" under fasakh).

Wanita dan Keluarga (LKBHIuWK, Indonesian Institute for Consultation and Legal Aid for Women and Families), mentioned the same problem: "Verses in the Qur'ân say that the wife must 'obey' (ta'at); what exactly does 'obey' mean? In a recent case we handled, the wife wanted a divorce through chuluk [with a payment; see below] and the husband contested it. He said that she did not 'obey' him, and the judge denied her the divorce" (interview, 1995). Musdah Mulia of the Human Rights Commission concludes that "the law is good, but the judges pay more attention to the husband's reasons for divorcing than to the wife's" (interview, 2000).

Divorce by ransom

If the defendant in a court case agrees to the divorce then the judge generally grants it; if not, the judge insists that the plaintiff prove that one of the stipulated conditions for divorce has been met. This situation leads defendants to offer to agree to divorce for a price, a "ransom" (Ind. tebus; Arabic chuluk). When a husband demands such a payment, he rarely offers any rationale, but wives usually offer specific reasons for requesting the money: he failed to complete the marriage payments, or has not repaid a loan from her. She may ask for support from the husband both for a specific time after the divorce takes effect (nafkah idd) and for time already elapsed during which he had failed to support her (nafkah yang lalu, "past support"). These payments to the wife can be ordered by the court, but a "ransom" (chuluk) to be paid to the husband usually has to be agreed to by the wife.

Either side may agree to make the payments if they do not have strong grounds for divorce. These possibilities for bargaining lead to calculations by the defendants as to how badly they wish to prevent the divorce (if at all) and how capable the spouse is to pay the "ransom." Judges frequently deny divorce requests when the grounds have not been proved and the defendant does not agree to the conditions proposed, so the threat is real.

Two back-to-back cases settled by the same judge, Salamuddin, in July 1994 illustrate how the burden of proof and the "ransom market" interact. In the first case, the couple had been married for five years and had two young children; the husband sought a divorce on grounds that they continually quarreled. After delivering a speech about the importance of both parents raising children, Judge Salamuddin asked relatives of the couple whether they thought the couple could be brought together; they did not think so. At that, he declared the session closed and all of us left except for the husband and wife.

When he reopened it and we all returned to the courtroom, the judge stated that the wife had demanded five grams of gold, a sofa set, sewing machine, a dinner set for six, and a wardrobe before she would agree to the divorce. She claimed that she was owed these objects as her "bride goods," agreed to but

never delivered by her husband. Judge Salamuddin then asked the husband if
he could pay what was demanded; he said no, he could not.

Judge Salamuddin then read his decision:

The plaintiff claims they are always fighting and that he can no longer lead the defendant.
The defendant states they never fight, but that if the plaintiff wants a divorce she will go
along if he pays the marriage payments that since our marriage in 1989 he has never paid.
The plaintiff says he won't pay it. Because the plaintiff cannot prove that they do quarrel,
he has not met the requirements set out in the Islamic Law Compilation, article 116,
his request to the court is not accepted, and he must pay the Rp 39,000 in court costs.

In the next case to be heard that day, Ramlah sued her husband, Ali, for
divorce. He said he would agree to the divorce but only if she paid him
Rp 500,000 as chuluk money, "because my rights have been taken from me."
She said, "I'll not pay one cent, because" – at which point Judge Salamuddin
cut her off, as he had cut off the husband earlier. He said to the crowd, "I guess
it's even now," at which everyone except Ramlah laughed. (Indeed, she was
clearly the least comfortable person in the courtroom, even though she won the
case.)

Judge Salamuddin then read out what the two sides had said so far. The wife
said that her husband would not go out and earn money but that she had to do so.
He would say he was sick but that was just an excuse. Then one day he ripped
her necklace off her neck to go and sell it, leaving red marks around her neck,
and that led her to ask for a divorce. The husband had responded by saying that
they had not had any major arguments. "I did ask for the necklace and then took
it from her; the red marks are from when she was roasting coffee." He said he
wanted them to reconcile. But his own witness agreed with the wife about the
source of the red marks; he said they came when the husband ripped off the
necklace.

Judge Salamuddin made his decision as follows. The husband had signed the
ta'lik talaq, and had done physical harm to his wife, one of the conditions for
automatic divorce. Therefore, based on the Compilation section, the first talaq
of divorce had been pronounced automatically and the couple was divorced.
The plaintiff, the wife, had to pay the court costs of Rp 54,000.

The two cases differed in their outcomes because, in the second case, the
judge considered the wife to have proved that she had been abused, whereas in
the first case, he considered the husband to have failed to have proved that they
had quarreled, despite the relatives' testimony that they could not be reconciled.
Although the one case was brought by the wife, the other by the husband, that
difference was not, I think, decisive. More important in Judge Salamuddin's
decision was the kind of treatment alleged – mere quarreling versus physical
abuse. Judges have very low tolerance for spouses who cause physical injury.
Judge Salamuddin may also have found the wife's request for back-payment of

marriage gifts more reasonable than the demands by the husband in the second case.

Along with deciding whether or not to accept the request for a divorce, the judge must set the terms of the settlement. In every case, he determines the support due the wife from the husband, the *nafkah*, by looking at the husband's income.[4] Plaintiffs may ask the court to divide their communal property (*harta bersama*) at the same time as the divorce is settled, or in a separate hearing thereafter, a right of the plaintiff or defendant formalized in the 1989 court organization law. Child custody is awarded according to the child's age: children below seven years of age remain with their mother unless she remarries, in which case they live with their father. Children older than seven may choose. "If needed we bring the child here and ask him or her with whom he or she would like to live" (Judge Hasan).

Moral discourses of divorce

Judges approach divorce petitions as moral issues at least as much as legal ones. In 1994 I heard Judge Hasan preside over a number of divorce cases. Judge Hasan's passions emerged when delivering advice in these cases. Islamic court judges are in an important way family law judges; all of their everyday work involves trying to sort out disputes within a family. I have found them to be family-minded, and sometimes gender-minded, concerned with the legal rights of wives and the moral duties of husbands. In the divorce cases that take up a large share of their time, the judges do at least as much social and religious counseling as they do fact-finding and statute-applying.

Judge Hasan most often displayed emotions when urging a couple to reconsider a divorce petition. Two cases from July 1994 show two of his set speeches on the evils of divorce. The first case was brought by the husband, Ali, forty-two years old, against his wife, Ema, aged forty-three. (Plaintiffs are referred to as "requesters," *pemohon*; defendants as "those requested," *termohon*.) They had been married for twenty-six years and had nine children. Ali claimed irreconcilable differences as the grounds for his petition for divorce.

After hearing the bare bones of the case, Judge Hasan gave a rather long speech, taking nearly fifteen minutes, in which he laid out some of his reasons why divorce, although permitted in Islam, was not a good thing.

You have nine children, and they have to be brought up by both parents. If they are brought up by just the father, they will never become close to their mother, and maybe even hate her. And if the mother brings them up they will not become close to their father. Who knows, when they ask where their father is, she may even say that he is a

---

[4] Parties often appeal divorce decisions to put off making the payments rather than because they hope to reconcile.

drunkard or a thief, and so they may come to hate him. The Prophet Muhammad said that children are like a white sheet of paper, you can write anything on them, either good things or bad things, or scratch all over so that they are filthy. And where would the children go? They cannot all be with the father: when would he ever have time to earn a living? He would not have time even to wash all their faces, and if they are sick, then what? Or if they are all with the mother, how will she care for them?

Maybe you'll marry again [to the husband], and maybe she will be pretty and wealthy, but maybe she'll be a thief and not good with the children. You have to learn how to have a good understanding with your wife, and you [turning to the wife] have to do the same with him. Because you have so many children you have to think first; I hope you will reconcile. If you had no children it would be no problem, we'd just arrange the divorce right now. But with children it is different. Because if the children have step-parents, they are never like the birth parents; they might hit a child until it bleeds or until it dies, and then what will you do? If the birth mother gets angry at a child, the child will seek out his father's lap, and then after a while laugh and return to the mother, but not with step parents.

He then asked the couple if they would not agree to reconcile their differences and remained married. The husband said he agreed with everything the judge had said, and he was clearly moved by Hasan's speech. He took a minute to think things over, but then said that no, he could not see them reconciling. The wife then said that yes, she would like to reconcile.

Judge Hasan asked for older relatives who could act as "reconcilers" (*wali*, which has the usual meaning of "guardian"). Each party had an elder sister in the court, and the judge said they could serve as the walis. He charged them and their husbands to try and reconcile the couple, but, failing that, to report back to him. "If they cannot be reconciled," he concluded, "then it is better to separate them; doing otherwise could lead to unwanted things happening later on." Several older people present nodded their assent to this observation. He set the next session for a week later, when he would ask each *wali* what they had to report. He would base his decision to grant the divorce or not on whether they said that the differences were indeed irreconcilable.

The second case presented Judge Hasan with the opposite extreme: a young couple, just married, with no children. Here he took a different tack. This time the plaintiff was the wife, Sulasteri, claiming irreconcilable differences with her husband, Armadan. She was eighteen, he twenty-one, and because they had been married only three months, Judge Hasan was especially reluctant to grant her the divorce.

He started his speech as above, emphasizing how much damage it does to one's life to divorce, but he continued in a different vein:

You are of such a young age, and have only been married three months, it is as if you are just playing around at marriage. It would be a different story if for years you had not been able to have peace in your household, but you haven't yet given marriage a chance. If you divorce now, you will not be giving Indonesia's youth a firm basis for the future; you will probably not be able ever to have steady married lives.

He then asked each if they could not reconcile to the other. "Perhaps you, Armadan, do things that are not pleasing to your wife, you should change them, and perhaps you, Sulasteri, do things that are not pleasing to him; you can change them. For marriage is not something to play with, we should just marry once, not marry twice."

But each said no. The husband said, "We do not have harmony in the family," and the judge noted that harmony (*kerukunan*) depends on the individuals concerned, and that a husband and a wife can make the atmosphere into one of harmony. He then noted that Armadan was a civil servant (he worked in a school), and that according to the law he had to get a recommendation from his superiors before he could be divorced. The judge continued, explaining the law to the audience as well as to the couple: "If it had been the husband who had asked for the divorce than he would have had to have his employer's *izin* (permission), which is a stronger requirement. Or if the wife, the plaintiff, had been a civil servant then she would have had to get permission; it is the same law for men or women."

"Recommendation," continued Judge Hasan, "means that perhaps the employer has seen the husband's work suffer because his home life is confused and troubled, and then he could say that it would be good for him to have a divorce." Judge Hasan had already sent a letter to the employer asking for the recommendation, but had received no answer, and so he was going to give the boy two weeks to obtain it himself. "This is in your interest," he said, "because according to today's regulations you can be fired if you divorce without the recommendation. If you still have not obtained it after two weeks, then I'll grant her request for the hearing, and then the risk will be yours."

On these and other occasions Judge Hasan would switch from time to time from the Indonesian that is the language of the court (as it is of all official transactions in Indonesia) to Gayo. People often addressed the judge in Gayo, and he would initially respond in Indonesian, switching to Gayo if he felt the person had trouble understanding his questions. This occurred especially with older men and women, and especially when the judge asked about kinship ties, for which the Indonesian kin terms and address terms were often misunderstood.[5] The Indonesian language also feels officious and less respectful than Gayo to many people. Judge Hasan clearly felt so at times, and would switch to a Gayo form of address with someone older than himself even if he communicated his main questions in Indonesian.

---

[5] For example, when Judge Hasan asked: "*Orang tua saudara di mana?*," which was intended to mean "Where are your parents?," with *saudara* serving as a status-neutral Indonesian "you," the petitioner misunderstood the question as "Where are your brother's parents?," because *saudara* can also mean "sibling" in Indonesian. Judge Hasan then repeated the question in Gayo and was easily understood.

Judge Hasan meant every word of his various "don't divorce" speeches. He repeated much of his longer speech to me in our discussions, adding to it a theory of proper child development: children should receive care from both sides, he told me, so that their character is built up by both father and mother. If not, then they will get only one aspect of character; for example, a boy will be too harsh without his mother. "I always try to get the couple to reconcile," he said,

but this only works in maybe two out of a hundred cases. Then I close the session to the public. I am required to do that by law, and anyway maybe the couple will get back together someday, and they would be very embarassed if they had spilled their secrets about boyfriends and girlfriends to everyone. Then, when it is just us, I ask whose idea it was to divorce, and what the reasons were. I want to see if others are involved – perhaps someone has put them up to this. Divorce must be the sincere intent of one party. And I do this in the same way whether the husband or the wife brought the request.

Although the judge is always careful to cite the appropriate laws when granting (or not) a divorce, the reasons he chooses to list in the written decision, in a section called "legal considerations," are moral rather than technical. They are in effect summaries of the speeches the judge would have already delivered in court. In a 1986 case (PA 181/1986), for example, Judge Hasan wrote that a husband who had left his wife for three years without sending her support "should have been responsible for his wife and children and goods. However, he left, abandoning them and never sending word or money, nor leaving them with wealth that they could have used for their needs."

Despite the judges' efforts, plaintiffs rarely back down from their requests to divorce. If they appear in court they have already resisted efforts to reconcile them by relatives, by the village headman, probably by their subdistrict religious official, the Kuakec (although they do not have to go through him), and finally by the court clerks. Indeed, Judge Hasan usually asks a divorce petitioner to see him in his office before accepting the case. As a clerk explained,

He could delegate that task to us, but he always wants to see the plaintiff. He asks what the grounds are, signs a form and sends the party to the clerk on duty, where they pay a fee, and then they come to see us for filing the petition. We help them write it in the correct way; it has to be from them, of course. Sometimes one party comes in and files, and the other does not know of it until called for the hearing!

As we were talking a young man entered and said he wanted to get a divorce. His wife had been yelling and breaking plates and he couldn't stand it. It turned out they had just been married. The clerk helping him was urging him to reconcile with his wife; he called over to me, in English, "They are on their honeymoon."

Current practices of "divorcing" would be almost unrecognizable to a Gayo man or woman of even fifty years ago. Among the most striking changes is the consideration of irreconcilable differences, implying no finding of fault. This change has occurred nationwide. In the 1970s, explained Achmad Djunaeni, the head of the Islamic division at the Supreme Court, judges sought to find fault. "The Court had held that even when the divorce was granted because of irreconcilable differences, syiqoq, and thus not because of a specific action by one party, if the party requesting the divorce had caused the problem, then their request should be refused and no divorce granted" (interview, 2000). By 1991, the Supreme Court had ruled that if a marriage has collapsed, then it was not proper (*tidak patut*) to search for fault on the part of one or the other of the spouses.[6]

Former Justice Busthanul Arifin, who authored the 1991 decision, claimed that he had been responsible for putting the no-fault idea into practice, and that in doing so he was enacting true Islam.

In the 1970s there was family law reform in many countries: Australia, Holland, elsewhere, and in all those countries, divorce law is returning to Islam. Now, in those countries, there is only one reason for divorcing, irreconcilable differences, marriage breakdown – in the language of the Qur'ân this is syiqoq, "breakdown." Those countries are more Qur'ânic, more Islamic than we are! I put the no-fault orientation into the marriage laws, but in a concealed way, via the costs of the lawsuit. In civil law the losing party pays court costs, but the marriage law [the Court Bill of 1989] has it that the party that brings the case pays the cost. In Islam, divorce is a "therapy," not a "penalty." The Prophet never asked who was at fault when someone brought a problem marriage to him, but would say they were divorced. If fault is ascribed, then a child later will see in the decision: "Oh, Mother played around" and be ashamed. (Interview, 2000)[7]

In justifying the movement toward no-fault, Arifin also reinforced the conception of marriage as essentially religious. The 1991 decision states that marriage is not an ordinary contract but a holy one, and, given this fact, its collapse cannot be followed by a search for fault. As we shall see in the next chapter, this conception of marriage as essentially religious has also been drawn on to justify forbidding marriage across religious lines.

Creating "marital property"

I have already mentioned the development of a national consensus on marital or common property. Both civil courts and religious courts throughout the country state that upon dissolution of a marriage through death or divorce a spouse has

---

[6] Case No. 38/1990, decided October 1991 and reported in *Varia Peradilan* 79, 1992:114–30.
[7] In a 1998 decision reported in *Varia Peradilan* (176, 2000:62–65), the Court affirmed this principle.

the right to one-half of all property acquired during the marriage. The marital property is not divided among heirs, and in towns and cities it is often far more valuable than the inheritance itself. Consequently, the national Women and Family Legal Aid Institute has given high priority to ensuring that widows and divorced women know of their rights and are able to obtain their share of this property.[8]

In many agrarian areas of Indonesia, in particular where the economy was based on wet-rice cultivation, older norms for dividing property were based on the assumption that wealth was relatively stable. After all, a ricefield that yielded six sacks of unmilled rice this year would do about the same a decade from now. Marriages brought in wives or husbands to work the field and consume its product, but they neither added to nor subtracted from its wealth. Death or divorce meant that the spouse left the village, but he or she had no claim to part of it. Islamic legal interpretations gave the wife no share of the husband's resources after divorce or death, only a short-term subsistence payment. Classical Islamic law only provided for maintenance of a divorced women for the three-month waiting (idda) period after divorce, or for up to two years if she was nursing a child.

From the standpoint of classical fiqh, the principle of equally dividing joint property is a major innovation. Ali Jadun, the Takèngën Muhammadiyah leader, explained the older Islamic rule and the change in "contextualizing" fashion, pointing to the conditions of work and production in the time and place where Islamic law was formulated: "Back in the time of Imam Shafii [the founder of the legal tradition followed in Indonesia] there were no gardens or ricefields, and so it made sense that the man kept everything" (interview, 1994). In the Gayo highlands, these ideas began to change when the material conditions of life shifted. North and west of Takèngën, in the 1920s and 1930s a growing number of households cleared forest land to make coffee gardens. They had created new wealth. Some of those households dissolved in divorce, and ex-wives began to complain to the colonial court, the Landraad, that they had the right to a share of such lands because they had contributed to the creation of the wealth.[9]

The legal response to this challenge took place at several levels. Local judges borrowed legal categories from other societies, where these change processes had already occurred. The Supreme Court also developed a jurisprudence of marital property, one that eventually superseded local innovations. In the Gayo highlands, courts created two sets of distinctions concerning family wealth, based on legal developments elsewhere. Wealth that was newly created was to be distinguished from wealth that had been inherited. Wealth that was created by the two spouses was to be distinguished from wealth created from only

---

[8] Interview with Institute director, Irawati Dasaad, SH, Jakarta, 1 June 1995.
[9] According to statements by older religious officials; I have not yet found records of Landraad decisions.

one spouse's labor or capital. The two categories are conceptually distinct – one may create new wealth without a spouse's assistance – but over time they were collapsed into one distinction, between marital property, acquired during the marriage and assumed to be jointly created, and property inherited by one person.

To label wealth that was newly created, the Takèngën Landraad borrowed an Acehnese phrase, *poh roh*, meaning "to work fallow [land]" and referring to the principle in both Gayo and Acehnese societies that the returns from long-fallow land go entirely to the laborer for some period of time, because of the high start-up costs involved. The opposite of poh roh wealth was inherited wealth, *pesaka*, and the distinguishing feature of the former was that the household created it through their *usaha diri*, "own efforts." At least by the late 1930s, "own efforts" land was divided according to the relative labor contributions of husband and wife. Inherited land was part of the capital contributed by the family in whose village the couple lived, and would remain with that family, and with the children of the couple.

These norms continued to be applied by the civil court after independence when faced with the question of whether land was to be divided among heirs or retained by a household as the fruit of their "own efforts" (PN Tkn 63/1959; PN Tkn 2/1969; PN 103/1964). In these suits, the issue before the court was not the relative claims of husband and wife, but whether or not the land in question had been inherited by the household or made into valuable property through their "own efforts." The phrase poh roh was appropriate in these cases for its imagery of clearing and planting land that had not been productive, at least not for a long while.

But how was "own efforts" land to be divided between husbands and wives? Here a second distinction was made, one that runs orthogonal to the first, concerning not the input of labor but the source of wealth. It separates wealth brought to a marriage by one party (*harta bawaan*, "wealth brought") and wealth created by both parties (*harta bersama*, "wealth together," or joint property). Whereas poh roh referred to fallow land that was made productive by the labor of husband and wife (and thus not inherited productive land in which the village would have a residual right), harta bersama referred to any wealth that did not clearly belong to only the husband or only the wife. Property that was neither brought to the marriage by one of the parties, nor purchased with money brought to the marriage, nor given to one of the spouses alone, would be declared as joint property. Often the Takèngën court used the Javanese phrase *gono-gini*, because the distinction had first been clarified by the Supreme Court with respect to Javanese practices.

Early Takèngën court decisions vacillated between awarding one-half and two-thirds of joint property to the husband. In a 1961 case (PN 31/1961), a woman sued her ex-husband for part of their jointly acquired wealth. The court awarded her one-third of the estate without seeming to feel the need to justify the formula. Three years later, in a similar suit (PN 45/1964), the judge ruled that in the Gayo area men and women work garden lands together, but men generally work harder than women, and thus the wife ought to receive less than the husband's share.

A series of Supreme Court decisions began to push the Takèngën civil court toward gender equality. In 1956, a divorced wife sued her ex-husband for re-covery of joint wealth in his possession. She asked for the wealth to be divided equally between them. The court agreed with her for part of the wealth, but found with the defendant that some of the lands had been brought by him to the marriage. In the absence of witnesses, the court relied on a decisory oath, which she challenged him to take, and he took. The Medan High Court affirmed the decision two years later, but the defendant sought to quash the ruling on grounds that adat law in Central Aceh divided joint property in thirds, with two-thirds for the husband. The Supreme Court heard the case in 1962 and sided with the lower courts, declaring that its own past decisions had already established that equal shares for husbands and wives was the norm for all Indonesia.[10]

The Supreme Court had already declared in 1956 that joint property included all wealth gained during marriage, regardless of who worked on the land and who worked at home (Katz and Katz 1975:679 n.160). The 1974 Marriage Law reaffimed the principle that husbands and wives had equal claims to wealth, and the Supreme Court, in a decision that they chose to reprint in their case review,[11] soon ruled that based on the 1974 law all wealth obtained during marriage must be divided equally between the husband and wife. The Takèngën civil court generally follows this ruling, citing the marriage law as its basis.

When does wealth begin?

The effect of these decisions was to bring about a consequential shift in how the fairness of a division was to be understood: from measuring the relative contributions of labor from each party, now judges were to look for the origins of wealth, to distinguish between wealth brought to a marriage and wealth created during the marriage. But does wealth begin when it starts to exist in its current form, or when the capital lying behind it is first acquired? As in so many other instances, this substantive issue was also a question of how the burden of proof was to be distributed between plaintiffs and defendants. In the 1960s and 1970s, an ex-wife suing for her joint property had to demonstrate that the husband had not owned the land before the marriage. In a dispute over land first

---

[10] The initial Takèngën case was PN 5/1956, the appellate hearing in Medan, PT Mdn 279/1958, and the Supreme Court case, MA 28/Sip/1962.
[11] The Supreme Court ruling was MA 1448/Sip/1974, reprinted in *Yurisprudensi Indonesia* 1977-II. Relevant Takèngën civil court cases include PN Tkn 9/1978 and PN Tkn 18/1979.

argued in 1951 and decided in 1963, it was sufficient for the plaintiff to show that the defendant, her ex-husband, had not possessed the contested wealth (riceland and water buffalo) before the marriage.[12] And yet, if the defendant could prove that although the wealth was acquired during the marriage, it was purchased with money given by his relatives, then the court would declare the wealth to have been brought to the marriage and therefore not joint property.[13]

In Takèngën, this approach was modified during the course of the 1980s, such that if you could show that something was purchased during the marriage, then you could win a ruling that the item in question was joint property. Underlying this shift in jurisprudence was the idea that the household buys and produces wealth as a unit; wealth, whatever its origin, "dissolves into" community property unless it can be clearly shown to have existed beforehand *in its current form*. Land brought to the marriage, for example as bride goods, could be claimed as solely owned by one party, but if money was used to buy land, the source of that money, whether it was, for example, earned by the husband before the marriage or given as a present to the wife, was now deemed irrelevant to the division.

Thus in *Ali vs Aisyah*, heard in 1988, the judge rejected arguments he might have accepted twenty years before. Ali married Aisyah in 1979, and they divorced in 1987. Ali asked for one-half of the joint property held by Aisyah. Aisyah replied that she had purchased some of the land with her own gold, and the rest had been given by her parents, though planted with coffee by the couple. Her argument was sound under the older logic of property categories, but the judge ruled that both land parcels had become joint property, to be divided equally between them.

Regarding the land bought with her gold, the judge stated that her very action of paying for the land with the gold showed that she was willing to merge her property into joint family property. "The 'brought property' has now dissolved, and merged with the joint property, the disputed coffee garden, because the defendant handed over her brought property in order to acquire the joint property

---

[12] Case PN 13/1963. The defendant replied that he had paid to have the riceland cleared during their marriage; this objection carried no weight and the court ordered the wealth divided in two. The defendant appealed to the Medan High Court in 1965; they ordered the lower court to reopen the case to hear the defendant's witnesses, whom he claimed would support his new claim that he had inherited the riceland from his father. No more on this case is in the court files, and given that the hearing would have been scheduled for the period of the massacres after Gerakan September 30 (GESTAPU, September 30th Movement, the coup attempt against Sukarno) in late 1965 to early 1966, the case may have been dropped.

[13] As in case PN 4/1979. The "joint" category could also work against a plaintiff. In 1979 (PN 18/1979) an ex-wife successfully sued for one-half of a coffee estate, and the husband was required to buy out her share of the land, based on land prices at the time the decision was reached. But the husband counter-claimed that he had given her a garden when he took a second wife, that she had enjoyed all the yield from this garden for four years, and that he was due one-half of that yield because it was joint property. He won this claim.

land voluntarily and when still happily married to the plaintiff. By responding that she did so her reply does not refute the plaintiff's claim but constitutes an admission that the disputed garden is joint property between the plaintiff and defendant."[14]

What under earlier interpretations would have been evidence for the "tainted" character of the purportedly joint property – that it had been purchased with outside money – now became evidence that Aisyah all along had considered her gold to be part of a general household fund. Similar logic underlies the judge's response to Aisyah's second argument, that the other parcel was purchased with money that came from her parents. The fact that she planted coffee seedlings on the land together with her husband showed that she thought of the land as jointly owned, said the judge.

The judge rejected two other arguments made by Aisyah: that Ali had married *angkap nasab*, and thus, according to Gayo adat, had no right to take property with him when the marriage dissolved, and that Ali had signed an agreement in 1986 after an earlier argument between them, in which they agreed that the party who kept to the agreement would keep all the wealth. The judge ignored the angkap argument, and said that the agreement had to be "measured according to feelings of justice and propriety."[15]

The judge made clear his general principle, namely, that wealth is transformed once it passes into the household domain, losing its traces of origin. Taking precedence over all the considerations advanced by the defendant – that it was her own money that was used to purchase the land, that the plaintiff was an angkap son-in-law with no property rights, that the reconciliation agreement guaranteed her the wealth – was the court's belief that household wealth was just that, household wealth, and that it was equally owned by husband and wife.

Thus, in the Takèngën civil court, judges gradually shifted, and as a result broadened their criteria for deciding that property was jointly owned by a couple. The older definition was in terms of effort; it considered property cleared and worked by the couple to belong to them jointly. The newer definition was in terms of the period when the the property was acquired; it assumed that households acquired and used wealth as a single unit. Because it is men who do the bulk of the labor on new fields, and because these fields tend to be planted in the more profitable cash crops, this change in legal reasoning substantially increased the share of wealth going to women. Under the older definition, a wife who kept house but did not work on a field received at most one-third of the field's value, but under the new definition she was guaranteed one-half of all new wealth.

---

[14] Case PN 23/1988.
[15] The plaintiff did not entirely win his case; he failed to prove that other wealth was joint property, and Aisyah successfully counter-claimed that a house and another garden were hers. (These matters were settled by the preponderance of witnesses' testimony.)

In 1994, Chief Judge Nazifli Sofyan of the Takèngën civil court refused even to speak in terms of respective contributions, rather speaking only in terms of the period during which property is acquired:

If property has been obtained while the couple is married, then it is joint property. It does not matter who worked it, nor from where the money came to buy it: wealth given to them is also presumed to be joint property unless one party can prove it was given only to him or her. So the origin of the property is not important, only the time when it was obtained.[16]

Turning practice into Islamic law

Until the Courts Bill of 1989, the religious court did not consider itself empowered to divide joint property, and all petitions for these divisions went to the civil court. But the same general principle followed in the civil court also was applied informally by the religious court judges. Tengku Mukhlis, the head of the religious court, would be approached for opinions (fatwas) and for his advice in dividing property, just as Takèngën ulama are today. "Tengku Mukhlis was the first to say that 'if poh roh, then divide equally,' " said Tengku Ali Jadun in 2000. Ali Jadun himself was, and is, frequently called on to divide property. "When people divorced, I would divide poh roh equally. People had to accept this; it was the law."

The most ideologically Islamic of judges in the 1950s were the members of the Darul Islam rebellion who operated in the hills, in the areas controlled by the rebels. These judges divided marital property much as did civil court judges. As Aman Kerna of Isak – the ex-village head who presided over the Kramil dispute described earlier – explained to me in 1994, the judge balanced different sets of norms in making his decision.

The D.I. judge would decide all cases according to religion. In inheritance disputes he would divide all the wealth among the children, with two shares to sons and one share to daughters, and he would divide joint property according to how much effort the wife had put into working the land. Generally it was divided as two shares to one, favoring the husband, but if the wife had worked the land along with her husband then it was one to one. For, there are three kinds of law: God's law, customary law, and the law of reason (*hukum akal*). In cases like these you have to use the law of reason and set aside religion and custom. You have to ask: How much did the wife work? Perhaps, as is often the

---

[16] The same view was expressed at the Islamic appellate court in Aceh: the chief judge of that court told me in an interview in Banda Aceh (25 July 1994): "Before 1974 we divided joint wealth according to who had worked it. If the wife had been at home, cooking, and taking care of the children, well then the wealth that the husband had worked was divided two shares for him, one for the wife; if they worked it together, then equally. But the 1974 marriage law says that all wealth obtained during the marriage is to be divided equally, and so we do that. All that has to be shown is that the wealth was not brought to the marriage, that it was obtained while they were married."

case, the husband would leave the wife on the ricefields and the garden, and he would go off somewhere else, so that she did more work than he did. But even then the division was never more than one to one.

Since 1989 the religious court has regularly divided property as part of divorce settlements, or upon separate petitions. The religious court judges employ substantially the same criteria as do the civil court judges, with one difference: they subtract from the value of the household wealth any capital brought to the marriage. In 1994, Judge Kasim explained:

The 1974 law makes clear that joint property is all wealth obtained during the time of the marriage. But we do look into where the money came from to buy the wealth. Let's say the couple buys a coffee garden during their marriage. If the money came from her bride goods that she was given at marriage, then we subtract the value of the bride goods and divide the rest as joint property (*harta bersama*); the bride goods are brought property (*harta bawaan*). But here as in the other matters each judge has discretion to decide the way he wishes, so there are different versions of all this.

As an example, a case decided in 1994 before the Islamic court of Takèngën (PA 273/1994) involved a sustained, item-by-item dispute over wealth remaining from a marriage. The plaintiff was the wife of the deceased, and the defendants, the deceased's children by a previous marriage, one that had ended before the remarriage. (These disputes are often the most protracted.) The plaintiff testified that there had been a *musyawarah*, a meeting to divide the property, but that she had received a small portion and that even that amount was accompanied by the threat of "take it or leave it." The two sides contested nearly every claim, and the disagreements were usually over whether an item of wealth had been purchased during one or another of the marriages, i.e., whether it was marital property shared by the husband and the first wife, in which case it was the inheritance due the children, or marital property with the second wife, in which case it was entirely due her. In resolving these disputes the court had to determine not only when wealth was acquired but also when the money was acquired to purchase items of wealth. For example, one coffee garden had been purchased with money from the sale of some riceland that itself had been part of the defendants' inheritance; therefore, the garden was part of that inheritance even though it was purchased during the period of the second marriage.

Difficulties of proof

But defendants have learned, or are told, how to make things difficult for widows seeking their share of joint property, by simply denying that land is joint property and forcing the plaintiff to prove its status. A good example of this tactic, and of its ultimate failure, is *Inën Aji Merah vs Inën Jafar* (PA Tkn 75/1982), a case that also shows how cases can be sent back and forth between the two court systems.

The plaintiff and defendant were the two wives of Jamin, Aman Aji Merah, who died in 1968. The plaintiff, his first wife, brought suit in the religious court. She claimed that most of the estate resulted from the joint effort of her and her husband. Each of the two wives controlled some of the estate, but the defendant had the choicest piece of land, about one hectare of riceland on the road just outside of town, a particularly valuable piece of land in the area with the fastest-rising prices. We will focus on this piece of the estate; some of the rest was admitted by the defendant to be joint property, some was not proved to be so. The defendant denied the claim, and countered that their husband had given her the riceland as a marriage payment. She had already turned ownership over to her three sons, who had obtained legal title in 1981.

Because the two sides contested the ownership of the riceland, the religious court was forced to send the case to the civil court. In the civil court, the plaintiff produced three witnesses to testify that they had farmed the disputed riceland in Dutch times (before the defendant's marriage to Jamin), and that the plaintiff had managed the land (they paid her the rent). One added that Jamin had bought the land after marrying the plaintiff and for some time he and she worked it together. The defendant had later been the one to work the land, he stated, but he had not heard that Jamin had given it to her. The defendant produced two witnesses, who said that the land had been given as a marriage payment to the defendant.

The civil court ruled that the burden of proof was on the plaintiff, and that she had indeed proved that Jamin bought the riceland when married to her, but not yet to the defendant, so it was the joint property of the plaintiff and Jamin. The plaintiff was awarded one-half of the land; the court ordered that the other half be divided among the heirs "following Islamic Law." The land deed held by the defendant's sons was declared void.[17]

Appeals followed. The Aceh High Court affirmed the decision but said that the lower court could not actually order the riceland to be returned to the plaintiff, because all she had asked for was for it to be divided, and the religious court should do that. The defendant sought cassation from the Supreme Court, making the intriguing argument that because both wives worked some of the lands between 1942 and 1968 with Jamin, these lands ought to be divided among the three of them. We do not get to hear the court's response, because, predictably, they ruled these claims as new substantive matters and thus inappropriate to a request for cassation.[18]

---

[17] Judge Hasan, who had the file of this case on his desk during one of our interviews, agreed that "it was up to the plaintiff to prove that the riceland indeed was joint property . . . Once she had done so, then it followed that Jamin could not have given it to the defendant as bride goods or a marriage payment, because one cannot give away joint property by oneself."

[18] Judge Hasan commented: "The second wife could not claim that she had a right through working on the land (a *hak poh roh*) even if she did in fact labor on it, because the land was already

These four hearings took three years, and three additional years passed before the plaintiff asked the Takèngën religious court to divide the land. In the meantime, the defendant, Inën Jafar, had died, and the plaintiff's children began to quarrel among themselves. The plaintiff's son, who had her power of attorney to represent her before the civil court, took control of all the land, in the Gayo fashion we already saw for Isak. In 1986 his sisters appealed to the civil court to let them work the portion of the land that they had worked prior to the litigation. The court's response is not in the files, but probably the matter was dropped once the religious court intervened.

In 1987 the religious court stated that the earlier decisions clarified that most of the disputed property, including the riceland, was joint property. They brushed off objections by various heirs that this or that item had already been inherited, and divided the entire estate, except for the garden and house that the plaintiff was unable to prove had been acquired during the marriage. The plaintiff was awarded one-half of the wealth, and the remainder was divided according to Islamic law among Jamin's eleven heirs, two wives and nine children. The riceland was divided as follows: of the whole, one-half to the plaintiff, one-half to Jamin; of Jamin's portion, one-eighth for the two wives divided equally between them; of what remained of Jamin's portion, each daughter received one-fifteenth and each son, two-fifteenths. One of the defendant's sons then appealed this decision to the Aceh Islamic High Court, which heard the appeal in 1990 and ruled that he had no legal standing to appeal because he was not the original defendant – who, of course, had died, making all appeals impossible by this reasoning.

Soon thereafter the plaintiff, Inën Aji Merah, died, and one of her daughters, Zulaiha Inën Fajar, came before the religious court to ask that she and a sister and a brother be declared to be the heirs. The court did so after hearing from witnesses that these and no others were the children of Inën Aji Merah. The brother died the following year, and his wife returned to the court for a ruling on his heirs, which she received. Neither request was contested; in each case the heirs, undoubtedly made skittish in these matters by the lawsuit they have grown up with, wished to guard themselves and their children from future lawsuits.[19]

The case of Inën Aji Merah illustrates just how difficult it may be for a wife or her children to obtain marital property, despite the clarity of the law. The division of labor between the two courts adds time and expense to the

the joint possession of the first wife and the husband when the second wife married him. Her working on it does not make it partly hers."

[19] Judge Hasan's determination, *penetapan*, of the heirs of Inën Aji Merah could have been contested, because it excluded the son of Aji Merah, Inën Aji Merah's son, who had died before his own son. Older Islamic jurisprudence excluded the children of predeceased heirs, but by 1991, when this ruling was made, the new Compilation was in effect, which awards such children the shares their parents would have received had they lived.

judicial path, as do the not infrequent mistakes made by judges that lead to their decisions being overruled and cases reheard.

Despite these efforts at preventing such awards, the effect of these judicial developments has been to enlarge the amount of wealth that falls into the category of marital property in both civil and Islamic law. The two court systems do cooperate with each other in preventing some litigants' efforts to endlessly stall. The religious court refuses to reopen questions settled by the civil court; the civil court forgoes the right to determine heirs or divide among them. These considerations are possible because the two courts follow parallel lines of reasoning.

Nationally, obtaining marital property upon divorce is one of the major tasks of women's legal advocacy groups.[20] Lawyers working for one such group told me that women often did not know their rights to property, and often approached the group only with the goal of obtaining a divorce in mind.[21] In 2000, a major women's legal advocacy group, APIK, had made women's rights to material resources during and after marriage its highest priority.[22]

Equality and polygamy?

In the early 2000s women's rights advocacy groups have created a "network of networks," as Ciciek Farha Assegaf of the NGO called P3M put it, in order to improve the legal situation of women and to change gender-biased interpretations of Islam. Each of the activists with whom I spoke in 2000 belonged to several working groups or organizations; the overlaps in membership meant that activities in a legal aid organization, for example, would profit from and inform activities in a religious discussion circle.[23] These overlaps also led these

---

[20] What constitutes "property" is of course increasingly hard to define. Just as the increase in cash crops led local courts to redefine marital property early in the twentieth century, at the beginning of the twenty-first century religious jurisprudence is challenged by stock options, insurance policies, and leasing arrangements. Wahyu Widiana, the head of the Directorate of Religious Justice at the Ministry of Religion, noted that these cases are the most complex arising in the larger cities, and increasingly with divorce comes a complicated web of economic rights and obligations to unravel. In September 2000 the Jakarta IAIN held a first-time semester course for religious court judges on economic legal reasoning, and a new field of study in Islamic economics has just been created at the same institute. "This is the one the students are choosing now because of the new opportunities, at banks for example," explained Wahyu, "whereas before they all chose the field of religious courts, because there was a great need for judges" (interview, 2000).

[21] Interview with lawyers working at the Lembaga Konsultasi dan Bantuan Hukum Indonesia untuk Wanita dan Keluarga, Jakarta, 1995.

[22] Interview with Ratna Batara Munti, at the LBH APIK (Lembaga Bantuan Hukum, Asosiasi Perempuan Indonesia untuk Keadilan, Legal Aid Body, the Indonesian Women's Association for Justice).

[23] Unless otherwise specified, quotations in this section are from interviews conducted in Jakarta in June 2000.

women (and men) to connect everyday women's problems to such high-profile issues as the question of whether a women should be president. Many in these groups see the issue of polygamy as of particular concern, because it stands for the inequality of women and men, because, although rare, it often leads to the maltreatment of the first wife (whose consent is often obtained through trickery), because it is an area where they fear "backsliding" in the post-Suharto era, and because men justify it on Islamic grounds, making opposition difficult without well-rehearsed arguments that engage the issue on religious grounds as well.

Musdah Mulia has written one of the key short tracts in this struggle (Mulia 1999), in which she advances an argument based on a contextual reading of the relevant Qur'ânic verses. In an analysis similar in style to those of Nurcholis Madjid and Ratna Batara Munti (see chapter 7), Mulia emphasizes that the Qur'ânic verse (4:3) authorizing polygamy is mainly intended to limit its extent (to four wives) and to place conditions on its exercise (that the husband treat each wife equally). It was revealed after the Muslims had been defeated at Uhud, leaving many widows and orphans. Some of the guardians of female orphans sought to marry their wards, for their wealth or for their beauty, and the verse was revealed in order to prevent them from so doing, according to a clarification given by the Prophet's wife Aisyah regarding the reasons for the verse (azbâb nuz ûl) (here Mulia follows interpretations made by the reformists Muhammad Abduh and Rasyid Ridha). "So the problem of polygamy is identical to that of the orphans" (1999:34). As for the example of the Prophet Muhammad: he was monogamous for twenty-eight years. Each additional marriage had to do with spreading Islam (Mulia 1999:17–27).

Polygamy thus appears as a context-specific resolution of a highly unusual situation, one that ought now to be done away with, as was recommended by (then-President) Abdurrahman Wahid (Mulia 1999:47–48). But as Mulia recognizes, the link between polygamy and helping orphans is cited as an argument for polygamy in Indonesia today, and "new Islamic tendencies, such as Usrah, Partai Keadilan, Partai Abuliyah Tama, say that polygamy is required (wajib), in order to save orphans. But I think that we don't have to marry the widows, we can help the orphans directly; so with friends from Solidaritas Perempuan [Women's Solidarity (organization)] I wrote a book to counter that [her 1999 publication]."

In the new era of "new tendencies" a number of individuals and groups have advocated restoring the "full rights" of Muslim men to take more than one wife. Civil servants currently are prohibited from so doing by an administrative regulation, but the civil servants corps, Korpri, has written a draft bill that would abolish this regulation. A number of key Muslim male leaders, including one leader of a pro-feminist Islamic organization, recently have taken second wives; others are rumored to be about to do so. Nursyabani Katjasungkana, SH, the director of the APIK legal aid organization, pointed out that the Partai Bulan Bintang, the party led by former Attorney General Yusril Izra Mahendra, had recommended that limits on polygamy be abolished, "on grounds that polygamy takes care of orphans and widows, and reduces prostitution – those are their reasons, though they don't make sense."

These women's rights activists and others are generally trying to work within the context of Islamic argumentation, to attack religious-based justifications. Ratna Batara Munti of APIK:

Polygamy contradicts the sexual rights of women and is discriminatory. The reasons given for it, that the wife cannot have children, that she does not receive her husband sexually, are all very stereotyping of women; it's disgusting. We want to do away with polygamy entirely. But it is hard because we face Islamic leaders, so we work with the Fattayat, a younger women's organization within NU, with Musdah Mulia, we prepare data about women and Islam as small-format books, in case we face opposition.

As Munti's statement indicates, activists working for gender-related reform from an Islamic perspective, such as APIK and Women's Solidarity, have found stronger footing within the the Java-based Nahdlatul Ulama (NU) association than with the other major Islamic organization, Muhammadiyah.

However, within NU circles there is far from uniform support for "analisis jender." Ciciek Farha: "We are relatively accepted in Javanese pesantrens, but some of the *kiyayis* [school heads] forbid us to enter, and censure our publications." Musdah Mulia reported that she went

to the field in 1993, as a head of the Fattayat NU, to a few pesantrens to try an analysis of gender, and, oh were the kiyayis angry with us: "What is this 'gender,' is it a Jewish concept to destroy us?" Then we reported to Gus Dur [Abdurrahman Wahid] and he said, "Yes, you're also wrong, you're too progressive, you need to use terms they understand." So I came back to Jakarta and redid the program with the title "exercise in equalizing status between men and women" (*latihan pemitrasejajahan laki dan perempuan*); we did not use "gender" because it is totally foreign to them, just as is "demokrasi," and then after two or three years we told the kiyayis that this was "gender analysis," and then they said, "Oh then it is in accord with Islamic teachings [she laughed]."

Within NU women's circles, "some would say that in some conditions polygamy is to be allowed, but not in others" (Munti). However, the NU Muslimat, an older women's association, issued a paper in 2000 opposing any relaxation of the restrictions on polygamy.

These activists find the other major Islamic organization, Muhammadiyah, more difficult to work with. Ratna Batara Munti: "There are women from Aisyah, the Muhammadiyah women's organization, who participate in the Women's NGO Forum, but they only do so as individuals; we have no contact with Aisyah itself. They have their Women's Crisis Center in Jogjakarta, Rifka an-Nisa, but they think within the framework of how to create a harmonious family, they do not work on issues such as polygamy." Ciciek Farha:

We do not work with Muhammadiyah; they have some good people but no organization; there is a lot of resistance; Amien Rais himself [head of Muhammadiyah] is resistant to these gender concepts, says they are Western and so forth. The Muhammadiyah women who started the Rifka an-Nisa had to create an NGO outside of Muhammadiyah to do it; they could not do it as a Muhammadiyah association. Amien was critical of the women's crisis center, saying that it is an "institute that tells people to divorce" (*lembaga suruh orang cerai*).

For a response from Muhammadiyah I talked with Prof. Dr. Maftuchah Yusuf of the Universitas Trisakti in Jakarta. Until 1995, she was the assistant head of the Muhammadiyah women's association, Aisyah. (She also had just celebrated her eightieth birthday when I saw her in June 2000, and was pulling copies of her Festschrift volume out of a box in her living room.) Maftuchah Yusuf established the National Commission on the Status of Women, and in that capacity has spoken at the United Nations and elsewhere on women's issues. I asked her specifically about polygamy.

Anything that is in the Qur'ân we have to follow, but according to the era in which we live. Five years ago I was in Mexico for the year of women, and a delegate from Chile attacked Islam, saying, "How can you speak of emancipation if you allow men to take a second wife?" And I arose and answered: "Men will always be men, with the positive and the negative. A man cannot do without a sexual companion, so you have polygamy here, but your husband is hiding that second wife – in America, wherever, you are hypocritical if you deny it." But we teach our husbands that this will be the consequence if you are with another woman, and Islam gives us the right to divorce. Islam lets him take another wife but only if he is fair, and if he is not he will enter hell.

She moved quickly to the topic of orphans, a central element in the historical self-understanding of Muhammadiyah. "I want to help them all, the orphans; I am giving all the money from the books to them."

When I asked another Muhammadiyah member, Dr. Muardi Chadib of the Majelis Ulama Indonesia, about Muhammadiyah activities regarding women and the law, he stressed that Muhammadiyah women were instrumental in building hospitals, orphanages, universities.

In many places the Muhammadiyah universities were the most important, that a new technique for clamping the heart without surgery is now available only in their hospital in Jakarta. There are five Muhammadiyah legal aid organizations in Jakarta, and they recruit lawyers from the Muhammadiyah law schools, so they do not need to go outside for lawyers. They handle all sorts of cases. The Muhammadiyah does not need NGOs because they have always had a lot of intellectuals; there have always been more there than in NU. Gus Dur [Abdurrahman Wahid] said that if he were not President the President would have been from Muhammadiyah, because all the other candidates were from there.

NU and Muhammadiyah do indeed have two different organizational cultures, and these have in turn affected policy.[24] NU was constructed around networks of mainly rural, Javanese religious schools and their leaders; these pesantrens are very tightly structured, requiring outside organizations to effect change, leading to the pressure to create NGOs. Muhammadiyah, by contrast, was built up as a hierarchy of scholars and activists from diverse regions of Indonesia claiming to bring new understandings from the Middle East. In its sense of "modernism" Muhammadiyah included a wide variety of social projects, many of them in urban areas, and in which women often played major roles.

This history of social activism may have contained the energies of Muhammadiyah social reformers, particularly women engaged in reform activities, within the organization's structure. It also led them to emphasize, in Maftuchah Yusuf's words, "independence over equality in the letter of the law." Muhammadiyah "modernism" has a built-in ambiguity, rationalistic but with a strict line of demarcation between religion and non-religion that prevents reinterpretation of, say, polygamy, but would promote its discouragement on worldly grounds. Nahdlatul Ulama's rural, pesantren-based structure was less adapted to promoting such activities as legal aid, and made it more likely that women and men would find a need to create new urban organizations. NU's institutional conservatism thus may have had the indirect effect of producing what today appears to be a more socially progressive set of new institutions than is the case among the "reformists" of Muhammadiyah.

Arguments about gender equality are themselves part of a broader debate, one could call it a meta-debate, about the relevant universe for debate, the grounds on which public reasoning and civil sociability ought to occur in Indonesia. Should Muslims deliberate over sociolegal issues entirely within the confines of Islamic sociolegal traditions, and only among themselves? Or should they and other Indonesians carry on these debates on a nationwide scale, and based on cross-religious principles such as human rights? This question underlies the disputes we have encountered so far; now we turn to it as a central topic.

---

[24] On Muhammadiyah, see Boland (1982) for an overall view, and Jamil (1995) and especially Noer (1978) for several perspectives from scholars involved in the organization. On NU, see Barton and Fealy (1996), van Bruinessen (1994), and Feillard (1995). Hefner (2000) discusses these and other organizations in the context of modern political history.

10   Justifying religious boundaries

In chapter 8, I discussed the ambiguities concerning the state's right to pronounce on matters of Islamic law. Now I turn to the state's involvement in setting boundaries: boundaries between Muslims and Christians, between Muslims and the larger world, and between what is *harâm* and *halâl*, forbidden and permitted, in food, marriage, and everyday sociability. What is at stake in policing boundaries between religious communities? Does boundary-maintaining contradict the desire for equal, universal citizenship? Can it be viewed as a way of regulating difference, sustaining tolerance, or only as a manifestation of intolerance? Here the state finds itself both claiming the autonomy of religious reasoning and asserting its right to determine religious norms.

Separating by fatwa

As in many countries with large Muslim populations, Indonesia has a national body of Islamic jurists, the Council of Indonesian Ulama (Majelis Ulama Indonesia, MUI).[1] The Council was created in 1975 by President Suharto during a period of a particularly high level of suspicion between religious leaders and the state. In a style that became typical of the New Order, Suharto tried to make the process appear as a bottom-up movement for change. Acting through his Minister of the Interior, Amir Machmud, Suharto first ordered each of the twenty-six provinces to create Councils of Ulamas, and only later developed the national council to coordinate the provincial bodies. As had happened in the case of the religious courts, Aceh already had created a provincial Council in December 1965 (whose first action was to demand that the government ban the Communist Party [Mudzhar 1993:47]).

At the time the MUI was established, a bad taste still lingered in the mouths of many Muslim political leaders from the 1971 elections. Former leaders of the Masyumi party, the party of reformist Muslims, had not been allowed to participate in the campaign. The Islamic parties did poorly in the election. In 1973, parties were "reorganized" into three megaparties, and the several

---

[1] For an overview of the history and nature of the fatwa as a religious genre, see Masud et al. (1996); for the Indonesian case see Mudzhar (1993, 1996).

Islamic parties and factions were shoe-horned into the state-controlled United Development Party, the Partai Persatuan Pembangunan, or PPP. We have seen the heated debates and protests following the government's introduction of a marriage bill. Given these unfavorable conditions, the government scored a major tactical victory in persuading the best-known Islamic scholar at the time, Hamka (Hadji Abdul Malik Karim Amrullah), to become the first chairman of the MUI, despite his earlier opposition to the institution on grounds that inevitably it would be manipulated by the government.[2]

The Council today is composed of a number of committees, one of which is devoted to issuing fatwas or legal opinions.[3] A fatwa (Ar. *fatwâ*, pl. *fatâwa*) takes the form of a response to a question, which may come from a lay person or from a government body. Islam-oriented newspapers usually carry a weekly column of fatwas delivered by Islamic scholars. In Indonesia, jurists and court judges have routinely issued fatwas (thus assuming the role of *mufti*, or fatwa-giver, usually without using that title). Fatwas can "stand in" for legal rulings, as they did, for example, in Java after 1937, when religious courts, deprived of legal jurisdiction over inheritance matters, continued to hear cases, issuing fatwas or "determinations" (*penetapan*) (Lev 1972a). Only in 1989 could they once more give legally binding "decisions" (*keputusan*). The Islamic organizations Nahdlatul Ulama and Muhammadiyah began to issue fatwas in the 1920s, and continue to do so. NU, for example, has a Fatwa Division of its Tarjih Council, which in 1999 debated the propriety of Viagra, wire tapping, and female presidents. These and other Muslim organizations (including regional associations and *dakwah* groups) are formally represented on the MUI. Scholars from both NU and Muhammadiyah occupy Council leadership roles, and fatwas from these organizations are discussed by the Council.

What is the MUI's legal status? Although created by the president, the acting general chairman, Muardi Chadib, described it as a private association of scholars (ulama) not subject to government decree. However, he also took pride in the attention the government has paid to its fatwas. The Council recently had ruled that chicken imported from the United States had not been properly killed and thus was *harâm*; the fatwa immediately was accepted by the Ministry of Trade, and the imports were banned (interview, 2000).[4] The committee has a

---

[2] Hamka served as general chairman from 1975 until he resigned in 1981. He was succeeded by Syukri Ghozali (1981–84), Hasan Basri (1985–98), and Ali Yafie (1998–99). In 2000–02 the office has rotated among several of the members.

[3] Other committees deal with education, Qur'ân study, *dakwah*, economics, women and children, and international relations; new committees may be formed in the 2000s. The fatwa committee was chaired by Syukri Ghozali from 1975 until 1981, when he became Council chairman, and then by Ibrahim Hosen from 1981 until the present.

[4] However, Muardi Chadib also lamented the lower level of respect given to the Council by the then president, Abdurrahman Wahid, compared with his predecessor, Habibie. He accounted for the difference by describing Wahid as believing that religion and politics should not mix.

subcommittee that evaluates the religious status of food and cosmetics.[5] Other fatwas have covered a broad range of topics, including matters of religious ritual, the acceptability of reproductive technology, HIV/AIDS, gambling, and banking.

In the generally critical atmosphere of the early Reform era, many Islamic scholars have faulted the Council for having taken orders from the New Order government. The head of the Aceh Council, Soufyan Hamzah, once said it should be called the *Majelis Ulama Istana*, the Council of "Court Ulama," referring (as many did) to the Suharto government (more precisely, Suharto's Jakarta home on Cendana street) as the "Istana." The MUI chairman campaigned for the government in the 1997 elections, the Council declined to prohibit the state from running a lottery in the 1980s, and it failed to support political reform efforts in 1998. There is little consensus on its future, however; among recent proposals for reform are both giving it greater independence and changing it into a State Fatwa Body.[6]

Sharî'a in Aceh

The ambiguous position of the Majelis Ulama is reproduced at the provincial level. The Council in Aceh has taken an active role in trying to change social life through its own fatwas. For example, in 1990 the Aceh Council issued a fatwa that women had to wear *jilbab*. They specified that in the presence of "marriageable men" this declaration meant that they had to cover all their body except for face, hands, and feet, and that when engaged in worship, women had to cover all but the face. They added that Muslims must not wear clothes associated with other religions. The fatwa since has been cited as authoritative in a local question and answer column (*Serambi Indonesia*, 9 June 2000).

This fatwa has been interpreted and justified in distinct ways. In Jakarta, Muardi Chadib stated that the fatwa was in response to a question about proper girls' attire at school, and that it only advised women to wear them. The fatwa was misunderstood by the common people, he added. "The fatwa is necessary, because males will be more likely to commit sex crimes if they are already tending in that direction; such crimes do not happen in religious schools, for example, nor do students fight there, because fights among students start with boys stealing each others' girlfriends, so it too is a matter of sex."[7]

---

[5] As of 2000, there are two subcommittees: one evaluates the religious acceptability of statutes, and the other deals with sharî'a more broadly.

[6] Many of these calls were voiced at an Islamic assembly called the Kongres Umat Islam, held in Jakarta in November 1998 (*Tempo* online, 17 November 1998; *Gatra* online, 14 November 1998).

[7] Interview, Jakarta, June 2000.

In Aceh, little has been done to "correct" this misunderstanding, however. There never was a government regulation to back up the fatwa, but the Aceh Council has continued to oppose efforts to make the jilbab a matter of individual choice. In early 2000, Musdah Mulia of the Department of Human Rights had spoken to the Acehnese Women's Congress to Give Voice to Women's Aspirations (Kongres Perempuan Aceh Untuk Menyuarakan Aspirasi Permepuan), attended, she said, by over 600 women. She and others from Jakarta argued that in Islam,

the jilbab was not a requirement but rather a way of keeping unwanted things from happening. We taught that during the Prophet's time not everyone wore a jilbab, that there is a hadîth that during the fasting month the women were told to wear jilbab for prayer, and those that did not have one were told to borrow them, which indicates that some women did not have them then. But the women thought that they needed to follow whatever the government, the Majelis Ulama, had told them to do. Religion gives freedom to choose, but here the MU Aceh opposed us, saying that women should not have a voice like that. But we just ignored them. (Interview, 2000)

And yet it is becoming harder to ignore such edicts. The Acehnese liberation movement, GAM, declared that all women would have to wear jilbab if they went out of their houses, and there were incidents of the edict having been enforced, "jilbab raids" (*razzia jilbab*). In the Gayo highlands, at Simpang Baliq, some Acehnese men cut the hair of girls not wearing jilbab in 1999. In Takèngën, I found nearly all girls and women wearing some sort of headcovering and long, flowing garments in 2000; village dress was more mixed.[8] Signs had been posted in parts of Takèngën proclaiming that Muslim dress should be worn there, and along the northern coast of Aceh I saw signs in villages saying Daerah Wajib Jilbab (Required Jilbab Area).[9]

There is an irony to sharî'a developments in Aceh. It has been the Indonesian state that has most vigorously promoted the implementation of Islamic law in the province. The then president, Abdurrahman Wahid, otherwise an outspoken opponent of expanding sharî'a, unsuccessfully attempted to "declare sharî'a" for Aceh in December 2000. His efforts were met with opposition from Acehnese leaders, who saw it as one more ploy to keep Aceh in Indonesia, an "unwanted gift," in the words of one Acehnese religious scholar.[10] Neither the independence movement, GAM, nor the various associations calling for Acehnese self-determination (in particular SIRA, the Sentral Informasi Referendum Aceh) have called for the implementation of sharî'a.

---

[8] As several friends commented, however, the clothing worn by teenage girls in Takèngën seemed to be closer-fitting than before.

[9] These signs also have been noted in other parts of Aceh (*Forum* online, 17–24 December 2000).

[10] See coverage in *Kompas* online, 5, 18 December 2000; *Serambi*, 18 December 2000; and *Forum*, 17–24 December 2000.

At issue is not the appropriateness of Islamic law in the abstract, but whether the Indonesian state ought to impose it on the Acehnese people. One has, at one and the same time, calls by GAM for women to dress and behave in Islamic fashion, and condemnations by them of the Indonesian police for enforcing the wearing of the jilbab.[11] There also has begun to appear an opposition between those religious figures who position themselves as present or future sharî'a enforcers, and those who see themselves mainly as scholars or jurists. Thus, the Aceh Council, and ulama connected to the main mosque in Banda Aceh, continue to support "jilbabization" (*penjilbaban*), whereas ulama associated with the IAIN Ar-Raniry have consistently advocated a more cautious approach. Interestingly, judges on the Islamic appeals court in Banda Aceh have played down the extent of eventual application of sharî'a.[12]

Pigs and enzymes

The MUI increasingly is asserting its role as a guardian of the Islamic community *vis-à-vis* the government as well as *vis-à-vis* external threats. In part, this new oppositional stance arose from the sense of antipathy between some MUI members and former President Abdurrahman Wahid; in part, it stems from a sense that, faced with increasing provincial autonomy and a fluid political situation, it is up to them to delineate the boundaries of the Muslim community.

The sense of opposition to the government appeared clearly in a controversy in 2001 over the monosodium glutamate additive Ajinomoto. The product, made in Indonesia by a Japanese-owned company, is widely used for cooking throughout the archipelago. But in January 2001, the MUI declared the product harâm, because its laboratory tests showed that an enzyme used as a catalyst in the production process comes from the pancreas of the pig. Even though pork is not itself present in the final product, "from the standpoint of Islamic law, it is used (*intifa*), and for that reason [the product] is declared harâm," was the announcement of the MUI's general secretary, Dien Syamsuddin.[13] Since 1994, the MUI has been issuing halal certificates, and has, to date, issued some 500 of these labels. Dien Syamsuddin took the occasion to suggest that such certificates be made mandatory for all food products.

Not long after the declaration, Jakarta police arrested eight Ajinomoto managers, of whom two were Japanese citizens, for having violated the interests of Indonesian consumers. The police also closed Ajinomoto factories, putting an estimated 3,000 workers out of work. Interestingly, the police acted without a

---

[11] Coverage in *Serambi*, 14 November 2000, 27 August 2001; *Tapol list-serve*, 29 August 2001.
[12] Interviews with Abdullah Nafi of the Islamic court (*Jakarta Post*, 5 January 2002), Soufyan Hamzah, the Imam Masjid Raya Baiturrahman in Banda Aceh (*Serambi*, 27 August 2001), and Al-Yasa Abubakar, vice-chancellor of IAIN Ar-Raniry (*Forum*, 17–24 December 2000).
[13] *Tempo* online, 8 January 2001; additional coverage was provided by the magazine over the period 8–15 January 2001.

court order, following the rationale that they were defending Islam. Responding to criticisms that the legal process was still underway, the head of the Jakarta metropolitan police force, Makbul Padmanagara, stated that "the case has offended the sensibilities of the Indonesian Muslim community" (*Tempo,* 8 January 2001).

But then the president weighed in, declaring on 9 January that the product was halâl, because laboratory tests showed that the pig pancreas substance was not detected in the product itself, a conclusion reaffirmed the following day by the chair of the biotechnology department at prestigious Gajah Mada University (and also conceded by the MUI). From that point forward, the issue became one of who had the authority to make such declarations, not the facts of any particular enzymatic matter. The disagreement was probably overdetermined by current political divisions: Dien Syamsuddin had been a strong supporter of former President Habibie, and was active in the government-shaped organization ICMI; he was also a political opponent of Wahid. Moreover, he had worked closely with K.H. Hasan Basri, once head of MUI (Hefner 2000:173, 177–78).[14] Abdurrahman Wahid thus had multiple political reasons to oppose the MUI fatwa, on top of his generally pluralistic, non-legalistic orientation towards Islam and his concern for the displaced Ajinomoto workers.

In the end, Wahid claimed that both he and the MUI were right, because it was a matter of ijtihâd, and, quoting a popular hadîth (that did not quite support his "both are right" statement), "he whose ijtihâd is true receives two merits; he whose ijtihâd is false receives one." But most personalities quoted in the news sided with the MUI; these included the popular scholar and preacher, K.H. Zainuddin M.Z., who said that the president's declaration could be the result of political thinking, about relations with Japan, for example. It is a matter of religion, not science, he said. "If one *kiai* (religious teacher) differs with 100 engineers about a prayer, then you have to follow the kiai's opinion, not that of the 100 engineers. We have to return to *profesionalisme*." The police, too, sided with the MUI, "because they are the ones given authority over matters of halâl and harâm." A member of Parliament warned the president not to enter into matters of religion (*Tempo* online, 10 January 2001).

The Internet chatter took both sides, with one commentator speculating that the president had received Japanese money in return for his stand in favor of Ajinomoto, another pointing out that what we now had was a conflict among authorities with no clear way to resolve it, and a third lamenting the fact that Indonesian housewives no longer know pepper from ginger, but depend on spice products made by foreigners.

---

[14] More recently, Dien Syamsuddin has been a promoter of Indonesians engaging in "jihad" in Afghanistan, a call regretted by others, and quickly "spun" by the MUI head as not implying armed conflict. Dien himself later said that he meant a "cultural jihad" (*Asia.CNN*, 25 September 2001; *Media Indonesia*, 1 October 2001; *Kompas*, 30 September 2001).

The matter was partly resolved when Ajinomoto agreed to substitute a vegetable substance for the porcine one, but the controversy pointed up the indeterminacy in Indonesian law regarding boundary maintenance on the cooking front. Is it in the power of the state to ban foods because they contain pork? And who has that power, if it exists? Does an MUI decree have the force of law, as the head of the Jakarta police force claimed, or is it only advisory to the government, and to Muslim citizens, as has generally been claimed heretofore?

Conversion and Christmas

The most noteworthy fatwas from the MUI have probably been those that concern Muslim–Christian relationships, which we might think of as the harâm–halâl issue transposed on to the plane of human social relationships. These fatwas reveal a particular concern among Indonesian Muslims for maintaining their community against the threat of conversion, or, perhaps, contamination, from what is perceived by some as a worldwide Christian missionary project.

Atho Mudzhar (1993) has observed that the Council's two most controversial fatwas in the 1980s dealt with Muslim–Christian relations. In 1981 it pronounced it to be forbidden (harâm) for Muslims to attend any Christmas celebrations, and in 1980 it opposed any marriages between Muslims and non-Muslims. The fatwa on Christmas claimed that all such celebrations were part of "ritual" and thus were not to be joined by Muslims. The jurists assembled extensive quotes from the Qur'ân that emphasized the importance to Muslims of remaining apart from the worship activities of other religions.

The fatwa came just as the government was intensively promoting inter-religious cooperation after a decade of sporadic conflicts between Muslims and Christians over the building of churches in Muslim areas and the use of foreign funds to convert Muslims to Christianity. The government position was that Christmas celebrations, which in Jakarta were normally held at offices and schools, were not "ritual" and thus could be attended by Muslims, and the Minister of Religion restated that opinion immediately after the Council fatwa. This was the only case from that period in which the Council and the ministry were unable to resolve their differences. The Council general chairman, Hamka, refused to revoke the fatwa, and was so furious at being asked to sign a letter limiting the circulation of the fatwa that he resigned his post.

Three other fatwas on family matters also were motivated by fears of Christian missionary activities. The 1980 fatwa against inter-religious marriages – the only one, incidentally, to be countersigned by the Minister of Religion – went far beyond the standard religious law texts in forbidding marriage between a Muslim man and a woman of the *ahl al-kitâb*, a marriage expressly permitted in the Qur'ân (5:5) and in Shâfi'î law. The fatwa drew on the doctrine of the "community interest" (*masâlih al-mursala*) to justify its abrogation of the Qur'ân, and cited the example of the second caliph, 'Umar, who had done the same (recall references to 'Umar by liberal reformers discussed in chapter 7). The "community interest" at stake was the fear of children of mixed marriages being raised as Christians.

Muzdhar (1993:90–93) argues that two other fatwas, both from 1984, were also motivated by fears of conversion. One stated that adoption neither breaks ties to biological parents nor creates new legal ties to the adoptive parents, and thus does not change limitations on whom one may marry, or one's status as an heir.[15] Fears of Christians adopting poor Muslim children prompted this fatwa (a link made explicit in a paper written by the then chairman of the fatwa committee, Syukri Ghozali). The second fatwa seems at first blush to have little to do with inter-religious relations. It urged Muslims not to parcel out their lands among their children, but to leave them as a unit for one of their heirs to receive (after duly compensating the other heirs), or to sell them to other Muslims in the village. The mention of Muslims here, in a fatwa on a strangely non-religious topic for the Council to take up, suggests the fear, widespread at the time, that Christians were buying up lands on which to build churches.[16] In principle, and particularly since a joint ministerial decree (of the Ministers of Religion and Interior) in 1970, no religion is allowed to proselytize in a region where another religion dominates. Yet Muslims frequently complain that Christians will point to the presence of a few Christians in a Muslim area as reason to build a church, which then serves as the base for attempts to convert others.

The MUI fatwas are symptomatic of a fear among some Muslims that they will lose their children to Christian missionaries. As Robert Hefner points out (2000:106–09, 140), by the 1960s, the Catholic and Protestant churches on Java had been successfully indigenized and were attracting relatively large numbers of converts, numbers that rose further when, after the massacres of 1965–66, it became dangerous not to belong to one of the five recognized religions. On Java, Christian churches were more sympathetic to ex-Communists released from prison, and had been less directly involved in the massacres than Muslim organizations. Churches were to benefit from their relatively positive responses with success in attracting converts, about 3 percent of the Javanese population in the 1960s, and continued increases in the subsequent decades (Hefner 2000:108).

Muslim responses to conversion activity have included propaganda campaigns, in some cases based on the MUI's authority. Since 1967, the Dewan Dakwah Islamiyah Indonesia (DDII, Indonesian Islamic Propagation Council),

---

[15] The fatwa in effect simply restated earlier Muslim objections to the first draft of the 1974 Marriage Law.

[16] Muzdhar (1993:93) makes the intriguing observation that when a fatwa is aimed at external threats to the Muslim community it relies almost exclusively on scripture, whereas a fatwa on internal matters relies on fiqh texts. Perhaps the degree of concern or alarm dictates the level of evidence felt to be required.

an organization led until his death by Muhammad Natsir, the former leader of Masyumi, has been energetic in preparing Muslims to propagate the faith (as *dâ'i*). In the mid-1990s the DDII made its *da'wa* manuals widely available. The same organization used its monthly magazine, *[Serial] Media Dakwah*, to remind readers of Christian missionization (coupled with the supposed "Jewish" presence in Indonesia), through stories of attempts to convert children through trickery, and even an effort to convert Muhammad Natsir through a stealthy invasion of his hospital room. The burning of churches, although not explicitly approved of, is stated to be the result of "excesses" by missionaries.[17]

Seemingly minor matters have become symbols of the threat to the Islamic community either from without or from within, from greeting Christians to translating focal Islamic terms. The magazine lambasted Nurcholis Madjid for his Indonesian rendering of the confession of faith, in which he translated the two occurrences of "god" in "there is no god but God" as *tuhan* and *Tuhan*, using the general Indonesian word (and the word used by Christians) rather than the specifically Islamic *Allah. Media Dakwah*'s editors complained that this way of translating these words weakened the boundaries between the two communities. (Of course, from an Islamic perspective, Muslims, Christians, and Jews *do* worship the same God.)[18]

For many years the DDII annually reprinted and distributed the MUI's fatwa on Christmas. These activities upset Suharto, who, it was said, did not want his Minister of Religion, Munawir Szadjali, whose daughter had married a Christian, further embarrassed. In 1989 several distributors of the leaflets were detained by the police. In 1990, Gideon International distributed Bibles at secondary schools in Jakarta, claiming they had permission from the Jakarta Office of Education and Culture. Muslim pupils reportedly ripped up the Bibles and dumped them into the trash. *Media Dakwah* (December 1990) cited this incident as proof of an aggressive Christianization campaign in Indonesia.

In August 1991, the Council of Ulama asked the attorney general to ban elementary school textbooks that suggested that people should attend the religious celebrations of people of other faiths. He did so. During the 1991 Christmas season, Nurcholis Madjid told the Islamic daily *Pelita* that while following Christian ritual was harâm for Muslims, saying "Merry Christmas" to Christians was not, for it was not part of ritual. Some other Muslim leaders consulted by the daily (including the prominent scholars Harun Nasution and Ali Yafie) agreed. However, the chair of the Council of Ulama, Hasan Basri, objected vigorously, reiterating the 1981 fatwa against attending Christian celebrations. *Media Dakwah* (January 1992:72) responded with a cartoon showing a mugger

---

[17] *Media Dakwah*, January 1993:54.
[18] Taufik Abdullah (interviews in 1994 and 2000) perceptively observed that Nurcholis's error was to forget that Indonesians think of words mainly as sounds, not writing. The distinction between "tuhan" and "Tuhan" was lost on most Muslims, some of whom drew the conclusion that Nurcholis was submerging the specificity of Islamic worship in a general concept of "deity."

wearing a cross (pointedly playing on popular associations of Christian Bataks with street violence) ordering a poor, ignorant Muslim to greet him; the Muslim responds with "Oh, what does ritual mean again? I'm just an ordinary person."

In January 1997, extended Internet discussion concerned whether a Muslim should send a Christmas card to a Christian friend, or even wish him or her "Merry Christmas." The discussion began with a statement by a Muslim that another participant in the discussion, a Christian, could send a *kartu Lebaran*, greeting card to mark the end of the fasting month and the celebration of Idhul Fitri, but that he should not hope to receive a Christmas card in return. Some of those who responded agreed with this comment, on grounds that Muslims had to keep a tight distinction between ritual and non-ritual (or, put in a different way, between "matters of this world," *masalah dunia*, and "matters of the afterlife," *masalah akhirat*). Others disagreed, saying that such greetings and wishes were matters of human relations (*silaturrahmi*) and not religious practice. The discussion quickly broadened to include the propriety of a Muslim's answering an "*Assalamu'alaikum*," the standard Arabic greeting, if it came from a Christian. Was it part of Islamic ritual, *ibadah*? Or was it simply a greeting that happened to be in Arabic and in any case preceded Islam? And some participants began to complain of the lack of tolerance exhibited towards other religions by some speakers on Islamic television programs. In December of that year, President Suharto attended Christmas celebrations. The festivities were staged so as to emphasize the "unity in diversity" cultural theme of the New Order, with Christmas songs in regional languages from Irian Jaya, North Sumatra, North Sulawesi, and, pointedly, East Timor.

Freedom of religion: choice or boundary-maintenance?

Boundary-maintenance took a more violent turn in the late 1990s, as law enforcement weakened and vigilantism expanded. In one notorious case from 1999 in West Sumatra, the homeland of the Muslim Minangkabau people, a Christian man was convicted in the civil court of having abducted and raped a sixteen-year-old Muslim girl in Padang, the provincial capital. His accused accomplices included the head of a Christian school where the girl was enrolled under a different name ("and without a headscarf," read the magazine account). Despite the conviction of the man, Salmon Melianus Ongirwalu, the judge who found him guilty of kidnapping and rape was attacked by Islamic associations for having not also found him guilty of trying to convert the girl to Christianity. According to a member of the West Sumatran Islamic Community's Jihad Forum, one of the groups that attacked the courtroom after the judge's decision, the judge's mistake was in not making explicit that "Salmon's action cannot be separated from Christianizing efforts in Minang[kabau] territory."[19]

---

[19] As reported in *Forum Keadilan*, 27 September 1999.

As noteworthy as the case itself is the way in which the newsmagazine *Forum Keadilan*, a non-sectarian weekly that focuses on issues of justice and law, presented the events. Rather than considering the possibility that the crowds could be ignoring freedom of religion, the report represented their actions as the logical response to the distribution of Bibles: "It is true that one cannot separate the Salmon case from the shock experienced by the residents of Padang at the recently growing efforts at Christianization in their area. Moreover, the people of West Sumatra also were startled at the circulation of Bibles in the Minangkabau language. So the anger of the masses was complete." Indeed, the article's authors suggest that the court may have erred in not heeding warnings from the police as well as from Islamic organizations that the sentence should be at least ten years (Salmon received eight).

There have since been efforts to regulate the expansion of Christianity. In 1970, the Ministers of Interior and Religion had issued a joint decree forbidding efforts to convert people already practicing one recognized religion to another; the distribution of Bibles in a Muslim area would violate this decree. However, the decree does not have legal sanctions attached to it. A law on "inter-religious harmony" (*kerukunan antaragama*) recently has been under parliamentary discussion. The law would give that decree the force of a statute, and also introduce limits on the construction of religious buildings, mandating a minimum distance from current buildings, the attestation of a minimum number of local worshipers, and the consent of local residents. In 2000, the Council of Ulama strongly supported the bill, and argued that the violence in Ambon and elsewhere between religious communities makes it necessary. Christian groups, the Alliance of Indonesian Churches (Persekutuan Gereja-gereja Indonesia, PGI) and the Indonesian Bishops' Conference (Komperensi Wali Gereja Indonesia, KWI) by and large opposed it, arguing that freedom of religion includes the right to spread their religious message, and that religion is not behind recent local conflicts, but only is manipulated by elites.[20] An objection from within NU was voiced by Masdar Mas'udi, who claimed that state intervention has created social conflict between religions, such as when the state regulates where churches can be built or when Idhul Fitri should be celebrated.[21]

[20] Coverage in *Republika*, 17 March 2000 and *Jakarta Post*, 17 March 2000.

[21] Reported in *Kompas*, 26 March 2000. The tension between freedom of religion and Islamic opposition to conversion appeared sharply in late 1998, in an event covered widely in the Indonesian press, when the influential Egyptian Muslim scholar Syekh Mohammaad Sayyed Thonthowy delivered a fatwa saying that under conditions of economic hardship a Muslim who converted to another religion need not be considered to deserve the death penalty. He reasoned that the Prophet Muhammad had interpreted the death penalty as deserved only by those who, in their conversion, insulted Islam. (No doubt the Salman Rushdie case came to the minds of many hearing or reading this fatwa.) The fatwa was delivered in Malaysia, on 20 August. As it happened, not long before Malaysia had passed a law permitting Malaysians over the age of 18 to freely choose their religion, and about 5,000 Muslims had responded by converting (*Gatra* online, 31 October 1998).

Debates about the state's role in regulating religion came to the fore at the beginning of President Abdurrahman Wahid's rule, largely because of his own position that religion and politics should be separated. Wahid made a point of attending celebrations held by other religions, much to the consternation of some Islamic groups. The heretofore recognized religions faced a dilemma, caught as they were between the desire to free themselves from state interference, and the reluctance to lose the power the state has provided to suppress movements considered by recognized religious leaders to be heterodox. Most spokespersons for major religious organizations and parties have hastened to agree that the state should not regulate religion, and that the New Order rules limiting recognizable religions to five should be abandoned. But then, each such spokesperson has added that the state's help will continue to be needed to suppress some sects – perhaps not on the grounds that they are heterodox, but because they conflict with Pancasila, or endanger social harmony. Thus, in February 2000, the acting chair of the Council of Ulama indicated that, although no religion should be banned because one of the "mainstream religions" objects to it, the Islamic sect Al-Arqam's teaching clearly conflicts with Pancasila, "so the government should ban it." The secretary general of the Christian PGI, J.E. Pattiasina, also expressed concern that a lifting of the prohibition would allow back into Indonesia the Children of God sect.[22]

These disputes signal a deep divide over the question of the community to which a Muslim belongs. The da'wa activities of the DDII and other activitist Muslim organizations stress the importance of solidarity among the the Islamic community, *ukhuwah Islamiyah*, against violations and intrusions. An alternative notion of *ukhuwah*, as an Indonesian community rather than an exclusively Islamic one, has been promoted by the pluralists, especially by Nurcholis Madjid and by former President Abdurrahman Wahid (Hefner 2000). These scholars invoke the Medina Constitution of the Prophet Muhammad, under which Jews and others lived together with Muslims, as a charter for an Islamic theory of religious pluralism. Jalaluddin Rakhmat (1991:37–38) has even proposed the concept of a *madhhab ukhuwah*, a "legal tradition based on community," in which Muslims would emphasize common effort and good works rather than theological debates – which he even more contentiously proposes as the *madhhab Ali*, the "tradition of 'Ali," the caliph mainly associated with Shi'ism by Indonesian readers.

Policing intermarriage

Intermarriage has been one of the battlegrounds on which these fears have been played out. Manipulating rules about the people with whom you may marry (or what you may eat) is a primary way to reinforce or transgress boundaries

---

[22] *Jakarta Post*, 21 February 2000.

between social groups. Mary Douglas, in her essays on the biblical prohibitions on eating certain foods, famously linked the sharp distinction of clean and unclean foods to the efforts by leaders of the Israelites to prevent intermarriage with other peoples. "Here is a people who prefer their boundaries to remain intact. They reckon any attempt to cross them a hostile intrusion" (Douglas 1975:304).[23]

The first sallies in Indonesian disputes over intermarriage came after the passage of the 1974 Marriage Law, which had created considerable confusion about the status of "mixed marriages." The term had been used in law and in everyday discourse to refer to marriages between two people subject to different laws, where "law" included religious laws. Marriages between citizens of different states or followers of different religions were "mixed." The right to enter into such marriages was guaranteed by law. Furthermore, Muslim jurists in Indonesia and elsewhere had generally acknowledged as valid the marriage of a Muslim man to a non-Muslim Christian (or Jewish) woman, citing the explicit permission given in the Qur'ân (5:5).

But the 1974 law redefined "mixed marriage" as referring only to different citizenships, and, as we saw in chapter 8, it stipulated that marriage was to be carried out according to the respective religions (article 2, clause 1). Did the new law mean that a couple had to be of the same religion before they could marry? Or that each had to satisfy his or her religious authorities? Or something else again?

Over the following few years, Jakarta residents of different religions who wished to marry continued to do so at the civil registry, as they had done previously (Katz and Katz 1978:315). This practice initially was endorsed by lower courts and in at least one Supreme Court decision.[24] However, in 1983, President Suharto directed the civil registries to register marriages only if they did not involve Muslims. In May 1986, the head of the Jakarta office of the Ministry of Religion sent a letter to the civil registrars stating that because marriage was a religious matter, the civil registries should refrain from registering any marriage involving a Muslim. After all, said the circular, Muslims have their own Office of Religious Affairs, which could marry a Muslim man to a Christian woman, so there was no need for the registries to be involved. Doing otherwise would be to "bow down to Western law."[25]

---

[23] A worry that continues to drive debates among Jews about the definition of a Jew and the requirements for conversion.

[24] See the Pengadilan Negeri decision PN 77/1977 of the Jakarta Utara Timur court, and the Supreme Court's decision in 1650/1974, dated 13 November 1979 (cited in Butt 1999:135, n.79).

[25] Suharto's decree was in the form of a presidential decision, *Keppres* No. 12, 1983; see also Pompe 1991. The Jakarta Council of Ulama followed up the 1986 instruction with its own letter, sent in July of that year, to the Governor of Jakarta, in which the Council asked him to forbid the civil registries to register or perform marriages between two people of different religions, if one was Muslim (both letters in Sukarja 1994).

The most celebrated, or reviled, decision on the matter was written by the chairman of the Supreme Court, Ali Said, in 1989. In the decision, referred to generally as the *Andy Vonny* case, Said wrote that the 1945 Constitution guaranteed people of different religions the right to marry, a right not revoked by the 1974 Marriage Law.[26] In the case, the Office of Religious Affairs in Jakarta had refused to marry a Muslim woman to a Protestant Christian man, saying that such a marriage was contrary to Islam. The civil registry also had refused to carry out the marriage, on grounds that the girl was a Muslim. The couple sued the Office of Religious Affairs and the registry, lost, and appealed to the Supreme Court.

The Court agreed with the Office of Religious Affairs' understanding of the 1974 law, but went on to say that the very fact that the woman had then gone to the civil registry, where the marriage could be performed but not in accord with Islam, showed that she "no longer heeds her religious status." The civil registry should then marry them or help them to marry, concluded the Court. The justices lamented that the 1974 law provides for no institution to handle inter-religious marriages, and stated that the law had created a regrettable "legal vacuum" (*kekosongan hukum*).

The decision was published in the official bulletin of case law, *Yurisprudensi Indonesia*, and elicited considerable reaction, mainly negative, from Muslim jurists. The Court's chief offense in their eyes was to have inferred from the bride's recourse to the civil registry that she had abandoned her religion. This inference confirmed fears that inter-religious marriages would lead Muslims to convert to Christianity. Even the jurist who edited the decision for the bulletin took the unusual step of complaining that this portion of the decision was regrettable.

Tightening the rules

Throughout the 1990s the editors of the Ministry of Religion's publication *Mimbar Hukum* carried out a campaign against mixed marriages, and against the *Andy Vonny* case. In a series of articles, jurists and judges argued that all religions oppose mixed marriage, and that Indonesia's laws merely codify this opposition. The 1974 Marriage Law states that marriage is valid when performed according to the religion of each party, they reminded their readers (largely judges and jurists), and both Islam and Christianity forbid such marriages. The Compilation of Islamic Law makes Islam's disapproval even more explicit. The civil registry is therefore only for registration, not for marrying, as marriage is a religious act. The legal situation is thus internally consistent (there is no "legal vacuum").

---

[26] The case, No 1400/1986 before the Court, was reported in *Yurisprudensi Indonesia* 2, 1989:93–103, and also in *Varia Peradilan* 45, 1989:73–86.

And, because inter-religious marriages are recognized in all societies to be undesirable, the laws now on the books produce the right social effects.

There was a problem, however, to the Islamic dimension of this argument, in that most Muslim jurists long had accepted the religious validity of marriages between Muslim men and Christian women (in the latter's status as *ahlul kitab*, "people of the book"). The response has been a variant of "contextualization": that such marriages indeed had received a "narrow dispensation" in the Qur'ân, but only because at that time there was a shortage of Muslim women, something which is not the case today (Daud Ali 1994b). Others pointed out that the problem was a general tendency to intermarry, that as many Muslim–Christian marriages in Jakarta were between Muslim women and Christian men as the reverse.[27] The historian Taufik Abdullah gave me an additional argument from social context (interview, 1994): "No one really debated this change in emphasis from 'OK for a Muslim man to marry a Christian woman' to 'neither way'; the latest theory to justify the change is that the religion of the mother is the more important since she is with the children more." He agreed with this theory, based on people he knew.

These steps taken to prevent Muslim–Christian marriages came at a time when Suharto was trying to attract Muslim support, by passing the 1989 Courts Bill, establishing the first Islamic bank, and appointing to the Cabinet ministers considered "Green," meaning pro-Islam. Suharto himself made the pilgrimage to Mecca in 1991. It was, as we saw above, also a time of increased concern about conversion to Christianity. A number of high-profile marriages between Christians and Muslims added to a sense of threat. The Ministry of Religion's 1986 letter forbidding civil registries from registering Muslims singled out for criticism "the procedure you followed in registering the marriage of the Muslim Djamal Mirdad to the Christian Lydia Kandou." If Megawati's efforts to remarry provided a symbol of Islamic legal disarray, the 1986 marriage of these two film stars brought together fears of the money and glamour behind Christianity, anxiety about secular urban life, and concerns that marriage was losing its religious character. The marriage continued to resonate for years thereafter in the public imagination and to trouble the jurists. In a 1992 letter, the Jakarta Council of Ulama urged civil registries not to register Muslims, acknowledging the role of that marriage in provoking their intervention. Even in 2000, judges and jurists with whom I spoke about inter-religious marriages repeatedly mentioned the Kandou–Mirdad marriage. In a polemic against inter-religious marriages (and against the then Minister of Religion, Munawir Sjadzali), *Media Dakwah* (February 1992:14–16) argued that pressure for allowing such marriages began with Jakarta artists, "who easily marry and divorce frequently."

---

[27] Between April 1985 and July 1986, 239 marriages were registered at the Jakarta civil registry of a Muslim to a non-Muslim, involving 112 Muslim men and 127 Muslim women (Sukarja 1994:19).

Muslim–Christian romances have involved politicians as well as film stars. Munawir Szadjali became a target of mixed-marriage opponents in part because his daughter married a Christian man. (To decrease the potential political fallout of the marriage, Szadjali asked a friend and former Cabinet colleague, Joop Ave, to replace him as his daughter's guardian at the wedding.) From time to time the children of other ministers have been rumored to be considering such marriages, and rumors flew in the early 1990s about a possible marriage between Christian singer Maya Rumantir with Suharto's son Tommy.

Since the mid-1990s it has been extremely difficult, if not impossible, to register inter-religious marriages, even if they have been performed according to Islamic law, without one party changing his or her religion. Some couples have married overseas, but they cannot then register their marriages in Indonesia. Not having a certificate of marriage registration causes problems for such couples. Both the 1989 law on religious courts and the 1991 Compilation of Islamic Law direct the religious courts not to recognize marriages where there is no marriage certificate. Certificates are needed to collect a deceased spouse's pension or bank account, or to be declared the heir of the spouse by the religious court. Nor does the conversion of one spouse always provide a satisfactory legal solution; the Supreme Court ruled in 1996 that a wife who had converted to Islam but then reverted to Christianity lost all rights to her children in case of divorce.[28]

The "vacuum" continues to produce legal anomalies. One of the many inter-religious marriages of Jakarta celebrities came to public attention because of a messy divorce. Emilia Contessa, a famous singer from a Muslim family, married a Christian man, Rio Tambunan, in 1976, after fleeing from a near-marriage to a Muslim businessman. They were married by a civil registrar who also happened to be a minister, and at that moment Emilia stated she was converting to her husband's religion. The couple separated after several years and two children, and in 1988 Emilia, saying she had returned to Islam, married a Muslim man. The problem was that neither the courts nor the church could find any evidence that she had ever divorced Rio, so, asked the newsmagazine *Tempo* (22 July 1989), was she living in a polyandrous situation? The head of the Council of Indonesian Ulama, Hasan Basri, said that her current marriage was perfectly legal because marriages at the civil registry were not recognized by the 1974 Marriage Law (and certainly not in Islam) and because when she returned to Islam her relationship with Rio (whatever it was) automatically ended.

The anxiety due to this "legal vacuum" led Minister Munawir Szadjali to call for new laws to regulate inter-religious marriages, a call echoed by Ali Said. But Munawir's voice had been weakened by his daughter's marriage, and some observers have suggested that this weakness allowed others, especially the head

---

[28] Case 210 of that year, originating in 1995 from Bandung, and reported in *Varia Peradilan* in 1996.

of the Compilation project, Justice Busthanul Arifin, to succeed in advancing the "strong" view that no mixed marriages should be considered religiously valid.

In the mid-1990s, when the controversy perhaps was at its height, a sample of liberal Muslim activists voiced a variety of views on the topic, indicating a certain generally shared ambivalence on the topic.[29] Psychologist Saparinah Sadli condemned the restrictions on marriage as "absolutely out of tune with the times. Our younger generation is motivated to broaden their social relationships, even more so for students who attend school overseas just when they start to date." However, three years earlier, her colleague in defending women's rights, the lawyer Nani Yamin, had taken the opposite position, coming out strongly against any legislation to permit mixed marriages on grounds that such laws would weaken religious values.[30] Her law colleague Irawati Dasaad also disapproved of a secularization of marriage: "We are a Pancasila society, so it is not possible to consider marriage only as a contract, because one of the *sila* (tenets) is belief in the one God."

The political scientist Dewi Fortuna Anwar, a Muslim from West Sumatra (and close aide to Habibie during his presidency), pointed to an unintended consequence of the prohibitions.

It is not a good idea to prohibit marriage between people of different religions. The idea was to prevent people from leaving Islam after such a marriage, but in fact the end result is that more people change religion in order to marry. It is not like in Egypt, where you cannot leave Islam. Even some Padang people [West Sumatran Minangkabau, generally assumed to be Muslim] have become Christian, and it is because of this change. In places where everyone is Muslim it makes no difference, but in the "open areas" [English, meaning large cities] people are grumbling about the rule.

Nurcholis Madjid found himself assuaging Muslim fears of marrying Christians. When asked whether it was still possible, in 1995, for people of different religions to marry, he responded:

Oh, yes, I perform marriage for quite a few myself, where the man is Muslim and the woman is Christian – but never vice versa. After all, the Qur'ân says that a Muslim man may marry a Christian: how can you forbid the marriage when the Qur'ân allows it? People then go to the civil registry so they have a marriage certificate, and they get it, still. Recently, a Christian girl wanted to marry a Muslim man. Her parents were in agreement, but he came to me, concerned, because his parents were unsure. Imagine, the parents were highly educated in Christian schools! I think that they felt social pressure. So I showed him the various religious law books and they all said it was fine.

---

[29] Unless otherwise indicated, the quotations are from interviews conducted in Jakarta in June 1995.

[30] As reported in the *INIS Newsletter* 7, 1992:24–25. At the time Yamin was head of the Indonesian Institute for Legal Consultation and Aid for Women and Families (Lembaga Konsultasi dan Bantuan Hukum Indonesia untuk Wanita dan Keluarga, LKBHIuWK).

But many others disagreed. Nurul Agustina, a woman in her twenties on the editorial research staff of the Islamic daily *Republika*, considers herself a feminist, a category she said meant that she tried to be aware of the role of women in Islam and the problems that alternative interpretations of religion make for women. "I agree with the government when they regulate marriage so that people of different religions cannot marry. Because religion is the foundation for everything – how could I have a husband who did not follow Muhammad or believe in the Qur'ân [she shuddered slightly to herself]; such marriages would be confusing." Sri Mulyati, with a masters degree in Islamic Studies from McGill University, concurred:

I think it's good that the government prevents those marriages because it is very difficult for people from different religions to have a successful marriage. Look, even people of the same religion and the same ethnic group have trouble! Ulama disagree on this issue: some say that you ought to be able to marry "people of the book"; others say that the original books of the Jew and Christians are lost, so there are no true "people of the book."

The argument that inter-religious marriage makes for a difficult family life is made by the Indonesian Council of Ulama as well. Muardi Chadib, of the Council's fatwa committee, defended the prohibition on grounds that such marriages "lead to problems in the home, because the husband and wife will behave differently. For example, when they have sex, the Muslim one will bathe afterwards and the other will not, and then the first will not want to have sex again because the other will be unclean (*najis*). Or when cooking, they won't both observe the dietary rules" (interview, 2000).

State–marriage–religion

The debate over mixed marriage is also a debate about whether marriage is primarily religious in character, or at least the debate can be couched in that fashion. Busthanul Arifin, one of the "hard-line" Supreme Court justices on mixed marriage, recalled only somewhat whimsically the time when Stevie Wonder was playing a concert in Jakarta, and one of his sidemen wanted to get married. Someone called up Arifin to see if he could help them find a church –

in the middle of the night! Of course, marriage in the church is the marriage for them, unlike the Dutch way, where it is first a civil marriage and only later in the church. So it is the fault of the Dutch that we have Christians thinking that marriage in a church, marriage being religious, is a threat to Christians . . . even Gus Dur [Abdurrahman Wahid] has said that the marriage laws make us sectarian. But I said no, if that is the case, then Europeans, Australians, they are sectarian, too, because they marry according to religion. (Interview, 2000)

The debate here joins that over human rights: the human rights lawyer Abdul Hakim G. Nusantara argued that the right to marry is a basic human right; Islamic opponents argue that just as basic is one's duty to God.

Furthermore, the "strong Muslim" position is also a statist one, that just as marriage is religious, so religion needs to be regulated by the state. In 2000, Arifin was supporting the proposed laws defining the bases of religion (*undang-2 berukun agama*), which would restrict marriage to those of the same religion, and extend to other domains as well.

Part of the laws will say that building churches and mosques must be done with permits. Catholics object that this is violating human rights (*hak asasi*), but you cannot just put a mosque anywhere; Catholics could not put a new church in the Vatican, so human rights have as their limit where you would infringe upon the human rights of another person. In the United States, you can't have prayers in school, it's limited.

The Catholic position is more welcoming of inter-religious marriages, and, in a fashion characteristic of such dialogues in Indonesia, the very openness incites suspicion from Islamic quarters. At the height of the public debate in 1989, Cardinal Justinus Darmojuwono stated that a Muslim could be married to a Catholic in church, without converting or reciting anything that implied conversion (no "Catholic *syahadat*," referring to the Muslim confession of faith). Indeed, conversion would be much more difficult for a Muslim than would be marrying a Catholic, as it would require a year or more of study, he said (*Tempo*, 30 December 1989).

One resolution of the conflict was proposed by Bismar Siregar, a Supreme Court justice at the time of my interview with him in 1994, and a widely read author of Islamic and legal essays. Bismar Siregar personally opposed inter-religious marriages but thought they ought to be legally available to Muslims and Christians.

The Qur'ânic verse says that it is permitted for a Muslim man to marry a non-Muslim woman, and verses are always true, eternally true. Back then the Arabs would kill daughters, so there were not enough women to marry, and so it was permitted to marry women "of the book," even though it was better to marry women of the same faith.

JB: But now they have to leave the country to get married; is that proper?

It should be permitted for the local Office of Religious Affairs to marry them, and I would approve their marriage as a judge, even though first I would speak to them as a Muslim and say I do not approve. You cannot force people in religion. There was a case that came to the Supreme Court, that of *Andy Vonny*, and the decision was that the civil registry was the right place for a mixed marriage. But I disagree, and I wrote that you should marry in the church if a Christian man marries a Muslim woman, and at the Office of Religious Affairs if the reverse.

Elsewhere (1994a:42–44), Bismar Siregar has sharply distinguished law from faith, writing that there are ways to make inter-religious marriages legal, and that is all that the state ought to concern itself with, but that does not mean that they are valid in the eyes of God. Thus, a marriage was valid when the Catholic Church gave the bride a dispensation to marry a Muslim man in an Islamic ceremony: "Halelulya," wrote Bismar, "but what about in God's eyes? Is it that easy to place love for another above love for God?"

A different sort of separation between law and religion is proposed by a number of lawyers and activists seeking to reform the Marriage Law. Ratna Batara Munti of APIK:

> We want to change the phrase "according to their religion (*agama*)" to read "according to the religion and the certainty (*keyakinan*) of each of those who hold a certainty and a belief (*kepercayaan*)." Then religion would be valid according to law even if not according to some views of religion. In Islam there is the Sufi element and the fiqh element. I find fiqh very modern, because marriage is a contract between the man and the woman; but the current Indonesian definition of marriage is very idealistic, very religious, "an outer and inner tie (*ikatan lahir-batin*) between a man and a woman," very Sufi, comes back to belief, makes marriage very *sakral*. People say we will have trouble with this reform, but Islam is very, very rational. (Interview, 2000)

Both Bismar Siregar and Ratna Batara Munti would allow freedom of marriage, but Bismar would associate Islam with faith, leaving marriage as a *merely* legal matter, whereas Ratna would associate Islam with the law of contracts, leaving faith as an individual matter.

Marriage according to what religion?

But what if a couple seeks to marry, not across religious boundaries, but according to a religion not recognized by the government? Under the New Order, religions were limited to five: Islam, Catholicism, Protestantism, Hinduism, and Buddhism. Left out were two other categories, other religions and "beliefs." Many other beliefs considered by their followers to be "religions" were nevertheless not on the list, Judaism and Confucianism being prime examples (Confucianism was officially recognized by President Abdurrahman Wahid in January 2000). The second such category is that of *aliran kepercayaan*, literally "currents of belief," associations and schools of practice and philosophy, including Pangestu, Subud, and Sapta Darma. The beliefs are not part of an "official" religion, although practitioners sometimes also adhere to one of those religions, often Islam (as did Suharto). These beliefs are most important on Java, among Javanese and Sundanese. They are quite publicly represented, and even enjoy a building in the Beautiful Indonesia theme park, alongside the buildings devoted to the state-recognized religions.

Despite some government denials after Suharto's fall that the state had never restricted the number of legitimate ones, in fact all citizens had been required to specify one of the five recognized religions on their identity cards. Moreover, by the late 1980s the civil registries had begun to require that prospective couples state their religion when requesting that a marriage be performed, and that the religion be one of those five. In the 1970s the Interior Ministry had stated that civil registries could marry people according to "beliefs," but in 1989 it reversed itself and instructed the registries not to do so.

And yet couples have continued to marry according to "beliefs" or "adat," not registering their marriages, and sometimes making the news. In one 1996 case, involving adherents of Sapta Darma from Central Java, the Supreme Court ordered the civil registry to register the marriage. But couples who married according to Confucianism (Konghucu), "beliefs," or adat continued to be turned away by their local civil registries (*Kompas* online, 6 May 1997).

By 1997 controversy over this policy was louder and hotter, as resistance to all sorts of heavy-handed government policies was growing. The case of Gumirat and Susilawati, known in the press as "Gugum and Susi," received the widest attention. Refused by the civil registry in East Jakarta after marrying according to Sundanese adat, the couple, already expecting a child and concerned about the child's future legal status, appealed to the Administrative Court.[31] Bismar Siregar wrote an impassioned public plea that the judge order the marriage registered. Legally, he argued that the marriage law mentioned "belief" as well as "religion" as an acceptable basis for marriage. Politically, he stated that all Indonesian citizens who do not deny God are to be protected under the Pancasila. In contrast, the attorney for the civil registry argued that not only was his client correct in refusing to register the marriage, because only marriages according to recognized religions should be registered, but that similar marriages approved in the past by his client should now be unregistered![32]

The Minister of Justice urged that registration be extended to the aliran kepercayaan, pointing to the Supreme Court's ruling the previous year as "jurisprudence" on the matter, but no one paid much attention to him. But he also remarked, fittingly, that much of the debate turned on how one interpreted the word "belief" in the 1974 Marriage Law. Recall that article 2 of the law states that "Marriage is valid if it is carried out according to the laws of the parties' religion and belief" (*hukum masing-masing agama dan kepercayaanya itu*). Does the word "belief" in this sentence refer to the parties' belief in their religion? Or does it legitimate the status of the aliran kepercayaan?[33]

Gumirat and Susilawati won this round; the Administrative Court judge ruled that their marriage was according to Sundanese adat, not aliran kepercayaan, and it was properly witnessed and reported to the village headman. The Marriage

---

[31] Because they had been refused by an administrative body, the civil registry, their appeal was properly to the Administrative Court; the next step would be to appeal to the Supreme Court.

[32] Coverage was in *Kompas* online, 15 May 1997.

[33] See coverage in *Forum Keadilan*, 2 June 1997:39.

Law's clarifications do mention adat, so, she concluded, the marriage should be registered. The decision predictably was strongly condemned by some Islamic jurists and activist groups. KISDI (Komite Indonesia untuk Solidaritas Dunia Islam, Indonesian Committee for Solidarity with the Muslim World), which in the meantime had become one of the strongest critics of "pluralistic" government policies, accused the court of legalizing marriage outside of religion, "even tending toward legalizing fornication."[34] More legalistic was the response of Busthanul Arifin, who appeared with KISDI head, Ahmad Soemargono, at a rally in opposition to the decision held the following day. Busthanul Arifin declared that "belief" in the marriage law was clearly linked to "religion"; he cited the English phrase "religious belief" as proof that the two ideas were closely linked. In any case, he said, the Administrative Court should never have agreed to make a ruling, because the civil and religious courts have jurisdiction over marriage disputes. Furthermore, "the five religions will be threatened if the aliran kepercayaan become new religions." Other Muslim jurists made similar statements in the days following the ruling.[35]

These responses ignored the Administrative Court's ruling that the marriage was conducted according to adat, not aliran kepercayaan. But Professor Ichtijanto of Universitas Indonesia responded directly, and critically, to the ruling. His concern was that there was no way of knowing whether the adat followed in the marriage ceremony was "really according to Sundanese adat." Ichtijanto's argument went further, applying the specific way that adat law maps on to people and territory in Indonesia that we considered in chapter 3. Even if the procedure was according to Sundanese adat, he said, the marriage could not be registered because it took place in Jakarta, rather than inside the Sundanese adat area of West Java. Adat is law for a specific territory, where people recognize it as applicable and "living," he continued. "Sundanese adat claimed by Gumirat does not apply in Jakarta. Even in Cigugur village [their village] it is only followed by a fraction of the residents." Aliran kepercayaan was simply masked as adat in order to claim legal status, he charged, and if this marriage were accepted, he could create his own aliran and adat, "Ichtijantoism," perhaps to be called "Javanese Adat from the slopes of Mount Merapi." He asked rhetorically: With roughly 157 aliran kepercayaan on Java, should each be considered to have its own marriage law?[36]

---

[34] Quoted in *Gatra*, 26 July 1997:7. For more on KISDI, and in general on the struggles between more "pluralistic" and more exclusionary Islamic movement, see Hefner (2000:207–10 and *passim*).

[35] Arifin's comments were reported in *Republika* online, 28 July 1997; for the similar pronouncements of Universitas Indonesia law professor, M. Daud Ali, former Minister of Religion Munawir Sjadzali, and Rector of the Jakarta IAIN, Quraish Shihab, all to the effect that couples must follow the law, and the law states that marriage must be according to religion see *Republika* online, 4 August 1997.

[36] The quotations come from *Gatra*, 26 July 1997:7, and *Republika* online, 28 July 1997.

Those supporting the court's ruling cited constitutional guarantees of equality before the law and freedom of religion, and a general sense of justice and of human rights. Munawir Sjadzali, who by this time had become head of the National Human Rights Commission (Komnas HAM), tried to undermine attempts to defend the registering of the marriage as a defense of the couple's human rights. "Human rights have to come after law, so that there is not anarchy," he stated. (Recall that 1997 was the beginning of international clamor for human rights protections in Indonesia and in East Timor.) Of course, Munawir Sjadzali was especially vulnerable to attack as soft on Islamic law after his support of what came to be framed as his "radical contextualization" (see chapter 6), but this statement won him fulsome praise from leaders of the Nahdlatul Ulama.[37]

The rhetoric adopted by most critics of the decision was heavily legalistic. Rather than facing the issue of whether or not the law ought to allow marriage on the basis of beliefs outside the "big five," nearly every Muslim commentator over the ensuing weeks made similar pleas to obey the law, avoid anarchy, and prevent mass fornication. Even some supporters of the couple's general right to marry on grounds of justice and equality, such as Universitas Gajah Mada law professor Sudikno Mertokusomo, said that the court was technically wrong, because the 1974 Marriage Law did require that couples marry according to religion. Similarly, a Supreme Court decision in March 2000 recognizing the right of a couple to marry as adherents of "Confucianism" (Konghucu), i.e., without having to declare themselves to be Buddhists, was made on the narrow ground that a 1965 law had included the religion on the list of those to be recognized.[38]

But these issues and cases can be represented in other ways, as involving human rights. It has become increasingly legitimate in the 2000s to argue on the basis of the international norms of religious freedom and universal human rights. Indeed, in November 2001, promoters of a bill that would guarantee the right to marry across religious boundaries sought to deflect religious-based criticism by arguing that the bill "is a matter of human rights, not religion."[39] Notably, those who had formed a Konsorsium to draft the bill included representatives from the National Commission on Human Rights, various NGOs, and UNICEF, but no representatives from the Ministry of Religion or religious organizations.

The controversy over mixed marriages combines fears of vertical and horizontal assaults on the *umma Islam*. Vertically, the danger comes from state institutions

---

[37] As reported in *Republika* online, 5 August, 1997.

[38] *Forum* online, 11 February 2001, an article that also noted that, eleven months later, those civil registries contacted on Java still refused to recognize Confucian religion as a legitimate category for a marriage.

[39] *Forum* online, 12 November 2001; Islamic parties equally declared the bill to be very much about religion, and objected to it.

that seek to supplant the ulama. If the state can legislate directly what counts as a marriage, rather than abdicating that authority to religious authorities, and if it can perform marriages without the consent of those authorities, then (say some) Indonesian Islam cuts itself off from the long tradition of acting according to the Qur'ân and the sunna. The horizontal danger follows from this state meddling, to the extent that permitting mixed marriages opens the door to a dissolution of community boundaries into an unfaithful Pancasila society, where a watered-down notion of general religiosity replaces the conscientious conformity to the word of God and the example of the Prophet. In this view, only by maintaining boundaries on all sides can Muslims preserve their religious integrity.

There is another view, of course, one that sees the hope for Muslims in their willingness to change their norms and their behavior in accord with the times, where "the times" means, most pointedly, an openness toward other Indonesians and toward other norms, from human rights and gender equality to legal uniformity. Under Suharto, a progressive advocacy of contextualization in religious interpretation, that religious norms change over time, fit with a conservative advocacy of state supremacy over civil society, including Muslim sectors of civil society. With the fall of Suharto, that powerful fit has fallen apart, and the relationships of Islam, law, and society, never agreed to by all, are ever more clearly up for grabs.

11   Public reasoning across cultural pluralism

"Justice is conflict," writes Stuart Hampshire (2000), pointing to the irreducibility of certain conflicts to consensus. Justice lies in the operation of "public reason," argues John Rawls (1999), claiming that citizens can agree on a minimal central set of principles. I find Hampshire persuasive, but I also find Rawls's challenge important. If social groups differ on the most fundamental political issues, how can they possibly coexist in a political community?

Irreducible pluralism

In the previous chapters, I have charted varied Indonesian efforts to coexist through sustained public reasoning, a restless, endless process of deliberation, intended sometimes to accommodate others, sometimes to exclude them. I began in Isak, a small enough place, where if there were to be normative resting-places in large nation-states, we might expect to find one. But Isak people, like their fellow citizens elsewhere, find themselves grappling with criss-crossing sets of norms, some of which have the backing of the state (and thus can be said to be "law"), others of which have their normative anchors in the past or the local present. The Isak case of the disputed houses, in which Aman Kerna created a web of complicated subterfuges and hedges to try and satisfy, or at least appease, everyone, dead ancestors and future judges alike, reminds us that village life is not normatively simple.

It also reminds us that law, dispute resolution backed by state authority, is only one element in a complex field of norms, feelings, livelihoods, and power. Sometimes raw power asserts its claims outside the law, as when Acim, the army man, convinced others, at least temporarily, that his land claims ought to be listened to. Sometimes a solution is accepted because it somehow strikes enough of the right people as attending sufficiently to each party's claims, as when Aman Kerna managed to speak in the name of Islamic law, adat, the deceased grandfather, his (also deceased) sister, the living father, and potential land title claimants.

The outcomes of these cases, and many others, are not *predictable* on the basis of norms, or rules, or law, for at least two reasons. First, norms themselves conflict. Acim argued on the basis of patrilineal rights; his opponents on the basis of past agreements; and both kinds of argument were legitimate. Second, power shapes outcomes, whether in the form of a threat (the army, or judges, might intervene), or in the form of rhetoric (Aman Kerna was unmatched in his ability to compose a convincing case). In these and other cases the outcomes were not *caused* by norms, but they were *reasoned* in normative terms. Threats or powerful rhetoric may select among the reasons a person chooses, but choose, and argue, he or she does. Enjoying an orderly social life in such a small-scale place as Isak depends on the prominence of public reasoning about social order, and the presence of commentary about how it is that we arrive at resolutions of conflicts, and how it is that we can work through the entanglement of commands.[1]

We can view the projects of colonial and postcolonial states in the same light as we view Aman Kerna's nighttime speech-making: as efforts to create discourses of social order that take into account normative pluralism. Each such project of "encompassing pluralism" has had its own characteristics. Dutch colonial mappings of adat law were designed to create a set of rules that could be appealed to in judicial settings, because they would look like the rules that made up civil law. But they also were intended as maps of how social processes did indeed work. The normative force of adat law came from its dual status as descriptive of social life *and* prescriptive of dispute resolution. Islamic law could be relegated to a quiet corner on grounds that it did not describe social life; that it was *only* prescriptive.

After independence this supposed match between life and rules began to break down. In an early burst of modernist enthusiasm, the Supreme Court pronounced a new adat for Indonesians, a prescriptive adat. Whether colonial constructions of adat described much of how disputes were resolved was not, a few university studies aside, a matter of great importance to the state. Much more important to a New Order state bent on uniformity of control was re-representing the diversity of adat as something *other than* politics and law, as a matter of "culture": of dress, dance, and marriage customs. Adat was now to be less something lived, than something seen on television, or visited at the Indonesian cultural theme park, Taman Mini. Islam could then gradually occupy or, depending on one's version of history, reoccupy a slot in the legal system, but on terms set by the state. The discourse of New Order politics was state-centered law and administration, within which a properly codified and state-administered Islam could exist.

Ironically, the New Order collapsed just as it had succeeded in constructing the edifice of a unitary legal system that could incorporate adat, Islam, and

---

[1] This point has been made in a number of ethnographic studies of language and politics, including the essays in Brenneis and Myers (1984) and Lutz and Abu-Lughod (1990), and by Joel Kuipers (1990, 1998) in his studies in eastern Indonesia.

statutory law. The collapse of the New Order allowed the return of the repressed, the other side of adat, the claims to provide a normative base for a local *political* community independent of the state. This return introduces new claims of political legitimacy into the public sphere. Yet the new mapping of adat is still very much in process. Each alternative way of thinking about adat has its own implications for the future. Adat may be thought of as local social norms, governing the conduct of all who choose to live in a region, as has been the case in much of eastern Sumatra. But it also may be thought of as a characteristic of a people (*bangsa*), an ethnic idea of adat that has rather chilling implications for social dislocation, if not ethnic cleansing, within provinces. This essentialistic idea is currently promoted by some at work in Aceh, who have killed or driven from the province people born in Aceh but of Javanese descent.[2] It also could mean the alienation of Gayo, Alas, Singkil, and other distinct ethnic groups within Aceh from a new provincial leadership.

Sharî'a seems to provide a basis for political and legal discourse that is entirely distinct from that of adat, but in Indonesia its legal life in courtrooms has been as one of several sources of law, to be combined and intertwined with adat and positive law by judges. Takèngën judges have constructed consistent forms of legal reasoning out of the material of adat and Islam, but the content of that reasoning has not remained the same. In the 1960s, judges were upholding claims that villagers had reached a social consensus over claims of rights under Islamic law, but by the early 1990s, judges were emphasizing the legal rights of the individual Muslim, usually the Muslim wife or daughter, over and against claims that disputes had been resolved through consensus. The weightings of competing commands were different, but in both cases decisions were reached through processes of legal reasoning that responded to current social conditions.

The main effect of the shift in Islamic legal thinking in the 1990s, at least in this part of Indonesia, was to foreground matters of fairness, agreement, and the legal rights of individual Muslims. From this perspective, what at first appeared to be a conservative legal decision by the Indonesian Supreme Court, limiting one's right to give away wealth, can also be understood as a mechanism for ensuring that women receive their share of an estate. Islamic legal interpretation provided a way to hold up existing social practices to criticism and suspicion. Only by inspecting the social context of such a legal change can we come to understand both why jurists and judges supported it and what its impact could be on the distribution of wealth in Muslim parts of Indonesia.

Some judges, jurists, and many others have attempted to construct an inclusive Islamic discourse that could take into account norms of gender equality,

---

[2] A letter supposedly written by "The State of Atjeh Sumatra, Peureulak District" in early 2001 ordered all of Javanese ethnicity (*suku*) to be driven out of villages in East Aceh, following which hundred of families left their villages for the city of Langkat (*Kompas* online, 11 April 2001). As in so many such cases, one does not know if the rebels or *agents provocateurs* were responsible.

the traditions of fiqh, and, selectively, adat social norms. When the history of human rights activity in Indonesia is written, one chapter must be these efforts to arrive, through Islamic legal reasoning, at a more gender-equal set of outcomes on grounds of individual rights. These battles continue to be fought by feminist Muslims, lawyers and social activists, against the patriarchal attitudes of some judges, jurists, and politicians. But they are battles fought as part of an internal debate, in the terms that have come to make sense to many Muslim Indonesians in their own public deliberations.

This project is far from accepted by all Indonesian Muslims. The attempts to embrace gender equality within fiqh have reached a limit of textual reinterpretation set by the current, transnational state of study of the Qur'ân. The failure of efforts such as Munawir Szadjali's to, in effect, abrogate certain gender-unequal provisions of the Qur'ân delimit the project of *contextualisasi*. Furthermore, a countertendency within Indonesian Islamic thinking has rejected an accommodationist project, and works instead to reaffirm the boundaries between the *ummat Islam* and everyone else. These Muslims propose their own discourse of encompassing pluralism, one that is transnational, in which Muslims of all countries are brought together as part of a worldwide community, Indonesian Muslims sharing only the barest elements of citizenship with their fellow Indonesians. From this perspective, Muslims define their lives through their own hukums about food, dress, speech, marriage, and general sociability, and thus ought to restrict their social intercourse with those of other religions. Law is a matter of regulating the community; the role of the state is external to hukum in this sense.

The efforts by some Muslims to create this sort of exclusionary discourse make critical the precise understanding of how state law effects, modifies, or elaborates Islamic law. Thus the furor over marriage laws in the 1970s reflected less a substantive disagreement than a fight over who was to say what Islamic law was, and who would apply its tenets. The state may seem to accommodate Islam and promote pluralism by taking Islamic law as one of several sources for a general, Indonesia-wide legal machine. But part of this effort has been to claim the exclusive right to define Islamic law and the exclusive right to apply it, in other words, to *erase* legal pluralism. A Muslim man who once could accomplish a talaq divorce on his own (the hukum of his constitutive divorce-pronouncing speech act) becomes, on the state's version of things, a mere supplicant to a state-appointed Islamic court judge. Even though the man might consider himself to have divorced his wife on his own, were he to marry again without approaching a court he would be, in the eyes of the state, a bigamist (at least according to the most recent Supreme Court view). A couple married according to the current interpretations of fiqh are not married unless their marriage is approved by a state agency (and by which one, the civil registry or, for Muslims, the local Religious Affairs Office, is itself at issue).

By the close of the New Order, then, the Indonesian state had partially succeeded in capturing law in its own declarations. Through the Compilation, it had positivized Islamic law and increasingly declared that only such law was "law." Fiqh became opposed to hukum, the disorganized decisions of jurists to the well-ordered statutes of the state. Adat remained a matter of common law, without ever being so called.

All this is now called into question, as the brute force of the state no longer has a clear moral or social objective. Adat's residual purchase in the local courts may turn out to have been the foundation for a more internally varied legal system in twenty-first-century Indonesia. As districts and provinces attempt to rebuild political life around new ideas of autonomy and local control, they could draw on the histories of legal interpretation in their local courts, both civil courts and Islamic ones (in Muslim regions). But claims based on adat must compete with claims based on other notions of political legitimacy, including equality, local control, sharî'a, and human rights, made by local political leaders, rebel movements, women's organizations, legal aid associations, human rights commissions, ethnic group associations, *masyarakat adat*, *perempuan adat*, religious organizations, and the many political parties and coalitions that appeared after Suharto's fall. These claims are made on grounds of local authenticity, international recognition, national tradition, or all three.

The pluralism in values and social norms this list suggests is an irreducible fact of Indonesian life. Whatever "rule of law" ought to mean in terms of transparency, adherence to procedure, protecting citizens from harm and loss, it must also incorporate this value-pluralism. The past decades of Indonesian efforts to do so indicate that public reasoning about law and values can begin from distinct starting-points – the fiqh of Umar, human rights, Gayo or Javanese adat – and approach a set of values and norms, such as gender equality, fairness, and agreement. "Approach" does not mean "arrive at"; there is always danger of backsliding, and the current violence and political crisis make Indonesia seem hardly a model for anything. However, the process shows one way in which value-pluralism can at least be imagined as the foundation for a political community.

Furthermore, what formally appear as distinct sets of norms – sharî'a, the many forms of adat, human rights, among others – in practice shape and reshape each other. More precisely, judges, jurists, and ordinary people employ and deploy elements from one normative set to challenge or refashion another: the norms of rural life are a resource for pushing sharî'a toward gender equality; the individualism of sharî'a is called on to reinterpret adat in individualistic terms; international legal changes concerning women's rights are cited in the effort to reform civil and religious law, but so is international recognition of religious rights in opposition to those reforms.

Here the present work joins a number of contemporary studies in anthropology that highlight the interconnected character of legal systems, morality, colonial projects of socioeconomic subordination, missionary projects of evangelical emancipation, and postcolonial projects of nation and state building (Comaroff and Comaroff 1997; Lazarus-Black and Hirsch 1994; Merry 2000). Building on the earlier insights of Moore (1986) about law as a "semi-autonomous" field, these studies have charted ways in which the concept of "law" is created and recreated as a normative object, and ways in which the practices of law are shaped and reshaped by religious, political, and moral values and forces.

Elements of Indonesian public reasoning

We have considered here the complexities of public reasoning both horizontally, across culturally constituted domains of law, religion, and politics, and vertically, along lines of communication and control that link village arguments to the institutions of towns and cities and to national-level cultural debates and legal processes. The issues most at stake change as we pass up or down along these lines. Are there general features to the public reasoning found across these domains and these levels of society? I would point to four such elements – the importance of precedent, principle, pragmatism, and metanormative reasoning.

Recall the way Aman Kerna crafted his intervention in Isak. He argued that people should not needlessly violate past agreements, either agreements among themselves or those with third parties, such as the ancestors. Doing so has negative social and cosmological results. These consequences are not because agreement is better than conflict, although this is true; it is because the past can have a morally and cosmologically "binding effect" on the present, a socially precedential value.

It was a similar notion of binding effect that Takèngën judges cited in the 1960s to justify their decisions upholding past estate divisions. Although the value of consensus sometimes was evoked, it was and is the binding nature of agreements that supplies the main force to these arguments. When, in the 1980s and 1990s, their successors reversed themselves and began to regularly strike down such past agreements, they justified their actions by claiming that any agreements entered into in the past must have been coercive, or done without the knowledge of some of the participants (usually daughters), as those individuals would not willingly have signed away their rights. In other words, although they *could* have argued that, agreement or no, Islamic law stipulates a certain division of an estate, in fact they felt it necessary to justify their decisions in terms of a logic of the continuing force of agreements, if only to counter arguments based on such force.

This first conception is closely related to a second, that general principles or values trump specific rules, or, more importantly, provide a normative ground for reinterpreting those rules. "Agreement" is, indeed, such a principle; jurists and judges reinterpeted adat and Islam so as to create new rules – for example, a rule of Gayo adat that a bequest requires the consent of the heirs. Across much of the preceding discussion, values of equality and fairness have played similar roles. Often it has been equality of men and women that has been at issue, but the equality of rights between "orphaned grandchildren" and other heirs similarly motivated Hazairin's reinterpretation of Islamic law. The Supreme Court reasoned from the general principle of fairness and agreement in justifying the new Islamic rule that limits gifts to one-third of an estate.

Not all would agree that general principles ought to govern the interpretation of Qur'ânic passages and fiqh traditions. For some, the argument from general values is based on an idea of God's consistency: if He held men and women to be equal, then He could not have intended a particular Qur'ânic verse to be interpreted in such a way as to lead to unequal outcomes. Such is the reasoning followed in contemporary feminist rejections both of polygamy and of the norm of exclusively male household headship. Responses to these arguments do not deny the validity of general principles, but point to the clarity of certain Qur'ânic passages, and to the impossibility for humans of ever fully grasping God's intentions.[3] In some cases claiming an actual convergence of norms is a supporting argument for claims in the name of general values, such as Hazairin's account of adat and Islam, or Busthanul Arifin's claim that no-fault divorce laws were a norm toward which Europe and Indonesia were converging. These empirical arguments buttress the felt normative force of the value under discussion.

Third, pragmatic arguments carry a certain weight. The central challenge faced by Aman Kerna was how to make the *status quo* valid in the eyes of the ancestors and in the eyes of judges and other state officials. His reasoning was pragmatic in the sense of experimenting with possible compromises, formulations, and terms, all with an eye to how they would be understood by specific other actors, "in the shadow of the law." So have been lines of reasoning employed by jurists, for example in arguing for the positive social value of a codification of Islamic law as opposed to the "disorder" created by fiqh, or the negative consequences of inter-religious marriages on domestic life as a justification for prohibiting them. Consistently, one finds people on opposite sides of debates about Islam invoking both a textual or historical account and a pragmatic account: the Qur'ân approves polygamy and here is what that practice accomplishes, or the Qur'ân disapproves of polygamy and here is why, or

---

[3] I have made a parallel analysis of two types of rationality in Islamic discourse on ritual (Bowen 1993b).

marriage across religious boundaries should be permitted (or not) because of what the law says, but the law is (or is not) appropriate because of the consequences of those marriages. Most of chapter 6 concerned how the Supreme Court explicitly justified its decision in legalistic terms, but couched its narrative in such a way as to justify the rule limiting gifts in terms of its desirable social consequences.

Finally, and in a logically related way, Gayo and other Indonesians have taken account of the necessity of moving upwards in their reasoning, to a level of deliberation where one can compare and weigh alternative arguments and arrive at compromise, even when the competing norms themselves do not easily admit of such compromise. We have examined metanormative reasoning across levels of society and institutions. Gayo adat did not dictate a solution to the problem of the Kramil houses; adat was recognized as one of several interpretive resources, open to multiple interpretations. Judges in Takèngën have justified their decisions, at least to each other and to the visiting anthropologist, in terms of the relative merits of following one or another set of norms. Sometimes, in discussing cases read in the archives, I have inferred this sort of metalevel reasoning process, for example in explaining why and how early judges avoided siding with Islam or adat. Whether jurists, such as Hazairin, or social activists, such as Ratna Batara Munti, those Indonesians arguing for new readings of laws and Islamic norms are arguing between normative sets, in a metanormative way.

Reasoning at this level often leads to an effort to ignore or sidestep conflict between norms. As I have emphasized elsewhere (Bowen 1993b), village life in Isak is about living next to people who may have tried to kill your daughter through sorcery, or, somewhat less dramatically, with whom you strongly disagree over the meaning of a ritual in which you participate, together, regularly. This tacit ignoring of differences is not limited to village life, as anyone who knows his or her neighbors sooner or later discovers. The intractable conflicts mentioned by Stuart Hampshire include such issues as abortion in the United States, where the irreducibility of principled conflicts to compromise means that, some of the time, anyway, the most successful solution may be silence. Indeed, legal reasoning may be generally a matter of deciding as little as possible, as I argued for the history of Takèngën court decisions, and as Cass Sunstein (1996) has argued for United States judges. Aman Kerna in Isak, judges on Indonesian courts, jurists formulating new statutes, and Indonesian Supreme Court justices sometimes, at least, have sought to craft resolutions to conflict among norms that would avoid deciding against any position.

Across social contexts, then, several elements appear consistently in public reasoning about conflicts between norms: the binding force of past agreements, taking general principles as grounds for interpreting specific texts, considering the social consequences of interpretations, and engaging in explicitly metanormative reasoning with compromise as a goal. The texture of the arguments changes, often with the position taken. For example, "contextualizing" readers of the Qur'ân often make the "reasoning from principles" element most explicit, because they can use it to argue directly on grounds of Qur'ân interpretation. If they choose to lead with a pragmatic interpretation they risk losing the Islamic argument. Those who resist those approaches often emphasize the binding force of past readings of the Qur'ân.[4]

These examples recall the strategic element of actors' argumentation. Strategy and principles are not mutually exclusive, and analyses of public reasoning must be attentive to both. The Indonesian case also shows how difficult it is to identify a single cultural style, or even a typology of styles or doctrines, through the study of justification and argumentation. The jurists, activists, and villagers we have listened to in this book develop arguments that present as evidence ideas about how the ancestors think, what God has said, 'Umar's fiqh reasoning, linguistic analyses of Qur'ânic Arabic, surveys and hunches about local norms, legal aid cases, village labor patterns, the diversity of adat, how ulama in fact divide their wealth, and whether Megawati Sukarnoputri could remarry. Different kinds of arguments and different kinds of evidence are marshaled for different audiences.[5]

Political theory and cultural pluralism

Let me now ask whether a socially embedded ethnography of Indonesian public reasoning has any bearing on contemporary debates in political theory about justice and cultural pluralism. A key question raised in such debates concerns the mechanisms through which constitutional democratic states can encompass cultural and religious diversity. In this final section I will argue that the answers provided by much political theory suffer from a narrow empirical range and a legalistic focus, and that comparative ethnographies of public reasoning point to a broader range of ways of developing politically coherent multicultural societies.

Liberal political theory

As several political theorists (Gray 2000; Hampshire 2000; Parekh 2000) emphasize, one major project of political theory as it has developed in the Western liberal political tradition has been to identify a single set of principles on which

---

[4] Elsewhere (Bowen 1999a) I argue that there has been a consistent association between legal reasoning and substantive position in Indonesian Islam.

[5] I note in passing that, despite the similarity of the approach taken here to that set out in Boltanski and Thévenot (1992), it would be difficult to sort the justifications discussed above into a typology of "orders of worth" as in their study, except perhaps as a heuristic, without losing the specificity of these arguments.

could be based all political systems: "the search for a rational consensus on the best way of life" (Gray 2000:1), or what Bhikhu Parekh (2000:16) calls "moral monism." This project is most easily traced to John Locke, for whom the best way of life was characterized by a certain set of economic, political, and religious orientations, including the rational accumulation of wealth, obedience to a sovereign, and belief in God. These theoretical positions had direct policy implications. For example, Locke held that only when people systematically worked a piece of land, mixing their own labor (something they could be said to own) with the land itself, could they claim property rights.[6] This belief left the lands of North America unowned, *terra nullius*, because they were not worked in this way (Locke did not consider whether the inhabitants of that land might hold different conceptions of ownership). Locke also based his appeal for religious toleration on a universal truth. He urged the sovereign to extend toleration to Protestant sects, but not to atheists or Catholics, as he considered belief in God (and not in the Pope) not only to be true, but also to be a precondition to the trustworthiness of an individual and to the successful rule of a sovereign.[7]

The centuries since Locke have seen a gradual narrowing of the scope of the monistic project. In the most recent work of the best-known contemporary political theorist, John Rawls (1996, 1999), the project is explicitly limited to defining a "political conception of justice," to be distinguished from the "background culture" where one finds distinct, and conflicting, "comprehensive doctrines" of the good life. Rawls argues that an "overlapping consensus" of all subgroups can be reached, within whose compass will be found a "basic structure of society." This structure must be "complete" in his view, that is, it must contain principles that can be extended to all issues of basic justice (1999:144–46). The structure does not reach into the internal workings of institutions, such as families and religious organizations, but it limits the capacity of internal arrangements within those institutions to have the force of law (1999:156–64). For example, patriarchal family arrangements could not become part of the basic structure. Once arrived at, this structure must then be made the unquestioned basis for all future political debate; in other words, it must become part of the constitution of the society (1996:227–30). Such are, for Rawls, the requirements of a well-ordered constitutional democratic society.

Rawls's formulations of justice are based on intuitions about North American institutions and sensibilities, in which values of individual autonomy and equality might be presumed to predominate, at least at a certain level of abstraction. But Rawls intends his account to be valid at least for all

---

[6] Most directly put in his *Second Treatise*, section 27 (Locke 1967 [1690]:287–88). As with many colleagues, I have long been guided in understanding these passages by the analysis of C.B. Macpherson (1962:194–221). For an example of Locke put into practice, see Comaroff and Comaroff (1997:365–95).

[7] See Locke (1983 [1689]) and the editor's introduction.

constitutional democratic societies; thus his effort to distinguish between a political conception of justice and the variety of religious and cultural beliefs held in different societies.

To his claims two objections have been made that are relevant to the present study. The first objection can be made by considering only Euro-American societies; it is that Rawls's basic liberties, those that are to form a coherent and complete constitutional core, frequently conflict among themselves (Gray 2000). For example, freedom of speech sometime conflicts with freedom from racist abuse. Although in the United States, judges generally strike down efforts to curb racist speech, and thus make intuitively plausible Rawls's argument that freedom of speech is part of the "basic structure," in many European states curbs on racist speech have been upheld as protecting basic liberties. In this and other instances, settling the issue involves conflicts *among* competing values within the political core, and one can expect different constitutional democratic societies to arrive at different ways of weighting these values.

The second objection concerns the limited cultural range within which the intuitions of Rawls and of other contemporary liberal theorists of political pluralism (for example, Kymlicka 1995; Raz 1994) are likely to hold. Liberal theorists give special value to the autonomy of the individual, and to his or her capacity to form and revise an idea of "the good life." As Parekh (2000) has argued, valuing autonomy and "the good life" are outcomes of a particular Western intellectual and social history, in which Greek philosophy, Christianity, and colonialism each contributed to liberal doctrine. People in other societies, or in new versions of Euro-American societies, might weigh values in different ways, for example, making autonomy and the capacity to form an idea of the good secondary to a proper understanding of God, or to the overall welfare of the community (Modood 1999; Sandel 1998).

So far, the argument is theoretical: liberalism rests on contingent assumptions, not universal human properties. We may add the empirical observation that a large number of societies are organized along lines based on competing, principled notions of justice. As we have seen, many Muslims argue that their religious texts provide a God-given set of political and social ideas, and do not see why they should be rejected in favor of liberal ideas. In many countries with large Muslim populations, these texts are one source of law.[8] Furthermore, in many such countries there is more than one "basic structure" of society, providing for different populations distinct principles of distributive justice, legal statuses of men and women, and, at a legal metalevel, the relationship between positive law and religious law. In other words, there is neither a single political

---

[8] Aside from the lengthy demonstration given here for Indonesia, see Dupret (2000) for an analysis of judicial decision-making in a country, Egypt, where sharî'a supposedly serves as *the* source of law.

structure regulating issues of basic justice, nor an overlapping consensus on the current pluralistic legal arrangements.[9] Do we then conclude that, *a priori*, such societies cannot be constitutional democracies? Or do we take such instances as material to be accommodated in the next iteration of political theory?

Creating *a* modus vivendi

At first glance, it appears that a second strand of political-theoretical reflections on difference would be more useful for an anthropological account of pluralism. This second strand, which, for the modern period, one can trace to Hobbes and Hume, looks for practical arrangements for accommodating differences, a *modus vivendi* that can allow groups to live in accord with their own ideas of justice within a larger state structure, "an ideal of a common life that does not rest on common beliefs" (Gray 2000:2).

Yet this approach also fails to take account of political and legal reasoning in pluralistic societies. I have argued that the "monist," liberal view of society underplays (not to say ignores) the problems of presuming that a particular, Western set of values can and ought to serve as the appropriate basis for politics in all societies. However, the *modus vivendi* view errs in the opposite direction. It pays too little attention to the role of values and reasoning as ways of reconciling differences in pluralistic societies. Individuals offer justifications for the practical arrangements they make in order to get along with others. These justifications are accepted (or not) as imposing *bona fide* moral obligations. These "bridging mechanisms" provide ways for adherents of incompatible comprehensive doctrines to support a common political project.

Rawls (1999:152–56) himself discusses one way in which adherents of different religions in a society seek to convince each other of the reasonableness of their beliefs, namely, by pointing to general values contained in one such doctrine that can be recognized as valuable by those who believe in a different one: for example, the idea of mutual aid, as found in the Good Samaritan parable and also in other religions. However, Rawls views this process as one of translating comprehensive doctrines into "political conceptions" as he understands them, so that they can then be expressed as a "public reason" properly shorn of its religious elements.[10]

---

[9] In a recent paper (1999:151 n.46), Rawls makes a positive reference to Islam, but does so by citing, not an actually existing arrangement, but the radical project of the theologian Abdullahi an-Na'im, who has proposed rejecting a large portion of the Qur'ân.

[10] Here I find a point of convergence between my own empirical-analytical project and the "conjectural" project endorsed by Rawls (1999:149–52), that theorists may conjecture that another people's religious (or other) beliefs could be interpreted so as to endorse a "reasonable political conception of justice." Our difference is that I think that the end-point is not Rawls's "political conception," but rather a much more complex set of principles and "bridging mechanisms."

As we have seen for Indonesia, much public reasoning *retains* its foundation in comprehensive doctrines, in specific understandings of Islam and particular adat conceptions of the world. The ensuing debates often concern the legitimacy, in Islamic terms, of efforts to interpret religious texts in such a way that they are compatible with other doctrines, for example, on the issue of gender equality. In these instances, the Indonesian Muslims in question endorse, not a political conception of justice as in Rawls, but a reasonable conception of justice that is *public and also Islamic.*

Taking account of internal debates

I argued above that the Euro-American political tradition underlying liberal political theory limits the relevance of much such theory for understanding other political traditions, elsewhere in the world. Such is the case for avowed proponents of multiculturalism, whose empirical focus has shaped their normative accounts, allowing them to skirt what I see as basic issues.[11] From the standpoint of an anthropologist, or, for that matter, any comparative social scientist, the range of the most frequently cited cases in political-theoretical studies of multiculturalism is strikingly narrow. These cases tend to share two features: they involve a distinction between a minority and a majority, and they are conceptualized in terms of cross-group differences.

First, the key cases for multicultural theorists usually involve a distinction between a minority group and a majority society, and the latter is nearly always in Europe or North America. The minority either enjoys a long-standing presence in the society (e.g., native North American or Australian groups), or has recently immigrated to the country in question (e.g., Muslims in Britain or France). Some cases are intermediate, such as the Amish in North America. The majority society is assumed to have formulated a clear set of values and principles, against which the minority is judged.

This feature leads theorists who otherwise disagree to converge on a certain model of cultural pluralism. For example, Kymlicka (1995) starts from a strongly liberal position, based on the idea of autonomy, to argue for multiculturalist policies that would set out limits to claims made by minority groups. In distinguishing among the claims made by different minorities in North America, he relies on the different histories of long-resident "national

---

[11] In the following discussion I draw from two recent and influential studies, by Will Kymlicka (1995) and Bhikhu Parekh (2000), chosen for their strong differences in viewpoint, their current importance, and the clarity of their work. Similar arguments could be made, with appropriate refashioning, regarding the work of Charles Taylor (1994), probably the most philosophically subtle and sophisticated of contemporary theorists of cultural pluralism, and Michael Walzer (1983, 1994, 1997), whose work is empirically much broader than the others, but who ends up rejecting an Indonesian-style approach to toleration. For a recent work in political theory that makes some of the points made here, see Levy (2000).

minorities" and immigrant groups. Long-term residence grants legitimacy to some claims to self-determination. Parekh (2000) would appear to offer the most strongly opposed position from among Kymlicka's contemporaries, in that he objects to liberalism, and in particular to Kymlicka's use of "autonomy," on grounds close to those I offered above, and offers a historically contextual analysis of each issue of value conflict. And yet, Parekh, too, is mainly concerned with the policies to be adopted in Great Britain with respect to norms followed by some recent immigrants. He ascribes to the majority society a set of "operative public values" (2000:268–73) against which minority values can be judged.[12] Although Parekh also urges British legislators to reexamine the rationales for and importance of particular laws and rules, his general approach, like Kymlicka's, can assume a background set of norms and values, to which immigrants will and should accommodate themselves.

This feature of the model also means that little attention need be paid to divergences and debates *within* the migrant communities, and may help explain the second striking feature of much of this writing, that is, that the question is posed in terms of differences across social groups, e.g., between Muslim Pakistanis and "native" Englishpeople, or between Hopi and non-Hopi.[13] That many of these frequently cited examples arose from court cases may help to explain why it has been easy to think of the differences in this way, in that the issue before courts has been whether anyone acting in a certain way *qua* "Muslim" or "Sikh" or "Amish" has the right to act in that way. Litigants have claimed to represent the beliefs and practices of a group, and respondents have claimed to represent the interests of the society as a whole.

But thinking about differences in beliefs and practices as mapping on to easily demarcated social groupings hampers our ability to understand cultural pluralism. The general cultural debates in any one society may divide members of those social groups, and individuals may also find themselves torn between two or more alternative positions. In other words, there is no reason *a priori* to pose the questions of pluralism of cultural or religious values and practices in terms of group differences.[14]

The key examples used by current multiculturalist theorists could easily be expanded to encompass these internal debates. Consider the case of Islamic headscarves worn in France, a case frequently discussed (e.g., Levy 2000:128–32;

---

[12] Parekh does describe some issues that arise in India as well, but limits his account of "operative public values" to British cases, making judgments about India on the grounds of general human values that do not receive the contextual analysis he calls for elsewhere (2000:280–82).

[13] This point has also been made by Gerd Baumann (1999); I differ with Baumann on his evaluations of work by Kymlicka and Taylor (a point to be taken up in future work).

[14] It is true that in discussing such legal cases political theorists, whether liberal or multiculturalist, sometimes mention diversity of opinions within a community, but these mentions are usually in terms of legal issues posed by, for example, the denial of rights of Hopi Protestants, and concern the relative rights of a minority community and those of the majority society.

Parekh 2000:249–54). Beginning in 1989, and continuing at full strength into the 2000s, some Muslim girls, usually in high schools (*lycées*) and more rarely in middle schools (*collèges*), have been sent to separate rooms or prevented from attending school because they wore headscarves generally identified, by them and by the teachers and principals, as signifying their personal commitment to Islam. In the early 1990s the French government wavered in its stance on the matter; currently, in principle the girls may wear the scarves, but school principals sometimes can find legal pretexts to exclude them from class.

Such are the bare legal facts; the case is used as an example of the conflict between Islam and French ideas of *laïcité*, and so it is, if we remain on the level of French legal wranglings and political discourse. But this focus on legal arguments ignores the widespread, virulent, and continuing debates *among French Muslims* about wearing headscarves, and about the broader relationship that Islam ought to have to *laïcité* in France. Some of the partisans in these debates seek to reinterpret Islamic jurisprudence in the context of France, and more broadly Europe. They argue that one can achieve gender equality, conduct oneself as a full citizen of France and of Europe, and at the same time preserve a public identity as a Muslim, through, among other actions, wearing modest dress. Others reject these claims, arguing instead that Islamic law must be set aside in favor of an emphasis on faith, or Muslim history, as the main feature of Islamic self-identity, and that to become full citizens, Muslims should dress in the same manner as do other French people. Many individuals are themselves ambivalent on these issues; they experience a conflict of norms in their own hearts and minds, and not only in law chambers or in the public press.[15] In other words, the French Muslim case must be understood in terms of the conflicts and ambivalence experienced by European Muslims as they seek to create new forms of Muslim life in France, and not as an instance of Islamic norms versus French ones.

It is at this point that we encounter a basic difference between liberal political theory and comparative social scientific inquiry. If the mission of the former is to formulate a systematic, principled account of how (some) societies ought to be organized, that of the second is to study how it is that they *are* organized. Thus, the stylized accounts of cases such as that of the French headscarves may suffice if the writer's goal is to pose a problem, sufficiently skeletonized for its legal issues, and to refer to that problem in discussing the appropriate legal frameworks for multicultural societies. An anthropologist, or other social scientist, however, looks toward giving an adequate account of the issues, institutions, and stakes for actors in a particular social setting. My intention

---

[15] I refer here to my own field notes from work in Paris in 2001, and to a series of recent studies of women, Muslim dress, and schools, in particular Gaspard and Khosrokhavar (1995); Venel (1999); and Weibel (2000), and the many normative works on the subject, for example, Abdallah (1995).

has been to offer not a competing version of political theory, in the sense of a reconstruction of society from first principles, but an anthropological account of the *reasonableness* of the ways in which citizens can take account of their own pluralism of values in carrying out their affairs – an account which might, in its turn, inform new versions of political theory.

The result, in the case of this study and I believe in others, is to destabilize certainties we may have arrived at through living in our own society, wherever that might be. There is no clear *telos* to the modern debates in Indonesia about what the "basic structure" of society might be: not liberal politics, not an Islamic state, not even each province its own adat. The diversities are multiple, and the tendencies centripetal, even as figures come forth with schemes for social unity. This is the aspect of social life on which the partisans of a *"modus vivendi"* approach have a firm grasp. But the diversities have engendered principled reflections, as well as vigorous disputes, about equality, religious commitment, political viability, and about how an internal debate might just arrive at the dreamed-of consensus. Perhaps all that can be hoped for is that the debate continue.

References

Abdallah, Dr. 1995 *Le foulard islamique et la république française: mode d'emploi* [The Islamic Headscarf and the French Republic: A User's Manual]. Bobigny: Editions Intégrité

Abdullah, Abdul Gani 1994 *Pengantar Kompilasi Hukum Islam dalam Tata Hukum Indonesia* [Introduction to the Compilation of Islamic Law in the Indonesian Legal Framework]. Jakarta: Gema Insani Press

1995 "Tinjauan hukum terhadap perkawinan di bawah tangan" [A legal view of marriage under the table]. *Mimbar Hukum* 23:46–51

Abdurrahman, H. 1992 *Kompilasi Hukum Islam di Indonesia* [The Compilation of Islamic Law in Indonesian]. Jakarta: Akademika Pressindo

Abubakar, Al Yasa 1991 "Beberapa teori penalaran fiqih dan penerapannya" [Several theories of jurisprudential reasoning and their application]. In Juhaya S. Praja, ed., *Hukum Islam di Indonesia: Pemikiran dan Praktek* [Islamic Law in Indonesia: Concept and Practice], pp. 173–208. Bandung: Remaja Rosdakarya

Adas, Michael 1995 "The Reconstruction of 'Tradition' and the Defense of the Colonial Order: British West Africa in the Early Twentieth Century." In Jane Schneider and Rayna Rapp, eds., *Articulating Hidden Histories: Exploring the Influence of Eric R. Wolf*, pp. 291–307. Berkeley: University of California Press

Anderson, Benedict 1991 *Imagined Communities: Reflections on the Origin and Spread of Nationalism*, rev. edn. London: Verso

Anderson, J.N.D. 1976 *Law Reform in the Muslim World*. London: Athlone

Antoun, Richard R. 1980 "The Islamic court, the Islamic judge, and the accommodation of the traditions: a Jordanian case study." *International Journal of Middle East Studies* 12:455–67

Assier-Andrieu, Louis 1987 "Le juridique des anthropologues." *Droit et Société* 5

Atkinson, Jane Monnig and Shelly Errington, eds. 1990 *Power and Difference: Gender in Island Southeast Asia*. Stanford: Stanford University Press

Aulawi, H.A. Wasit 1993 "Analisis yurisprudensi: tentang kewarisan" [Analysis of jurisprudence: concerning inheritance]. *Mimbar Hukum* 8:114–45

1994 "Analisis yurisprudensi: tentang kewarisan" [Analysis of jurisprudence: concerning inheritance]. *Mimbar Hukum* 16:112–35

Baidlowi, Drs. 1999 "Kententuan hak waris saudara dalam konteks hukum Islam" [Determining a sibling's inheritance rights in the context of Islamic law]. *Mimbar Hukum* 44:12–19

Barth, Fredrik 1987 *Cosmologies in the Making: A Generative Approach to Cultural Variation in Inner New Guinea*. Cambridge, UK: Cambridge University Press

Barton, Greg 1995 "Neo-modernism: a vital synthesis of traditionalist and modernist Islamic thought in Indonesia." *Studia Islamika* 2(3):1–75

Barton, Greg and Greg Fealy, eds. 1996 *Nahdlatul Ulama: Traditional Islam and Modernity in Indonesia.* Clayton, Australia: Monash University, Monash Asia Institute

Basyir, Ahmad Azhar 1994 "Corak lokal dalam hukum positif Islam di Indonesia (tinjauan filsafat hukum)" [Local content in Islamic positive law in Indonesia (a view from the philosophy of law)]. *Mimbar Hukum* 13:29–35

Baumann, Gerd 1999 *The Multicultural Riddle: Rethinking National, Ethnic, and Religious Identities.* New York: Routledge

Benda-Beckmann, Franz von 1979 *Property in Social Continuity: Continuity and Change in the Maintenance of Property Relationships Through Time in Minangkabau, West Sumatra.* The Hague: Martinus Nijhoff

Benda-Beckmann, Keebet von 1984 *The Broken Stairways to Consensus: Village Justice and State Courts in Minangkabau.* Dordrecht: Foris Publications

Boland, B.J. 1982 *The Struggle of Islam in Modern Indonesia*, rev. 2nd edn. The Hague: Verhandelingen van het Koninklijk Instituut voor Taal-, Land-, en Volkenkunde, No. 59

Boltanski, Luc and Laurent Thévenot 1991 *De la justification: les économies de la grandeur.* Paris: Gallimard

Bourdieu, Pierre 1984 *Distinction: A Social Critique of the Judgment of Taste.* Cambridge, MA: Harvard University Press

1987 "The force of law: toward a sociology of the juridical field." *Hastings Journal of Law* 38:209–48

1990 *The Logic of Practice*, trans. Richard Nice. Stanford: Stanford University Press (originally published in French, 1980, Paris: Editions de Minuit)

Bowen, John R. 1984 "The history and structure of Gayo society: variation and change in the highlands of Aceh." Ph.D dissertation, University of Chicago

1988 "The transformation of an Indonesian property system: adat, Islam, and social change in the Gayo highlands." *American Ethnologist* 15:274–93

1991 *Sumatran Politics and Poetics: Gayo History, 1900–1989.* New Haven: Yale University Press

1993a "A modernist Muslim poetic: irony and social critique in Islamic verse." *Journal of Asian Studies* 45:629–46

1993b *Muslims Through Discourse: Religion and Ritual in Gayo Society.* Princeton: Princeton University Press

1995 "The forms culture takes: a state-of-the-field essay on the anthropology of Southeast Asia." *Journal of Asian Studies* 54:1047–78

1996 "The myth of global ethnic conflict." *Journal of Democracy* 7(4):3–14

1998 " 'You may not give it away': how social norms shape Islamic law in contemporary Indonesian jurisprudence." *Islamic Law and Society* 5(3):1–27

1999a "Legal reasoning and public discourse in Indonesian Islam." In Dale F. Eickelman and Jon W. Anderson, eds., *New Media in the Muslim World: The Emerging Public Sphere*, pp. 80–105. Bloomington: Indiana University Press

1999b "The role of microhistories in comparative studies." In John Bowen and Roger Petersen, eds., *Critical Comparisons in Politics and Culture*, pp. 230–40. Cambridge, UK: Cambridge University Press

2002 *Religions in Practice: An Approach to the Anthropology of Religion.* Boston: Allyn & Bacon

Bowen, John R. and Roger Petersen 1999 "Introduction." In John Bowen and Roger Petersen, eds., *Critical Comparisons in Politics and Culture*, pp. 1–20. Cambridge, UK: Cambridge University Press

Brenneis, Donald Lawrence and Fred R. Myers, eds. 1984 *Dangerous Words: Languages and Politics in the Pacific*. New York: New York University Press

Brown, Daniel W. 1996 *Rethinking Tradition in Modern Islamic Thought*. Cambridge, UK: Cambridge University Press

Brown, Nathan J. 1997 *The Rule of Law in the Arab World: Courts in Egypt and the Gulf*. Cambridge, UK: Cambridge University Press

Bruinessen, Martin van 1990 "Kitab Kuning: books in Arabic script used in the pesantran milieu." *Bijdragen tot de Taal-, Land- en Volkenkunde* 146:226–69

　1994 *NU: Tradisi, Relasi-relasi Kuasa, Pencarian Wacana Baru* [NU: Tradition, Power Relations, and the Search for a New Discourse]. Yogyakarta: LKiS

Buskens, Leon 1993 "Islamic commentaries and French codes: the confrontation and accommodation of two forms of textualization of family law in Morocco." In Henk Driessen, ed., *The Politics of Ethnographic Reading and Writing: Confrontations of Western and Indigenous Views*, pp. 65–100. Fort Lauderdale: Plantation

Butt, Simon 1999 "Polygamy and mixed marriage in Indonesia: the application of the marriage law in the courts." In Timothy Lindsey, ed., *Indonesia: Law and Society*, pp. 122–44. Leichhardt, NSW: The Federation Press

Cammack, Mark 1989 "Islamic law in Indonesia's New Order." *International and Comparative Law Quarterly* 38:53–73

　1997 "Indonesia's 1989 Religious Judicature Act: Islamization of Indonesia or Indonesianization of Islam?" *Indonesia* 63:143–68

Cammack, Mark, L. Young and T. Heaton 1996 "Legislating social change in an Islamic society – Indonesia's marriage law." *American Journal of Comparative Law* 44:45–73

Chanock, Martin 1985 *Law, Custom, and Social Order: The Colonial Experience in Malawi and Zambia*. Cambridge, UK: Cambridge University Press

Christelow, Allan 1985 *Muslim Law Courts and the French Colonial State in Algeria*. Princeton: Princeton University Press

Comaroff, John L. and Jean Comaroff 1997 *Of Revelation and Revolution, vol. II: The Dialectics of Modernity on a South African Frontier*. Chicago: University of Chicago Press

Comaroff, John L. and Simon Roberts 1981 *Rules and Processes: The Cultural Logic of Dispute in an African Context*. Chicago: University of Chicago Press

Coulson, N.J. 1964 *A History of Islamic Law*. Edinburgh: Edinburgh University Press
　1971 *Succession in the Muslim Family*. Cambridge, UK: Cambridge University Press

Das, Veena 1994 "Cultural rights and the definition of community." In Oliver Mendelsohn and Upendra Baxi, eds., *The Rights of Subordinated Peoples*, pp. 125–37. Oxford: Oxford University Press

Daud, Habibah 1982 "Peranan pengadilan agama dalam menyelesaikan masalah kewarisan di Indonesia" [The role of religious courts in resolving inheritance disputes in Indonesia]. In Muchtar Zarkasyi, ed., *Laporan Hasil Seminar Hukum Waris Islam* [Report of the Results of the Seminar on Islamic Inheritance Law], pp. 40–53. Jakarta: Departemen Agama

Daud Ali, Muhammad 1993 "Asas-asas hukum kewarisan dalam Kompilasi Hukum Islam" [Principles of inheritance law in the compilation of Islamic law]. *Mimbar Hukum* 9:1–17

1994a "Pengembangan hukum Islam dan yurisprudensi peradilan agama" [The development of Islamic law and religious legal precedent]. *Mimbar Hukum* 12: 17–23

1994b "Peraturan perkawinan Indonesia dan kedudukan wanita di dalamnya" [Indonesian marriage regulations and the place of women therein]. *Mimbar Hukum* 15:26–36

Departemen Agama 1992/93 Kompilasi Hukum Islam di Indonesia [The Compilation of Islamic Law in Indonesian]. Jakarta: Direktorat Pembinaan Badan Peradilan Agama, Departemen Agama

1996/97 *Kompilasi Hukum Islam di Indonesia* [Compilation of Islamic Law in Indonesia]. Jakarta: Direktorat Jenderal Pembinaan Kelembagaan Agama Islam, Departemen Agama R.I.

Departemen Kehakiman 1973 *Masalah-masalah Hukum Perdata di Takengon* [Civil Law Issues in Takèngën]. Jakarta: Direktorat Jenderal Pembinaan Badan-Badan Peradilàn, Departemen Kehakiman

Dobbin, Christine 1983 *Islamic Revivalism in a Changing Peasant Economy: Central Sumatra, 1784–1847*. Scandinavian Institute of Asian Studies, Monograph Series, No. 47. London: Curzon Press

Douglas, Mary 1975 "Self-evidence." In Mary Douglas, *Implicit Meanings: Essays in Anthropology*, pp. 276–318. London: Routledge & Kegan Paul

Dupret, Baudoin 2000 *Au nom de quel droit*. Paris: Maison des Sciences de l'Homme

Effendy, Bachtiar 1995 "Islam and the state in Indonesia: Munawir Szadjali and the development of a new theological underpinning of political Islam." *Studia Islamika* 2(2):97–121

Eickleman, Dale F. 1985 *Knowledge and Power in Morocco*. Princeton: Princeton University Press

1992 "Mass higher education and the religious imagination in contemporary Arab societies." *American Ethnologist* 19(4):1–13

Eickelman, Dale F. and James Piscatori, eds. 1990 *Muslim Travelers*. London: Routledge

1996 *Muslim Politics*. Princeton: Princeton University Press

Ellen, Roy F. 1983 "Social theory, ethnography, and the understanding of practical Islam in South-East Asia." In M.B. Hooker, ed., *Islam in South-East Asia*, pp. 50–91. Leiden: E.J. Brill

Elster, Jon 1995 *Local Justice*. New York: Russell Sage Foundation

Errington, Shelley 1989 *Meaning and Power in a Southeast Asian Realm*. Princeton: Princeton University Press

Esposito, John L. 1982 *Women in Muslim Family Law*. Syracuse: Syracuse University Press

Evans-Pntchard, E.E. 1937 *Witchcraft, Oracles and Magic among the Azande*. Oxford: Clarendon Press

Fearon, James D. and David D. Laitin 1996 "Explaining interethnic cooperation." *American Political Science Review* 90(4):715–35

Feener, R.M. 1999 "Developments of Muslim jurisprudence in twentieth century Indonesia." Ph.D dissertation, Boston University

Feillard, Andrée 1995 *Islam et armée dan l'Indonésie contemporaine*. Paris: L'Harmattan

1997 "Indonesia's emerging Muslim feminism: women leaders on equality, inheritance, and other gender issues." *Studia Islamika* 4(1):83–111

Fox, James J., ed. 1980 *The Flow of Life: Essays on Eastern Indonesia*. Cambridge, MA: Harvard University Press

1988 "Origin, descent, and precedence in the study of Austronesian societies." Lecture delivered at Leiden University, 17 March 1988

ed. 1997 *The Poetic Power of Place: Comparative Perspectives on Austronesian Ideas of Locality*. Canberra: Research School of Pacific and Asian Studies, The Australian National University

Gaspard, Françoise and Farhad Khosrokhavar 1995 *Le foulard et la république* [The Headscraf and the Republic]. Paris: La Découverte

Geertz, Clifford 1983 "Local knowledge: fact and law in comparative perspective." In Clifford Geertz, *Local Knowledge: Further Essays in Interpretive Anthropology*, pp. 167–234. New York: Basic Books

Giddens, Anthony 1979 *Central Problems in Social Theory: Action, Structure and Contradiction in Social Analysis*. Berkeley: University of California Press

Goffman, Erving 1974 *Frame Analysis: An Essay on the Organization of Experience*. New York: Harper & Row

Gray, John 1996 *Isaiah Berlin*. Princeton: Princeton University Press
2000 *Two Face of Liberalism*. Cambridge, UK: Polity Press

Greenhouse, Carol J. 1982 "Looking at culture, looking for rules." *Man* 17(1):58–73

Griffiths, J. 1986 "What is legal pluralism." *Journal of Legal Pluralism* 24:1–55

Griswold, Wendy 1992 "The writing on the mud wall: Nigerian novels and the imaginary village." *American Sociological Review* 57:709–24

Gupta, Akil and James Ferguson, eds. 1997 *Culture, Power, Place: Explorations in Critical Anthropology*. Durham: Duke University Press

ter Haar, Barend 1948 *Adat Law in Indonesia*, trans. E.A. Haebel and A.A. Schiller. New York: Institute of Pacific Relations (originally published in Dutch, 1939, Batavaia/Groningen)

Haeri, Shahla 1989 *Law of Desire: Temporary Marriage in Shi'i Iran*. Syracuse: Syracuse University Press

Hallaq, Wael B. 1989 "Non-analogical arguments in Sunni juridical Qiyâs." *Arabica* 36:286–306
1995 "Model Shurût works and the dialectic of doctrine and practice." *Islamic Law and Society* 2(2):109–34
1997 *A History of Islamic Legal Theories: An Introduction to Sunnî usûl al-fiqh*. Cambridge, UK: Cambridge University Press

HAMKA [Haji A. Malik Karim Amrullah] 1984 *Islam dan Adat Minangkabau* [Minangkabau Islam and Adat]. Jakarta: Penerbit Panjimas

Hampshire, Stuart 2000 *Justice is Conflict*. Princeton: Princeton University Press

Hamzah, Andi 1986 *Kamus hukum* [Legal Dictionary]. Jakarta: Ghalia Indonesia

Hanan, Damsyi 1995 "Pengertian yuridis sahnya suatu perkawinan" [Judicial understanding of the validity of a marriage]. *Mimbar Hukum* 23:23–45

Harahap, M. Yahya 1988 "Praktek hukum waris tidak pantas membuat generalisasi" [The practice of inheritance law ought not to lead to generalizations]. In Iqbal Abdurrauf Saimima, ed., *Polemik Reaktualisasi Ajaran Islam* [Polemic about Reactualizing Islamic Teachings], pp. 124–48. Jakarta: Pustaka Panjimas
1994 "Informasi materi kompilasi hukum Islam: mempositifkan abstraksi humkum Islam" [Information about the source for the compilation of Islamic law: rendering as "positive" the abstraction of Islamic law]. In Tim Ditbinbapera [Team from the Directorate for Promoting Religious Justice Institutions], *Berbagai Pendangan Terhadap Kompilasi Hukum Islam* [Diverse Perspectives on the Compilation of Islamic Law]. Jakarta: Yayasan Al Hikmah

1995a "Kedudukan wanita dalam hukum kewarisan" [The position of women in inheritance law], Part One. *Mimbar Hukum* 18:89–103

1995b "Kedudukan wanita dalam hukum kewarisan" [The position of women in inheritance law], Part Two. *Mimbar Hukum* 19:95–105

1995c "Kedudukan wanita dalam hukum kewarisan" [The position of women in inheritance law], Part Three. *Mimbar Hukum* 20:91–102

Hatem, Mervyn 1986 "The enduring alliance of nationalism and patriarchy in Muslim personal status laws: the case of modern Egypt." *Feminist Issues* 6:19–41

Haverfield, Rachel 1999 "Hak Ulayat and the state: land reform in Indonesia." in Timothy Lindsey, ed., *Indonesia: Law and Society*, pp. 42–73. Leichhardt, NSW: The Federation Press

Hazairin, Dr. 1950 Hukum Baru di Indonesia [New Law in Indonesia]. Jakarta: Bulan Bintang

1962 *Hukum Kekeluargaan Nasional* [National Family Law]. Jakarta: Tintamas

1964 *Hukum Kewarisan Bilateral Menurut Al-Qur'ân* [Bilateral Inheritance Law According to the Qur'ân]. Jakarta: Tintamas

Hefner, Robert W. 2000 *Civil Islam: Muslims and Democratization in Indonesia*. Princeton: Princeton University Press

Hirsch, Susan F. 1998 *Pronouncing and Perserving: Gender and the Discourses of Disputing in an African Islamic Court*. Chicago: University of Chicago Press

Holleman, J.F. 1981 *Van Vollenhoven on Indonesian Adat Law*. The Hague: Martinus Nijhoff

Hooker, M.B. 1978 *Adat Law in Modern Indonesia*. Kuala Lumpur: Oxford University Press

Horowitz, Donald L. 1985 *Ethnic Groups in Conflict*. Berkeley: University of California Press

2001 *The Deadly Ethnic Riot*. Berkeley: University of California Press

Hosen, K.H. Ibrahim 1994 "Taqlid dan ijtihad: beberapa pengertian dasar" [Obedience and interpretation: some basic understandings]. In Budhy Munawar-Rachman, ed., *Kontekstualisasi Doktrin Islam dalam Sejarah* [The Contextualization of Islamic Doctrine in History], pp. 319–37. Jakarta: Paramadina

1995 "Jenis-jenis hukuman dalam hukum pidana Islam dan perbedaan ijtihad ulama dalam penerapannya" [Types of penalties in Islamic criminal law and differences in scholars' interpretations in their application]. *Mimbar Hukum* 20:7–29

Hourani, Albert 1983 *Arabic Thought in the Liberal Age, 1798–1939*. Reissue, with new preface, of 1962 edn. Cambridge, UK: Cambridge University Press

Humphreys, Sally 1985 "Law as discourse." *History and Anthropology* 1:241–64

Ichtijanto, Dr. 1995 "Al-Qur'an tentang perkawinan dan kelurga" [The Qur'ân on marriage and family]. *Mimbar Hukum* 19:7–14

Ilmie, H. Muhammad Bahrul 1996 "Kompilasi hukum Islam (KHI) dalam konstelasi politik hukum nasional" [Compilation of Islamic law in the constellation of national law policy]. *Mimbar Hukum* 24:18–26

Ilyas, Yusuf 1995 "Masalah ijtihadiyah dalam hukum waris Islam (sebuah kajian singkat)" [The problem of ijtihâd in Islamic inheritance law (a brief discussion)]. *Mimbar Hukum* 21:62–65

Jamil, Fathurrahman 1995 "The Muhammadiyah and the theory of Maqâsid al-Sharî'ah." *Studia Islamika* 2(1):53–68

Jaspan, M.A. 1965 "In quest of new law: the perplexity of legal syncretism in Indonesia." *Comparative Studies in Society and History* 7:252–66

Just, Peter 2001 *Dou Donggo Justice: Conflict and Morality in an Indonesian Society.* Lanham, MD: Rowman & Littlefield

Kansil, C.S.T. 1979 *Pengantar ilmu hukum dan tata hukum Indonesia* [Introduction to Legal Studies and the Indonesian Legal System]. Jakarta: Balai Pustaka

Kasrori, Dr. S. 1999 "Kalalah." *Mimbar Hukum* 44:40–48

Kastoryano, Riva 1997 *La France, l'Allemagne et leurs immigrés: négocier l'identité.* Paris: Armand Colin

Katz, June S. and Ronald S. Katz 1975 "The new Indonesian Marriage Law: a mirror of Indonesia's political, cultural, and legal systems." *American Journal of Comparative Law* 23:653–81

1978 "Legislating social change in a developing country: the new Indonesian marriage law revisited." *American Journal of Comparative Law* 26:309–20

Kuipers, Joel C. 1990 *Power in Performance: The Creation of Textual Authority in Weyewa Ritual Speech.* Philadelphia: University of Pennsylvania Press

1998 *Language, Identity, and Marginality in Indonesia: The Changing Nature of Ritual Speech on the Island of Sumba.* Cambridge, UK: Cambridge University Press

Kymlicka, Will 1995 *Multicultural Citizenship.* Oxford: Oxford University Press

Laitin, David 1992 *Language Repertoires and State Construction in Africa.* Cambridge, UK: Cambridge University Press

Lamont, Michèle 1992 *Money, Morals, and Manners: The Culture of the French and American Upper-Middle Class.* Chicago: University of Chicago Press

Lamont, Michèle and Laurent Thévenot, eds. 2000 *Rethinking Comparative Cultural Sociology: Repertories of Evaluation in France and the United States.* Cambridge, UK: Cambridge University Press

Lapidus, Ira 1975 "The separation of state and religion in the development of early Islamic society." *International Journal of Middle East Studies* 6(4):363–85

Layish, Aharon 1983 "The Maliki family *waqf* according to wills and *waqfiyyât.*" *Bulletin of the School of Oriental and African Studies* 46:1–32

1991 *Divorce in the Libyan Family: A Study Based on the* Sijills *of the Sharî'a Courts of Ajdâbiyya and Kufra.* New York: New York University Press

Lazarus-Black, Mindie and Susan F. Hirsch, eds. 1994 *Contested States.* New York: Routledge

Lev, Daniel S. 1962 "The Supreme Court and Adat inheritance law in Indonesia." *American Journal of Comparative Law* 11:205–24

1965 "The lady and the banyan tree: civil-law change in Indonesia." *American Journal of Comparative Law* 14:282–307

1972a *Islamic Courts in Indonesia: A Study in the Political Bases of Legal Institutions.* Berkeley and Los Angeles: University of California Press

1972b "Judicial institutions and legal culture in Indonesia." In Claire Holt, ed., *Culture and Politics in Indonesia,* pp. 246–318. Ithaca: Cornell University Press

1973 "Judicial unification in post-colonial Indonesia." *Indonesia* 16:1–37

1976 "Origins of the Indonesian advocacy." *Indonesia* 21:135–69

1978 "Judicial authority and the struggle for an Indonesian Rechtsstaat." *Law and Society Review* 13:37–71

1985 "Colonial law and the genesis of the Indonesian state." *Indonesia* 40:57–74

1999 "Between state and society: professional lawyers and reform in Indonesia." In Timothy Lindsey, ed., *Indonesia: Law and Society*, pp. 227–46. Leichhardt, NSW: The Federation Press

Levy, Jacob T. 2000 *The Multiculturalism of Fear*. Oxford: Oxford University Press

Libson, Gideon 1997 "On the development of custom as a source of law in Islamic law." *Islamic Law and Society* 4(2):131–55

Liddle, R. William 1996 "Media Dakwah scripturalism: one form of Islamic political thought and action in New Order Indonesia." In Mark R. Woodward, ed., *Toward a New Paradigm: Recent Developments in Indonesian Islamic Thought*, pp. 323–56. Tempe, AZ: Arizona State University, Program for Southeast Asian Studies

Lindsey, Timothy 1999 "From rule of law to law of the rulers – to reformation?" In Timothy Lindsey, ed., *Indonesia: Law and Society*, pp. 11–20. Leichhardt, NSW: The Federation Press

Locke, John 1967 [1690] *Two Treatises of Government*. Peter Laslett, ed. Cambridge, UK: Cambridge University Press

1983 [1689] *A Letter Concerning Toleration*. James H. Tully, ed. Indianapolis: Hackett Publishing

Lombard, Denys 1990 *Le carrefour javanais: essai d'histoire globale*. 3 vols. Paris: Editions de l'Ecole des Hautes Etudes en Sciences Sociales

Loudoe, John Z. 1981 *Beberapa Aspek Hukum Materil dan Hukum Acara* [Aspects of Substantive and Procedural Law]. Jakarta: Bina Aksara

Lubis, Ali Basya 1981 *Kamus Hukum Jurisprudensi* [Dictionary of Legal Precedent]. Jakarta: n.p.

Lubis, Nur Ahmad Fadhil 1994 "Islamic justice in transition: a socio-legal study of the *Agama* court judges in Indonesia." Ph.D dissertation, University of California, Los Angeles

1995 "Institutionalization and the unification of Islamic courts under the New Order." *Studia Islamika* 2(1):1–51

Lubis, Todung Mulya 1999 "The Rechsstaat and human rights." In Timothy Lindsey, ed., *Indonesia: Law and Society*, pp. 171–85. Leichhardt, NSW: The Federation Press

Lutz, Catherine A. and Lila Abu-Lughod 1990 *Language and the Politics of Emotion*. Cambridge, UK: Cambridge University Press

Macdonald, Charles, ed. 1987 *De la hutte au palais: sociétés "à maison" en Asie du Sud-Est insulaire*. Paris: Editions du CNRS

Macpherson, C.B. 1962 *The Political Theory of Possessive Individualism: Hobbes to Locke*. Oxford: Oxford University Press

Madjid, Nurcholis 1979 "The issue of modernization among Muslims in Indonesia: from a participant's point of view." In Gloria Davis, ed., *What is Modern Indonesian Culture?*, pp. 143–55. Papers in International Studies, Southeast Asia Series, No. 52. Athens, OH: Ohio University

1992 *Islam: Doktrin dan Peradaban* [Islam: Doctrine and Civilization]. Jakarta: Paramadina

1994a "Konsep asbab al-nuzul dan relevansinya bagi pandangan historis segi-segi tertentu ajaran keagamaan" [The concept of the "reasons for revelation" and its relevance for a historical view of certain religious teachings]. In Budhy

Munawar-Rachman, ed., *Kontekstualisasi Doktrin Islam dalam Sejarah* [The Contextualization of Islamic Doctrine in History], pp. 24–41. Jakarta: Paramadina

1994b "Sejarah awal penyusunan dan pembakuan hukum Islam" [The early history of assembling and refining Islamic law]. In Budhy Munawar-Rachman, ed., *Kontekstualisasi Doktrin Islam dalam Sejarah* [The Contextualization of Islamic Doctrine in History], pp. 237–50. Jakarta: Paramadina

Malinowski, Bronislaw 1926 *Crime and Custom in Savage Society.* London: Routledge & Kegan Paul

Manan, Abdul 1995 "Masalah taklik talak dalam hukum perkawinan di Indonesia" [The problem of the ta'lik talak in Indonesian marriage law]. *Mimbar Hukum* 23:68–92

Mardjono, Hartono 1995 "Syarat manakah yang menentukan sahnya perkawinan?" [Which conditions determine the validity of a marriage?]. *Mimbar Hukum* 23:33–45

Margalit, Avishai 1996 *The Decent Society.* Cambridge, MA: Harvard University Press

Masud, Muhammad Khalid, Brinkley Messick, and David S. Powers, eds. 1996 "Muftis, fatwas, and Islamic legal interpretation." In Muhammad Khalid Masud, Brinkley Messick, and David S. Powers, eds., *Islamic Legal Interpretation: Muftis and their Fatwas*, pp. 3–32. Cambridge, MA: Harvard University Press

Matardi, Drs. E. 1996 "Kompilasi hukum Islam sebagai hukum terapan di pengadilan agama" [Compilation of Islamic law as applied law in the religious courts]. *Mimbar Hukum* 24:27–35

Mehdi, Rubya 1994 *The Islamization of the Law in Pakistan.* Nordic Institute of Asian Studies, Monograph Series, No. 60. Richmond, UK: Curzon Press

Meliala SH, Djaja S. and Aswin Peranginangin SH 1979 *Hukum Perdata Adat Karo dalam Rangka Pembentukan Hukum Nasional* [Karo Civil Adat Law in the Framework of Forming National Law]. Bandung: Tarsito

Merry, Sally Engle 1988 "Legal pluralism." *Law and Society Review* 22:869–96

1992 "Anthropology, law, and transnational processes." *Annual Review of Anthropology* 21:357–79

2000 *Colonizing Hawai'i: The Cultural Power of Law.* Princeton: Princeton University Press

Merryman, John Henry 1969 *The Civil Law Tradition.* Stanford: Stanford University Press

1985 *The Civil Law Tradition*, 2nd edn. Stanford: Stanford University Press

Messick, Brinkley 1993 *The Calligraphic State: Textual Domination and History in a Muslim Society.* Berkeley and Los Angeles: University of California Press

Mir-Hosseini, Ziba 1993 *Marriage on Trial: A Study of Islamic Family Law.* London: I.B. Tauris

1999 *Islam and Gender: The Religious Debate in Contemporary Iran.* Princeton: Princeton University Press

Modood, Tariq 1999 "Multiculturalism also in, Secularism, and the State." In Richard Bellamy and Martin Hollis, eds., *Pluralism and Liberal Neutrality*, pp. 79–97. London and Portland, OR: Frank Cass

Moore, Sally Falk 1978 "Law and social change: the semi-autonomous social field as an appropriate subject of study." In Sally Falk Moore, *Law as Process: An Anthropological Approach*, pp. 54–81. London: Routledge & Kegan Paul

1986 *Social Facts and Fabrications: "Customary" Law on Kilimanjaro, 1880–1980.* Cambridge, UK: Cambridge University Press

Moors, Annelies 1995 *Women, Property and Islam: Palestinian Experiences, 1920–1990*. Cambridge, UK: Cambridge University Press

Mudzhar, Mohammad Atho 1993 *Fatwa-fatwa Majelis Ulama Indonesia* [The Fatwas of the Indonesian Council of Ulama]. Jakarta: INIS

  1996 "The Council of Indonesian 'Ulama': on Muslims' attendance at Christmas celebrations." In Muhammad Khalid Masud, Brinkley Messick, and David S. Powers, eds., *Islamic Legal Interpretation: Muftis and their Fatwas*, pp. 230–41. Cambridge, MA: Harvard University Press

Mulia, Musdah 1999 *Pandangan Islam tentang Poligami* [The Islamic Perspective on Polygamy]. Jakarta: Lembaga Kajian Agama dan Jender

Munawar-Rachman, Budhy, ed. 1994 *Kontekstualisasi Doktrin Islam dalam Sejarah* [The Contextualization of Islamic Doctrine in History]. Jakarta: Paramadina

  1996 "Rekonstruksi fiqh perempuan dalam konteks perubahan zaman" [Reconstructing a women's fiqh in changing historical context]. In Budhy Munawar-Rachman, et al., *Rekonstruksi Fiqh Perempuan dalam Peradaban Masyarakat Modern* [Reconstructing a Women's Fiqh in a Modern Society's Culture], pp. 13–32. Jakarta: Ababil

Mundy, Martha 1988 "The family, inheritance, and Islam: a re-examination of the sociology of Farâ'id law." In Aziz al-Azmeh, ed., *Islamic Law: Social and Historical Contexts*, pp. 1–123. London and New York: Routledge

  1995 *Domestic Government: Kinship, Community and Polity in North Yemen*. London: I.B. Tauris

Munti, Ratna Batara 1999 *Perempuan Sebagai Kepala Rumah Tangga* [Women as Household Heads]. Jakarta: Lembaga Kajian Agama dan Jender

Murdoch, Lindsay 2000 "Religious killing fields spread across the ugly new Indonesia." *Sydney Morning Herald*, June 29, online

an-Na'im, Abdullahi Ahmed 1990 *Toward an Islamic Reformation: Civil Liberties, Human Rights, and International Law*. Syracuse: Syracuse University Press

an-Nawawi, Syekh Muhammad bin Umar 1995 *Terjemah Uqudulijain: Etika Berumah Tangga* [Translation of the "Uqudulijain": Ethics of Married Life]. Jakarta: Pustaka Amani

Noeh, Zaini Ahmad 1994 "Lima tahun undang-undang peradilan agama" [Five years of the religious judiciary laws]. *Mimbar Hukum* 17:12–29

Noer, Deliar 1973 *The Modernist Muslim Movement in Indonesia, 1900–1942*. Kuala Lumpur: Oxford University Press

  1978 *Administration of Islam in Indonesia*. Modern Indonesia Project, Monograph Series, No. 58. Ithaca: Cornell University

Nuzul, SH, Drs. A. 1999 "Kompromistis hukum waris KHI dengan ilmua faraid, hukum waris adat dan barat" [A compromise between inheritance law as in the Indonesian Compilation of Islamic Law and the inheritance laws of Islam, adat, and the west]. *Mimbar Hukum* 44:20–27

Parekh, Bhikhu 2000 *Rethinking Multiculturalism: Cultural Diversity and Political Theory*. Cambridge, MA: Harvard University Press

Peletz, Michael G. 1993 "Knowledge, power, and personal misfortune in a Malay context." In C.W. Watson and Roy Ellen, eds., *Understanding Witchcraft and Sorcery in Southeast Asia*, pp. 149–78. Honolulu: University of Hawaii Press

  1996 *Reason and Passion: Representations of Gender in a Malay Society*. Berkeley: University of California Press

Peters, F.E. 1994 *Muhammad and the Origins of Islam*. Albany: State University of New York Press

Petersen, Roger Dale 2001 *Resistance and Rebellion: Lessons from Eastern Europe*. Cambridge, UK: Cambridge University Press

Pompe, Sebastiaan 1988 "Mixed marriages in Indonesia: some comments on the law and the literature." *Bijdragen tot de Taal-, Land- en Volkenkunde* 2–3:259–75

  1991 "A short note on some recent developments with regard to mixed marriages in Indonesia." *Bijdragen tot de Taal-, Land- en Volkenkunde* 2–3:261–72

  1996 *The Indonesian Supreme Court: Fifty Years of Judicial Development*. Leiden: Leiden University, Faculty of Law

  1999 "Between crime and custom: extra-marital sex in modern Indonesian law." In Timothy Lindsey, ed., *Indonesia: Law and Society*, pp. 111–21. Leichhardt, NSW: The Federation Press

Powers, David S. 1986 *Studies in Qur'an and Hadîth: The Formation of the Islamic Law of Inheritance*. Berkeley and Los Angeles: University of California Press

  1990 "The Islamic inheritance system: a socio-historical approach." In Chibli Mallat and Jane Conners, eds., *Islamic Family Law*, pp. 11–29. London: Graham & Trotman

  1993 "The Maliki family endowment: legal norms and social practices." *International Journal of Middle East Studies* 25:379–406

  1994 "Kadijustiz or Qâdî-Justice? A paternity dispute from fourteenth-century Morocco." *Islamic Law and Society* 13:332–66

Prawiranegara, Syafruddin 1988 "Reinterpretasi sebagai dasar reaktualisasi ajaran-ajaran Islam" [Reinterpretation as the basis for reactualizing Islamic teachings]. In Iqbal Abdurrauf Saimima, ed., *Polemik Reaktualisasi Ajaran Islam* [Polemic about Reactualizing Islamic Teachings], pp. 28–42. Jakarta: Pustaka Panjimas

Rahman, Fazlur 1965 *Islamic Methodology in History*. Islamabad: Islamic Research Institute

Rais, M. Amin 1995 "Islam and Christianity in Indonesia." *Studia Islamika* 2(1): 69–71

Rakhmat, Jalaluddin 1988 "Kontroversi sekitar ijtihad Umar r.a." [Controversy around the ijtihâd of "Umar"]. In Iqbal Abdurrauf Saimima, ed., *Polemik Reaktualisasi Ajaran Islam* [Polemic about Reactualizing Islamic Teachings], pp. 43–59. Jakarta: Pustaka Panjimas

  1991 *Islam aktual* [Today's Islam]. Jakarta: Penerbit Mizan

  1994 "Tinauan kritis atas sejarah fiqh: dari fiqh tabi'in hingga madzhab liberalism" [Critical review of the history of jurisprudence: from the tabi'in fiqh to the school of liberalism]. In Budhy Munawar-Rachman, ed., *Kontekstualisasi Doktrin Islam dalam Sejarah* [The Contextualization of Islamic Doctrine in History], pp. 251–310. Jakarta: Paramadina

Rasjid, H. Sulaiman 1954 *Fiqh Islam*. Jakarta: Attahirijah

Rawls, John 1996 *Political Liberalism*, 2nd edn. New York: Columbia University Press

  1999 *The Law of Peoples, with "The Idea of Public Reason Revisited."* Cambridge, MA: Harvard University Press

Raz, Joseph 1994 *Ethics in the Public Domain: Essays in the Morality of Law and Politics*. Oxford: Clarendon Press

Reid, Anthony 1988 *Southeast Asia in the Age of Commerce, 1450–1680, vol. I: The Lands below the Winds*. New Haven: Yale University Press

1993 *Southeast Asia in the Age of Commerce, 1450–1680, vol. II: Expansion and Crisis*. New Haven: Yale University Press

Repp, Richard C. 1988 "Qânûn and Sharî'a in the Ottoman context." In Aziz al-Azmeh, ed., *Islamic Law: Social and Historical Contexts*, pp. 124–45. New York: Routledge

Rodgers Siregar, Susan 1983 "Political oratory in a modernizing southern Batak homeland." In Rita Smith Kipp and Richard D. Kipp, eds., *Beyond Samosir: Recent Studies of the Batak Peoples of Sumatra*, pp. 21–52. Athens: Ohio University Center for International Studies

Rosen, Lawrence 1989 *The Anthropology of Justice*. Cambridge, UK: Cambridge University Press

1995 "Law and custom in the popular legal culture of North Africa." *Islamic Law and Society* 2:194–208

ar-Ruhaily, Ruway'i 1994 *Fikih Umar* [The Jurisprudence of Umar]. Jakarta: Al-Kautsar

Sabrie, Zuffran 1990 *Peradilan agama dalam wadah Negara Pancasila (Dialog tentang RUUPA)* [Religious Justice Contained in the Pancasila State (Dialogue about the Draft Bill on Religious Justice)]. Jakarta: Pusaka Antara

1993 "Editorial." *Mimbar Hukum* 9:v–vi

Sabrie, Drs. H. Zuffran 1996 "Editorial" [unsigned]. *Mimbar Hukum* 24:5–6

Sahlins, Marshall 1985 "The stranger-king; or, Dumézil among the Fijians." In Marshall Sahlins, *Islands of History*. Chicago: University of Chicago Press

Sandel, Michael J. 1998 *Liberalism and the Limits of Justice*, 2nd edn. Cambridge, UK and New York: Cambridge University Press

Santos, Boaventura de Sousa 1987 "Law: a map of misreading, toward a postmodern conception of law." *Journal of Law and Society* 14:279–302

Schacht, Joseph 1964 *An Introduction to Islamic Law*. Oxford: Clarendon Press

Schelling, Thomas C. 1960 *The Strategy of Conflict*. Cambridge, MA: Harvard University Press

Shaham, Ron 1997 *Family and the Courts in Modern Egypt: A Study Based on Decisions by the Sharî'a Courts, 1900–1955*. Leiden: Brill

ash-Shiddieqy, T.M. Hasbi 1950? *Dasar-dasar Fiqih Islam* [The Foundations of Islamic Law]. Medan: Tokobuku "Islamyah"

1953 Pengantar Hukum Islam [Introduction to Islamic Law]. Jakarta: Bulan Bintang

1973 Fiqhul Mawaris [Inheritance Law]. Jakarta: Bulan Bintang

Siegel, James T. 1969 *The Rope of God*. Berkeley: University of California Press

Siregar, Bismar 1994a *Bunga Rampai Hukum dan Islam* [Collection on Law and Islam]. Jakarta: Grafikatama Jaya

1994b "Kata sambutan" [Foreword] to Ruway'i ar-Ruhaily, *Fikih Umar* [The Jurisprudence of Umar], pp. 5–7. Jakarta: Al-Kaut Sar

Slaats, Herman 1988 "A continuing story: the use of state courts in Indonesia." *Review of Indonesian and Malaysian Affairs* 122:133–53

Slaats, H. and M.K. Portier 1986 "Legal plurality and the transformation of normative concepts in the process of litigation in Karo Batak society." In Keebet van Benda Bechman and Fons Strijbosch, eds., *Anthropology of Law in the Netherlands*, pp. 217–39. Dordrecht: Foris

Slaats, Herman and Karen Portier 1993 "Sorcery and the law in modern Indonesia." In C.W. Watson and Roy Ellen, eds., *Understanding Witchcraft and Sorcery in Southeast Asia*, pp. 135–48. Honolulu: University of Hawaii Press

Snouck Hurgronje, C. 1903 *Het Gajoland en Zijne Bewoners*. Batavia: Landsdrukkerij 1906 *The Achehnese*, trans. A.W.S. O'Sullivan. 2 vols. Leiden: E.J. Brill (originally published in Dutch, 1893–94)

Supomo, Dr. Rd. 1967 [1933] *Hukum Perdata Adat Jawa Barat* [The Civil Adat Law of West Java]. Jakarta: Penerbit Djambatan

Steedly, Mary Margaret 1993 *Hanging Without a Rope: Narrative Experience in Colonial and Postcolonial Karoland*. Princeton: Princeton University Press

Stiles, Erin 2002 "Marriage, divorce, and the Islamic legal tradition in Zanzibar." Ph.D dissertation, Washington University in St. Louis

Subadio, Maria Ullfah 1981 *Perjuangan Untuk Mencapai Undang-undang Perkawinan* [Struggle to Realize the Marriage Laws] Jakarta: Yayasan Idayu

Subekti, R. 1964 *Hukum Pembuktian* [Law of Evidence]. Jakarta: Prakarsa 1977 *Law in Indonesia*. Bandung: Karya Nusantara

Subekti, R. and J. Tamara, eds. 1965 *Kumpulan Putusan Mahkamah Agung* [Collection of Supreme Court Decisions], 2nd edn. Jakarta: Gunung Agung

Subekti, R. and R. Tjitrosudibio, eds. 1961 *Kitab Undang-undang Hukum Perdata* [translation of *Burgerlijk Wetboek*]. Jakarta: Pradnja Paramita

Sukarja, Ahmad 1994 "Perkawinan berbeda agama menurut hukum Islam" [Inter-religious marriage according to Islamic law]. In Chuzaimah T. Yanggo and Hafiz Anshary, eds., *Problematika Hukum Islam Kontemporer* [Contemporary Problems in Islamic Law], pp. 1–33. Jakarta: PT Pustaka Firdaus

Sunstein, Cass R. 1996 *Legal Reasoning and Political Conflict*. New York: Oxford University Press

Swidler, Ann 1986 "Culture in action: symbols and strategies." *American Sociological Review* 51:273–86

Syafe'i, H. Rachmat 1999 "Kajian terhadap putusan Mahkamah Agung tentang kewarisan saudara kandung dengan anak perempuan" [Discussion of the Supreme Court's decision on inheritance by siblings and daughters]. *Mimbar Hukum* 44:5–11

Syamsuddin, M. Din 1995 "The Muhammadiyah Da'wah and allocative politics in the New Order." *Studia Islamika* 2(2):35–71

Szadjali, Munawir 1991a "Landasan pemikiran politik hukum Islam dalam rangka menentukan peradilan agama di Indonesia" [Conceptual foundations for Islamic legal policy in determining the religious judicial system in Indonesia]. In Juhaya S. Praja, ed., *Hukum Islam di Indonesia: Pemikiran dan Praktek* [Islamic Law in Indonesia: Concept and Practice], pp. 41–67. Bandung: Remaja Rosdakarya

1991b "Reaktualisasi ajaran Islam" [Islamic teachings for today]. In Juhaya S. Praja, ed., *Hukum Islam di Indonesia: Perkembangan dan Pembentukan* [Islamic Law in Indonesia: Development and Formation], pp. 83–93. Bandung: Remaja Rosdakarya

1993 *Islam: Realitas Baru dan Orientasi Masa Depan Bangsa* [Islam: New Reality and the Orientation for the People's Future]. Jakarta: Universitas Indonesia

1994 *Bunga Rampai Wawasan Islam Dewasa ini* [Collection on the Scope of Islam Today]. Jakarta: Universitas Indonesia

Tarrow, Sidney 1995 "Cycles of collective action: between moments of madness and the repertoire of contention." In Mark Traugott, ed., *Repertoires and Cycles of Collective Action*. Durham: Duke University Press

Taylor, Charles 1994 *Multiculturalism: Examining the Politics of Recognition*. Princeton: Princeton University Press

Thalib, Sajuti 1982 *Hukum Kewarisan Islam di Indonesia* [Islamic Inheritance Law in Indonesia]. Jakarta: Sinar Grafika

Tilly, Charles 1997 *Durable Inequality*. Berkeley: University of California Press

Tucker, Judith E. 1998 *In the House of the Law: Gender and Islamic Law in Ottoman Syria and Palestine*. Berkeley and Los Angeles: University of California Press

Urban, Greg 2001 *Metaculture: How Culture Moves through the World*. Minneapolis: University of Minnesota Press

Venel, Nancy 1999 *Musulmanes Françaises: des pratiquantes voilées à l'université* [French (Female) Muslims: Veiled Practitioners at the University]. Paris: L'Harmattan

Vergouwen, J.C. 1964 *The Social Organisation and Customary Law of the Toba-Batak of Northern Sumatra*, trans. Jeune Scott-Kenball. The Hague: Martinus Nijhoff (originally published in Dutch, 1933)

Vogel, Frank Edward 1993 "Islamic law and legal system studies of Saudia Arabia." Ph.D dissertation, Harvard University

Walzer, Michael 1983 *Spheres of Justice: A Defense of Pluralism and Equality*. New York: Basic Books

    1994 *Thick and Thin: Moral Argument at Home and Abroad*. Notre Dame: University of Notre Dame Press

    1997 *On Toleration*. New Haven: Yale University Press

Watson, C.W. 1992 *Kinship, Property and Inheritance in Kerinci, Central Sumatra*. Canterbury: Centre for Social Anthropology and Computing, University of Kent at Canterbury

Watson, C.W. and Roy Ellen, eds. 1993 *Understanding Witchcraft and Sorcery in Southeast Asia*. Honolulu: University of Hawaii Press

Weibel, Nadine B. 2000 *Par-delà le voile: femmes d'Islam en Europe* [Beyond the Veil: Women of Islam in Europe]. Brussels: Editions Complexes

Whyte, Susan 1997 *Questioning Misfortune: The Pragmatics of Uncertainty in Eastern Uganda*. Cambridge, UK: Cambridge University Press

Wolters, O.W. 1999 *History, Culture, and Region in Southeast Asian Perspectives*. Southeast Asia Program Publications. Ithaca: Cornell University

Yafie, Ali 1994 "Nasikh-mansukh dalam al-Qur'an" [Abrogation in the Qur'ân]. In Budhy Munawar-Rachman, ed., *Kontekstualisasi Doktrin Islam dalam Sejar at* [The Contextualization of Islamic Doctrine in History], pp. 42–51. Jakarta: Paramadina

Zein, Satria Effendi M. 1992 "Analisis yurisprudensi: tentang wasiat" [Analysis of jurisprudence: concerning bequests]. *Mimbar Hukum* 7:47–57

    1993 "Analisis yurisprudensi: tentang hibah" [Analysis of jurisprudence: concerning gifts]. *Mimbar Hukum* 9:72–99

    1994 "Analisis yurisprudensi: tentang sengketa hibah" [Analysis of jurisprudence: concerning a dispute over gifts]. *Mimbar Hukum* 15:110–41

    1996 "Analisis yurisprudensi tentang warisan: analisis fiqh" [Case analysis concerning inheritance: analysis of fiqh]. *Mimbar Hukum* 24:106–13

    1997 "Analisis fiqh" [Fiqh analysis]. *Mimbar Hukum* 30:104–12

Index

COURT CASES